Being Young and Muslim

RELIGION AND GLOBAL POLITICS SERIES

SERIES EDITOR
John L. Esposito
University Professor and Director
Center for Muslim–Christian Understanding
Georgetown University

ISLAMIC LEVIATHAN
Islam and the Making of State Power
Seyyed Vali Reza Nasr

RACHID GHANNOUCHI
A Democrat Within Islamism
Azzam S. Tamimi

BALKAN IDOLS
Religion and Nationalism in Yugoslav States
Vjekoslav Perica

ISLAMIC POLITICAL IDENTITY IN TURKEY
M. Hakan Yavuz

RELIGION AND POLITICS IN POST-COMMUNIST ROMANIA
Lavinia Stan and Lucian Turcescu

PIETY AND POLITICS
Islamism in Contemporary Malaysia
Joseph Chinyong Liow

TERROR IN THE LAND OF THE HOLY SPIRIT
Guatemala under General Efrain Rios Montt, 1982–1983
Virginia Garrard-Burnett

Being Young
and Muslim

*New Cultural Politics in the Global
South and North*

Edited by

LINDA HERRERA

ASEF BAYAT

OXFORD

UNIVERSITY PRESS

2010

OXFORD
UNIVERSITY PRESS

Oxford University Press, Inc., publishes works that further
Oxford University's objective of excellence
in research, scholarship, and education.

Oxford   New York
Auckland   Cape Town   Dar es Salaam   Hong Kong   Karachi
Kuala Lumpur   Madrid   Melbourne   Mexico City   Nairobi
New Delhi   Shanghai   Taipei   Toronto

With offices in
Argentina   Austria   Brazil   Chile   Czech Republic   France   Greece
Guatemala   Hungary   Italy   Japan   Poland   Portugal   Singapore
South Korea   Switzerland   Thailand   Turkey   Ukraine   Vietnam

Published by Oxford University Press, Inc.
198 Madison Avenue, New York, New York 10016

www.oup.com

Oxford is a registered trademark of Oxford University Press

Library of Congress Cataloging-in-Publication Data

Being young and Muslim : new cultural politics in the global south and north / edited by Linda
Herrera and Asef Bayat.
   p. cm.
Includes bibliographical references.
ISBN 978-0-19-536921-2 (hardcover)—ISBN 978-0-19-536920-5 (pbk.) 1. Muslim youth. 2. Muslim
youth—Attitudes. I. Bayat, Asef. II. Herrera, Linda.
BP188.18.Y68B45 2010
305.235088'297—dc22   2009031486

9 8 7 6 5 4 3 2 1

Printed in the United States of America
on acid-free paper

Acknowledgments

This book originated from two international workshops on the "Making of the Muslim Youth," which took place in Leiden in February 2005 and in The Hague in October 2006. The first workshop was organized by the International Institute for the Study of Islam in the Modern World (ISIM) in the context of the research subprogram on the Making of the Muslim Youth coordinated by Asef Bayat. The sequel workshop held in The Hague was a cooperative endeavor between ISIM and the International Institute of Social Studies of Erasmus University Rotterdam (ISS) where Linda Herrera is convenor of the Children and Youth Studies Master of Arts specialization. We are grateful for the support given by ISIM and the ISS Innovation Fund that made possible an extremely fruitful intellectual exercise and exchange with colleagues from around the globe. We particularly thank the ISIM secretariat and ISS student assistant Kristian Tamtomo for their part in the excellent organization of the events. Thanks are due also to Ramzy Kumsich for preparing the book's index. A number of colleagues and scholars contributed to the richness of the discussions by way of acting as chairs, discussants, and participants and we thank them all. Although the bulk of chapters in this volume were produced for the two workshops, others have been solicited to ensure a balanced representation of themes and regions. In this context, we acknowledge the journal of *Comparative Studies of South Asia, Africa and the Middle East*, Palgrave, as well as Stanford University Press for granting permission to reprint the articles "Muslim Youth and the Claim of Youthfulness" (chapter 2), Securing Futures: Youth, Generation, and Muslim Identities in Niger (chapter 14), and "Negotiating with Modernity: Young Women and Sexuality in Iran" (chapter 17), respectively.

An exciting feature of the authors of this volume is their intergenerational profile. Senior scholars worked with their mid-career and younger counterparts in a fruitful and cooperative way to produce this exciting volume. All of our work has benefited from hundreds of youth whose voices we hope to echo in this book, even though we do not identify them by name. We wish to register our deep appreciation to these young people whose stories, struggles, visions, despair, and hope inform our analyses and theorizing. We dedicate this book to them.

Linda Herrera, The Hague
Asef Bayat, Leiden

Contents

About the Authors, xi

1. Introduction: Being Young and Muslim in Neoliberal Times, 3
   Asef Bayat and Linda Herrera

Part I: Politics of Dissent

2. Muslim Youth and the Claim of Youthfulness, 27
   Asef Bayat

3. The Drama of Jihad: The Emergence of Salafi Youth in
   Indonesia, 49
   Noorhaidi Hasan

4. Moroccan Youth and Political Islam, 63
   Mounia Bennani-Chraïbi

5. Rebels without a Cause?: A Politics of Deviance in Saudi Arabia, 77
   Abdullah al-Otaibi and Pascal Ménoret

6. The Battle of the Ages: Contests for Religious Authority in The
   Gambia, 95
   Marloes Janson

7. Cyber Resistance: Palestinian Youth and Emerging Internet
   Culture, 113
   Makram Khoury-Machool

Part II: Livelihoods and Lifestyles

8. Young Egyptians' Quest for Jobs and Justice, 127
    Linda Herrera

9. Reaching a Larger World: Muslim Youth and Expanding Circuits
    of Operation, 145
    AbdouMaliq Simone

10. Being Young, Muslim, and American in Brooklyn, 161
    Moustafa Bayoumi

Part III: Strivings for Citizenship

11. "Also the School Is a Temple": Republicanism, Imagined Transnational
    Spaces, and the Schooling of Muslim Youth in France, 177
    André Elias Mazawi

12. Avoiding "Youthfulness?": Young Muslims Negotiating Gender
    and Citizenship in France and Germany, 189
    Schirin Amir-Moazami

13. Struggles over Defining the Moral City: The Problem Called
    "Youth" in Urban Iran, 207
    Azam Khatam

Part IV: Navigating Identities

14. Securing Futures: Youth, Generation, and Muslim Identities in Niger, 225
    Adeline Masquelier

15. "Rasta" Sufis and Muslim Youth Culture in Mali, 241
    Benjamin F. Soares

16. Performance, Politics, and Visceral Transformation: Post-Islamist
    Youth in Turkey, 259
    Ayşe Saktanber

17. Negotiating with Modernity: Young Women and Sexuality in Iran, 273
    Fatemeh Sadeghi

Part V: Musical Politics

18. Fun^Da^Mental's "Jihad Rap", 291
    Ted Swedenburg

19. Maroc-Hop: Music and Youth Identities in the Netherlands, 309
Miriam Gazzah

20. Heavy Metal in the Middle East: New Urban Spaces in a Translocal
Underground, 325
Pierre Hecker

21. Music VCDs and the New Generation: Negotiating Youth, Femininity,
and Islam in Indonesia, 341
Suzanne Naafs

22. Conclusion: Knowing Muslim Youth, 355
Linda Herrera and Asef Bayat

Notes, 365

References, 391

Index, 421

About the Authors

Schirin Amir-Moazami holds a professorship for Islam in Europe at the Department of Islamic Studies at Free University Berlin. Prior to that she worked as a researcher at Europa-Universität Viadrina in Frankfurt/Oder. Her research interests include gender, political theory, Islamic movements in Europe, and politics of religion and the secular. Her publications include "Euro-Islam, Islam in Europe, or Europe revised through Islam? Versions of Muslim solidarity within European borders" (2007), "Islam und Geschlechtunter liberal-säkularer Regierungsführung—Die Deutsche Islam Konferenz" (2009), and, with Jeanette Jouili, "Knowledge, Empowerment and Religious Authority among Pious Muslim Women in France and Germany" (2006).

Asef Bayat is professor of sociology and Middle East studies and holds the chair of society and culture of the modern Middle East at Leiden University, The Netherlands. His research areas range from social movements and nonmovements; to religion, politics, and everyday life; Islam and the modern world; urban space and politics; and international development. His books include *Street Politics: Poor People's Movements in Iran* (1997), *Making Islam Democratic: Social Movements and the Post-Islamist Turn* (2007), and *Life as Politics: How Ordinary People Change the Middle East* (2009).

Moustafa Bayoumi is an associate professor of English at Brooklyn College, City University of New York. He is the coeditor of

The Edward Said Reader (2000) and the author of *How Does It Feel to Be a Problem?: Being Young and Arab in America* (2008), winner of a 2008 American Book Award.

Mounia Bennani-Chraïbi is associate professor at the Institute of Political and International Studies, at the University of Lausanne. Her research deals with youth, mobilizations (associations, elections), and militants in Moroccan political parties. She coedited the volumes *Jeunesses des sociétés arabes: Par-delà les menaces et les promesses* (2007), *Scènes et coulisses de l'élection au Maroc: Les législatives* (2002), and *Résistances et protestations dans les sociétés musulmanes* (2003).

Miriam Gazzah received her PhD from the International Institute for the Study of Islam in the Modern World in Leiden, the Radboud University in Nijmegen in September 2008. Her dissertation, "Rhythms and Rhymes of Life: Music and Identification Processes of Dutch–Moroccan Youth," was published by Amsterdam University Press (2008). She is currently a postdoctoral fellow at the Amsterdam School for Social Science Research at Amsterdam University, working within a research program called Islamic Cultural Performances: New Youth Cultures in Europe.

Noorhaidi Hasan is associate professor at Sunan Kalijaga State Islamic University of Yogyakarta, Indonesia, and also serves as the director of the Centre for the Study of Islam and Social Transformation at the university. His research interests include transnational Islam, youth, and political mobilization in contemporary Indonesia. Among his publications are *Laskar Jihad: Islam, Militancy, and the Quest for Identity in Post-New Order Indonesia* (2006); "Saudi Expansion, Wahhabi Campaign and Arabised Islam in Indonesia," (2008); and "Ambivalent Doctrines and Conflicts in the Salafi Movement in Indonesia" (2009).

Pierre Hecker holds an MA in Middle East studies from the University of Erlangen-Nürnberg and recently completed his dissertation on Turkish heavy metal at the Department of Oriental Studies at the University of Leipzig. He is the author of several articles on heavy metal in the Middle East and coeditor of the book *Muslimische Gesellschaften in der Moderne* (Muslim Societies in Modernity, 2007).

Linda Herrera is a senior lecturer in international development studies at the International Institute of Social Studies of the Erasmus University Rotterdam

and convenor of the Children and Youth Studies (CYS) Master of Arts specialization. Her research interests lay at the intersection of youth and international
development, the social history of education in the Middle East and North
Africa, and critical pedagogy. Her publications include the coedited volume,
Cultures of Arab Schooling: Critical Ethnographies from Egypt (2006), "A Song
For Humanistic Education: Pedagogy and Politics in the Middle East"(2008),
and "Education and Empire: Democratic Reform in the Arab World?" (2008).

Marloes Janson earned her PhD in cultural anthropology from Leiden Univer-
sity in 2002. Her published PhD dissertation is titled *The Best Hand Is the
Hand That Always Gives: Griottes and Their Profession in Eastern Gambia* (2002).
She is currently working as a researcher at Zentrum Moderner Orient in Berlin,
Germany, and was affiliated as a visiting lecturer in anthropology at Brandeis
University during spring semester 2009. Her research focuses on youthful
participation in the Tabligh Jama'at, a transnational Islamic missionary
movement originating from India, in The Gambia, and has resulted in several
journal articles and book chapters. She is currently working on a monograph of
the Gambian branch of the Tabligh Jama'at.

Azam Khatam is an Iranian independent sociologist who works on issues of
space and society, urban structure, and movement in the developing world. Her
main research interests during the past two decades have been urban change
and geography in postrevolution Iran and the role of women in the labor market. She is a member of the editorial board of the quarterly journal *Goftogu*
(Dialogue). Her edited book, *City and Earthquake: Why Earthquake Is Lethal in
Iran,* is forthcoming.

Makram Khoury-Machool specializes in media and politics. He was a fellow at
the university of Oxford and formerly taught at the School of Oriental and African
Studies, London, Bedfordshire and Anglia Ruskin. He has been teaching and
supervising at the University of Cambridge since 2003. He is also the head of
mass media communications studies at the University of Hertfordshire. He
was the journalist who announced the outbreak of the first Palestinian *Intifada*
in 1987 and was a Reuters Award prize winner in 1990. His textbook on Arab
media, *Arab Media: From the First Press to New Media* is forthcoming.

Adeline Masquelier is professor of anthropology at Tulane University and director of the religious studies program. She is currently executive editor of the
Journal of Religion in Africa. She has written on a range of topics including spirit
possession, Islam and Muslim identity, witchcraft, twinship, dress, and medicine

based on her research in Niger. She is author of *Prayer Has Spoiled Everything: Possession, Power, and Identity in an Islamic Town of Niger* (2001) and *Women and Islamic Revival in a West African Town* (2009), and editor of *Dirt, Undress, and Difference: Critical Perspectives on the Body's Surface* (2005). Her current interests are centered on Muslim youth, romantic love, and popular culture in Niger.

André Elias Mazawi is an associate professor in the Department of Educational Studies, Faculty of Education, University of British Columbia, Vancouver, BC, Canada. His fields of interest are sociology of education, schooling and higher education policy, and comparative education. He is currently interested in the schooling of Muslim youth in France within the larger contexts of deregulatory policies, spatial segregation, multiculturalism, and European politics in post-9/11. His publications include "Dis/integrated Orders and the Politics of Recognition: Civil Upheavals, Militarism, and Educators' Lives and Work" (2008) and the coedited volume *Education and the Arab "World": Political Projects, Struggles, and Geometries of Power* (2010).

Pascal Ménoret is a postdoctoral research associate at the Institute for the Transregional Study of the Middle East, North Africa, and Central Asia (Princeton University). Between 2005 and 2007, he was a visiting researcher at the King Faisal Center for Research and Islamic Studies in Riyadh. He is currently writing a book on deviance and politics in Saudi Arabia.

Suzanne Naafs is a PhD candidate at the International Institute of Social Studies of Erasmus University Rotterdam. She is writing her dissertation on how young people in an Indonesian industrial town engage with globalization and negotiate the processes and relations that influence their access to and inclusion in education, lifestyles, and livelihoods.

Abdullah al-Otaibi graduated from the Institute of Public Administration in Riyadh. He is currently working on a documentary movie on *tafhit*.

Fatemeh Sadeghi obtained her PhD in political science from Tarbiyat Modarres University, Tehran, in 2004 and was a fellow of the International Institute for the Study of Islam in the Modern World in Leiden in 2008. She is currently a member of the editorial board of the Persian quarterly *Goftogu* (Dialogue). Her book, *Gender, Nationalism, and Modernity in the First Pahlavi Iran*, was published in Persian, and *Gender and Power: A Study of Ethics from the Third to Ninth Century Iran* is forthcoming.

Ayşe Saktanber is professor and chair in the Department of Sociology at the Middle East Technical University, Turkey. Her major research interests are in cultural studies, gender and women's studies, media studies, and Islam in the Middle East. Her publications include *Living Islam: Women, Religion and the Politicization of Culture in Turkey* (2002) and the coedited volume *Fragments of Culture: The Everyday of Modern Turkey* (2002).

AbdouMaliq Simone is an urbanist and professor of sociology at Goldsmiths College, University of London. Since 1977 he has had many jobs in different cities across Africa and Southeast Asia, in the fields of education, housing, social welfare, urban development, and local government. His best known publications include *In Whose Image: Political Islam and Urban Practices in the Sudan* (1994), *For the City Yet to Come: Urban Change in Four African Cities* (2004), and *Movement at the Crossroads: City Life from Jakarta to Dakar* (2009).

Benjamin Soares, an anthropologist, is a senior research fellow at the Afrika-Studiecentrum in Leiden, The Netherlands. He has recently been a visiting professor at the University of Cape Town and at Northwestern University in Evanston, Illinois. His publications include *Islam and the Prayer Economy* (2005) and the edited volumes *Islam and Muslim Politics in Africa* (2007), *Muslim–Christian Encounters in Africa* (2006), and "Islam, Politics, Anthropology," the 2009 special issue of the *Journal of the Royal Anthropological Institute*.

Ted Swedenburg is professor of anthropology at the University of Arkansas. He is the author of *Memories of Revolt: The 1936–39 Rebellion and the Palestinian National Past* (1995; 2003), and coeditor of *Displacement, Diaspora and the Geographies of Identity* (1996) and *Palestine, Israel, and the Politics of Popular Culture* (2005). He is working on a book about the transnational flows of Middle Eastern and Islamic music titled *Radio Interzone*. He serves on the editorial committee of *Middle East Report*.

Being Young and Muslim

I

Introduction:
Being Young and Muslim
in Neoliberal Times

Asef Bayat and Linda Herrera

The current demographic shift heavily tilted toward a young population
has caused a remarkable change in the social composition of Muslim
majority countries. Youth have assumed a central, if complex, place in
the politics and cultures of these societies, as well as in societies where
Muslims make up a sizable minority. As a result of a combination of the
shifting moral politics at home, the relentless process of neoliberal
globalization, the geopolitics of neo-imperialism, the rise of a
civilizational discourse in which "Islam" is positioned in opposition to
the "West," and unprecedented levels of school and university graduates
combined with crises of unemployment, youth cultures are developing
in novel ways with consequences of historical significance. Their
expressions of interests, aspirations, and socioeconomic capacities
appear to be producing a new cultural politics. In other words, the
cultural behavior of Muslim youths can be understood as located in the
political realm and representing a new arena of contestation for power.

While often referred to as the *builders of the future* by the power
elite, the young are also stigmatized and feared as "disruptive" agents
prone to radicalism and deviance. Although gender, class, and
cultural divisions may render untenable a homogenous treatment of
youths, or even call into question "youth" as an analytical category, it
is equally true that the young undeniably share a certain important
habitus and historical consciousness that is recognized by both the
young themselves as well as by the political establishment and

moral authorities. The complex status of Muslim youths in these neoliberal times is what we intend to explore in this book.

The objective of this volume, then, is to address questions about the cultural politics of Muslim youth from the perspective of the youths themselves; from the viewpoint of political and moral authorities who consider it their role to discipline, control, and formulate policies for the young; and from an understanding of market and media forces in which youths are both consumers and producers. Furthermore, this volume explores intersections of the global with the local, with special attention on how specific attitudes, cultural behaviors, and tendencies are instigated among the young, and how these may have changed since September 11, 2001. The "construction" of Muslim youth, therefore, represents a dialectical interplay between different forces and actors.

Youth are at times described as the *new proletariat* of the 21st century. A combination of the youth bulge (when young people from 15–29 years comprise more than 40% of the adult population), youth unemployment, and exclusion is believed by many to be a dangerous recipe that leads to political instability and civil wars, especially in the global South. Major civil conflicts from the 19th century to recent times are attributed to a youth bulge during conditions of scarce livelihoods (Cincotta et al. 2003: 45–48; UN Office for West Africa 2005). Recent studies suggest that young men account for "about 90% of arrests for homicide in almost all countries" surveyed, and more than three quarters of violent crimes worldwide (UN Office for West Africa 2005: 44). Currently, the world's most "extreme" youth bulge societies, where cohorts between 15 to 29 years make up more than 50% of the population, are located in 27 counties in sub-Saharan Africa, the Middle East, and South and Central Asia, 13 of which are Muslim majority states and several of which contain sizeable Muslim minorities (ibid).

There is a general feeling that the marginality of a very large young Muslim population incurs not only major economic human capital costs (in education, health, and training for employment), but also accounts for a new age of instability (Chaaban 2008). A prevailing claim made in media and policy circles is that Muslim youth constitute the driving force behind radical religion and politics in the Islamic mainland and in Europe, and hence pose a serious security threat worldwide (Beehner 2007). Youth marginality, in short, is said to be responsible for Islamism, *Jihadi* trends, and a range of illiberal extremist behavior among the young—all of which stand against commonly perceived youthful interests. Such assumptions position Muslims as "exceptional" in relation to their global counterparts. These exceptionalist claims about Muslim youth are made not simply because of their objective marginalization, but especially because of their "Muslimness"—an attribute often equated with religious

fundamentalism, outdated notions about gender relations, insularity, and proclivities toward violence.

The post-September 11, 2001, "war on terrorism" rhetoric, for instance, is
replete with assumptions about how conditions of poverty and unemployment
in Muslim majority countries are apt to lead Muslim youth on paths of radicalism and violence. Esposito and Mogahed (2007: 67–68) write in *Who Speaks for
Islam? What a Billion Muslims Really Think*: "The conventional wisdom, based
on old and deeply held stereotypes and presuppositions about extremists, has
often fallen back on an intuitive sense that a combination of religious fanaticism, poverty, and unemployment drive extremism and terrorism." Their
analysis of a Gallup World Poll representing 90% of the world's Muslims (1.3
billion people) in 35 countries, call these assumptions into question. They concur that although unemployment and poverty are both major social problems,
"neither unemployment nor job status differentiate radicals from moderates.
No difference exists in the unemployment rate among the politically radicalized and moderates; both are approximately 20%" (Esposito and Mogahed 2007:
71). Similarly, the realization after 9/11 that some of the perpetrators of the
attacks and their leaders were highly educated, employable, from well-connected
families, and not all observant Muslims, was evidence that other explanations
were needed to understand youth involvement in not only radical groups, but
also in the spectrum of movements.

How exceptional, then, are Muslim youth when compared with their global
cohorts? The chapters in this volume, which take a cross-cultural perspective
that spans the global North and South, question sweeping assumptions about
the threats posed by Muslim youth. They demonstrate that although segments
of the young are certainly drawn into radical Islam and make up the foot sol-
diers of militant Islamist groups such as the Indonesian Lashkar Jihad, Moroccan Society of al-Adal wal-Ehsan, or Egyptian al-Gama'a al-Islamiya, many
others from similar backgrounds opt for different kinds of politics, if at all.
Broadly speaking, there is more to the lives of Muslim youth (whether in the
Muslim mainland or societies in which they make up minority communities)
than mere religiosity, conservative cultural politics, and extremism. Despite
common elements of identification and cultural specificities, Muslim youth
have as much in common with their non-Muslim global counterparts as they
share among themselves. While there exist many lines of demarcation within
the category of "Muslim youth" along lines of class, gender, education, and
cultural divides, to name a few, there are also certain common attributes that
make the category of "Muslim youth" meaningful. But what is meant by the
notion of "youth" in general? How can we make sense of the term if we do not
wish to be bogged down by empirical messiness?

The Young, Youth, and Youth Movements

Pierre Bourdieu (1993) has famously contended that *youth* is "nothing but a word," because young people of different social classes have too little in common to warrant a single category. But Bourdieu's contention refers largely to the times and places where schooling was the privilege of elites, a situation very different from the current era of mass schooling—one that produces and prolongs "youthfulness" on a very broad national and global scale. We are not suggesting, of course, that people from different gender and cultural backgrounds carry identical experiences of being (or even not being) young, because they do not. What we are suggesting is that despite important differences, certain fundamental dispositions, a particular *habitus* (to use Bourdieu's own term) renders "youth" a meaningful analytical category.

To elaborate, "youths" in the sense of "young persons" is, in part, an age category and thus bears an essential biological attribute in the same way that "woman" constitutes a biological category. But *youth*, like *woman*, is also a socially constructed category that carries certain time and culture-bound sociopsychological characteristics. In the second instance, "youth" represents a sociological reality. In this sense, it describes social conditions in human development, a "life stage" where the individual stands between childhood (as the stage of vulnerability, innocence, need of protection) and adulthood (the time of responsibility for self and others). Theoretically, a young person should experience a life of "relative autonomy"—a social condition in which the individual is neither dependent nor totally independent. Mass schooling is instrumental in the production and prolongation of being young, because it sets youngsters apart from the world of work and responsibility, while at the same time generating some degree of self-reliance where the individual makes choices and expresses autonomous ideas.

Youth, in the sense of being young, represents a kind of Bourdieuian "habitus" that consists of a series of dispositions, mental and cognitive structures, and ways of being, feeling, and carrying oneself that are not consciously or rationally designed, yet follow a structure associated with the biological fact of being young. As habitus, young people are often involved in everyday practices of cultural politics, exemplified in negotiating with adults, carving out their own social and cultural spaces, rebelling against the establishment, forming subcultures, innovating, and worrying about their future adult status. These practices and ideas are, in the first instance, individual, expressed in families, neighborhoods, and schools, but they also take collective form in the realms of youth slang, fashion, or in the more durable subcultural activities of, for example, music.

The actual expressions and the reality of being young (or experiencing youth) are more complex and vary across cultural, class, gender, and other divides. Although middle class youths (both male and female) of rich industrialized nations, the "global North," have a chance to experience relative autonomy, many rural youngsters (especially female) in poor countries, the "global South," may have little opportunity to undergo "youthfulness." For they have to move rapidly from the status of childhood into the world of work, responsibility, and parenting—all markers of adulthood. Some youngsters, thus, are excluded from the stage of youth by virtue of their lack of participation in, or access to, education, youth leisure activities, media, and markets, key axes around which youth cultures and politics crystallize and modes of youth consciousness form.

Young persons would thus be unable to forge a collective challenge to assert their youthful status and act as collective agents without first turning into the social category of youth. Cities play a crucial role in turning young people into youth, by cultivating a particular consciousness about being young (Bayat, chapter 2, this volume). Schooling, mass media, and urban spaces (public parks, shopping malls, or street corner spots, to name a few locales) provide key venues for the formation of youth identities. Some scholars have spoken about the formation of "rural youth" (distinct from "young people"), without acknowledging that the rural areas to which they refer have, in reality, assumed some major features of urban life, such as the spread of schooling, expansion of information and communication technology (ICT), spread of fashion trends and consumer products, specialization, and the spread of the nuclear family that, taken together, have transformed the countryside's social structure and political economy. Although youth as a social category remains an essentially urban phenomenon, as rural areas urbanize, distinctions between rural and urban become more blurred.

What about youth movements? It is curious that social movement theory has little to say about the nature of youth movements. The general assumption seems to be that youth movements are those in which mostly young people take central stage, such as the student activism or antiwar mobilization of the 1960s in Europe and the United States. This is not to say that youth do not get adequate attention in scholarly circles. On the contrary, recent years have witnessed numerous websites and conferences on various themes ranging from HIV/AIDS, new media, religious activism, conflict, marginalization, and music that in one way or another relate to the life of young people. Yet in these intellectual endeavors, "youth" remains accidental or at best peripheral to the central focus of these studies. Our point is that a study that investigates religious radicalism or political protests in which young people happen to participate is not necessarily about youth per se, unless the youthful implications of such movements or protests are examined. Consequently, forms of youth activism that do not fall into the frame of classical social movements are viewed largely from the prism of social problems or subcultural studies. At best, youth activism gets subsumed under the category of student protests or larger political movements, rather than being treated in their own right as, specifically, youth movements.

As Bayat elaborates in chapter 2 of this volume, even though most young people are students and most students are young, youth movements should conceptually be distinguished from student activism. Whereas student activism embodies the struggles of a student collective to defend or extend student rights (such as decent education, fair exams, or accountable college management), a youth movement is about claiming and reclaiming youthfulness, or defending or extending youth habitus. Yet a thorough understanding of youth subjectivities and youth movements remains incomplete without placing the young in their historical setting where they share common experience and common sensibilities. The concept of "generation" can offer an especially constructive framework for understanding why the young espouse particular subjectivities during a certain historical period.

Generation and Generational Consciousness

Whereas the concept of habitus captures the spaces, dispositions, and ways of being young, the sociological literature on generations provides insights into how youth develop historical consciousness. Generational research, from studies on the interwar period that viewed German youth movements and cultures as a factor in the rise of fascism in the 1920s and '30s (Wohl 1979); to the antiwar, consumer-oriented, and politically progressive generation of the 1960s in the United States and Europe; to the postcolonial (Camaroff and Camaroff 1999) and "lost" generation (O'Brien 1996) in Africa, are examples of how a generational lens can allow for an understanding of larger social processes and the role of youth as a potential generative force for cultural and political change (Cole and Durham 2007; Durham 2000; Edmunds and Turner 2002, 2005; Eisenstadt 2003). To understand the features of a global generation, as well as the subset, or "generational unit" (Mannheim 1952) of Muslim youth, requires understanding key historical factors—economic, political, and cultural, as well as issues relating to lifestyle and livelihood—that contribute to shaping a generational consciousness.

The youth represented in this volume are roughly between 15 to 29 years old, born in the years ranging from 1979 to 1993. They are "the most highly educated generation in human history" (UN Department of Economic and Social Affairs 2005: 13). Education, however, has not necessarily translated into better opportunities, security, or livelihood. This generation has had to maneuver in an economic order of mature neoliberalism that has seen the dismantling of welfare states and public provisioning of all sorts, and the rise of insecure labor arrangements. Youth, especially those from low- and middle-income countries, continuously confront an array of insecurities and hurdles with regard to their current lives and future prospects (Herrera 2006a). Some 90% of the world's young are located in the global South, in regions that experienced massive transformations and political upheavals during the decades following World War II and leading up to national independence from colonial rule. The youthful revolutionary generation who took part in the anticolonial, nationalist, and Third World nonalignment movements from the 1950s to the '70s gained not only a political consciousness about the power of collective movements to engender change, but also lived during an historical moment of global upheaval when change was not only possible, but inevitable. Those youths who were leaders and active participants in various independence struggles that now date back to more than half a century, are now elder statesmen; members of religious, business, and government establishments; and leaders of the political opposition parties. Whether in opposition movements or ruling parties, political elites do not have a good record of allowing the current younger generation, with the exception of their own kin, into the corridors of power, opportunity, and privilege.[1] In Egypt, for example, as in many other states on the continent and in the region, there is a veritable battle of generations as today's "historic" leaders from the 1950s and 1960s (who are well into their 70s and 80s) hold on to their power monopolies.

This generation has come of age in a post-Cold War era, a supposedly more unipolar world with a highly militarized United States at its head (although the rise of competing powers cannot be disputed). At the same time, the fall of the Berlin Wall in 1989 provided the iconic imagery for a new era when human rights would become the moral and political compass for the world's nations and peoples—the "official ideology of the new world order" (Douzinas 2007: 32). Hopes were raised for the spread of a global order steeped in principles of rights, justice, democracy, gender equity, and participation. School systems worldwide in which these youth have participated have seen an unprecedented convergence on educational reforms that promote—at least on the formal policy level, if not always in practice—children's rights, global citizenship, and youth participation (Herrera 2008). Whereas educational institutions provide a vertical and formal pedagogic space to promote a changing consciousness about citizenship and rights, burgeoning ICT offers a more horizontal pedagogic space.

Muslim youth, like their global counterparts, have come of age during a technological and communications revolution. New information communication technologies (ICT), from the mobile phone to the Internet, have changed the landscape of youth learning, culture, sociability, and political engagement. This generation, the "e (electronic)-generation" or "Internet generation" "operates in a more interactive and less hierarchical way, and there is greater scope for mutual influence" (Edmunds and Turner 2005: 569). Clay Shirky calls this dual role of being both a producer and a consumer "symmetrical participation," which means that "once people have the capacity to receive information, they have the capability to send it, as well" (2008, p. 107). On a massive and growing scale, youth use the new media as a tool for peer interaction, leisure, consumption, generating and consuming information, and an array of direct and indirect political action—uses that are not mutually exclusive. Global youth cultures spread and interact by means of satellite television (Lynch 2006), blogging (Etling et al. 2009, Ulrich 2009), texting, sharing videos which they themselves have often created through a process of mixing through YouTube (created in 2005), and social networking sites of Facebook (launched in 2004), My Space (2002), and Twitter (2006). As the communication sphere becomes more linguistically plural (Arabic, for instance, was introduced into Google and Facebook in 2009), youth navigate between different linguistic, spatial, and cultural communities with growing ease[2] (fig. 1.1).

Insofar as they have come of age in a common "world time" and take part in the cultural politics of a global youth culture, Muslim youth are part of a global generation. However, the fateful events surrounding the terrorist attacks of September 11, 2001; longer standing geopolitical conflicts in the Muslim Middle East, Asia, and Africa; debates and policy changes in Europe and North America with relation to Islam, integration, and multiculturalism—combined with situations of marginality and crises of livelihood for Muslim youth throughout the South and North—has set apart Muslim youth in some significant ways as a generational subset. Muslim youth today are struggling to assert their youthfulness, claim rights, and make life transitions in a highly fraught post-9/11 global moment in which they are subject to media scrutiny, surveillance, a range of policy interventions to contain them, influence them, and cultivate in them a strong Islamic identity. But these youths diverge radically among themselves in how to turn their common sentiments into action, how to respond to their status of "subordination."

FIGURE I.I. An event at Cairo University introducing Google's Arabic Knol program. (Ahmed A. Gaballah, 2009)

Among global youth in general, but Muslim youth in an even more pronounced way, there appears to be a growing generational consciousness, diffused in part through the new media, about issues of social justice and human rights accompanied by a profound moral outrage at the violation of fundamental rights. Young people blog, sing, protest, agitate, join formal and informal organizations, and find myriad other ways to claim their rights and assert their will for justice, livelihoods, and lifestyles. The fundamental question that the authors in this volume address, is how does this generation of Muslim youth operate within the multiple constraints and opportunities of being young, Muslim, marginalized, and subjects of social control?

Livelihoods and Lifestyles

The demands and desires of many youth are simple. As Dina, a 20-something Egyptian explains when discussing the aspirations of her generation: "The ambitions of young people are modest. We want to live at a decent level (' ala mustawa karim), get a job, find love, and get married."

Yet for scores of youth, these simple goals seem hopelessly out of reach (Herrera, chapter 8). Economic exclusion, political corruption, underemployment, and deprivation prevail among a vast segment of youth, which means "the transformation into adulthood is something increasingly problematic" (Simone, chapter 9).

Youth unemployment and underemployment stand among the towering challenges of these times. Youth unemployment rates (15–24 years) are the highest in the Middle East region, where they have reached 25% (the world average is 14%). In Iran, for instance, the rate rose from 19% in 1996 to 24% in 2006, while a staggering 77% of Syrian young (compared with 12% of the total workforce) in 2002 remained without jobs (Chaaban 2008). Similar kinds of marginalization have gripped Muslim minorities in Europe. British Asian male Muslims, who reside in segregated and oftentimes dreary housing units, suffer from unemployment three times higher than their white male counterparts; similar trends can be found among ethnic Arab/Muslim youth in France and the Netherlands.

For an average middle class youngster, not having a job means little income, slight chance of having an independent accommodation, and low chance of marriage—in sum, no meaningful autonomous life. Precisely because of their youth status and the lack of steady employment, youngsters face far greater difficulties in securing credit to plan for a new life and marriage. Simply put, the high cost of marriage in regions like the Middle East and North Africa, combined with lack of jobs and affordable housing, prevent the young from experiencing the transition to adulthood and independence (Salehi-Isfahani and Dhillon 2008).

Most young people, then, seem to be trapped in this maze of structural constraints and power relations. How does it feel to be in such a desperate predicament? Linda Herrera offers a taste of what is like to be part of the middle class youth in today's Egypt. Those in the most difficult circumstances, who struggle without connections, means, and opportunities, can suffer from an overwhelming sense of "being stuck," of not being able to see a way out of the state of liminality in which they find themselves.

To be sure, social justice issues and the right to a livelihood are not the exclusive concerns of young people. Adults too often express similar claims, but the young remain disproportionately more disadvantaged. The fact is that deprivation from livelihood not only affects a young person's general well-being, but it also has undeniable bearing on the expression of specifically youthful desires—for example, to have enough income to acquire consumer goods, pursue youthful dreams, and be free from anxiety about their adult future. The right to a livelihood—one that also secures a youthful habitus—is certainly a key demand of low-income youngsters, something that differentiates them from their well-to-do counterparts.

Yet Muslim youths from almost all social classes (rich, poor, and middle class), in settings where they make up minorities (as in Europe and Africa) and majorities (in the Middle East and parts of Asia), share a broader kind of concern: the violation of rights to a lifestyle, a concern that involves the young population as a whole. In states with repressive moral regimes, hardships for the young go beyond the fact that large proportions of them cannot find work. In regimes such as in Iran, Saudi Arabia, or Afghanistan, the young—whether male or female, rich or poor, rural or urban—have been undergoing systematic forms of social control and disciplining by the state. Through different types of policing, states mandate what the young can wear, how they should look, who they can associate with (especially if unmarried), where they can go, what they can listen to, and so on. Azam Khatam describes in this volume the elaborate ways in which the state attempted to discipline youth in the name of fighting "immorality," "westernization," and "cultural invasion."

While religious states regulate youth behavior in the name of "religious values," Turkish and French secular states do so in the name of "secular values." André Mazawi shows how the French state systematizes the "regulation" of Muslim youth through schooling and its policy of laicité. Within the backdrop of a French and European public sphere in which Muslim citizens occupy a growing space, Mazawi examines how debates around Muslim confessional schools and republican secular schools offer a lens to understand competing notions of Muslim youth, citizenship, and forms of political action. Likening the school to a temple, he elaborates how the school functions as political ritual. The imagined sacred experience of schooling is where French Muslim youth are thought to become transformed into citizens of the French republic and "Europeanized" members the Islamic umma. The schooling of Muslim youth thus provides insights into debates concerning integration, social diversity, and multiculturalism in Europe.

The religious activity and appearance of Muslim youth in public arenas inevitably place them in sites of struggle for equality and recognition for citizenship. The feeling of alienation and "otherness" among the Muslim youth in France is particularly strong, because these youths consider themselves as French, the legal citizens of a nation that, however, shuns them as "outsiders". They are quite different from the Muslim youth in Germany, who find the host country more "tolerant," precisely because they already assume themselves immigrant "outsiders" who are nevertheless "tolerated" by the host nation. In both France and Germany, however, many young Muslims are involved in the kind of religious appearances and activities—putting on the headscarf, refraining from drinking and premarital sex, or pursuing modesty—that the mainstream society considers "unyouthful."

Schirin Amir-Moazami offers a provocative argument by suggesting that the piety of Muslim young women in Germany or France actually challenges or redefines "youthful dispositions" like individuality, autonomy, joy, and fun; because these youths "confine themselves to forms of piety, which consciously attempt to overcome certain youthful temptations". Indeed, the religious sensibilities of these Muslim youngsters are not dissimilar to their conservative Christian counterparts in the United States who dislike MTV, refrain from premarital sex, and live a pious life. But, is such "countercultural" behavior necessarily "unyouthful," considering that autonomy, individuality, or adventurism may be expressed not simply in terms of "wild hedonism," but also counter to it? The truth is that both veiling and unveiling may express an instance of "youthful" acts if they symbolize challenges to dominant norms, defy the older generation, and express autonomy. In addition, can one not interpret the headscarf in France or the *chador* in Iran in terms of Bourdieuian "distinction," as a set of cultivating virtues and bodily behavior that distinguish the young from the rest? As Amir-Moazami argues in chapter 12, for French and German Muslim young girls, "searching to please God, fulfilling religious duties and cultivating piety are the touchstones of their way to adulthood. While these women simultaneously negotiate freedoms within intergenerational conflicts with their parents or extended family, it is not sexual liberation, but rather the contrary—the avoidance of the temptations of dominant sexuality norms outside of the framework of matrimony" to which they aspire.

Whatever the forms of expressions—going pious in France and Germany or defying piety in Iran or Saudi Arabia—Muslim youth are inevitably placed in the arena of struggles for citizenship and the right to pursue a lifestyle. What shapes the cultural politics of Muslim youth is not any intrinsically rebellious nature of such pious or unpious conducts, nor, for that matter, the particular disposition of *Muslim* youth; primarily, it is the behavior of the states in violating youth rights. But what kind of reactions do Muslim youth exhibit when confronted with the seemingly desperate conditions of exclusion in economic, political, and social arenas?

From Radical Religion to Minimal Life

Do Muslim youth exhibit necessarily a more intense propensity toward radicalism and religious politics than their non-Muslim counterparts? Is there a direct link between being young and militant Islamism? To what extent do the conditions of exclusion play a role in a young person's choice toward radicalism? And what is the role of Islam as a political theology? The discussion of diverse national cases in this book confirms that the analytical links between deprivation and political response, between youth and radicalism, and between youth and religiosity are extremely complex and that a simple conclusion cannot be drawn. Indeed, youth respond to similar conditions in a variety of ways, depending on the setting and a host of other factors; they may engage in radical politics, withdraw from public life out of frustration, or pursue a minimal life.

In Indonesia during the late 1990s, a segment of Muslim youth joined a flamboyant armed militia, Laskar Jihad, which upheld a Salafi ideology. Even though Indonesia emerged from the Asian crisis during the late 1990s with more than 70% youth unemployment, the correlation between the economy and youth radicalism remains incidental, at best. Laskar Jihad, with some 7,000 militant youngsters ranging in age from 20 to 29 years, half of them university students or graduates, reflected, according to Noorhaidi Hasan not simply an irrational fanaticism of the lower class young, but a "rational choice in their attempt to negotiate identity, and thus claim dignity". The group could be seen to be carrying out a "drama," a sort of "performative practice of youth to demonstrate, in face of powerful opponents, a hitherto marginalized youth". These were the youngsters who saw the horizon for upward mobility to be quite limited. By cultivating the idea of the "total Muslim," the Salafi ideology of Laskar Jihad provided an alternative community and a distinct identity in which the lower class Indonesian youth found meaning, purpose, and dignity in life.

Mounia Bennani-Chraibi's study of Moroccan youth makes it clear that religious positioning is less a matter of age, than a matter of education and dispositions gained through becoming an "educated person." Thus, educated young and old converge in their views and stand apart from those less educated people. Herrera's life history of an educated but disenfranchised Egyptian youth gives life to Bennani's sociological argument. Karim, an unemployed Egyptian youth waits in what seems like a permanent state of limbo. Despite having the "profile" of a would-be radical, he opposes extremist religious ideas, and by so doing confirms that radicalism is not the inevitable trajectory of dis- enfranchised youth. However, he expresses a degree of understanding, if not empathy, with those who choose an alternate path when he says: "I want to emphasize that the young person who becomes a terrorist sees his life as a closed path. It is closed in its past, its future, its material and moral aspects. This person needs someone to help him but doesn't find anyone. He doesn't belong to a powerful family that can protect him from failed laws. The social and economic conditions don't provide him with any opportunities. He is angry that all the important things in his life—work and love—have failed. He doesn't believe in the social structure since it's neither just nor legitimate. He considers this system responsible for his own failures and problems of his society. . . . This person has nothing to do but to escape".

Yet despite these variations in attitudes toward radical Islam, there does exist among the young in Morocco, Egypt, Turkey, and indeed throughout the Muslim world, a general sentiment that they share as "Muslim youth"—an identity that is reinforced primarily by international processes such as western "Islamophobia" or Palestinian victimhood.

Adherence to political Islam represents only one venue that some pursue. The fact is that beyond biographical trajectories (family background, educational level, ideological baggage, and so forth), the morally outraged Muslim youngsters need a political opportunity—a permissible political climate and a catalyst for social action—to be able to mobilize. Otherwise, they might opt for exit, accommodation, or everlasting waiting for something to turn up, if they do not pursue the path of underground activism.

In Palestine, cyber activism has provided an outlet for vigorous youth political engagement because it functions outside physical constraints of space and, although to a lesser extent, under the radar of surveillance and censorship. Makram Khoury-Machool documents in this book how Palestinian educational institutions and nongovernmental organizations, given the many constraints they faced operating under conditions of occupation, seized the opportunities offered by the World Wide Web for teaching, organizing, and communicating with each other and the outside world. The Internet has become increasingly central to everyday Palestinian life and is used as a means not only for information, commerce, and social organization, but also for forming international solidarities around issues of Palestinian rights and justice. Palestinian youth in particular have became highly skilled in ICT and have been pioneers in using the Web for emerging forms of peaceful youth activism.

How do the young operate in a society such as Saudi Arabia, where the state imposes high social control and political surveillance, including censorship of cyber space? Here, a segment of youth has joined in the radical Sahwa movement, whereas others sympathize with Jihadi groups. An alternative form of expression is symbolized in "fatal fun"—a highly dangerous past-time during which the young get involved in car skidding. Called *tahfit*, this trajectory of rage is seen often as a response to social vacuum and boredom, or *tufush*, in a nation that allows little possibility of public fun and collective joy. But as al-Otaibi and Ménoret argue in chapter 5, *tufush* "is not mere boredom and emptiness, but rage that overwhelms young when they realize that structures of opportunities are violently unfair". Coming largely from lower middle class,

Bedouin, and marginal countryside backgrounds settling in Riyad, these youths encounter the incredible wealth and opulence from which they feel they are deprived. A product of the oil-induced modernization of 1980s (mass automobile ownership), the urban boom, anonymity, and declining parental control, *tahfit* represents the rebellion of the street against the Saudi "anarchical modernization" and consumerist bourgeois utopia.

In postpopulist societies in which neoliberal economies operate alongside some sort of multiparty democracy, the resulting economic disparity often finds stiff and open opposition by the relatively free media, and political dissent. In Muslim societies, this dissent often assumes religious language, expressed in Islamic associations and civil activism, especially when traditional secular ideologies and parties lack credibility. However, the form of dissent varies. In Mali, the disenchanted youth have embraced Islam as a moral and political frame, by engaging either in violent Islamist dissent, nonviolent cultural–religious associations, or, in the case of those "tea-drinking" Sufi-orientated youth, spending their abundant free time (because they are unemployed) in tea houses (Soares, chapter 15).

Islam may still play different parts in the lives of Muslim youth. In search of jobs, or any opportunity for that matter, young Muslims circulate cities of the South, oftentimes below the radar. For some, Islam serves as a faith-based community that offers trust, support, and networks, especially for transient youth in non-Muslim environments, within which the young can enhance their life chances. In Bangkok, for instance, Islam serves as a medium through which the migrant Muslim youth intensely associate, build networks, forge trust to do better in society, and work as business partners and as entrepreneurs. For the less fortunate others, those dispossessed youth who cannot afford the "normal" mode of livelihood, Islam may offer what AbduMaliq Simone calls spaces of "minimal" life. These are the Muslim youngsters such as those in Cameroon who do not see Islam as a radical mode of resistance, but as a religious frame that helps them survive the harsh realities of their lives. A mode of minimal life means that youngsters have to forgo many facets of the "standard" globalized "youthfulness," such as acquiring consumer goods, being up to date on the latest youth trends, or being mobile. Yet they find ways to assert their youthful tastes by resorting to what Michael Mann (2001) calls "cheap globalization," such as appearing in the fake but globally typical brands such as Nike baseball caps or listening to pirated international CDs. The truth is "across the world," as Doreen Massey (1998: 122) notes, "even the poorest of young people strive to buy into an international cultural reference system: the right trainers, a T-shirt with a western logo, a baseball cap with the right slogan." In short, even in desperate conditions, these youngsters tend to make the best of what is perceived to be possible (fig. 1.2).

Maneuvering within the constraints and making the best of what is available has become the the art of being young. This "politics of possibility," as Bayat explains, extending between accommodation and subversion, finds particularly remarkable expressions in societies in which the young with a strong youth consciousness face the type of moral and political authorities that tend to deny people's youthful claims. In many Muslim majority countries such as Iran, Saudi Arabia, and, to a lesser extent, Egypt, youthful lifestyles, sexuality, and individualities receive strong hostility on the grounds that they defy prevailing Islamic codes, moral sensibilities, and the ethical well-being of their societies. How do these youngsters manage such constraining conditions? To negotiate their sense of freedoms and to assert youthful habitus within the constraints, some youth groups utilize what looks like "accommodating" strategies, which nevertheless can be transformative. One such strategy is what Bayat calls *subversive accommodation* where youth operate within and thus use the dominant (constraining) norms and institutions, especially religious rituals, to accommodate their youthful claims, but in so doing they creatively redefine and subvert the constraints of those codes and norms. This mode of subversive accommodation is best expressed in the way groups of youths in Iran, for instance, treat

FIGURE 1.2. Young people shopping for bargains outside a mall in Jakarta, Indonesia. (Asef Bayat, 2008)

the highly charged ritual of Muharram, which commemorates the death of Imam Hussein, the grandson of Prophet Muhammed. By inventing what is popularly labeled *Hussein parties*, the young tend to turn this highly austere occasion of mourning into an evening of glamor, fun, and sociability. Boys and girls often dress in their best, stroll through the streets, join parades of mourners, and use the occasion to stay out until dawn to socialize, exchange phone numbers, and arrange dates secretly.

In comparison, in Egypt, where the political authority is less restrictive and youth less assertive, young Egyptians often resort to *accommodating innovation*— that is, they take advantage of the prevailing norms and traditional means to accommodate their youthful claims; they do not depart radically from the dominant system, but make it work for their interests. The relatively widespread practice of *urfi* (informal) marriage since the late 1990s exemplifies this strategy. *Urfi* marriage is a religiously accepted but unofficial oral contract that requires two witnesses and is carried out in secret. In essence, the young utilize this traditional institution to pursue romance within, but not outside or against, the moral and economic order to get around the moral constraints on dating and economic constraints on formal marriage. The practice continues even though it has caused much fear and fury within the state and institutions of establishment Islam, such as al-Azhar in Egypt (Abaza 2001).

Being Young, Muslim, and Modern

All these examples of youthful accommodation, subversion, and rebellion are indicative of the intricate relationship between the young, youth identities, and Islam, and how different youth groups deploy different strategies to maneuver between being young and Muslim. Thus, against common claims, radical religion is neither an essential disposition of Muslim youth, nor is religion foreign to youth habitus or to a "modern" identity. The fact is that Islam has become an important identity marker for many young Muslims, whether modern or traditional, rich or poor. The ways in which the young relate to this religious identity is by no means straightforward. In secular Turkey, as Ayşe Saktanber shows in chapter 16, against all expectations, even high-achieving university youth consider themselves Muslims first. In contrast, in the Islamic Republic of Iran, Muslim youth exhibit such seemingly liberal sexual and moral behavior that their religiosity is cast in doubt. In both secular Turkey and Islamist Iran, religion for these Muslim youths is more a matter of negotiation than some immutable normative codes. These youths strive to perceive and interpret their Islam in ways that can accommodate their youthful habitus. Whatever their approach to Islam—whether expressed with pride, ambiguity, or remorse—the young generate a youthful Islam, one that is more plural, open, ambiguous, and seemingly contradictory. In Niger, as described by Adeline Masquelier in this volume, Muslim youths do not see a conflict between listening to their favorite radio programs and hip-hop tunes, between wearing an American–style baseball cap on the one hand and being concerned with what happens in their prayer halls on the other. "Youth restrict Islamic practices to specific spaces and temporalities, apart from the realm of 'secular,' western-inspired practices, and they carefully negotiate their way between these two domains". These youth simultaneously support what they consider Bin Laden's "punishment of the US" in the 9/11 attacks, as they harbor a keen desire to immigrate to the United States, a country they characterize as "arrogant" and the cause of much misery in different parts of the world. Unlike the more purist and exclusivist youth of the Izlah trend in Niger, most youth have become "pragmatic Muslims."

The seeming ambiguities, the shifting identities, of these young "pragmatic Muslims" exhibit themselves in not simply how "truly Muslim" they are, but also in how truly "modern" they strive to be. Do the radically unconventional youth behaviors—say, the practice of premarital sex—in Muslim societies represent a break from conservative traditions of the past? Drawing on the contradictory behavior and attitudes of young Iranian females (including fully veiled and badly veiled), Fatemeh Sadeghi in chapter 17 suggests that such rather daring and unconventional youth behavior (as premarital sex) under the Islamic Republic does not necessarily point to youth subjectivity as modern actors. Rather, there seems to be a deep mismatch between youths' public claim of modern lifestyle and their inner conservatism. She argues that although these young women are not as docile to traditional norms as their parents' generation, they continue to uphold deeper social conventions of the past—gender hierarchy and male dominance. Thus, young Iranian women may be engaging freely in premarital sexual relationships, but they do so in a social context that privileges male desire over female sexual expressions. In sum, young women defy the traditional and moral authority by wearing loose veils, not necessarily to express free will, but primarily to satisfy the male gaze.

Just as the practices and pretensions of modernity among Muslim youths may be a consequence of global flows of ideas and models, their Islamic identity may also be an outcome of international politics. Internal processes in Muslim majority countries certainly play an important role in generating a religious identity among the young, the "9/11 generation," as is clear in such cases as the Laskar Jihad young activists in Indonesia. It is crucial, however, to note that in the current juncture, global politics has played a crucial part in constructing Islamic identity among the Muslim youth. Whether as radical or moderate, principled or pragmatic, the current cohort of young Muslims constitutes the globalized generation of the post-9/11 era that has felt, experienced, and been overwhelmed by the overbearing politics and discourse in the West that prejudice Islam and Muslims. Very simply put, the recent Islamophobia in the West has rendered even "secular" youth in Muslim societies to identify with Islam.

The construction of identity of this sort is even more critical among Muslim minorities in Europe or the United States, where Muslims are circumvented by the non-Islamic surroundings that deride them. In the United States, for instance, young (Arab) Muslims have been compelled to come to terms with their religious identity, as Bayoumi illustrates. Youth did not ask for Islam; rather, in post-9/11 America, everyone defined them as Muslims. Thus, instead of escaping from or hiding such identity, the Arab Muslim youths have visibly and proactively embraced it, by redefining (and educating) themselves as Muslims. They embraced such an identity because they had to live and get by as Muslims in a hostile climate in which survival depended on establishing a recognition that it is okay to be young, Muslim, and American. Theirs, then, was radically different from their parents' generation, for whom seeking an Islamic identity was not imbued with so much weight.

Musical Politics: Faith, Rage, and Fun

Clearly, the construction of Muslim identity among the youths of minority groups in the West is more complex than that among the youth in Muslim majority countries. Given their non-Islamic cultural and religious surrounding, Muslim minority youth in Europe and North America tend to forge sharper (and imposed) identities than their counterparts, say, in the Middle East. Yet, they are freer to express youthful desires as they face far less social control and moral constraints than in the Islamic mainland. In these complex conditions, perhaps no medium expresses the intricacy of multiple identities among Muslim youth more vividly than music. Because of its location between the real and fictional, serious and sarcastic, musical mediation provides a wider space for expression than even verbal discourse or behavior. Musical bands can insult, be outrageous, cross boundaries, build unusual solidarities, and reach audiences of millions, Muslim and non-Muslim alike. Musical idioms are perhaps the most effective venue for outraged and excluded youth who feel the overbearing inequities of host societies, and find, through music, a way to attain a social capital of hipness and respect on the streets.

Youth music, which has historically constituted an important site of dissent, embodies one of the theaters in which youth politics takes place (Blackman 2005; Hesmondhalgh 2005). The spread and growth of musical youth subcultures are indicative of movements in the political realm and can be seen as a "thermometer for a society's political climate" (Garrat 2004: 146). In the Netherlands, as Miriam Gazzah shows in chapter 19, *sha'bi* Moroccan music acts as a crucial channel for youth to articulate their Moroccan origin in response to experiences of multiple forms of exclusion by the host society. It serves as a long-distance cultural community in which youth can feel at home even though they live on the margins. This feeling does not necessarily utter the love of Morocco. What matters, rather, is constructing a Dutch–Moroccan identity—one that signals a feeling of solidarity, collective sentiment, a space for interconnectedness in a land that repels them as "outsiders." The emerging genre in the Netherlands of "Maroc-hop" (Moroccan hip-hop) takes this "other-ing" to even greater extremes. The very self-naming of the most popular rapper, Ali B (a proper first name and initialized surname refers to the way criminals are identified to the public) reflects how Moroccan youth feel about their status in Dutch society. These secular hip-hop groups were pushed to rap in defense of Islam and Muslims when, beginning in 2000, the demeaning ethnic desig-nation of immigrants (e.g., "Moroccans" or "Turks") changed to a demeaning of religion—Islam (e.g., "Muslims").

A similar pattern can be seen in Britain among South Asian Muslim youth who spearhead such musical groups as Fun^Da^Mental. As Ted Swedenberg posits here, contrary to what has been claimed, the group Fun^Da^Mental is not merely a Muslim rap band, but a kind of mobile political and cultural coalition whose members are united musically and politically by a "hatred of inequality" rather than a common religious faith. The rise of such musical groups should be seen against the political background of the increasing Islamophobia in Britain after the 9/11 and the July 7, 2004, terrorist attacks, during which Mus-lims as a whole were shunned as "immigrants" and dangerous, despite most being born in and citizens of the United Kingdom. They were labeled as hostile to European values, ghettoized, and involved in gang violence and drug use. British Asian ("BrAsian") Muslim youth in particular are seen as Britain's cul-tural other, the enemy within. In this hostile climate, Fun^Da^Mental reflects the frustration of BrAsian youth about what they see as the hypocrisy of British secularism, reflected, for instance, in the British flag, which carries the symbol of English crusaders. It rejects mainstream judgments about the Muslim head-scarf and claims of nonintegration. The lyrics and songs expose the double standard of mainstream views that condemn suicide bombing, but remain silent about the mass killings of people in Iraq, Lebanon, or Palestine. "Militant yet inclusive and open, rejectionists yet deeply concerned with education and dialogue, Muslim and black and British/punk, and global in their concern, [the group] provides a very different, multiplex, and more useful vision of what it might mean to be 'Muslim' [and young] in today's Britain".

For Muslim youth in general, music is not merely the political language of protest as noted here. Whether they make up the majority or minority, young Muslims also show a great interest and involvement in the kinds of globalized genres—pop, rock, rap, and heavy metal—that their non-Muslim counterparts in different parts of the world enjoy. Global musical genres have become important identity markers of urban youth, Muslim and non-Muslim alike. Yet there are ongoing negotiations between the use of these cultural products and the habitus of "Muslimness." Suzanne Naafs (chapter 21) looks at the images that circulate through the highly popular video compact disks of popular female performers in Indonesia. Pop artists promote not only their music, but a youthful lifestyle, and thereby play a part in the cultural negotiations that take place over questions of what it means to be young, female, and Muslim in contemporary Indonesia. As young women are exposed to the global youth flows, they find new ways of incorporating older codes of decency and virtuosity into a modern image and lifestyle.

The Turkish heavy metal bands and youth hang-out "metal spaces" that Pierre Hecker so vividly describes, tell us how segments of Muslim youth, with their deviant appearance of long hair, black clothing, tattoos, piercings, and drinking habits, push the cultural boundaries. Turkish metal heads engage in a musical, social, and moral endeavor that stands counter to traditional norms and religious teachings. Such countercultural trends seem to be gaining ground since the 1990s in the bustling urban quarters of Istanbul among segments of the urban youth. Metal groups and their supporters reflect a love of music among the "unconventional" youth; they engage in the kind of solidarity building among the youth of the Middle East that conventional politics is unable to accomplish. Under the platform of peace (between Arabs and Israel), several bands in the region have been linked to one another, thus galvanizing their fans in Egypt, Lebanon, Syria, Dubai, and Israel to develop transnational networks via the Internet to promote debate on peace in the region. Hecker suggests that, in fact, Islam has played a minor role in the uncommon practice of heavy metal in the Muslim Middle East. The source of youth rebellion and resistance cannot be traced to restrictions arising from Islam and the religious order, but from political repression, lack of economic opportunities, and the dearth of cultural travel.

What, then, is the status of Muslim youth in these neoliberal times? In the conventional wisdom, a combination of youth bulge, unemployment, marginality, and a general sentiment of deprivation has given the young an exceptional status as the harbinger of radicalism and threat to stability. Radical Islam, in this view, marks the ideological shield through which Muslim youth fight their excluders while protecting themselves from the relentless flow of global cultural goods and values. As we have demonstrated in the preceding discussions, although the majority of youth in Muslim societies and communities share many common social, political, and economic misfortunes, they exhibit remarkably diverse responses to their situations. Whereas groups of them have been drawn into radical Islam, others have embraced their religion more as an identity marker. While some take Islam as a normative frame and then subvert it to express and reclaim their youthfulness, their counterparts assert themselves and express discontent through a music of rage. Through such mediations, Muslim youth remain in constant negotiation between being Muslim, modern, and young. Thus, far from being "exceptional," young Muslims in reality have as much in common with their non-Muslim global counterparts as they share among themselves. And as they migrate, forge networks, make and change culture, and assert themselves in a multitude of ways, it is clear that Muslim youths have emerged with a consciousness that they are simultaneously major objects, agents and victims on a world stage. This may very well be a moment of historical significance for Muslim youth.

PART I

Politics of Dissent

2

Muslim Youth and the Claim of Youthfulness

Asef Bayat

There seems to be a great deal of both alarm and expectation about the political weight of Muslim youth in the Middle East. Although many express anxiety over the seeming desire of the young in the Arab world to act as foot soldiers of radical Islam, others expect youth (as in Iran or Saudi Arabia) to push for democratic transformation in the region (Gorton Ash 2005; Sami 2005). Thus, youths are projected to act as political agents and social transformers, whether for or against Islamism. Indeed, the recent history of the region is witness to the political mobilization of the young, as scores of Muslim youth have been involved in radical Islamist movements, such as in Saudi Arabia, Egypt, and Morocco; or, alternatively, have defied the moral and political authority of the doctrinal regimes in the region such as the Islamic Republic of Iran.

What do these events and involvements tell us about the nature of youth politics in general and youth movements in particular? Do they point to the necessarily transformative role of the young? Are youth movements revolutionary or, ultimately, democratizing in orientation? How far can the prevalent social movement theory help us understand the nature of youth politics in general, and that of the Muslim Middle East specifically?

Although studies on youth-related themes such as HIV/AIDS, exclusion, violence, or religious radicalism have flourished in recent years, *youth* as an analytical category appears in them, for the most part, incidentally. Thus, many studies on youth religious radicalism, for example, are primarily about religious radicalism per se, where the young people (like others) only *happen* to be involved. This is different from an approach that takes *youth* as the point of departure, as the central category, to examine religious radicalism. On the other hand, *youth* as a social category has curiously been absent from the prevalent social movement debates. In general, scholarly attempts to conceptualize meanings and modalities of youth movements remain rare. At best, it is assumed that such conceptual tools as ideology, organization, mobilization, framing, and the like would be adequate to assess youth as a collective body. Consequently, forms of youth activism, those that do not fall into the frame of classical social movements, have fallen into the realm of and are viewed largely from the prism of *social problems* or *subcultural studies*. Although historical studies and journalistic accounts do talk about such collectives as youth movements (referring, for instance, to the political protests of the 1960s or the subcultures of hippies or punks), they presume a priori that youth movements are those in which young people play the central role. Thus, student activism, antiwar mobilization, and counterculture trends of the 1960s in Europe and the United States, or youth chapters of certain political parties and movements such as Communist youth, are taken to manifest different forms of youth movements (Mao 1967).[1] What I propose here differs from these approaches.

I suggest that a discussion of the experience of youth in the Muslim Middle East, where moral and political authority impose a high degree of social control over the young, can offer valuable insights into conceptualizing youth and youth movements. By comparing youth activism in the Muslim Middle East, we can productively construct "youth" as a useful analytical category, which can then open the way to understand the meaning of a youth movement. Rather than being defined in terms of the centrality of the young, youth movements are ultimately about "claiming or reclaiming youthfulness." And *youthfulness* signifies a particular habitus, behavioral and cognitive dispositions that are associated with the fact of being "young"—that is, a distinct social location between childhood and adulthood, where the youngster experiences "relative autonomy" and is neither totally dependent (on adults) nor independent, and is free from responsibility for other dependents. Understood as such, the political agency of youth movements, their transformative and democratizing potential, depends on the capacity of the adversaries, the moral and political authorities, to accommodate and contain youthful claims. Otherwise, youth may remain as conservative as any other social group. Yet, given the prevalence of the doctrinal religious regimes in the Middle East with legitimizing ideologies that are unable to accommodate the youth habitus, youth movements have great transformative and democratizing promise.

Young People, Youth, and Youth Movements

The idea of youths as a revolutionary class is not new. The widespread mobilization of young people in Europe and the United States during the capitalist boom of the 1960s convinced many observers that youth (then active in universities and antiwar movements, and in producing alternative lifestyles) were the new revolutionary force of social transformation in western societies. For Herbert Marcuse in the United States and Andre Gortz in France, youths and students had taken the place of the proletariat as the major agents of political change (Marcuse 1969). In this vein, youth movements have often been equated and used interchangeably either with student movements or with youth chapters or branches of this or that political party or movement (Bundy 1987). Thus, the youth section of the Fascist party in Germany is described as the *German youth movement* (Liqueur 1984); and the youth organization of the Iraqi Ba'ath Party is assumed to be the youth movement in Iraq.

I suggest that a youth movement is neither the same as student activism, nor an appendage of political movements, nor is it necessarily a revolutionary agent. First, movements are defined not simply by the identity of their actors (even though this factor affects very much the character of a movement), but by the nature of their claims and grievances. Although in reality students are usually young, and young people are often students, they represent two different categories. "Student movements" embody the collective struggles of a student body to defend or extend "student rights," decent education, fair exams, affordable fees, or accountable educational management (Cockburn and Blackburn 1969). On the other hand, activism of young people in political organizations does not necessarily make them agents of a youth movement. Rather, it indicates youth support for, and their mobilization by, a particular political objective (democracy, Ba'athism, or Fascism). Of course, some youth concerns may be expressed in and merge into certain political movements, as in German Fascism, which represented aspects of a German youth movement, or in the current pietism of Muslims in France, which partially reflects the individuality (through veiling) of Muslim girls. However, this possibility should not be confused with the situation when young people happen to support a given political organization or movement.

But is the political ideal of the young necessarily revolutionary? By no means. Indeed, the political conservatism of many young people in the West after 1960, which compelled Marcuse to retreat from his earlier position, shattered the myth of youths as a revolutionary class. If anything, the political or transformative potential of youth movements is relative to the degree of social control their adversaries impose on them. For instance, a political regime, such as that in present-day Iran or in Saudi Arabia, which makes it its business to scrutinize individual behavior and lifestyle, is likely to face youth dissent. Otherwise, youth movements may pose little challenge to authoritarian states unless they think and act politically. Because a youth movement is essentially about *claiming youthfulness*, it embodies the collective challenge, with a central goal that consists of defending and extending the youth habitus, by which I mean a series of dispositions and ways of being, feeling, and carrying oneself (e.g., a greater tendency for experimentation, adventurism, idealism, autonomy, mobility, and change) that are associated with the sociological fact of "being young." Countering or curtailing this habitus, youthfulness, is likely to generate collective dissent.

But, as the experience of today's Saudi Arabia shows, the mere presence of young people subject to moral and political discipline does not necessarily render them carriers of a youth movement, because "young persons" (as an age category) are unable to forge a collective challenge to the moral and political authority without first turning into "youth" as a social category—that is, turning into social actors. When I was growing up in a small village in central Iran during the 1960s, I of course had my friends and peers with whom I talked, played, cooperated, and fought. However, at that point we were not "youth," strictly speaking; we were simply young persons, members of an age cohort. In the village, most young people actually had little opportunity to experience "youthfulness," as they rapidly moved from childhood (a period of vulnerability and dependence) to adulthood (a world of work, parenting, and responsibility). Many youngsters never went to school. There was little "relative autonomy," especially for most young girls, who were rapidly transferred from their father's authority to that of the husband and were effectively trained in their roles as housewives long before puberty (boys were usually exempted from such responsibility, an indication of how gender intervenes in the formation of youth).

It is partially in this light that Bourdieu (1993) has famously contended that *youth* is "nothing but a word," suggesting that talking about youth as a social unit is itself a manipulation of the young. How can we imagine youth as a single category, he argues, when the youngsters of different classes (rich and poor) have little in common? Indeed, I must add, the difference in the life-worlds of male and female youngsters may be even more remarkable. Yet, Bourdieu's contention pertains primarily to the era prior to mass schooling, when young persons experienced radically different life-worlds. However, as Bourdieu himself acknowledges, in modern times mass schooling has changed all this. It has produced "youthfulness" on a massive national and global scale.

"Youth" as a social category, as collective agents, is an essentially modern, indeed, urban phenomenon. It is in modern cities that "young persons" turn into "youth" by experiencing and developing a particular consciousness about being young, about youthfulness. Schooling, prevalent in urban areas, serves as a key factor in producing and prolonging the period of youth while it cultivates status, expectations, and, possibly, critical awareness. Cities, as loci of diversity, creativity, and anonymity, present opportunities for young people to explore alternative role models and choices, and offer venues to express their individuality. Mass media, urban spaces, public parks, youth centers, shopping malls, cultural complexes, and local street corners provide arenas for the formation and expression of collective identities. The fragmented mass of young individuals might share common attributes in expressing common anxieties, demanding individual liberty, and in constructing and asserting subverting identities. Individuals may bond and construct identities through such deliberate associations and networks as schools, street corners, peer groups, and youth magazines. However, identities are formed mostly through "passive networks," the undeliberate and instantaneous communications among atomized individuals that are established by the tacit recognition of their commonalities and that are mediated directly through gaze in public space, or indirectly through the mass media (Bayat 1997: 16–19). As agents present in the public space, the young recognize shared identity by noticing (seeing) collective symbols inscribed in styles (T-shirts, blue jeans, hair style), types of activities (attending particular concerts, music stores, and hanging around shopping malls), and places (stadiums, hiking trails, street corners). When young persons develop a particular consciousness about themselves as youth and begin to defend or extend their youthfulness in a collective fashion, a youth movement can be said to have developed.

Unlike student movements, which require a good degree of organization and strategy building, youth (non)movements augment change by their very public presence. With their central preoccupation with "cultural production" or lifestyles, the young may fashion new social norms, religious practices, cultural codes, and values, without needing structured organization, leadership, or ideologies. This is because youth (non)movements are characterized less by *what the young do* (networking, organizing, deploying resources, mobilizing) than by *how they are* (in behavior, dress, speaking fashions, ways of walking, in private and public spaces). The identity of a youth movement is based not as much on collective *doing* as on collective *being*, and the forms of their expression are less collective protest than *collective presence*. The power of Muslim youth movements in the Middle East lays precisely in the ability of their atomized agents to challenge the political and moral authorities by the persistence of their merely alternative presence. Even though youth movements are, by definition, concerned with the claims of youthfulness, nevertheless they can and do act as a harbinger of social change and democratic transformation under those doctrinal regimes with legitimizing ideologies that are too narrow to accommodate youthful claims.

I will elaborate on these propositions by a comparative analysis of the dynamics of youth activism in Iran and Egypt since the 1980s. In Iran, where moral and political authority converged, draconian social control gave rise to a unique youth identity and collective defiance. Young people both became central to and were further mobilized by the post-Islamist reform movement. The assertion of youthful aspirations, the defense of their habitus, lay at the heart of their conflict with moral and political authority. With the state being the target of their struggles, Iranian youths engendered one of the most remarkable youth nonmovements in the Muslim world. The struggle to reclaim youthfulness melded with the struggle to attain democratic ideals. In contrast, Egyptian youth, operating under the constraints of passive revolution, opted for the strategy of accommodating innovation, attempting to accommodate their youthful claims within existing political, economic, and moral norms. In the process, they redefined dominant norms and institutions, blended divine and diversion, and engendered more inclusive religious mores. Yet this subculture took shape within, and neither against nor outside, the existing regime of moral and political power. Egyptian youth remained distant from being both a movement and an involvement in political activism; only by the end of 2000s did a new type of youth politics (in the web world and civic institutions) seem to emerge in Egypt.

Iran's "Third Generation"

The spectacular activism of young people in the Islamic revolution,[2] the war with Iraq, and in the new revolutionary institutions earned them a new, exalted position, altering their image from "young troublemakers" to "heroes and martyrs." This was the image of the "spectacular male youth" drawn sociologically from lower and middle class families. At the same time, the young were seen as highly vulnerable to corrupting ideas and, therefore, required protection and surveillance. To reproduce an ideal "Muslim man," the Islamic regime launched, in 1980, the "cultural revolution" program to "Islamize" educational culture and curricula. Universities were shut down for two years, Islamic associations were set up in schools, and all public places came under the watchful gaze of morals police and proregime vigilantes.

What sustained this regime of surveillance for a decade were revolutionary fervor, preoccupation with war, and the repression of dissent. Young men were either on the war front or fleeing the country, preferring the humiliation of exile to "heroic martyrdom" in a "meaningless" battle. Although adolescents sought refuge in schools, often by deliberately failing exams to postpone graduation, they lived in anxiety, gloom, and depression. One out of every three high school students suffered from a behavioral disorder. Girls in particular were more susceptible to stress, fear, and depression (*Aftab* July 30, 2001: 9). The poetic reflections of a young girl talking to herself capture the depth of her inner gloom as she witnesses the gradual erosion of her youth:

> My father never recognizes me on the street.
> He says, "All of you look like mourners."
> Yes, we dress in black, head to toe in black.
>
> Sometimes, I get scared by the thought of my father not
>   recognizing me in this dark colorlessness . . . .
> I stare at the mirror
> And I see an old woman.
>   Am I still sleepy?
>   Oh . . . I feel aged and unhappy.
>   Why should I be so different from other 20-year-olds?
>
> They liken my joy to sin,
> They close my eyes to happiness,
> They stop me from taking my own steps . . .
>   Oh . . . I feel like an old woman . . . .
> No, no, I want to be young,
>   Want to love,
>   To dress in white, be joyful, have fun,
>   And move to fulfill my dreams . . . .
> I look at myself in the mirror.
> I look so worn out and aged . . . (*Nowrooz*, September 15, 2001)

Few officials noticed this inner despair in youngsters' lives. Blinded by their own constructed image and by their doctrinal animosity toward joy, Islamist leaders failed to read the inner minds and hearts of this rapidly growing segment of the population. The shocking truth emerged only during the postwar years, when some officials noticed "strange behavior" among the young. With the war over and postwar reconstruction underway, the young began to express their selfhood publicly both individually and collectively. The media carried stories about the "degenerate behavior" of Iranian youth. Boys were discovered disguised as women walking on the streets in the southern city of Shiraz. Tomboy girls wore male attire to escape the harassment of morals police. College students refused to take religious studies courses,[3] and "authorities in an Iranian holy Muslim city launched a crackdown on pop music, arresting dozens of youths for playing loud music on their car stereos."[4] Other reports spoke of groups of young males dancing in the streets next to self-flagellation ceremonies on the highly charged mourning day of Ashura. Young drivers had fun by crashing their cars into each other, or by playing a driving game by racing while hand-cuffed to the steering wheel and trying to escape before flying off a cliff (Qotbi 2000). Drug addiction soared among school children. The average age of prostitutes declined from 27 years to 20 years old, expanding the industry by 635% in 1998.[5]

Yet alongside individual rebellion, the young took every opportunity to assert open and clandestine subcultures, defying the moral and political authority. The severe restriction on music did not deter them. When the reformist mayor of Tehran, Gholam Hussein Karbaschi, established numerous cultural centers in south Tehran, young people comprised 75% of those who rushed to fill classical music classes and concert halls. Smuggled audio and video recordings of exiled Iranian singers filled big city main streets, and MTV–type music videos found widespread popularity. The young blared loud music from speedy cars to the dismay of Islamists. Across the capital, underground pop and rock bands thrived at covert late-night parties. Teenagers enjoyed not only the music, but also its culture and fashion—tight or baggy pants, vulgar English slang, tattoos—acquired through smuggled videos (Yaghmaian 2002: 65–71). Rap and heavy metal music, in particular, became popular. By 1999, music subcultures had become so widespread that the reformist ministry of culture was compelled to recognize and even organize the first concert of "pop music" in the Islamic Republic. Some ran away from home to join rock bands, attracted by a sense of belonging, although many were incarcerated by the morals police.

Indeed, teenage runaways became a major social problem. In 2000, Tehran was reportedly faced with an "escalating crisis of runaway girls frequently becoming victims of prostitution rings and human trafficking" (*Aftab* January 16, 2003: 9). Between 1997 and 1998, the number of reported runaway teenagers tripled. In Tehran in 2000, 900 girls ran away; the number reached well more than 4,000 by 2002 (IRNA August 5, 2001), when the total number was reported to be 60,000.[6] Assertion of individuality—freedom to have a male partner (42%) and freedom from family surveillance—seemed to be the main causes.[7] "I want to leave Iran," lamented a young female who had been arrested for leaving home. "I don't like Iran at all. I feel I am in prison here even when I am sitting in the park."

Openly dating had become a prime casualty of Islamic moral code, although the young devised ways to resist. Well-to-do young boys and girls made contacts not only at private parties and underground music concerts, but also in public parks, shopping malls, and restaurants, often discreetly arranged by cell phone. In such "distanciated dating," Muslim girls and boys stood apart but eyed each other from distance, chatted, flirted, and expressed love through electronic waves. To seek privacy and yet appear legitimate, young couples hired taxis to drive them around the city in anonymity, while they sat back for hours to romance or take delight in their companionship. The popularity of Valentine's Day revealed an abundance of "forbidden love" and relationships in which sex, it seemed, was not excluded. In fact, scattered evidence indicated widespread premarital sex among Iran's Muslim youths, despite the high risk of harsh penalties. An academician claimed that one out of three unmarried girls and 60% in North Tehran had had sexual relations. Of 130 cases of AIDS cases reported in hospitals, 90 were unmarried women (Mahmoud Golzari 2004). An official of Tehran Municipality reported "each month at least 10 or 12 aborted fetuses are found in the garbage" (Farahi 2003). Although public information did not exist, researchers and medical professionals were alarmed by the extent of unwanted pregnancies. Doctors unofficially spoke of the fact that "not one week passes by without at least two or three young girls coming in for an abortion."[8] Reportedly some 60% of patients requesting abortions were unmarried young girls. United Nations Population Fund officials in Tehran referred to a survey on "morality" (meaning sexuality) among young people, but the results were so "terrible" that they had to be destroyed.[9] Attention to self, physical appearance, clothing, fashion, and plastic surgery became widespread trends among young females.

Clearly, sexuality among the young posed a major challenge to the Islamic state, testing the capacity of Islamism to integrate youths, whose sensibilities were inherently subversive to it. During the early 1990s, President Rafsanjani came up with the idea of "temporary marriage" as an "Islamic" solution to the crisis. It meant controlling sexual encounters through fixed short-term (as short as a few hours) relationships called "marriage." Ayatollah Ha'eri Shirazi proposed "legitimate courtship" (without sex) (*Payman-e Doust-ye Shar'i*), an openly recognized relationship approved by parents or relatives (*Salam* September 17, 1996). Others called for some kind of official document confirming the legitimacy (*halaliyyat*) of such relationships, meaning something like temporary marriage in which the couple would not live together (*Iran* November 9, 1996). Young men purely seeking sex were to "temporarily marry" prostitutes to "legitimize" their encounters.

The young's desperate cultural politics shattered Islamists' image of them as self-sacrificing individuals devoted to martyrdom and moral codes.

By challenging the regime's moral and political authority, the young subverted the production of "Muslim youth." Anxiety over the increasing bad *hijabi* (laxity in veil wearing) among school and university girls haunted officials: "We are encountering a serious cultural onslaught. What is to be done?" they lamented.[10] More than 85% of young people in 1995 spent their leisure time watching television, but only 6% of them watched religious programs; of the 58% who read books, less then 8% were interested in religious literature.[11] A staggering 80% of the nation's youth were indifferent or opposed to the clergy, religious obligations, and religious leadership,[12] whereas 86% of students refrained from saying their daily prayers.[13] Official surveys confirmed the deep mistrust separating the young from the state and whatever it stood for. The vast majority (80%) lacked confidence in politicians, and most (more than 70%) saw the government as being responsible for their problems (Ministry of Culture and Islamic Guidance 1994).

Yet this distrust of the Islamist authorities did not mean that the young abandoned religion. Indeed, they expressed a "high religiosity" in terms of fundamental religious "beliefs" and "feelings" (Serajzadeh 1999), with some 90% believing in God and the idea of religion, according to one study.[14] However, youth remained largely indifferent to religious practices; religious belief and knowledge seemed to have little impact on their daily lives. God existed, but did not prevent them from drinking alcohol or dating the opposite sex. To them, religion was a more philosophical and cultural reality than it was moral and doctrinal. Although most refused to attend mosque ceremonies, they flocked to public and private lectures given by the "religious intellectuals," which spread during the mid 1990s. Like their Egyptian counterparts, the globalized Iranian youth reinvented their religiosity, blending the transcendental with the secular, faith with freedom, divine with diversion.

Many youngsters utilized the prevailing norms and institutions, especially religious rituals, to accommodate their youthful claims, but in doing so they creatively redefined and subverted the constraints of those codes and norms. This mode of *subversive accommodation* was best expressed in the way the North Tehrani youths treated the highly charged ritual of Muharram, which commemorates the death of Imam Hussein, the grandson of Prophet Muhammed. By inventing "Hussein parties," the young turned this highly austere occasion of mourning into an evening of glamour, fun, and sociability. Boys and girls dressed in their best, strolled through the streets, joined parades of mourners, and used the occasion to stay out until dawn to socialize, flirt, exchange phone numbers, and secretly arrange dates (Yaghmaian 2002: 61–65). In a similar spirit, they reinvented the *sham-e ghariban* (the 11th night of the month of Muharram), the most dreary and sorrowful Shiʻi ritual in Islamic Iran, as a blissful night of sociability and diversion. Groups of 50 to 60 girls and boys carried candles through the streets to large squares, where they sat on the ground in circles, often leaning on one another in the romantic aura of dim candlelight, and listened to the melancholic *nowhe* (sad religious songs) while chatting, meditating, romancing, or talking politics in hushed tones until dawn.[15]

These rituals of resistance did not go unpunished by organized, violent *basiji*, bands of "fundamentalist" youth who attacked the participants and disrupted their assemblies, and in so doing turned their subversive accommodation into political defiance. The cultural became overtly political. In January 1995, 100,000 young spectators of a Tehran soccer match went into a rampage following a disagreement on the result of the competition. Riots destroyed part of the stadium and led to a mass protest of youths chanting: "Death to this barbaric regime." "Death to the *pasdaran.*" (*Al-Hayat* January 22, 1995). And in 2004, more than 5,000 youths battled with violent vigilante groups in North Tehran. Much earlier, the city of Tabriz had witnessed thousands of young spectators raging against *basiji* bands for objecting to the "improper behavior" of a few individuals in the crowd.

Even more than collective grief and violence, collective joy became a medium of subversion, for the mass expression of "happiness" not only defied Puritan principles of grief and gloom, but also circumvented its aura of repression. The success of Iran's national soccer team in Australia in November 1997, and again at the World Cup in France against the United States in June 1998, sent hordes of young boys and girls into the streets in every major city to cheer, dance, and sound their car horns. For five hours security forces lost control, stood aside, and watched the crowd in its blissful ecstasy.[16] In the city of Karadj, the crowd overwhelmed the *basijies* by chanting, "*Basiji* must dance!" But even defeat was a pretext to show collective defiance. Hours after Iran's team lost to Bahrain in 2001, hundreds of thousands took to the streets, expressing deepfelt anger at the Islamist authorities. In 54 different areas of Tehran, young people marched, shouted political slogans, threw rocks and hand-made explosives at police, vandalized police cars, broke traffic lights, and lit candles in a sign of mourning for the defeat. Other cities—Karadj, Qom, Shiraz, Kashan, Isfahan, and Islam Abad—also witnessed similar protests. Only after 800 arrests did protesters go home (*Nowrooz*, October 23, 2001: 3).

But perhaps nothing was more symbolic about the young's defiance than setting off fireworks to celebrate Nowrooz, the coming of the Iranian New Year. The Islamic state had outlawed this ancient Persian tradition, but by setting off millions of firecrackers, youngsters turned urban neighborhoods into explosive battle zones, scorning the official ban on the ritual and the collective joy that went with it. The "mystery of firecrackers," as one daily put it, symbolized outrage against officialdom that the young saw as having forbidden joy and jolliness.[17]

The Making of a Youth (Non)Movement

The younger generation's defiance deepened the conflict between reformists and conservatives in government. Reformists attributed it to the "suppression of joy," the "need for happiness," and they set off a public debate over joy and fun (shadi) by sponsoring studies, organizing seminars, and publishing numerous articles supporting the idea that "joy was not sin, but a deeply human emotion." Some called for a "definition" and even "management of joy" to develop a culture of festivity among a population that lacked that experience and its norms (Nowrooz October 21, 2001). Scores of public events discussed the meaning of "leisure" and the modalities of "fun among women," who had been suffering from depression more than other social groups.[18] Psychologists and journalists called for a "love of life," emphasizing that "living with joy is our right . . . . A depressed and austere society cannot have a solid civility," they argued.[19] Crying out, "Laughter is not deviance!," reformists lashed out at Islamists who had shunned fun and laughter, human pursuits that invigorate the society (Iran March 18, 2001: 4). In so doing, the reformists supplied the young with a platform, political support, and moral courage.

Supported by reformist friends at the top, the young further pushed for their claims not only through defiance, but also through engagement in civic activism. In 2001, some 50 youth nongovernmental organizations (NGOs) were registered in Tehran and 400 in the country (Hayat-e Nou April 30, 2001: 11; Nowrooz August 6, 2001: 9). Within two years they reached 1,100, of which 850 participated in the first national congress of youth NGOs in 2003 (Iran Emrooz August 11, 2003). Still thousands more flourished informally throughout the country, working in cultural, artistic, charity, developmental, and intellectual domains. They organized lectures and concerts, did charity work, and held bazaars, at times with remarkable innovation. On one occasion, a group of youths presented President Khatami with a plan for alternative young cabinet members to form a "government of youths." However, reclaiming public space to assert their youthful sensibilities remained the major concern of those whose globalizing subcultures (expressed in sexuality, gender roles, and lifestyle) were distancing them even from post-Islamists' commitment to largely traditional moral conventions (Hayat-e Nou April 30, 2001: 21; Nowrooz August 6, 2001: 9). This infuriated conservative Puritans, who clamored against what they considered a "cultural invasion," "hooliganism," and "anti-Islamic senti-ments," blaming Khatami's failure to ameliorate "unemployment, poverty and corruption" (*Resalat* October 23, 2001: 2).

Thus, in August 2001, the conservative judiciary began a new crackdown, by public flogging, of those committing or promoting immorality, "depravity," and "indecency" in the public space. The police closed down boutiques, cafés, and restaurants that exhibited signs of depravity.[20] They outlawed neckties, photographed girls wearing loose veils, and flogged men for drinking alcohol or being seen with unrelated women. The campaign was meant not only to rebuff Khatami's second presidential victory, but also to restrict cultural open-ness by putting a halt to the normalization of "forbidden" conduct. The crack-down did little to change the behavior, however, and instead caused a public uproar in which the fundamentals of Islamic penal code came under further attack, as scores of reform-minded clerics questioned its application in this modern age. Failing to bring much fruit, the cultural crackdown took a new turn a year later. Some 60 "special units," including several hundred men wearing green uniforms and toting machine guns and hand grenades, drove up and down the streets chasing young drivers listening to loud music, women wearing makeup or loose veils, party-goers, and drinkers of alcoholic beverages (Recknaged and Gorgin 2000).

This simultaneous condition of both suppression (of youthfulness by the political–moral authority) and opportunity (valorization and encouragement of the young) offered youth a spectacular sense of self and the possibility to act collectively, a status their Egyptian or Saudi counterparts lacked. But there was more to the emergence of a national Iranian youth movement than politics. Sweeping social change since the early 1980s had helped the formation of "youth" as a social category. Demographically, by 1996, Iran had experienced a dramatic rise in its number of young people, with two thirds of the population younger than the age of 30. Of this, a staggering 20 million, one third of the population, were students (an increase of 266% since 1976). Most lived in cit-ies, exposed to diverse lifestyles with spaces for relative autonomy, extrakinship identities, and social interactions on a broad scale. In the meantime, as urban-ity was permeating into the countryside, an "urbanized" generation of rural youth was in the making. The spread of Open University branches throughout the country, for instance, meant that, on average, every village had two univer-sity graduates, a very rare phenomenon in the 1970s. Rural youth began to acquire legitimacy based on competence and merit, and became major decision makers, which the dominance of seniority had previously made unthinkable. With sweeping social changes in the countryside and expanding communica-tion technologies that facilitated the flow of young people, ideas, and lifestyles, social barriers separating rural and urban youth began to crumble, giving the country's young a broader, national constituency. Meanwhile, the weakening of parental authority over the young (resulting from the state's valorization of youth) and the reinforcement of child-centeredness in the family (an outcome of increasing literacy among women and mothers) contributed to the individuation of the young and their militancy.[21]

By the mid 1990s, Iran's postrevolutionary young had turned into becoming "youth"—a social agent. But theirs was not a conventional social movement, an organized and sustained collective challenge with articulated ideology or a recognizable leadership. Rather, theirs was a nonmovement, the "collective conscience" of the noncollective actors, whose principal expression lay in the *politics of presence*, tied closely to the young's everyday cultural struggles and normative subversion. This fragmented mass of individuals and subgroups shared common attributes in expressing common anxieties, demanding individual liberty, and in constructing and asserting their collective identities. The individual youngsters were tied together not only within dispersed subgroups (youth magazines, NGOs, peer groups, and street corner associations), but more commonly through "passive networks"—those undeliberate linkages formed by the youngsters tacitly recognizing their commonalities through gaze in public spaces, by identifying shared symbols displayed in styles (T-shirts, blue jeans, hair), types of activities (attending particular concerts, music stores), and places (sport stadiums, shopping malls, hiking trails). Thus, the birth of youth as a social category of national scale, operating in unique simultaneous conditions of both repression and opportunity, drove Iranian youths to reclaim their youthfulness in a battle within which the state became the target. Reclaiming youth habitus from state control and moral authority defined Iran's youth (non)movement.

Politics of Egyptian Youths: "Accommodating Innovation"

"Youth" as a social category also developed in Egypt. Quite similar to Iran, in 1996, about half of Egypt's 60 million people were younger than 20 and 64% were younger than 30 (CAPMAS 1996). Although the total student population in 1996 (11.6 million) was only just more than half of Iran's, Egypt had the same number of college students (1.1 million) (CAPMAS 1999). Similarly, the peculiarity of the Egyptian countryside (with comparatively large villages concentrated along the Nile Valley and Delta, and in close proximity to each other and large cities) contributed to the increasing urbanity during the 1980s and '90s. The abundance of electricity; new means of communication; commercialization;

the flow of people, goods, and information; and increasing occupational specialization marked the shifting social structure of post-Infitah rural settings
(Denis and Bayat 2001). The spread of mass schooling provided the raw materials to produce educated youth. And urban institutions such as college campuses, coffee shops, shopping malls, concert venues, mulid (celebration of
saints'birth) festivals, and street corners provided spaces for social interaction,
active and passive networks, and the construction of youth identities. In brief,
the young as social actors had emerged in both Iran and Egypt in a more or less
similar pattern.

However, the simultaneous processes of urbanization, Islamization, and
globalization had fragmented the young generation in Egypt. Alongside actively
pious and provincial adolescents had emerged new generations of globalized
youths who had been increasingly exposed to the global cultural flows. Clearly,
different class and gender experiences had given rise to multiple youth identities. Whereas harsher social control in the Islamic Republic had pushed male
and female youth to develop closer aspirations, gender distinction in Egypt
remained more evident. For example, the difference in social aspirations
between adolescent boys and girls in Egypt was so pronounced that observers
spoke of "more separate male and female cultures than a single youth culture."
Especially crucial were the male perceptions of women, which seriously threatened their identity as youths' shared habitus. Men would rarely (in Egypt only
4%) marry a woman who had premarital sex (Khalifa 1995: 6–10) "No one
goes out with a girl and marries her. Ninety-nine percent of men would not
marry a girl they ever touched," stated a university student in Egypt. And the
girls felt this bitter truth. "This is what we hate about the boys; they rarely marry
the girl they go out with."[22]

But in both Iran and Egypt, the mainstream young attempted to assert
their habitus, to exert their individuality, to aspire for change and create youth
subculture. They did so by recognizing the existing moral and political constraints,
and trying to make the best out of the existing institutions. However, compared
with their Iranian counterparts, Egyptian youth remained for the most part
demobilized in the political and civic domains. Although they showed interest
in political participation, they lacked the means to do so. Unlike in Iran, where
ageism was breaking down and the youth were remarkably valorized, the elders
and political elites in Egypt did not trust the young in the political arena. Egyptian
politics, both governmental and oppositional, continued to remain in the grip
of very old men (average age of 77 in 2002).[23] Meanwhile, the young distrusted
party politics, which happened to be the only legitimate channel for activism.[24]

Lack of trust in electoral games pushed the young further away from
politics, and restrictions on campus activism put a damper on youth political

mobilization. The mobilization of middle and lower middle class youth in the Islamist movement during the 1980s did not repeat itself in other political fields. During the late 1990s, political activity on campuses was paltry, as state security intervened to prevent Islamist, Leftist, and Nasserist candidates from running for student unions. Only Israel's reoccupation of the Palestinian territories in early 2000 galvanized social and political mobilization (Hammond 1998: 7). The remarkable involvement of Egyptian youths in collecting food and medicine for Palestinians was indeed a watershed in youth volunteerism, but it was the result of the unique political and moral aura of the siege of Palestinians by Likud's repressive incursions. Otherwise, the young showed slight interest in public service or volunteerism. Even the youths of elite families whose social and financial resources often make them the prime source of donations remained indifferent. Of 20 hand-picked students of Egyptian universities, only one had engaged in any volunteer activities (Khalifa 1995: 6–10). Genuine youth initiatives, such as Fathi Kheir NGO, were exceptions. The prevailing notion was that the state, not citizens, was to take charge of social provisions.

Clearly, the young were bearing the brunt of Egypt's "passive revolution," in which the "seculareligious" state had appropriated the initiative for change through a remarkable blend of concession and control. Egyptian youth were not under the same moral and political control as their counterparts in Iran or Saudi Arabia. Depending on their social and economic capacities, they were able to listen to their music, follow their fashion, pursue dating games, have affordable fun, and be part of global trends as long as they recognized their limits, beyond which their activities would collide with the moral authority and the state. Youths were to be integrated and guided by the state.

To do so, the state would provide the young with "scientific advancement" or technical education to catch up and compete in the world, and at the same time guide them into religious piety to withstand both foreign cultural influences and home-grown political Islam.[25] Indeed, the 1999 presidential decree to rename the Supreme Council of Youths (established in 1965) the Ministry of Youths and Sports, displayed official anxiety over the "youth problem."[26] Their protection from political and moral ills had become a matter of "national security." The Ministry of Youths, with its control of 4,000 youth centers, was to help materialize these objectives. Government loans were established to enable the young to settle down and marry by purchasing housing,[27] to provide access to information and communication technology, and to acquire technical training through NGOs.[28] Meanwhile, the youth centers, some kind of state-controlled NGOs, would organize summer camps, debates, entertainment, training programs, religious education caravans, and sporting events. However, the deplorable state of most of these centers, their poor amenities, garbage-infested athletic fields, poor libraries, and the state's control rendered them inadequate to carry out this enormous task. Often, only lower class youngsters, almost entirely male, attended the centers. Many remained "youth centers without youths," as an official weekly put it (Fuad 2001: 2; Shalabi 2003).[29] If the televised annual "dialogue" of the president with "Egyptian youths" was any indication, a deep distrust separated youths from the state.[30] The young took solace in nonstate spaces that infringed only marginally on political and moral authorities. They resorted to the cultural politics of everyday life where they could reassert their youthful claims.

For more than a decade, young Egyptians were seen in the image of Islamist militants waging guerrilla war, penetrating college campuses, or memorizing the Quran in the back street mosques (*zawaya*) of sprawling slums. Moral authorities, parents, and foreign observers expected them to be characteristically pious, strict, and dedicated to the moral discipline of Islam. Yet in their daily lives, the mainstream young defied their constructed image, often shocking moral authorities by expressing defiance openly and directly. "The youth of this country are rebelling against the old traditions," stated a 20-year-old female student in Cairo. "We are breaking away from your chains; we are not willing to live the lives of the older generations. Women smoking *shisha* is the least shocking form of rebellion going on. Face the changes and embrace our generation, do not treat us as if we are children. Our generation is more exposed than yours, and this is a simple fact".[31]

Reports of "satanic youth" in January 1997 demonstrated not only prevailing moral panic over the alleged vulnerability of youths to global culture, but those youths' emerging self-assertion. Every Thursday night, hundreds of well-to-do youngsters gathered in an abandoned building to socialize, have fun, and, above all, dance to heavy metal music. Six weeks of sensational media and the arrest of dozens accused of "Satanism" (later released for lack of evidence) proved the existence of underground subcultures that few adults had noticed. The music subculture, however, did not die out after the Satanist myth. It reappeared in the form of raving. Egyptian raves began with small bands and small crowds, but after 1998, professional organization and commercialization helped them grow rapidly. They encompassed music genres from around the world, including Egyptian pop, and catered to young elites of "glamour, high fashion and life style" (Matar 2002: 16).[32] For many, the rave became "a community which you have grown to know, at least recognize, centered around a common interest in the music" (Matar 2002: 19). The Egyptian rave was largely sex free, but it did involve alcohol and (unofficially) drugs (in the form of Ecstasy). Indeed, studies indicated that experimentation with alcohol went beyond the well-to-do young. One out of every three students in the cities had drunk alcohol, mainly beer.[33] Although just over 5% admitted experimenting with drugs (85% with cannabis), the problem became more severe during the early 1990s. Law enforcement professionals warned that the use of Ecstasy, in particular, was on the rise.[34]

Although in general a "culture of silence" prevailed regarding sexuality (Population Council 1999), premarital sex seemed to be fairly widespread among Muslim youth, despite normative and religious prohibition. In an approximate but indicative survey of 100 high school and college girls in various Cairo districts, 8% said they had had sexual intercourse, 37% had experienced sex without intercourse, 23% had kissed, and 20% had only held hands. In a survey of 100 school and college male students in Cairo, 73% said they would not mind having premarital sex as long as they would not marry their partners (Khalifa 1995). A more comprehensive study found "substantial rates of premarital sex among university students" (Ibrahim and Wassef 2000: 163). In AIDS education classes, students posed questions about specific sexual practices that surprised health educators (Cairo Times, May 15-8, 1997:12).[35] Although comprehensive surveys did not exist, the use of pornography by males appeared to be quite widespread.[36] Ninety out of 100 respondents said

FIGURE 2.1. Youth out on a Friday afternoon in Al Azhar Park, Cairo. (Linda Herrera, 2009)

they masturbated regularly, and 70% of those 90 thought they were doing something religiously and physically wrong (Khalifa 1995). Beyond influences from satellite dishes or illicit videos, the changing structure of households seemed to facilitate youth sexual practices. The father figure, once so important, was changing even in villages. One out of three families was fatherless, resulting from divorce, abandonment, and, mostly (20% to 25%) fathers working abroad. Children might use the home for romance when their mothers went out. Otherwise, lower class Cairo couples found romantic solace on the benches of inconspicuous metro stations, where they sat and talked or romanced while pretending to wait for trains.[37]

Most of these young people were religious. They often prayed, fasted, and expressed fear of God. Many heavy metal "Satanists" whom I interviewed considered themselves devout Muslims, but also enjoyed rock music, drinking alcohol, and romance. The mainstream young combined prayer, partying, pornography, faith, and fun. Notice how, for instance, a lower class young man working in Dahab, a tourist resort where many foreign women visit, blended God, women, and police in pursuit of his mundane and spiritual needs: "I used to pray before I came to Dahab. My relationship to God was very strong and very spiritual. Now, my relationship to God is very strange. I always ask him to provide me with a woman and when I have a partner, I ask him to protect me from the police" (Abdul-Rahmna 2001: 18)

This might sound like a contradiction, but it expresses more a consolation and accommodation. The young enjoy dancing, raving, having illicit relationships, and fun, but find solace and comfort in their prayers and faith. "I do both good and bad things, not just bad things. The good things erase the bad things," said a law student in Cairo.[38] A 25-year-old religious man who drank alcohol and "tried everything" also smoked "pot in a group sometimes to prove [his] manhood." He prayed regularly, hoping that God would forgive his ongoing misdeeds. Such a state of liminality, this "creative in-betweeness," illustrates how the young attempted to redefine and reimagine their Islam to accommodate their youthful desires for individuality, change, fun, and "sin" within the existing moral order. Not only did they redefine their religion, they also reinvented notions of youthfulness. "During adolescence," a 19-year-old student said, "all young men do the same; there is no *haram* or *halal* at that age."[39] Similarly, many young girls saw themselves as committed Muslims, but still uncovered their hair or wore the veil only during Ramadan or only during fasting hours. Many of those who enjoyed showing their hair found consolation in deciding to cover it after marriage, when their youthful stage was over.

To assert their habitus under the prevailing moral and political constraints, Egyptian youths resorted to *accommodating innovation*, a strategy that redefined and reinvented prevailing norms and traditional means to accommodate their youthful claims. The young did not depart radically from the dominant system, but made it work for their interests. The relatively widespread practice of *urfi* (informal) marriage since the late 1990s exemplified this strategy. *Urfi* marriage is a religiously accepted but unofficial oral contract that requires two witnesses and is carried out in secret. The Minister of Social Affairs spoke of 17% of university female students going through *urfi* marriage, causing a public uproar over this "danger" to "national security." (*Al-Wafd*, May 4, 2000) Officials cited declining social authority, absence of fathers, and the employment of mothers as the cause of this "frightening phenomenon." Experts pointed to the lack of housing and, especially, absence of a "religious supervision" over youth (*Al-Wafd*, ibid; *Al-Ahram*, May 6, 2000:13). But in essence, the young utilized this traditional institution to pursue romance within, but not outside or against, the moral and economic order, to get around the moral constraints on dating and economic constraints on formal marriage.[40] With the same logic, lower class youth resorted to, but also transformed, such religious occasions as Ramadan, Eid al-Adha, and Mulids of Saints as occasions of intense socializing and diversion.

Indeed, the phenomenon of Amr Khalid, Egypt's most popular young lay preacher who, since the late 1990s, spoke about piety and the moralities of everyday life, should be seen in similar sense of a reinvention of a new religious style by Egypt's globalizing youth.[41] In a sense, Egyptian cosmopolitan youths fostered a new religious subculture—one that was expressed in a distinctly novel style, taste, language, and message. It resonated the aversion of these young from patronizing pedagogy and moral authority. These globalizing youth displayed many seemingly contradictory orientations; they were religious believers, but distrusted political Islam if they knew anything about it; they swung back and forth from (the pop star) Amr Diab to Amr Khalid, from partying to prayers; and yet they felt the burden of a strong social control of their elders, teachers, and neighbors. Because young Egyptians were socialized in a cultural condition and educational tradition that often restrained individuality and novelty, they were compelled to assert them in a "social way" through "fashion." Thus, from the prism of youth, this religious subculture galvanized around the "phenomenon of Amr Khalid" was in part an expression of "fashion" in the Simmelian sense of an outlet that accommodates contradictory human tendencies—change and adaptation, difference and similarity, individuality and social norms. Resorting to this type of piety permitted the elite young to assert their individuality and undertake change, and yet remain committed to collective norms and social equalization.

Although innovative, these strategies conformed to the prevailing regime of power, meaning that Egyptian youth stood largely demobilized in social and political arenas. Egypt's "passive revolution" ensured this demobilization by offering room to exercise a limited degree of innovation but only within the political discipline of the "secularreligious" state. In Egypt, unlike in Iran, a youth movement did not develop. It was only at the end of the first decade of the 2000s that a youth civic activism seems to emerge. The decline in the appeal of political Islam in Egypt pushed a segment of the religious-oriented youths to embrace voluntarism and organized charity work as a venue for social mobilization and doing something good. This kind of civic activism in addition to the April 7th movement, the collective mobilization of the young through Facebook and YouTube to support striking textile workers in 2008, heralded a new stage in Egypt's youth politics.

What, then, of youths as a political force in the Muslim Middle East? Do youth movements possess the capacity to cause political and democratic transformation? If, indeed, the youth movements, as I have suggested, are ultimately about claiming and reclaiming youthfulness, then their transformative and democratizing potential would depend on the capacity of the moral and political authorities to accommodate youthful claims. If their youthful claims are accommodated, youth movements would, by definition, cease to exist, and young people may remain as politically conservative as any other social groups. To become political agents, the young will need to think and act politically, as the Egyptian "April 7th movement" in 2008 illustrates. Yet, because the current doctrinal religious regimes in the Middle East have limited capacity to contain the increasingly global youth habitus, youth movements consequently retain a considerable transformative and democratizing promise. Muslim youth, perhaps similar to their non-Muslim counterparts, remain in constant struggle to assert, claim, and reclaim their youthfulness, by taking advantage of available venues, including resorting to religion or subverting it. Negotiating between their youthfulness and Muslimness against the general backdrop of modernity marks one of the most enduring elements in Muslim youth habitus.

3

The Drama of Jihad: The Emergence of Salafi Youth in Indonesia

Noorhaidi Hasan

Youth and Crisis in Indonesia

The Asian economic crisis of 1997 brought about the dramatic meltdown of the Indonesian currency, inflation, and mass dismissals, which eventually contributed to the collapse of Suharto's New Order authoritarian regime that had been in power for more than 32 years in May 1998. As the crisis deepened, more and more people in the world's largest and most populous Muslim country were thrown into the harsh reality of joblessness. The group most severely affected by the lack of employment was youth. They constituted 72.5% of the total unemployed in Indonesia in 1997, the highest in the list of global unemployment. A decade later, 70% of the total unemployed in Indonesia are still from the younger generation, male and female, having nothing to sell but their own muscles (Hendri 2008).

This fact apparently cannot be disassociated with the current politics of youth in Indonesia involved in street politics and mobilization for violence. The hallmark was the rise of a number of Muslim paramilitary groups with names like the Laskar Pembela Islam (Defenders of Islam Force), the Laskar Jihad (Holy War Force), and the Laskar Mujahidin Indonesia (Indonesian Holy Warriors Force), whose membership consisted mainly of youth between the ages of 15 and 29 years old. Characterized by their distinctive appearance, these groups achieved notoriety by organizing protests and a variety of other radical actions in the Indonesian public sphere. Not only did they demand the comprehensive implementation of the *shari'a* (Islamic law), but they also raided cafés, discotheques, casinos, brothels, and other reputed dens of iniquity, and most important, called for *jihad* in the Moluccas.

The backdrop of the call was bloody communal conflict between Muslims and Christians, which erupted in the islands of the Moluccas located in the eastern part of Indonesia in January 1999, and cost hundreds of casualties and displaced thousands of people. Facing the threats of mass killing, many were forced to flee to adjacent provinces. In addition, hundreds of buildings, including schools, mosques, and churches, were gutted. At the height of the conflict, the two combating parties tried to attract wider national attention. They circulated photos, video compact disks, and amateur movies of atrocities committed by their respective enemies. Rumors circulated about a revival of the old Dutch-sponsored RMS (South Moluccan Republic), now in the form of a separatist movement supported by a Zionist–Christian conspiracy working to "Christianize" the Moluccas islands.[1]

Among the groups, the Laskar Jihad might be considered the most exclusive and phenomenal paramilitary organization uniting thousands of young members, militants who call themselves *Salafis*, followers of the *Salaf al-Salih* (pious ancestors). Active under the umbrella organization *Forum Komunikasi Ahlus Sunnah wal-Jama'ah* (Forum for Followers of the Sunna and the Community of the Prophet), henceforth called FKAWJ, whose establishment was officially inaugurated in the palpably religious mass gathering *tabligh akbar* held in Yogyakarta in January 2000, it emerged on the scene as an undoubtedly militant Islamic organization and impressed the public through the onward march of its members willing to martyr themselves for the cause of God. Under the leadership of Ja'far Umar Thalib (b. 1961), this largest and best organized paramilitary group claimed to have dispatched more than 7,000 voluntary *jihad* fighters to the Moluccas. Deployed in different places to confront Christians, their presence undoubtedly changed the map of the communal conflict occurring in the islands.

This chapter examines why thousands of young men, roughly half of whom are university students and graduates between the ages of 20 to 35 years old, were so eager to welcome the call for *jihad* announced by Ja'far Umar Thalib and compete to risk their lives by enlisting to venture to the front lines and fight against Christians. To what extent does this religiously sanctioned repertoire of violence represent their attempts to consolidate identity during the contemporary period of rapid social transformation sometimes described as globalization? And in what way does their collective activism reflect a process of cultural interactions between the local and the global, the hegemonic and the subaltern, and the center and the periphery? Unlike the popular perception that associates *jihad* simply as an expression of religious fanaticism, an outrageous act of irrational, insane individuals driven by their firm belief in radical religious doctrines, this chapter argues that the determination of the youths to fight *jihad* in the Moluccas is more a form of rational choice in their attempt to negotiate identity, and thus claim dignity. To some extent it can be conceptualized as drama, a sort of performative practice of youths to demonstrate, in the face of powerful opponents, a hitherto marginalized power and to challenge the hegemonic global order.

Youth and the Global Salafi *Da'wa* Campaign

Laskar Jihad's success in mobilizing thousands of young men to fight *jihad* in the Moluccas has its roots in the so-called global Salafi *da'wa* campaign that deliberately and specifically targeted youth. In fact, their participation in the mission was generally preceded by their association with the Salafi *da'wa* movement that began to gain ground in Indonesia during the mid 1980s and initially developed on university campuses, which, similar to many other countries of the Middle East, had witnessed the proliferation of *halqas* (religious study circles) and *dauras* (a type of workshop). This so-called "Campus Islam" phenomenon started with mosque-based *da'wa* activities pioneered by youth activists of the Salman Mosque of the Institute of Technology in Bandung (Aziz et al. 1989). Under the leadership of Imaduddin Abdurrachim, who had been appointed the general secretary of the Kuwait-based International Islamic Federation of Student Organizations in the 1970s, they introduced the program of the *Latihan Mujahid Dakwah* (Training of *Da'wa* Strivers), which aimed to train new cadres among university students prepared to undertake *da'wa* activities. Thanks to the support of Muhammad Natsir, the leader of Dewan Dakwah Islamiyah Indonesia ([DDII] Indonesian Council for Islamic Propagation), a *da'wa* organization that served as the local representative of the Saudi Arabia–based Rabitat al-'Alam al-Islami, the program developed very fast.[2] It not only provided a model for Islamic activism on college campuses, but also facilitated the popularity of a variety of programs for the study of Islam organized by religious activity units, such as *Mentoring Islam* (Islamic Courses) and *Studi Islam Terpadu* (Integrated Study of Islam) (Aziz et al. 1989; Aziz 1995; Rosyad 2006).

President Suharto (1967–1998), following his policy of marginalizing political Islam, attempted to depoliticize university campuses through the implementation of the Normalization of Campus Life (*Normalisasi Kehidupan Kampus*) in 1978, thus prohibiting university students from playing an active part in politics. This restrictive policy stimulated growing numbers of students to turn toward Islamic *da'wa* activities, and this trend reached its pinnacle after the Iranian Revolution in 1979. There can be little doubt that the spirit and euphoria inspired by the success of the revolution affected youth in general and university students in particular, to the extent that they became keen in their endeavors to "cleanse" and "purify" the society from the alleged vices and evils of "westoxication," and to base their lives according to Islamic ideological and social values. More than that, the revolution provided inspiration for Muslims all over the world to struggle for the creation of Islamic states. In the years that followed, the Muslim world witnessed what Esposito (1983: 17) calls an "Islamic resurgence," marked by an increasing interest among Muslims in implementing religious teachings into all aspects of life.

Indeed, the growth of the Campus Islam phenomenon coincided with the dissemination of global revival messages, which revolves around the slogan "Islam is the solution" (*Islam huwwa il-hal*). This vague call puts an emphasis on the need to return to the model of the Prophet Muhammad and the example of the first generation of Muslims (*Salaf al-Salih*), considered to be the purist form of Islam. In this context, Islam is underscored as a complete system governing all religious, social, political, cultural, and economic orders, and encompassing all things material, spiritual, societal, individual, and personal. Battles over dress, morality, marriage, celebrations, entertainment, sexuality, and faith as well as conflicts over governance and law are thus at the center of the call (Ayubi 1991; Eickelman and Piscatori 1996; Kepel 2002). As a result, university campuses witnessed signs of Islamization, as appeared in the increase in students' observation of Islamic obligations, in their wearing of *jilbab* (headscarf) and other Islamic symbols, and in the spread of Islamist books. The translations of the books by the Islamist (Sunni and Shi'ite) theoreticians, including Hasan al-Banna, Abul 'Ala al-Mawdudi, Sayyid Qutb, Mustafa al-Shiba'i, Ayatollah Khomeini, Murtada Mutahhari, and Ali Shariati, were circulated widely among university students. This situation undoubtedly provided a precondition for the growing influence of transnational Islamic movements, including the Ikhwan al-Muslimin (Muslim Brotherhood), the Hizb al-Tahrir (the Party of Liberation), and the Tablighi Jama'at (*Da'wa* Society).[3]

The Salafi *da'wa* movement began to develop on university campuses during the mid 1980s and succeeded in establishing itself as an important current of Islamic movements at the beginning of the 1990s. Its proliferation was pioneered by Saudi Arabian graduates who had undergone their baptism of fire in the Afghan War. Adopting the most puritanical Saudi style of Islam, Wahhabism, it distinguished itself with other branches of Islam by its strict adherence to an extreme Puritanism, manifested in the members' inclination to adopt a typical Arab–style dress (*jalabiyya*) and let their beards grow long in their enforcement of religious observance.[4] Nevertheless, by adhering to the doctrine of the *Salaf al-Salih* of the Saudi Wahhabi model, which focuses on the purification of Muslim belief, it avoided discussing politics, or, more precisely, engaging questions of political power.[5] Instead, it concentrated on re-Islamizing society at a grassroots level by insisting on the correct implementation of the *Shari'a* by individuals, particularly through preaching and the establishment of Islamized spaces. This stance of apolitical "quietism" was developed in accordance with the Saudi Arabian policy to suppress radical expressions of political Islam, while demonstrating its commitment to religious propagation and a puritanical life style.[6]

The Salafi *da'wa* movement had to compete with all the other movements that had found fertile soil at university campuses to recruit university students. Upon return from Saudi Arabia, Abu Nida, the early proponent of the movement, chose to live in Yogyakarta, the city known as the main destination of students wanting to study at a university. At the beginning of every academic year, thousands of students from almost all the provinces pour into the city. Here, Abu Nida began to propagate Salafi *da'wa* activities, targeting university areas with the goal of attracting students. Supported by Saefullah Mahyuddin, the then head of the DDII branch office in Yogyakarta known for his close relations with the Jama'ah Shalahuddin (Shalahuddin Community), a religious activity unit attached to the Gadjah Mada University, one of the largest universities in Indonesia, Abu Nida lectured at Islamic study forums organized by the community and promoted Wahhabite doctrines among students.

Abu Nida believed that the growth of the Salafi *da'wa* movement in Indonesia was dependent upon successfully recruiting university students into his circles. To him, university students are the most educated and, thus, the most important layer of the younger generation of Indonesian Muslims that can serve as agents of change to direct Indonesia into a more Islamized country.[7] As interest in the Wahhabite doctrines spread, Abu Nida expanded his influence by independently organizing Salafi *halqas* and *dauras* both inside and outside university campuses. In developing his activities, Abu Nida gained support from his colleagues who had also completed their studies in Saudi Arabia, including Ahmad Faiz Asifuddin, Aunur Rofik Ghufron, Dahlan Basri, Abdul Hakim Abdat, Masrur Zainuddin, Muhammad Yusuf Harun, Ahmad Zawawi, Yazid Abdul Qadir Jawwas, Yusuf Usman Baisa, and Ja'far Umar Thalib. The efforts made by these new graduates to spread the Salafi *da'wa* proved fruitful. Salafi communities, with a membership that consisted mainly of university students between the ages of 18 and 30, proliferated. The multiplication of the Salafi communities led seamlessly to the emergence of foundations that received considerable financial support from Saudi Arabia, Kuwait, and other Gulf countries, particularly the Mu'assasat al-Haramayn al-Khayriyya (Haramayn Charitable Foundation), known as al-Haramayn, and the Jam'iyyat Ihya' al-Turath al-Islami (Reviving of Islamic Heritage Society).[8]

It is worth noting that the burgeoning of the Salafi foundations was made possible by the shift of the state policy toward political Islam. At the end of the 1980s, Suharto introduced an Islamization strategy that focused particularly on the accentuation of Islamic symbols in public discourse and accommodating religious sociopolitical powers. A number of organizations and institutions that made use of Islamic symbols appeared on the scene, including the Ikatan Cendekiawan Muslim se-Indonesia (Indonesian Muslim Intellectual Association), which was established under Suharto's patronage. While thousands of mosques were built under the sponsorship of the state, the Islamic Court Bill was introduced, followed by the Presidential Decree on the Compilation of Islamic Law.[9] The Bank Muamalat Indonesia, which holds as its slogan the words *pertama sesuai syariah*, or "the first [bank in Indonesia] in accordance with the *shari'a*" was set up, and its establishment initiated the mushrooming of Islamic *shari'a* banks and insurance companies. No doubt, these policies were part of Suharto's political strategy to hold on to power (Liddle 1996). In fact, various Islamic (opposition) groups saw the New Order's accommodation of Islam as a promising opportunity to enter the political arena of the state. They believed that through this way they would be able to change the fate of their society, their nation, and their state—not to mention bringing about changes at the personal level. Nasr (2001) refers to this sort of strategy as "Islamic leviathan" and perceives it as a facet of the state's drive to establish hegemony over society, and to expand its power and control, which hardly bears any positive result. Although regimes in the states that applied such a strategy could remain long in power, they hardly succeeded in bringing prosperity into society and providing participatory spaces, which is the prerequisite for the augmentation of democracy.

Living in a Risk Society

The plea of the Salafi *da'wa* movement—a strict religious organization that demands sacrifice and forces members to suffer from social stigma as a result of an unwavering belief and rigid adherence to the distinctive lifestyle—among Indonesian Muslim youths can be seen as one of the consequences of the fast current of social changes set in motion by the processes of modernization and globalization. Even though this accelerated process has opened up social, economic, and cultural possibilities, it has simultaneously ushered in a pleth-ora of problems and uncertainties. Problems such as the widening social gap and unequal access to education and economic opportunities resulted in high unemployment rates, worsening poverty, poor human resource quality, and low productivity. These problems affected mainly youths, whose upward mobil-ity was blocked by the state policy to accelerate unprecedented economic growth through the hands of conglomerates and multinational corporations, at the expense of the popular economy. No doubt, this situation has created a risk society faced with the problem of a dysfunctional social system.[10] For youth, who have to be mobile and ready to reap opportunities, living in uncertain con-ditions is often frustrating. The core of the problems lies in the fact that the horizon for upward mobility is quite limited (Leccardi and Ruspini 2006).

The whole story began when Suharto introduced the program of develop-ment in 1966; since then, Indonesia has been caught up in the government's attempts to accelerate the process of modernization and globalization. To achieve this purpose, the government initiated *Pelita*, the five-year planned development program, in 1969. One of the most important goals of New Order development was to increase the rate of literacy, which motivated the government to spend large amounts of money on the infrastructural development of primary schools. New schools were constructed across the entire archipelago, enabling villages to have full access to basic education. Since 1974, primary school education has been compulsory for children between the ages of 7 and 12. In making education more affordable, attractive, and accessible, the new system also brought absen-teeism under control (Leigh 1999). As a result, between 1965 and the early 1990s, the percentage of young adults with basic literacy skills rose from about 40% to 90% (Jones and Manning 1992).

To absorb the number of children finishing primary school, the government was forced to set up new junior and senior high schools. These schools were no longer confined to cities and large towns, which were difficult for villagers to reach; they were also built in small towns near villages in remote areas. In response to this availability, the numbers of young people attending junior high and senior high school rose significantly from year to year. Keeping pace with the improvement in societal economic prosperity, the ambition of the pupils finishing senior high school to continue their studies at the university level also increased. This spurred an increase in participation in modern education and higher education, with a growth that marginalized an older, nonmodern, tradi-tional form of schooling, such as *pesantren* and *madrasa*. Throughout the years, more and more people from small rural villages have enrolled in the newer national schools and universities in large urban areas such as Jakarta, Bandung, Semarang, Surabaya, Yogyakarta, and Makassar.

Needless to say, youth emerged as the group that felt most directly the impact of development. Having completed their basic and secondary education, many of them had the opportunities to migrate to big cities for a better education. The growing opportunities for youths coming from either small country towns and rural areas or from the urban lower middle classes to migrate to big cities for a better education have created certain problems that continue to trouble those young people who make the attempt. As appeared in a dozen case studies I collected among the Laskar Jihad members, in contrast to the students from the urban upper middle class, those from rural areas usually do not receive sufficient support from their families to enable them to cope with the heavy burdens of living as university students in the cities. Forced to rely on their own resources, they shoulder not only academic burdens, but also responsibility for their own basic living costs and tuition fees. Hampered by economic constraints, they are prevented from enjoying the "real" campus life that remains the prerogative of affluent students. Some have been forced to board in cramped quarters with limited facilities, located on narrow streets. Indeed, most of their parents generally live as peasants who own limited farmland. Because the economic policies of the state have tended to neglect agricultural development, it has become increasingly difficult for this stratum to improve their socioeconomic status (Hasan 2006).

Other village youths who had no hopes of undertaking a university education followed in their footsteps. Attracted by portrayals of cities disseminated by electronic media (most notably television), these youths came to find jobs in the cities and formed something resembling a new proletariat class, trying their luck by working as factory laborers, petty traders, shopkeepers, tailors, or artisans. They usually live very simply because of their ambition to transfer as much money as possible to their families in the countryside or to save for the future.[11]

These two segments of newly urbanized youths who came from slightly different social backgrounds had to experience a multiplicity of delicate, unsettled problems. By migrating to urban settings that strike them as unfriendly and intimidating, these people have become detached from the community of their villages. This heightens their sensitivity to psychological shocks and weakens their ability to deal with them. They have been used to living in a relatively predictable manner within the bounds of a community with members who could easily communicate with one another. Kinship ties are particularly useful in providing solidarity and protection, and their ubiquitous presence in a village means that problems are not carried on a single individual's shoulders, but are resolved collectively. In cities, on the other hand, a person is more likely forced to live independently in relative isolation. They are forced to live in overcrowded urban neighborhoods that the state has failed to organize either with respect to infrastructure or in terms of cultural or political structures, but at the same time witness unattainable modern luxuries in the shop windows of stores located in vast impersonal super- or hypermarkets.

It is apparent that the inequitable conditions that pervade the cities have disturbed the *habitus* of the newly urbanized youths. *Habitus* is a concept introduced by Bourdieu (1977: 78-79) to refer to a "system of durable, transposable dispositions which, integrating past experiences, functions at every moment as a matrix of *perceptions and actions,* and makes possible the achievement of infinitely diversified tasks." Bourdieu contends that people experience a particularly comfortable sense of place through sharing a *habitus.* Calhoun (1995) points out that one of the crucial features of *habitus* in traditional societies is that it radically limits the range of options available to rational actors. From his point of view, every increase in a person's range of options creates greater complexity and unpredictability for a person's decision making, a circumstance that is antithetical to the maintenance of stable traditional patterns of social relations. *Habitus* thus informs the selective act of choosing and determines the relation between social conditions of existence, the formation of the person, and the practice of consumption as a construction of a life-world (Friedman 1994; Sweetman 2003).

Exacerbating the feeling of dispossession is New Order Indonesia's climate of widespread corruption, economic stagnation, and bureaucratic incompetence. Shortly after taking power from Sukarno through a drama preceded by an abortive communist coup, Suharto began the construction of an extensive patronage system that, by the 1980s, distributed benefits and bought support throughout the country. In such a system, corruption from the top down was not only a temptation, but also the essence of political strategy. Bureaucrats were kept on board through job-based patronage, and military officers found it easy and lucrative to go into business. In the absence of an autonomous, effective state framework, personal political networks became the key institution of the New Order regime (Johnston 2005: 178–179). As a result of the corrupt system, many were alienated and were denied entrance into the central corridors of power or were disenchanted by the New Order arbitrary rule and by rampant corruption (Robison and Hadiz 2004: 120–130).

The government has seemingly failed to balance the supply of and demand for workers, engendering increasing competition in job markets. Although the majority of Indonesians achieved a higher standard of living under Suharto's New Order, problems of equity and distribution remain on the horizon, arising primarily as by-products of growth—a greater concentration in urban areas and the increasing expectation of the better educated. With the labor force growing by more than two million a year, the government faces an uphill struggle finding them jobs. About 600,000 university graduates could not find employment in 1988 through 1989. More than 60% of the labor force between the ages of 15 and 19 with a high school education were looking for work during the same years (Vatikiotis 1998: 57–58). In fact, youth appeared to be the most vulnerable social group that represents three quarters of the total unemployed population. Those working are forced to work in the informal economy, where they lack adequate income, social protection, security, and representation (Abdullah 2004). Predictably, this problem will get worse during the next 10 years because the bulk of the 11 million unemployed will be between 15 and 24 years old. Indonesia's unemployment rate could even increase to 20% of its roughly 150 million person workforce by 2015, whereas the number of poor families, currently estimated at 19.2 million, could double.[12]

All these problems have undermined the more conventional anchors of social life that provide a measure of reassuring stability for the youth. They experienced a sort of identity crisis, or more precisely, a relativization or fluidity of identity, when identity can be gained or lost, depending on individual volition and accomplishment. As a source of meaning for social actors, identity organizes meaning by determining how the purpose of certain actions is symbolically identified. Melucci (1989) refers to the "homelessness of personal identity" when describing the sort of alienation people experience when identities are relativized, and he proposes that this condition requires individuals to reestablish their identity and thus their "home" continually. In a similar analysis, Castells (1999: 20) suggests that the need to reconstruct an identity shaken by the swift current of social change encourages global, modern people to return to a primary identity established by working on "traditional materials in the formation of a new godly, communal world, where deprived masses and disaffected intellectuals may reconstruct meaning in a global alternative to the exclusionary global order."

In Search of an Alternative Channel

The Salafi da'wa movement and other exclusive Islamist organizations came to offer an alternative channel and protective cover for the Indonesian Muslim youth who migrated to cities for education and employment, through which they had the opportunity to consolidate their basic identity and thus find more security in facing the future. More than any other movements, the Islamist organization provided an alternative communal system and offered illusory social security and protection. It introduced a new vision of Islam that emphasized the formalization of religious expressions and provided a channel through which basic social and political questions as well as dissatisfaction and frustration could be articulated in a new way. The basic message is that to be Muslim alone is not enough to guarantee success in dealing with future challenges. There is no choice for any Muslim but to become a Muslim *kaffah* (total Muslim) that practices and applies Islam in all aspects of his life. The identity as a total Muslim is quite crucial in a sense a Muslim cannot be considered a (faithful) Muslim without believing in and applying the totality of Islam. A total Muslim is in turn required to show his commitment to uphold the principle of *al-amr bil ma'ruf wa-nahy 'an al-munkar*, a Quranic phrase meaning "enjoining good and opposing vice,"[13] and to become the most committed defenders of Islam. It is believed that this commitment is badly needed during a moment of history when Islam is under attack by the western world.

At certain levels, the commitment to become a total Muslim requires that youth conduct a sort of conversion to true Islam. Young men between the ages of 25 and 35 originally from rural areas now living in cities with university education typically described the years prior to their conversion as their *jahiliyya* (pagan ignorance) period, which they said had been dominated by the sins of *shirk* and *bid'a* (reprehensible innovations), and they regretted that the light of true Islam came so late to change their lives, a reminiscence of Qutb's interpretation of the concept of *jahiliyya* popular among Indonesian university students active in the campus *da'wa*. This sort of consciousness encouraged them to study Islam seriously. Even when faced with great difficulties, they always seemed enthusiastic to embark on a study of how to recite the Quran and how to perform the ablutions (*wudu'*) and prayers (*salat*) properly. Those who could already recite the Quran still felt it necessary to improve their skills. Their failures to pronounce some letters of the Arabic alphabet, such as *'ayn*, correctly, embarrassed them. Among Javanese, *'ayn* is usually pronounced as *ngain*. To polish their pronunciation, they eagerly listened to cassettes of Quran recitation (*murattal*) by well-known reciters from Saudi Arabia; these recordings were available everywhere, from traditional markets to luxurious modern supermarkets. As a result of the Islamic resurgence that has made religious symbols an important social indicator, such commodities have gained popularity and prominence in Indonesia.

As part of their social struggle to gain control over spatial behavior, initiates adopted a new, Arab–style costume and let their beards grow long. This move was usually accompanied by a commitment to distance themselves from their previous social environment, joining a sort of enclave in which they have the opportunity to undergo an internal *hijra* (migration) to shelter themselves from the stains and temptations of the outside world. They felt that, by doing so, they could more readily assert their claim to be true Muslims. Subsequently, they usually traded their Javanese (*abangan*) names for Arabic (Islamic) ones. Names like Sutarto, Hartono, Raharjo, Suryanto, Haryanto, Sumarjono, and Wardoyo were replaced by Ahmad Haris, Muhammad Chalid, Abdullah, Abdul Wahhab, Hamzah, Ibn Usman, and Ibn Rasyid. When they married and had children, they would adopt their children's Arabic names and insert "Abu" before them, becoming Abu Khalid, Abu Ahmad, Abu Mash'ab, and Abu Sulaiman.

When asked to explain this decision, they argued that as Muslims they should practice the Sunna of the Prophet Muhammad consistently. From their point of view, the adoption of a new name indicated a person's commitment to implement the Sunna. They insisted that their new names had been used by the *Salaf al-Salih* during the early period of Islam. Others acknowledged that the newly adopted names were "the names of the *hijra*," an echo of Qutb's idea. They asserted that the move from the *jahiliyya* culture dominated by *shirk* and *bid'a* into a genuine Islamic culture should be total, and taking on an Arabic name signaled a person's commitment to leave the *jahiliyya* culture. At the same time, they tried hard to use as many Arabic terms as possible in their daily conversations. They usually preferred, for instance, to call their friends by the terms *akhi* (brother) or *ukhti* (sister) or the plural *ikhwan* (brothers) or *akhawat* (sisters).

In the enclave, a member's pride in being different is emphasized, and a sense of certainty is reached. Inclusivity is particularly crucial for the consolidation of an identity that has been disrupted by the excesses of modernization and globalization. It is not surprising that the impulse to seek certainty is the driving force behind a person's consent to sacrifice and suffer from social stigma. Certainty is apparent in the way they organize their lives. The collectivity the group offers is appealing, as members stress the need to gather at every opportunity, particularly at prayer times. They usually wake up early in the morning and soon after take a bath. They then go to a mosque, or *musalla*, a smaller place to pray, to perform a morning prayer collectively. The *musalla* does not always belong to them. In many instances, they symbolically take control of a *musalla* where they live and make it the center of all their activities. This way of operating automatically consigns local people to the sidelines. The enclave culture reflects what Castells (1999: 9) describes as "the exclusion of the excluders by the excluded." Yet, in the face of the hegemonic capitalist global system that engenders problems of equity and distribution, this sort of resistance remains rhetorical and hardly produces any tangible results.

The frustration affecting youth arising from their inability to adjust to all the disparities and developmental paradoxes might be transformed into actual mobilization, especially when the political opportunity structure is available for social actors to organize contention. To achieve sufficient responses, the actors need to frame their action by producing, arranging, and disseminating discourse, which sometimes involves the utilization of irreverent symbols and violence.[14] Herein lies the significance of *jihad* as a language with a symbol and discourse that provide an aura of sacredness and righteousness, and that serves as a vehicle to resist impotence and frustration, and thereby establish identity and claim dignity. Seen from this perspective, *jihad* might be conceptualized as a drama. As in the case of the Laskar Jihad's mission in the Moluccas, thousands of young men poured into the spice islands of the Moluccas to fight *jihad* against the Christians blamed to have waged a crusade against Muslims. Spread in a dozen command posts in Ambon and surroundings, they impressed the public as militant youths willing to martyr themselves for the cause of God. Wearing the distinctive uniform of the Salafis (white *jalabiyya* and turban), complete with arms on proud display, they portrayed themselves as the most heroic combatants, aching to venture to the front lines. This process began with the spectacular gathering at the Senayan Stadium, a strategic and prestigious site close to the political and business centers of Jakarta. Through the media, millions of Indonesians watched participants shout and cry together, displaying their determination and capacity to defend the Moluccan Muslims from the attacks of Christian enemies. Imbued with such a theatrical dimension, this apparently frenzied action was motivated not so much by the hope for a resounding victory as by an ambition to fabricate a heroic image (Hasan 2006).

Jihad is appealing among youths, because it functions as an identity marker crucial for acquiring as much social status and reputation as comradeship and excitement. It might be seen as an attempt made by youths to claim spaces on the national level, using Massey's terminology, so that they can capture the geography of influences and the power relations they embody (Massey 1998). To reach this end, they do not hesitate to package and propagate their mission by utilizing global, modern media like the Internet. They interconnect two extremely different, and indeed competing, things into particular forms of hybrid cultures, generating the so-called *cyber jihad*, for instance. In fact, as in the case of the Laskar Jihad's mission in the Moluccas, the skillful use of global technology informed the success of youth in staging and propagandizing their collective actions. They not only published the *Maluku Hari Ini* (*Moluccas Today*), a pamphlet printed on a single double-sided sheet of paper presenting information about day-to-day developments in the Moluccan conflict, and the *Buletin Laskar Jihad Ahlus Sunnah wal Jama'ah*, a 16-page, large-layout weekly bulletin, but also set up a radio station named *Suara Perjuangan Muslim Maluku* (the Voice of the Struggle of Moluccan Muslims), and took a leap into cyberspace by setting up *Laskar Jihad Online*, extolling the slogan "*Berjihad di Dunia Maya*" (*Jihad* in Cyberspace).

No doubt, *jihad* of this kind emerges as a product of the creative processes of young people to synthesize the local and the global in the constitution of their reflexive biographies.

Transforming Frustration

The readiness of thousands of young men, roughly half of whom are university students or graduates, to participate in the *jihad* mission in the Moluccas pioneered by the Salafi leaders cannot be disassociated with the global Salafi *da'wa* campaign that deliberately targeted youth. Thanks to the financial support from Saudi Arabia, this campaign succeeded in establishing an exclusivist current of Islamic movement and in recruiting dedicated young followers into its core circles. The government attempts to accelerate the process of modernization and globalization provided the opportunities for youths to pursue a better education, thus opening the chances for them to attain social, economic, and political mobility. Yet, the modernization the government initiated stumbled and failed to achieve the promised economic development. Instead, it created not only corruption, nepotism, poverty, and unemployment, but also society's alienation and dependency. In view of this situation, youth felt threatened and insecure toward their fate and their future. They thought that to get out of this delicate situation they need to seek an alternative channel that offers a remedy. One such alternative is to join the exclusive Salafi *da'wa* movement and similar organizations that found fertile soil among university students. The exclusiveness offered by these movements facilitated youths' attempt to consolidate their identity and achieve some sort of certainty *about their future*. In tight-knit exclusive communities, they developed a passive resistance against the existing—hegemonic—world order, and this resistance ends in failure as the walls of the order remain stout. Caught in this situation, it was not a difficult decision for many of them to join the Laskar Jihad mission in the Moluccas, because *jihad* provided an opportunity to break out of their own frustration and, at the same time, claim identity and dignity.

4

Moroccan Youth and Political Islam

Mounia Bennani-Chraïbi

The Promise and Menace of Youth

Youth in the Middle East and North Africa represented a promise of change during the postindependence period, but they were soon depicted as a menace (Bennani-Chraïbi and Farag 2007). During the years following independence, youth have represented the "dangerous classes."[1] In Morocco, youth are both the victims of the "failure of the state" and globalization, and rebels confronting the hegemony of the American empire. Youth use Islam as a form of identification and action. The attacks in Casablanca on May 16, 2003,[2] as well as the role played by Moroccans during the attacks of September 11, 2001, on the United States and those in Madrid on March 11, 2004, have contributed to a triangulated image of youth, Islamism, and violence. These constructions are echoed in academic literature.

Since the independence of Morocco in 1956, research and analysis on youth have been carried out essentially using quantitative surveys. During the 1960s, youth were seen as transformative actors in history. Echoing theories of modernization and development, youth were characterized as being "modernist" and avant-garde in their "resistance to tradition" (Adam 1962: 163). The "spearheads for change," youths distinguished themselves from the older generation by rejecting polygamy and by adopting their "westernized" cultural preferences. However, in a famous study on rural youth, sociologists Paul Pascon and Mekki Bentaher (1969) qualified them as "conventional" and unquestioning of the social order, particularly with regard to the family and the position of women. At the same time, they considered youth "the motor of society," because young people were becoming numerically important. Despite being better educated, they were more destitute and more exploited than adults, and they were engaged in a generational conflict with their "retrograde elders" of the "patriarchal society." From 1980 to 1990, the perspective was inverted. From then on, the numerical weight of youth has been greater than any time in the past. The unemployment of university graduates has been recognized on the political agenda as a public problem. (See Boudarbat and Ajbilou 2007: 16–9).

Beginning in the 1980s, the "return of the religious" began to worry the elite, who feared that dissatisfied youth could become more receptive to political currents with Islamic references. In this context, a survey was conducted on high school and university students by the Rabat Group of research and sociological studies. It concluded that a predominant feature of youth was a "retraditionalization of mentalities," because of their positive attitude on issues such as polygamy and the place of religion in society (Bourqia et al. 2000). For example, 55.7% of those surveyed replied "lots" to the question: How much weight should religion occupy in administrative and political life? All these studies were strongly influenced by the dominant paradigms of the times. Furthermore, "youth," meaning those younger than 30, were falsely homogenized.

More recently, studies from the media and academia have played a role in restoring the idea of the diversity of Moroccan youth, albeit in two general groupings. Upon a suicide attack, or the dismantling of a "terrorist" group, the Moroccan "secular" press is alarmed by "spreading Islamic fanaticism" throughout Moroccan society, and, most notably, among marginalized youth. However, at other moments, the globalized "youth" appears hip with "alternative music" festivals (rap, R&B, hip-hop). Although Islamic movements denounce the "westernization" of Muslim youth, others rejoice that it is a protective barrier. An example of this polarization is demonstrated in a recent issue of the secular French language Moroccan newspaper *Tel quell* (Hamdani 2007). The front cover represents young men with the cool "Nayda" look, and a young girl, veiled, who turns her back to them. The title is "Morocco against Morock: The Liberty of Some Offends Others." The article begins: "Some pray, others dance. Some dare, others accuse. And the cleavage is becoming wider. . . . Will there be a clash soon?"[3] The producers of meanings compete over images to their society at different moments of its trajectory.

In this chapter I will look, on the one hand, to what degree young Moroccans maintain a homogeneous relationship with political Islam and assess whether they are really different from their elders in this domain. To address this issue, I use the data from several qualitative surveys conducted in Morocco. During the past 20 years, I have conducted interviews (ranging from 90 minutes to 3 hours) that have systematically contained questions on religious aspects (Bennani-Chraïbi 1994). Those interviewed were educated urban people, age 15 to 56 years. I will specifically analyze the repeated interviews conducted between 1998 and 2007 with young people from Casablanca, age 16 to 28 at the time of the first meeting. When they were first interviewed, the vast majority lived in working-class areas and had a general education. All were single, some were high school students, others were university students, and still others were unemployed. I met them near their schools, in youth community centers, in neighborhood associations, or during the electoral campaign in 2002.

By *youth* I refer to the phase of transition during which a person becomes more autonomous in the domains, for example, of housing (the fact of leaving the family home), on an emotional level (building a new family group by marriage or having a child), and at an economic level (integration into the labor market). It should be emphasized that with the phenomenon of extended youth, the thresholds are not necessarily simultaneous. For example, in Morocco, the average age for a first marriage has been pushed back; it is currently 26.3 years for women and 31.2 years for men.

First of all, I would like to show the diversity of the Moroccan political–religious scene. In quantitative surveys, certain Moroccan youth express a favorable opinion concerning religion in politics, even supporting the "application of the *shari'a*." I will focus on this category of young people. Next, it is not evident that opinions translate to political actions. Political Islam is not a flag behind which the masses of young Moroccans would be ready to move as one homogenous and united group. I will present data questioning the idea that "youth" are necessarily more sensitive than their elders to political tenets with an Islamic reference.

The Moroccan Political and Religious Sphere: A Battlefield

It has often been emphasized that the Moroccan religious arena is fundamentally dominated by the monarchy. However, the religious "legitimacy" of the Moroccan monarchy is not "natural," but has been the product of struggle, work, and a process of "naturalization" (Hammoudi 2007). In Morocco, a complex "religious field," to use Bourdieu's concept (1971), has enabled the Moroccan religious arena to be perceived as a terrain in which a whole series of players (monarchy, religious scholars [*ulamâ*], brotherhoods, political actors, and so forth) compete in the appropriation and interpretation of religion (Tozy 1999).

As some historians remind us (Berque 1982; Burke 1972; Laroui 1977), attempts by the monarchy to control the religious field date to the late 19th century. The domination imposed by the French protectorate (1912–1956) slowed the competition. However, since independence, the monarchy has applied itself to constructing hegemony by subjecting all its potential competitors to division, "clientelism," and dominance. More precisely, concerning religion, the king has tried to subordinate the *ulamâ*.

During the 1970s, the Islamists' questioning of the royal monopoly on religion[4] led King Hassan II to reassert control of the religious arena. A series of measures, including control over Friday sermons and the creation of the High Council of *Ulamâ*, were taken during the early 1980s to restrict the progress of any spontaneous religious movement. Later, in a style comparable with that adopted to deal with the leftist opposition, the monarch also set about to co-opt a group of Moroccan Islamists.[5] The parliament of 1997 included nine Islamist deputies. At the beginning of his reign in 1999, Mohammed VI liberalized speech, which benefited many players and revealed the presence of "self-proclaimed" preachers and *ulamâ* who were produced en masse by the various establishments created under Hassan II (Zeghal 2003). Moreover, in September 2002, acknowledged Islamists became the third largest parliamentary force.[6] Although the new king had given the impression that he was no longer playing his role as Commander of the Faithful, the attacks of May 16, 2003, led him to attempt to regain this status. It is on this basis that he presented his draft reform of the Code of Personal Status to Parliament.[7] This act subsequently gave rise to intense polarization led by feminists.[8] The Code was adopted after a reframing influenced by the concept of the *ijtihâd* (interpretation in God's way). This brief outline shows that the Moroccan political and religious arena is very fluid and remains a battlefield. Its frontiers, players, and issues have not been determined once and for all, and continue to be contested and negotiated. Throughout the reign of Hassan II, this struggle for hegemony over the production of religious meaning, which takes place at mosques and in law, media, and education establishments, had repercussions. It contributed to the shaping of an image of "official Islam."

From a legislative point of view, Islam, the state religion, is one of the fundamental principles of the monarchy. This was confirmed in 1962 by article 19 of the Constitution: "The King, *amir al-mu'minin* [Commander of the Faithful], supreme representative of the nation, symbol of its unity, guarantor of the stability and continuity of the State, shall ensure respect for Islam and the Constitution. He is the protector of the rights and liberties of the citizens, social groups and communities." Nevertheless, religious legislation has essentially inspired the Code of Personal Status of 1956, drawn up in accordance with the Malikite rite. On the other hand, proven adultery (*zîna*), public drunkenness, nonobservance of the fast, apostasy, and antireligious propaganda constitute disturbances of the peace and are punishable under penal law.

On a completely different level, schoolbooks are another important carrier of the official ideology of the kingdom. The curriculum analysis carried out by Mohamed El Ayadi gives a particularly revealing insight into this. On the basis of an analysis of nine schoolbooks dealing with Islamic education, the Arabic language and literature until the 1995–1996 scholastic year, he shows that "the religious discourse in school is not a simple presentation of religious dogma but an idealization of a religion . . . , by means of an appeal to glorification and apologetics" (El Ayadi 2000: 117). This discourse presents the Islamic system as the best, by putting it in competition with the West and even Communism. The scriptural sources (the Quran, the *Hadîth*) are sometimes accompanied by doctrinal texts produced by influential Islamic thinkers such as the Egyptian Sayyid Qutb (1906–1966) or the Pakistani Mawlana Mawdudi (1903–1979).[9] Repudiation, polygamy, the "natural" preeminence of the head of the family, wearing of the *hijâb* (veil), and the separation of opposite sexes on the beach are among the practices that are justified and idealized. On the political level, it emerges that "Islam is a totalizing religion" (*al-islâm dîn ash-shumûl*), and that it is both "religion and state" (*dîn wa dawla*). However, it is also stated that, "the political values appreciated by humanity today have long been proclaimed by Islam" (El Ayadi 2000: 133). This is particularly related to democracy and human rights. At the transnational level, Arab and Muslim unity are promoted and division is decried. Moreover, Islam and Muslims are frequently portrayed as being victims of various "conspiracies," and as having been so throughout history. This vision of Islam spread by schoolbooks does not seem to be in total contradiction with that of the Islamists.

Today, the two principal Moroccan Islamist factions follow a reformist tradition and condemn the use of violence. The Al-Adl wa Al-Ihsân (Justice and Benevolence) group forms a junction between mysticism and contemporary political Islam (Tozy 1999). It has opted for the education of the masses, refusing co-optation into the official political scene. The Justice and Development Party (JDP) resolved to integrate into the system. It recommends a kind of Islamic democracy under the umbrella of the monarchy, in a pragmatic and "open-minded" perspective. Moreover, its leaders prudently declare not to claim a monopoly on representing Islam They aspire to occupy the platform of the official opposition, regarding both the social and political problems of the country (violations of human rights, social injustice, unemployment) and also when "the Islamic features of the country must be preserved." Indeed, one should not forget the religious discourse of the "self proclaimed" *ulamâ*, who are sometimes close to the groups responsible for attacks like those of May 16th. It is also important to emphasize the importance of the Islamic satellite television channels, often quoted by my interviewees.

This short summary would be incomplete without mentioning the political, associative, and cultural actors who have no Islamic reference, but also play an important part in the configuration of Moroccan "Muslim politics."[10] They indeed contribute to its heterogeneity and to the number of dissonant voices. Moreover, this arena is far from being closed to what occurs outside its geographical borders. Neither the government nor its opponents are indifferent to what the U.S. State Department may think, to the possible reaction of the foreign media, and to the support or the withdrawal of international organizations.

If I have taken the time to set the arena, it is, first, to show that there are many hegemonic narratives about Islam, but there is no standardized production of Islamic meanings. It would be remiss to leave out the "ordinary" actors (the ones I interviewed), and dissociate them from this scene to which they have differential access and do not perceive uniformly. Nevertheless, I do not imply complete determinism, nor insinuate a boomerang effect between the meanings circulating in the Moroccan religious arena and the representations of those interviewed.

Youth and the "Confusion" between Islam and Politics

When one extols the virtues of the presence of religion in the city, how are its boundaries and modalities drawn? The implementation of the *shari'a* (religious law) does not mean the same thing to each individual. Likewise, the positive a priori assumption regarding this law does not automatically refer to the same content. Furthermore, when a student at the Faculty of Law states, "as we are Muslims, we cannot refuse something that is in its dogma," one must not immediately deduce that he wants to abolish interest rates, cut off the hands of thieves, or stone adulterous women. Behind the same declaration of principle, several constructions of meanings are possible.

In my sample, the hard-liners are represented in two ways. First, there are those who sympathize with Islamic movements, such as the JDP or Al-Adl wa Al-Ihsân, and, more generally, those who could be termed as *ordinary Islamists*— that is to say, those who share a similar vision of the world without necessarily translating it into political affiliation or commitment. For both of these groups, Islam is a total system that follows the principle of *ijtihâd* (the authority to interpret religious questions). This allows religion to adapt through the course of time and to acclimatize to all environments. From their point of view, the "gray areas," the legislative "loopholes" of the *shari'a* are indicative of a great deal of flexibility in legislative matters. In addition, this process of interpretation must be progressive. It is necessary to convince rather than impose.

Second, there are interviewees who maintain weak religious practices and are distinguished by a high degree of accommodation, pulled between several "programs of truth" (Veyne 1982). During the course of our discussions, they sometimes advocate a strict Islamization imposed from the top, while also expressing regret at being born Muslim! They present themselves as products of a corrupt society, eaten away by "debauchery" and decadence. In other words, Muslim male interviewees consider that if they consume alcohol or hashish, if they chat up girls coming out of school, it is the fault of society. In order for them to reform themselves individually, the state must safeguard their morality: close bars, veil women, prevent them from exhibiting their charms, apply "the laws of God and not those of the slave" in courts, in banks, in "all areas." Furthermore, to reconcile with themselves and society, these young people feel the need for a "totalizing" structure (embracing all aspects of their life) that would be imposed from above.

An intermediate position consists of considering the *shari'a* as an ideal, while noting the obstacles that face such a project. Some emphasize that Morocco is part of an international system and cannot opt for an Islamist economic approach in the context of globalization. In the same spirit, suppression of interest rates, closure of bars, as well as the eradication of cannabis production—which are all sources of revenue required for the survival of the country—would plunge the kingdom into an even more critical crisis. Also, the high levels of poverty and unemployment in Morocco do not provide favorable conditions for the implementation of the law of God, or the harsh *hudûd* punishments (for example, amputating the hand of a thief or the stoning of adulterous women)—an argument that is shared by the Islamists of the JDP and the Al-Adl wa Al-Ihsân.

The minimalists state that the *shari'a* is already implemented. For them, the issue consists of progressing on a path to democracy that preserves the "fundamentals of Islam" (*at-tawâbith*). They define democracy in terms of respect for differences and pluralism, and advocate that others establish a democratic system based on the Islamic principle of *shûra* (consultation),[11] a concept that is used in a vague, fluid manner and carries different meanings. Some interviewees consider the profession of faith as the "zero grade" of the belonging to the nation. The national motto "God, homeland, king" implies, in the words of one interviewee, "Respect the dimension of Islam, the state religion, and respect its fundamentals; there is only one God and the religion of God is Islam."

Dissent is legitimate, as long as there is a consensus about the Islamic creden-tials of all the players. For others, the conditions for observing the "fundamen-tals" are not related to the intrinsic qualities of community members; they are in relation to external characteristics. Morocco is a Muslim state through its own constitution. The presence of a commander of the faithful at its head represents a sizable guarantee that Islam will be protected and propagated in society. Institutions such as the state television announce prayer time and broadcast religious programs.

Last, the country's "Islamness" is sometimes reduced to an individualist conception of religion in which everyone can freely make his or her own choices. A whole set of comments support this position. As stated by inter-viewees: "The *shari'a* is implemented with or without [the Islamists]; there is the bar and the mosque. On the day of the last judgment, all will be judged according to their acts." "Religion must not be imposed." "Each one must try to reform oneself." "I like people who are religious for themselves." These state-ments suggest that religious practice and the sacred are relegated to the sphere of private life, to a direct, unmediated relationship between the individual and God. In the sample observed, there appears to be a real diversity behind the affirmation of the necessity of implementing the *shari'a*. On another level, I will show that some respondents adhere to a principle of the active presence of religion in the political scene, a position that has multiple manifestations.

The Gap between Religious Ideals and Religious Practice

In social movement theory, the distance between the spread of ideas and their crystallization into collective action is far. According to the approach developed by William Gamson (1992), three dimensions of collective action frames should be articulated: the existence of feelings of indignation when faced with "injus-tice"; "identity," which designates the constitution of an "us" in opposition to "them" in relation to values and interests; and "agency," which is the feeling of being able to settle the problem by collective action. On the other hand, mobi-lization occurs at the intersection of several variables located in space and time (local, national, transnational) through "recognition circles" (Pizzorno 1986). In other words, the inscription of different actors in the same "political oppor-tunity structure" does not necessarily produce a similar impact. Of fundamen-tal importance is the way actors perceive the world. Social movement theory throws light on the diversity of paths and the variability of intensity with regard to identification and political commitment. I shall illustrate this point by giving some profiles of "hard-liners" from my sample.

Mahfoudh was 28 years old at the first interview (1998). He was living in the same popular area in which he was born and belonged to the first generation of his family born in the city. After studying physics and chemistry for two years at the university level, he became a technician. He presented his trajectory as a continuity; his was a conservative upbringing in a neighborhood "still" soaked in religious values, and especially by the spirit of solidarity. He claimed to have an "Islamic orientation," but expressed worries about religious "extremes." He read publications on Islam from Morocco and elsewhere in the Arab world. He especially admired Youssef Al-Qardâoui,[12] who, according to him, considers democracy as compatible with *shari'a*. On the other hand, he disapproved of violent groups as well as movements like al-Adl wa al-Ihsân who "exclude the others" (he met some of them at university). Convinced by the necessity of legal, organized, and gradual action, he identified himself with the ideas of the JDP. One of his friends introduced him to Mustapha, a teacher of Arabic literature who was especially active when their area was flooded two years earlier. Mahfoudh had already seen him in the mosque. When Mustapha ran as the JDP candidate for the legislative elections of 1997, Mahfoudh campaigned with him. On this occasion, he had the opportunity to admire him more closely. When provoked by adversaries who unfairly treated him like a "terrorist," Mustapha stayed calm and dignified. Once elected, Mustapha founded a social development association and Mahfoudh "naturally" committed himself to it. In the frame of this association, Mahfoudh met other members of the JDP. In 2002, he converted his sympathy for the JDP into party membership. In this case, several circles and experiences consolidated (readings, friends and neighborhood circles, electoral campaigning, and association), without being experienced as a break either with the familial background or with the national and political context, because the JDP enjoyed legal legitimacy. Before his commitment to the party, Mahfoudh already had political markings, but his political orientation materialized only after microexperiences grounded in ties of action and trust. In this case, Mahfoudh experienced a strong identification with actors in a movement that was articulated to a feeling of being able to change the situation through collective action. However, this articulation between ideas and commitment is far from systematic.

Khadija was 26 years old when I first met her in 2002. An accountant, she is from the same social and geographical background as Mahfoudh. The charismatic Mustapha was her teacher and played a central role in her adolescent life. Thanks to him, she abandoned love stories in favor of religious books. Under his influence she adopted the headscarf. When Mustapha was a candidate in the 1997 elections, she gave him her vote. When he founded the association in 1998, she, along with her high school friends, joined him. She recognized herself as having an "Islamic orientation," but under the influence of her parents, expressed mistrust toward "politics." By "politics," she meant both the official and underground movements. In the frame of the association, she became more politically sophisticated. For the first time, she took part in demonstrations (first against the reform of the Code of Personal Status in March 2000 in Casablanca and then in support of Palestinians in April 2001, in Rabat). These forms of participations constituted an interlude of socialization. During the initial stages, her interest was aroused by the events and discussions preceding collective decision making. The later experience of demonstrations, the atmosphere, the slogans chanted were all elements that contributed to uphold and unify a distinct vision that was unfocused and vague up to that point. Even so, during the elections of 2002, she left her ballot blank (Mustapha was not a candidate in her constituency). She was not ready to transfer the faith she had in a person involved in the JDP to the whole party. Moreover, she was convinced that a large distance separated the world of ideas from the world of action. In 2007, she once again left her ballot blank, because she did not personally know any candidate. Once again, she did not vote for the JDP. Following her experience in the association, she observed that the JDP members were "good people," but not sophisticated enough politically, that "we don't do politics only with good intentions." She formed this opinion while observing the association's breakup, which she attributed to a lack of experience and of "long-distance vision." Furthermore, she expected that members of government should exhibit "sophistication in all fields" and efficiency in developing the country, which included struggling against unemployment and corruption; it did not matter what their ideology was. After she left the association, she stopped being interested in "politics" and even stopped following the news. She justified this decision by saying, "as I am not in position to bring any solution, I don't need to get worked up about it. If I can offer something, I do it; if it's far from me . . . ."

Khadija was influenced by her former teacher and her involvement in the association, but in a precise field—what she framed under the "social" label (in the promotion of the Islamic Moroccan family, in solidarity at the neighborhood level, and in solidarity with Palestinians). These experiences contributed to increasing her political sophistication, without making her want to engage directly in politics. Her relationship to politics seems close to what Nina Eliasoph observed in some American associations: "They wanted to care about *people*, but did not want to care about *politics*. Trying to care about people but not politics meant trying to limit their concerns to issues about which they felt they could 'realistically' make a difference in people's lives" (Eliasoph 1998: 12–13). For Khadija, there was a lack of political identification and of "agency" on the national level.

Ali, a 16-year-old high school pupil in 2002, expressed a great interest in politics. His socialization was particularly heterogeneous because he kept a distance from any single political commitment. He was critical toward both transnational and national political scenes, which he thought exhibited strong feelings of injustice. According to him: "The United States of America exerts a strong pressure on the Muslim world. They support Israel; they kill our children and our old people. . . . The big fish devours the smallest." On the national scale, he rejected the monarchy and considered it as monopolistic and dictatorial—at least under the rule of Hassan II—and as very expensive for the country. His model was a democracy like France, but soaked in "Islamic values." He describes his position saying, "I am an Islamic democrat. We must take the positive things from democracy: freedom of expression, of circulation. . . . [In the spirit of] Islam, group interest comes before individual interest. . . . If I observe that you are on the wrong path, I intervene."

He shaped this vision of the world after moving through different circles. He was the youngest child of a large family and recalled his drunkard brother-in-law and his brother who dreamed for a better life in the western world. He particularly admired another brother-in-law, a graduate in religious law, who frequented several Islamist groups without tying himself to any one in particular. Ali also attended summer camps organized by different Islamic groups. In this frame, he listened to lectures given by their leaders and closely mixed with members from these groups. Despite these experiences, Ali did not identify with any one Islamist Moroccan movement. He globally associated them with *khubzawiyya* (opportunism moved by the quest for bread),[13] by opposition to (the Salafiyya) *Jihâdiyya* from elsewhere. Indeed, he felt admiration for Osama bin Laden, who "defies those more powerful than him" and who "abandoned palaces for caves." At the same time, he disapproved of civilians attacks. If Ali developed a strong feeling of injustice, his identification remained diffused and hindered by mistrust toward all Moroccan political actors. Moreover, he was not convinced he could remedy the situation: "According to me, if you want to make the *jihad*, make it in your own ideas. If there is some one stronger than me, I am not going to fight him; I will stay hidden at home, until the day I will reach his level."

Mistrust is sometimes expressed toward the self. Such was the case of a group of male adolescents (17 years old on average) I met during spring 2002 in front of a girl's high school. They used to meet every afternoon to chat up the girls. They had the same feeling of injustice as Ali about transnational conflicts, and legiti-mized the *jihad*, defined as a defensive war act against those who attack Muslim majority territories. Furthermore, they had just taken part in high school strikes in support of Palestine. Nevertheless, they did not have faith in themselves:

> "[Our relation to religion is] very marginal. Few of us pray, even though praying is a foundation of religion. To tell you the truth, all of us lie. . . . Do you know what striking means for us? It means not studying from Monday to Monday [laughs]. Sincerely, it isn't solidarity . . . making the *jihâd*, not being afraid of death, submission to God. . . . Nobody from our group is ready for the *jihâd*. . . . Killing oneself isn't easy. You need strong self-confidence, faith in your homeland."

> "No, sorry, some people do want to go to heaven."

> "So what? Even a junkie wants to go to heaven, but we have not the faith, the strength of faith; we haven't been raised in it."

> "I, I want to go [to the Jihad]."

> "You, you want to go?! Do you think your mother is going to let you go?"

> "I swear she will encourage me."

> "She should tell you to go to the port to jump [the frontier]."[14]

> "If your mother loves you, do you think she would accept to let you die? . . . You do not have the strength of faith which would push you to go. Personally, I am not a true believer. We are too attached to material goods, to here below (*dunyâ*)."

Conscious of the disharmony in their discourse and of the variety of their "programs of truth," the majority of these high school pupils asserted their preference for "life's pleasures"; they expressed, with derision, their weak self-esteem. In this case, too, there is a big gap between supporting an ideal and passing to action.

A year later, I met one of these high schools pupils who was considering Jihad as the only possible weapon for Palestinians. The attacks of May 16, 2003, constituted a turning point for him, an intense moment that contributed to transform his frame of values. The violence stopped being abstract, virtual, only watched on television, after it entered his physical space. Terrorized, he finished by rejecting the whole idea of martyr operations, even those conducted in Palestine.

Thus, beyond the identification with formal political Islam, there are many degrees and materializations of Islamic identity. Furthermore, the socializa-tion of this youth has not occurred once and for all; it is in process. It remains to be seen whether these configurations and attitudes are particular to young people.

The Young and Old: A Congruence?

During my fieldwork, I did not observe any real cleavages between the youngest and the oldest of my sample regarding the relations between politics and religion, political commitment and noncommitment. A recent representative survey conducted with 1,156 persons spread over the 16 regions in Morocco gives a more precise vision (El Ayadi 2007). First, the family appears as the main locus of socialization. Next, contrary to what was asserted by the media and by some academic studies, it seems that "the assertion of religious values and practices is a general phenomenon, which concerns all categories: age, social, and economic" (El Ayadi 2007: 105). Moreover, according to this survey, "the Islamist expression is an undeniable reality within youth . . . , it is not the majority, nor more pronounced than in the other categories of age. [It] is nevertheless more radical among a minority of young people" (El Ayadi 2007: 160). Tables 4.1 and 4.2 illustrate these results numerically.

At the level of declared intentions, religious action within the associative frame is valued by all age categories. Nevertheless, concerning the segment of persons 60 years old and older, it comes in first position (23.4%); and, for the 18- to 24-years-old, it is in the third position (15.7%), after charity associations and human rights (El Ayadi 2007: 159).

In fact, the variable of education seems to be more deterministic than age. Effectively, the answers of educated people converge, whatever the age. They contrast with noneducated people who answer the question concerning politics and religion, with high rates of "do not know," "indifferent" (El Ayadi 2007: 174).

TABLE 4.1. "In your opinion, should religion guide only personal life, or also political life?"

Age, y	Only Personal Life, %	Also Political Life, %
18–24	26	28.8
≥60	23.4	17.9

Source: El Ayadi (2007: 161).

TABLE 4.2. "Do you agree or not with the Jihadist movement?"

Age, y	Agree, %	Disagree, %
18–24	21.8	31.4
≥60	9.7	20

Source: El Ayadi (2007: 163).

Conclusion

I have shown that the plurality of religious reference, a taken-for-granted feature of the global North, also exists in Morocco, a country situated in the Middle East region. As elsewhere, "young" Moroccans do not constitute a coherent, uniform, or isolated unit. The place of religion in the city is renegotiated at the junction of internal and external dynamics—in a battlefield where frontiers, issues, and players are continually moving. It is within this framework that problems and arenas are constituted, and that even "young" people position and reposition themselves in the process. They may identify themselves as "Muslim youth" by their support of Palestinians or involvement in other "Muslim causes." Their "imagined community" is revealed by conflicts in which Muslims are in a weak position. They could also assert an "Islamic" political orientation. "Muslim youth" is neither a transparent or monolithic category nor an explanatory variable. The context and meaning of Muslim youth always need to be clarified.

Furthermore, as everywhere, the perception of injustice is not sufficient in and of itself to provoke a passage to collective action. Action comes about as the result of a particular type of socialization, involvement in networks, and experience in microevents that allow ideas to translate into actions. Finally, Moroccan young people do not have a greater concern to build God's City on Earth than the older generations. Admittedly, they have been more exposed to the medium of Islamist socialization. There is surely a generational effect that remains to be studied. Despite this, there is not an Islamist steamroller. Moroccan "youth" are subject to the same cleavages that run throughout the global society.

5

Rebels without a Cause?: A Politics of Deviance in Saudi Arabia

Abdullah al-Otaibi and Pascal Ménoret

'The class war is fought out in terms of . . . crime, riot, and mob action.

—E. P. Thompson (1963)

The Death of Sharari

On March 15, 2006, young Mish'al al-Sharari died in a car accident on the al-Ghurub (twilight) avenue, in the low-income district (*al-dakhl al-maḥdūd*) of Riyadh. Six people died with him: the three passengers in his car, two pedestrians, and a pickup truck driver who had involuntarily triggered the accident. The death of an ordinary Saudi citizen had rarely provoked so many reactions and echoes. A rapid survey of the discussion forums on the Internet gives an image of the importance of this event in the eyes of young Saudis, in whose pantheon Sharari had joined the late King Fahd, Shaykh Abd al-'Aziz bin Baz[1] and the pro-Chechen Saudi fighter 'Umar al-Khattab. Neither a monarch, nor a religious scholar or a *jihad* fighter, Sharari shared with some 300 other young Saudis[2] the envied and shameful privilege of being a "car skidder" (*mufaḥḥaṭ*), a car skid enthusiast (*muhajwil*), a professional destroyer of vehicles, an entertainer of idle young people, and an enemy of public morality. He died during a skid session (*tafḥīṭ* or *hajwala*[3]). Yet Sharari had first refused to follow his fans who had gathered and urged him "to throw the iron" (*siff al-hadīd*) and to "domesticate" it (*ta'dīb al-hadīd*). He instead preferred to drift around in his car with another *mufahhat*, "Shaytani" ("Diabolical"). His fans then organized a procession of several dozens cars and drove at top speed in Riyadh until they eventually caught up with him. Won over by their enthusiasm, he performed daring skids and figures (fig. 5.1) for spectators who turned up in the hundreds from all over the city (fig. 5.2).

He eventually died. His car somersaulted several times, crashing into some of the fans who were clustered on the sidewalk, before bursting into flames. The car's four occupants were burned alive before the gaze of his powerless public Deeply moved by Sharari's screams of pain, five of the *mufahhatin* in attendance repented and decided to become pious Muslims.

On that evening, a local legend was born. From the poignant details relayed by witnesses to the cold and impersonal comments conveyed in the local press, the death of Sharari became a narrative of major proportions.[4] The elements of the story included Sharari's initial refusal to satisfy the desire of his admirers, the mass of fans ultimately catching up with their hero, even the name of the fatal avenue ("al-Ghurub" [the twilight])—all elements of a good plot. Everything

FIGURE 5.1. "Al-Sagri" a member of the last generation of Mufahhatin. He is seen here during a show. His name is written on cardboard while one of his assistants dances for the public on the other side of the road. (Pascal Ménoret, 2006)

FIGURE 5.2. "Al-Sagri" greets his fans before getting back on track. *Tafhit* emerged out of the suburban landscape of the postoil boom in Saudi Arabia. (Pascal Ménoret, 2006)

was present except the love story. This indispensable ingredient of any good session of *tafḥīṭ*, for *mufaḥḥaṭīn* are expected to address younger boys with feelings approximating chivalrous good companionship or Greek love. But on that day, the drama itself was sufficient, and no one felt the need to color the story with the paintbrush of passion.

This chapter is dedicated to understanding some of the dynamics that are made clear by this and other events related to the world of *tafḥīṭ*. It aims at drawing a clear picture of the Saudi disenfranchised and urban male youth who cope with the reality of being young in Riyadh today. The least one can, indeed, say is that the academic interest for youth in the Middle East has had more to do with Islam and variously described processes of "Islamization" than with the issues confronting youths and the many responses to them youths try to invent on a daily basis. This main trend explains why studies focus less on youth practices than on the institutions that deal with youth (family, school, association, club, party, and so forth), and less on deviances than on the supposedly straightforward processes of inculcation of norms. In particular, politicization of youth is understood mainly as a process of normalization and socialization, be it through official education or Islamic institutions—hence the somewhat exaggerated interest in the issue of school curricula for instance.

We show here that politicization may also result from processes of deviance and desocialization. We, therefore, describe *tafḥīṭ* in Saudi Arabia—its dynamics, its challenges, and the variety of players involved in it—to propose another way of dealing with the wider issue of the politicization of youth in Saudi Arabia.

Becoming a *Mufaḥḥaṭ*

The *tafḥīṭ* milieu in Riyadh is not homogeneous. It mainly attracts young men whose ages range from 15 to 30, who dropped out of school and/or who are job seekers, and who come from lower middle class, lower class, and Bedouin backgrounds. It is also the gathering ground of sometimes older, well-educated people who have not lost touch with the world of the street, and may as well fund some of the *mufaḥḥaṭīn*, when they do not themselves steer the wheel. One of the most revered *mufaḥḥaṭīn* of Riyadh, Badr 'Awadh (nicknamed "al-King") was in his mid 30s when he retired from the street and started a new career as a religious preacher. But *tafḥīṭ* also attracts well-off people, such as young princes and offspring of the bourgeoisie, who like to fill their lives with some feeling of danger and occasionally fund this or that street hero. Nevertheless, the majority of my interviewees are young countrymen whose families have recently settled in Riyadh or who themselves came to the capital for study purposes or to find work opportunities. They usually come from marginalized regions such as the South or the Bedouin areas, and their brilliant tribal heritage strongly contradicts their poor housing and urban living conditions. The opportunities of the big city have often proved to be mere mirages, and many are those who either have quit studying or who are long-term job seekers. Bedouins hold also a heavy burden—namely, their more "liberal" and nomadic identities toward townspeople who claim to be more religious and less kin oriented, and who have benefited in a more direct way from the modern Saudi state.

At a crossroads between the countryside and the town, *tafḥīṭ* gathers many deviances and is seen by many families as the final stage of a relentless process that leads ineluctably from consumption of tobacco and alcohol to car robbery, then to homosexuality, drug addiction, trafficking of drugs, and sometimes to death in a car accident. From a once innocent pastime, *tafḥīṭ* has thus become an important public issue related to the emergence of criminalized practices (trafficking and consumption of drugs and alcohol, car robbery, homosexuality). Since the end of the 1990s, the *tafḥīṭ*'s prevention has become a socially and politically resonant issue and is the object of articles, criminology studies, preaching efforts under the guidance of the Ministry of Islamic Affairs and eradication campaigns by the Ministry of Interior. Many institutions directly or indirectly fight *tafḥīṭ*: the media has to be socially responsible and regularly denounces the "*tafḥīṭ* dissent[5]" (*fitna al-tafḥīṭ*) or the "street terrorism[6]" (*irhāb al-shawāri'*) (fig. 5.3).

Various research centers, often funded by the Ministry of Interior, study "the *tafḥīṭ* phenomenon" (*ẓāhira al-tafḥīṭ*) and publish articles and studies (Al-Rumayh 2006: 228–229). Many officers of the traffic police hold sociology and criminology diplomas.[7] Health institutions such as the al-Amal psychiatric hospital[8] are dedicated to fighting drug addiction and the behavioral problems of many youth who ended up in *tafḥīṭ*. Last but not least, many Islamic institutions fight the socialization related to *tafḥīṭ* through preaching campaigns at the very locations used by *mufaḥḥaṭīn*.

How does one fall into *tafḥīṭ*? When one asks the *mufaḥḥaṭīn* or their fans about the context in which they were initiated to this activity, the answer is unanimous: It is because of what young people in Riyadh refer to in colloquial Arabic as *ṭufush*. This word is translated by Saudi sociologists into the classical Arabic *faragh* or *malal* (vacuum, boredom), and this linguistic shift is, in itself, the source of many misunderstandings. The state-funded war on delinquency will indeed concentrate on idleness, without trying to understand

FIGURE 5.3. Mufahhatin and their fans have adopted an odd dress style. For security reasons, and out of coquetry, they veil their faces like Jihadists—and women—do. (Pascal Ménoret, 2006)

what young low-class people say when they talk of *ṭufush*. Rather than vacuum or boredom, *ṭufush* denotes the feeling of social impotence that over-whelms young people when they realize the incommensurable distance between the economic and social opportunities of Riyadh, the capital of the richest state in the region, and their own condition (unemployment or low income, split-up families because of rural migration, poor housing, and so on). *Ṭufush* may then be understood as the feeling of being deprived of social or relational capital (Bourdieu 1980) in a city where all opportunities are within reach, provided that one has a good "connection" (*wāsta*). If boredom is "vacuum, nothing," *ṭufush* is "what drives you to do anything, what drives you into being an *'arbajī* (hooligan)" (interview, Riyadh, March 2006)—in other words, "to sell the entire world for a bicycle wheel's price" or "to take the whole world as a [cigarette] butt and to step on it."[9] This malaise seems specific to the lower class youth, who experience much more difficulties in terms of education, jobs, and housing than the other sectors of the Saudi society. Being *ṭufshān*, experiencing *ṭufush* is to experience in one's everyday life a discrepancy between subjective hopes and objective opportunities (Bourdieu 1997: 336). *Ṭufush* therefore is not mere boredom or emptiness, but the rage that overwhelms young people when they realize that structures of opportunities are violently unfair.

Joining a *tafḥīṭ* is an easy task. Pupils living in a mainly Bedouin neighbor-hoods compare the group of Islamic awareness (*jamā'at at-taw'iyya al-islāmiyya*), which had been set up in their high school by the Saudi Islamic movement (*ṣaḥwa*), with the groups of *tafhit* that recruit from the street, neighborhoods, and schools. The Islamic group is extremely selective and recruits primarily good pupils, described in a pejorative way by their schoolmates as *dawāfīr* (nerds). *Tafḥīṭ* groups recruit every kind of pupils and effectively utilize various means of communication—flyers, mobile phones, and the Internet—to gather their public and organize their shows. The Islamic groups themselves can hardly compete with the attractiveness of *tafḥīṭ*. "We were all obsessed by it: you had to become a skidder!" says a ninth grader in a Riyadh high school. He (and others) continue:

> *First pupil*: I feel like 1% of the people are destined for the preaching group. [. . .] As for *tafḥīṭ* groups, they are larger. At the beginning of middle school, *tafḥīṭ* fans distribute master keys to the pupils, the keys we use to steal cars. I remember this one day, I was walking back home and I saw two pupils, new ones. They said they wanted to steal a car; they had a key. That's their way of recruiting people; they distribute keys to the pupils. And they gather important groups.

Second pupil: Entering *tafḥīṭ* is easier than joining a preaching group, though. I mean, you watch them from your window, maybe you gonna get down in the street and there, in front of the door, you find a guy, you chat with him, and this guy, maybe, he'll let you in his car the day after. It's easier! (Interview, Riyadh, March 2006)

For their shows, *mufaḥḥaṭīn* use stolen or rented cars, which explains why it is so simple to join a *tafḥīṭ* group. By the nature of their activities, *mufaḥḥaṭīn* need the assistance of many little hands who will manage the material aspects of *tafḥīṭ* and "borrow" the main instrument of *hajwala*. Contrary to low riders or drag racers, *mufaḥḥaṭīn* do not customize their cars. They work on raw material. They love, in particular, banal cars such as regular Japanese sedans that are seen everywhere in Saudi Arabia, and did not develop the sort of car-oriented youth subculture one may expect of them. *Mufaḥḥaṭīn* are more interested in the figures and the skidding techniques than in cars, whose management is abandoned to younger newcomers. At the lowest echelon, the master key is a challenge to the pupil. Were he to accept it, he should soon be confronted with other challenges to get closer to the *mufaḥḥaṭīn* himself and his circle of close attendants. Should the pupil decline the offer, he would immediately be confined to a subordinate position in the peer group. From the first step onward, a series of tests leads to the constitution of clear hierarchies inside the group.

A History of *Tafḥīṭ*

Islamic groups and *tafḥīṭ* groups do not have much in common. Pious well-organized elitist young people belonging to the middle classes—or aspire to it—on the one hand, and young deviant people addicted to drugs and alcohol and who come from a lower class background, on the other, clearly do not have the same interests or the same goals. The Saudi Islamic movement, better known inside Saudi Arabia as the *ṣaḥwa islāmiyya* or "Islamic awakening," appeared during the 1970s as a preaching movement dedicated to resist the unexpected consequences of an anarchic modernization of the country. After many failed attempts at influencing the local political status quo—namely, in 1979, 1991 to 1993, and 2002 to 2003—the *ṣaḥwa* took refuge in a prudent and elitist pietism that would protect it from repression. Islamists and *mufaḥḥaṭīn* cannot be further from each other than they actually are. Yet this does not mean that both universes do not cross. At least, both groups share the same chasing ground (i.e., school and neighborhood). It is true that the *ṣaḥwa* cannot gather as many partisans as the *tafḥīṭ* group, which is explained by the somewhat severe mode of socialization and the ascetic ethos of the Islamic groups. They try, nevertheless, to bring back pupils on the right path, or to prevent them from falling into the many moral traps of the street and the neighborhood, even if they frequently fail to do so. Football matches and desert excursions are indeed not attractive enough to divert the pupils from the more adventurous games of *tafḥīṭ*.

Tafḥīṭ and *ṣaḥwa* developed during the same historical period, one of tremendous change for Saudi Arabia: the economic and social boom (*ṭafra*) of the 1970s and 1980s (al-Ghazzami 2004: 149–173). Moreover, these youths grew up in the same places, around the newly built schools and streets of Riyadh, Jeddah, and Dammam—those places that had been devastated and dehumanized by the sudden increase in oil prices.

> There was a huge gap between the construction of the place and the construction of the man; the spatial development hindered the human development. The human aspect had been overlooked in a way that makes you feel the inhumanity of the place. Visit our large, asphalted streets, with all their hoardings, signs, lights, and skyscrapers, and look for the man: you will only find the noise of cars and the swish of tires. Who looks for a place of his in this chilling splendour will feel alone. (al-Ghazzami 2004: 172)

This inhuman place has been invested both by the *ṣaḥwa*, on the one hand, which has been trying to bring up the youth despite the anarchic changes, and by the *tafḥīṭ* groups, on the other, which have grown up with the urban boom and the massive imports of cars in the country. The *ṣaḥwa* developed in schools around the extracurricular activities, in mosque libraries (*maktabāt*), and Quranic circles (*mufaḥḥaṭīn al-Qur'ān*) (Ménoret 2008: 156–167). The politicization of extracurricular and Islamic activities was the result of an overt strategy of the many Islamic groups. They aimed at investing any space left available by political repression on the one hand and the banning of any political activity on the other.

The *ṣaḥwa* was clearly aiming the category of "youth" that the economic and social boom had newly constituted. Young males had been freed from absorbing and tiring daily tasks by the economic boom, and freed from the exiguousness of space, and the social and familial surveillance by the urban boom. They represented an energy that could have been invested in political or unionist activism, had political parties and unions been authorized and popular. Since it was—and still is—not the case in the country, a whole generation, the "boom generation" (*jīl al-ṣaḥwa*) was hanging out in streets and empty neighborhoods, overwhelmed by *ṭufush* and intensely trying to find a way out. *Tafḥīṭ* and *ṣaḥwa*, although being totally different and even antagonistic ways of socialization, appeared with the economic boom and the urbanization of Riyadh as possible answers to the powerful sentiment of impotence and disorientation. "There is no *tafḥīṭ* in Najran, because everybody knows everybody," as one young man put it (interview, Najran, April 2006). Located on the Saudi–Yemeni border, Najran is a relatively small town where powerful local networks somewhat cushioned the economic boom, whereas the more heterogeneous society of the big urban centers was atomized and proved incapable of preventing either the formation of an ideal and ascetic countersociety, or the deviant practices of *tafḥīṭ*.

It is in this context that *tafḥīṭ* developed as a celebration of individual courage toward machines, these most visible testimonies of modernity—toward society as a rapidly changing and at times threatening body, and in front of violent death or state repression. The death of Sharari was not the first time *tafḥīṭ* was threatened with large-scale repression and disappearance. A few months earlier in Jeddah, the fatal accident of "Abu Kab" had led the *tafḥīṭ* leaders in Riyadh to warn their fans in all the provinces of the country to avoid their usual gathering sites for a few weeks because of an exceptional police presence.[10] Since its emergence in the early 1980s on the large avenues of the kingdom, *tafḥīṭ* has known several of these moments of crisis, each time surviving what at the time was thought to be a decisive blow. The first star of *tafḥīṭ*, Husayn al-Harbi, was imprisoned in 1985. The torch was quickly taken up by Sa'd Marzuq, who, arrested in 1990, ceded his place to Sa'ud al-'Ubayd (alias "al-Jazura") and to Badr 'Awadh (alias "al-King"). Technical standards had evolved in the meantime, even if *tafḥīṭ* was not originally thought of as a speed race or a competition. The anonymous Internet writer Rakan remembers that at the beginning, "they were doing *tafḥīṭ* to widen their souls (*li-wisā'at al-ṣadr*), they did not have to win (they always reached a tie)."[11] The also aimed to gather the largest possible number of fans.

If at the time of Husayn al-Harbi, the skids and figures were carried out at 140 kmph on Japanese sedans, the end of the 1980s saw the domination of American cars. These required special control skills, being automatic rear-wheel-drive cars. After this period of "*tafhit amiriki*," during which Sa'd Marzuq was the uncontested champion, the fashion for Japanese sedans returned, culminating in 1995 with the arrival of the new Toyota Camry, which could largely exceed the speed limit of 200 kmph. During the period of al-Jazura and al-King reigns, the tiniest error in piloting could no longer be countenanced, and fatal accidents began to multiply. Al-Jazura would die in an accident in 2001 and al-King was to make his repentance a few years later. Both destinies illustrated one of the *mufaḥḥaṭīn's* proverbs: "The end of *tafḥīṭ* is either death or repentance" (*iā al-mawt, iā at-tawba*) (interview, Riyadh, August 2005).

The Socioeconomic Structures of *Tafḥīṭ*

Tafḥīṭ and *ṣaḥwa* have not only developed in the same places and during the same period, they also are the products of the same socioeconomic conditions. In very specific circumstances, the *ṣaḥwa* attempted to influence the Saudi political scene. From 1992 to 1993, and 10 years later from 2002 to 2003, Islamic intellectuals and activists presented petitions to the government. Yet this activism did not do much to enhance the socioeconomic conditions in which a majority of Saudis live; it did not manage to modify even slightly the effective structures of power in Saudi society either. After these outbursts of political awareness, the economic power was still in the hands of the princes, the real estate investors, and the car dealers.

Since the 1973 oil boom, real estate has been the main arena of distribution of the oil-generated wealth, through the allocation of lands and the attribution of public loans (Bonnenfant 1982: 682–693). Connections (*wāsṭa*) with the royal family have proved the more effective means of enhancing one's economic position, since the princes literally own the country and may delegate this possession to their circle of flatterers—and sometimes to perfectly unknown brokers whose only merit is to be there. This anarchic distribution of wealth has led to the formation of what popular voices in Riyadh call "the six families who own the city." When the son of one of those six real estate pioneers, Badr bin Saidan, runs for municipal election on the theme of "decent housing," people quickly recall how he and his family have contributed for 30 years to the burst of the real estate market in the capital, and thus to the indecent living conditions of many household in Riyadh (interview, Riyadh, February 2005). Public life is thus made of repeated real estate scandals and of popular impotence about them, as made clear by the following scene. One of my interviewees—a lawyer with an activist Islamic background—brought with him one day the property act of lands located in one of the fastest growing neighborhoods of the city. The lands, which had been seized years ago by one of the sons of the late king Abdelaziz, had now incredible value and "could welcome the population of Kuwait." Hearing this, one of the Islamists who were with us evoked the name of the second caliph Omar bin al-Khattab, grumbling: "Those were real Arabs," while the lawyer said: "What can we do against this?" Of course, nobody answered the question, and the feeling of *ṭufush*, of political powerlessness, became tangible in the room.

Real estate is but one of the sources of enrichment in Riyadh. In a city in which only 2% of trips are made using public transportation and 93% with personal cars[12] the car is nearly the only mean of mobility, and the car market is dominated by the foreign companies' agents (*wukalāʾ*), who exert a powerful monopoly over the sale, credit, spare parts, and maintenance of cars. Like the allocation of plots of lands, the attribution of importation licenses has been monopolized since the early 1950s by a handful of people, the most famous of them probably being Abdellatif Jameel. This wealthy businessman started his career as the owner of a filling station in Jeddah and a small subcontractor of Aramco; he then became, as the official Toyota dealer in Saudi Arabia, one of the richest commoners in the country. His commercial skills can be inferred from this anecdote: During the 1950s, when roads were more hazardous than they now are, it was one of his employees' tasks to warn by microphone passing drivers that Abdellatif Jameel's station was the last one for 700 miles, thus exhorting them to fill up all the tanks that were at their disposal.

Mufaḥḥaṭīn refers roughly to these monopolistic structures of distribution when they try to justify themselves, saying, for example: "We have only the streets and cars. Where do you want us to go?" (interview, Riyadh, January 2006). The "real estate projects" (*mukhaṭṭaṭāt*), with their broad empty avenues and lines of street lamps, are the very spatial conditions of possibility for *tafḥīṭ*.

Mufaḥḥaṭīn's performances and figures are not possible elsewhere. The author of an ironic and truculent history of hooliganism tells of the *mufahha-tin*'s enthusiasm for the real estate boom: "By the way, [the *mufahhatin*] don't want to hear about the stock market boom. Why? Because when the share prices go up, the real estate market stops or slows down. And if real estate slows down, projects (*mukhaṭṭaṭāt*) are stopped as well as new broad avenues.... You know how the story ends."[13] The huge power of car dealers has also led some *tafḥīṭ* fans to articulate a rebellious discourse: "It is with our oil that you build cars. And you sell them to us at top prices. And us, we destroy them." "It is a Zionist and American plot. They import cars to kill our youngsters" (interview, Riyadh, August 2005).

Tafḥīṭ represents an apex of the over-consumption prevalent in Saudi culture, and at the same time expresses a grassroots revolt against it, through subversion of private property (car robbery), of public order and space (dangerous figures at top speed on the avenues, the systematic challenge of the police), violation of the family-centered Saudi ideology (through homosexuality), and violation of social and religious prohibitions (consumption of drugs and alcohol). *Tafḥīṭ* subverts the authority of the police by "jumping traffic lights, speeding like crazy, losing the police and slaloming between cars" (interview, Riyadh, January 2006). The relationship of *mufaḥḥaṭīn* with the police and the bourgeois consumption culture is captured, for example, in one of the *kasrāt* (songs[14]) that are popular in the *tafḥīṭ* milieu:

Play the horn. Skid and disturb your beloved's neighborhood
o Bubu!
Let the patrols die of disgust and let them give up the chase,
give up![15]

In the eyes of one of the Islamic activists who founded, in 1993, the Committee of Defence of the Legitimate Rights,[16] *tafḥīṭ*, despite its obviously deviant nature, represents "the zero degree of political activism" (interview, Riyadh, March 2006), because of its rebellion against the residential and consumerist philosophy or "bourgeois utopia" (Davis 1992: 169–170) of the Riyadh bourgeoisie and middle classes. Similar to the bread and food riots in 18th-century England, *tafḥīṭ* is thus directed toward the source of economic power and social injustice. This rebellion against monopolies may even be seen as a contemporary version of older mob actions and popular indignation—as a true car and land riot.

From *Mufahhat* to Islamic Preacher

Tafḥīṭ and *ṣaḥwa* developed during the same period and in the same place, reacting in various ways to the same socioeconomic conditions. Some who repented *mufahhatin* also became influential Islamic preachers, sometimes after a fatal accident they provoked while doing *tafḥīṭ*. The first well-known "hooligan preacher" (*zāḥif dāʿiya*) was Abu Zegem (photo 6), who started doing *tafḥīṭ* in 1986 and repented at the beginning of the 1990s.

He quickly became popular among youth for his radically new style in preaching: "He was always joking, and people rushed on to his taped lectures, because he was funny; he was not as serious and moralizing as the other preachers, who were always talking of death and hell and the afterlife, of stuff that really break your heart" (interview, Riyadh, July 2006). This youthful preaching style and his paradoxical identity as former *mufaḥḥaṭ* and Islamic preacher allowed Abu Zegem a nationwide reputation as the redeemer of deviant youth. He soon joined the al-Amal psychiatric hospital as a religious consultant, and his taped sermons became best-sellers. Abu Zegem created a group of preachers and attempted to gain the other *mufaḥḥaṭīn* in order to attract their fans. Through public lectures organized near the *tafḥīṭ* sites in itinerant tents, Abu Zegem and his disciples led some very famous *mufaḥḥaṭīn* to repentance. Al-King, Bubu, Wiwi, Sirri li-1-ghaya (aka Top Secret), and al-Mustashar (aka The Councilor) became preachers after having "thrown the iron" for sometimes as long as 16 years. Yet despite the increasing number of fatal accidents and the subsequent augmentation of those who repented, Abu Zegem's strategy was not totally successful, perhaps because the fans soon found new *mufaḥḥaṭīn* and followed them. Sometimes the *mufaḥḥaṭīn* and their fans organize *tafḥīṭ* shows around the preaching tents, in order to have a ready-made excuse in case they were to be arrested by the police: "When they come for *tafḥīṭ*, they don't have any way out and they are caught immediately by the cops. [Imitating the policeman:] 'Why did you come around here?' While if they say they came to the lecture . . . ." (interview, Riyadh, July 2006). Formerly, the fans requested their star "to domesticate steel"; now it was the star who requested his fans to follow the right path—but with limited success.

Having failed to attract as many young people as they first hoped, the repented *mufaḥḥaṭīn* soon became brokers between different people and institutions, such as the *tafḥīṭ* milieus, the police, Islamic charities and organization, and sometimes even the prisons, where they propose activities and lectures. They are known to help the traffic police to design effective anti-*tafḥīṭ* strategies: "Abu Zegem is considered to be the head of a very powerful network, a network better than the traffic police or even the secret police [*al-baḥth*]. They know everybody, who is doing *tafḥīṭ*, who is a beginner, who is a fan, who is filming *tafḥīṭ* . . ." (Interview, Riyadh, July 2006) Preachers failed in their peaceful and religious combat against *tafḥīṭ*; if they could not manage to work in Islamic or health institutions, they were soon driven to become mere police informants. If *tafḥīṭ* eventually decreased, it had more to do with the more and more violent accidents—such as the one in which Sharari died—and the offensive strategies of the traffic police than with the preachers themselves. Yet some of the repented are the best analysts of *tafḥīṭ*. If Bubu states briefly, for instance, that "the rich provide cars and play on us" (interview, Riyadh, April 2006), the argumentation of Abu Zegem is more detailed. In a conference on video, he shows how Abu Hasan, his preaching buddy, "former hooligan and addict," started following his path of deviance at primary school, when he was expelled for stealing a sandwich. At the age of 10, he was subjected to the *falaqa* (*bastinado*) in the school. Abu Hasan would later declare that "the school was the beginning of perdition."[17]

Madness Is an Art (*Al-Junūn Funūn*)

We have provided a merely political interpretation of *tafḥīṭ* as being a rebellion of youth against the Saudi consumption patterns and anarchical modernization. It would nevertheless be an exaggeration to politicize too quickly what, in the eyes of the *tafḥīṭ* aficionados, is first and foremost a living subculture. *Al-junūn funūn*" is one of *tafḥīṭ*'s most famous slogans and is found on Riyadh's walls as well as on fans' websites. It is true that some *mufaḥḥaṭīn* transited directly from urban rebellion to *jihad* in Afghanistan[18] or more recently in Iraq (interview, Riyadh, August 2005), making up enthralling cases of nonideological radicalization. Yusuf al-'Uyairi, who led al-Qaeda in the Arabian Peninsula from 1998 to his death in 2004, was skidding every Wednesday in Dammam under the nickname of Abu Saleh before flying to Afghanistan in 1991[19] (Ménoret 2008: 414–418). Equally true is that the very management of *tafḥīṭ* nights, from the gathering of vast moving groups to the challenging by police, allows for the acquisition of truly effective subversive techniques, ready to be used in other contexts. But revolt is formulated in apolitical terms, in part because of the restricted repertoires that are available for mobilization and action, in addition to the limited social and cultural level of *tafḥīṭ* fans. A majority of them "have fallen into *tafḥīṭ*" (interview, Riyadh, July 2006) without even desiring it, being unable to belong to more rewarding or more prestigious social networks.

This enforced apolitical attitude does not exclude the use of narratives drawn from the contemporary history of Saudi Arabia. For the young Bedouins who form the vast majority of the *tafḥīṭ* groups, *hajwala* is first and foremost the perpetuation of an older moral code, a code that relies on the notion of honor that is transmitted through oral poetry or by the accounts by elders (*sawālif al-shayyabīn*). These notions form the background of many rivalries between *mufaḥḥaṭīn*, who represent either a particular tribe (Shaharin, 'Utban, Mutran, Hurub, and so forth) or, more and more frequently, a district of Riyadh (e.g., al-Nasim, al-Nazhim, al-Dakhl al-Mahdud, al-Janadriyya). At its beginnings, as well as in the case of Los Angeles's lowriders gang culture, *tafḥīṭ* offered "cool worlds of urban socialization for poor young newcomers" from rural areas (Davis 1992: 293). This was especially the case for young Bedouins who, coming from the steppes of northern Najd or from the southern mountains, were in search of a job in the bulging metropolis and who, for the first time in their lives, had rid themselves of the heavy patronage and control of their family. Gradually, the groups of *mufaḥḥaṭīn* became re-territorialized around districts that host a strong Bedouin population, and *tafḥīṭ* became an assertion of Bedouin pride vis-à-vis a modern society that was funded and managed by sedentary people.

A long anonymous *kasra*[20] about the glory of the *mufaḥḥaṭīn* shows in which social context the Bedouin reference is utilized, as well as the melancholy awareness that members of these groups have about the lowly nature of their own social and family status. The author of the song attributes this, in part, to what he terms the treason of time:

Go fast, burn tires! Cars make you the Antar[21] of this time
For your time has betrayed you
The beautiful boys applaud you and prove your value
The cop beats you
No wonder he insults you, humiliates you
Since you failed in everything
Nothing betters your position
You left school and roam with bad boys
You did not obey your father when he cried because of you
Nor your mother when she shouted and exhorted you
You neglected her, you turned your back to her and you
 wanted her humiliation
Go, vanish and let your Lord dissolve your crises
Go fast, burn tires until your ears explode.[22]

The *mufahhatīn* are thus indefinitely re-playing the tragedy that has been, for the Bedouin tribes, the establishment of the modern Saudi state by the sedentary oasis dwellers of lower Najd. The raids are not launched any more for the beautiful eyes of the Bedouin ladies, but for those of some fine young man. If some fearless girls dare to attend the *tafhīt* meetings, they are a rare exception. Bubu "threw the steel" for Sultan's eyes (*li-'uyūn Sulṭān*), whereas other *mufahhatīn* beat asphalt for one of the attending young fans. The passive boy (*wir'*) occupies a central place in the *tafhīt* phenomenon. It is for his eyes that death is challenged, for his eyes that crowds are put into motion. Badr 'Awad once made turn a whole *mawkib* (procession) of 70 cars around his boyfriend's house, in a popular and narrow southern district of Riyadh (interview, Riyad, July 2006). It is also to charm high-school pupils that the *mufahhatīn* bring their fans and show around schools, particularly after the end of the examination period. If *ṭufush* is regularly taken as an excuse for falling into *hajwala*, the *wir'ān* (passive boys) provide a positive reason to do *tafhīt*: "We know *tafhīt* is bad, but it gives you the sense of time and space. And there are the boys (*wir'ān*)" (interview, Riyadh, January 2006).

Hamad asked me and told me: Why?
Why do beings fall into *tafhīt*?
I pointed my finger at him and said, Look at you!
A beautiful boy stretching at the rhythm [of the tires]

The love of younger boys is frequently used to stigmatize the *mufahhatīn* as both Bedouins and homosexuals. "Their aspect is frightening. They look like crap, as if they came out from under the earth, with their standing hair and their moustaches. I know that I am not very handsome or attractive, but I would not like to find myself alone with one of them," declares a young man who is passionate about drag racing and comes from an upper middle class background. He adds: "Us, we have goals; we know what we are doing. Them, they are acting like fools; it is total confusion (*hamajia*) and accidents" (interview, Riyadh, May 2006).

The apparent confusion about *tafḥīṭ* should not be misleading. There is art in its madness. Its rules are published on the Web (in the form of technical advice to young *mufaḥḥaṭīn*), its figures are carefully codified and judged by "referees" during competitions between *mufaḥḥaṭīn*, its songs (*kasrāt*) are recorded and diffused by informal bands, and its poems are published on the Internet and memorized by a very large number of young fans. The apparent disorder of a moving procession corresponds, in fact, to a meticulous organization, managed by a pivotal character—the "guide" (*muajjih*)—whose task is to coordinate the movement of the cars, to centralize information on the deployment of police patrols, and to modify the trajectory of the procession if necessary. In opposition to the police as well as in rebellion against the family, the apparent disorder and extreme speed are tactics to combat against the partitioning and monitoring of an urban area that has become a disciplinary space, a space where visibility plays a central role (Foucault 1979: 187). Becoming a *mufaḥḥaṭ* therefore means having to acquire a true discipline through the acquisition of certain techniques in an environment characterized by the omnipresent risk, an intense competition between individuals, and an informal but overwhelming publicity. The senior *mufaḥḥaṭ* does not drink or smoke, and does not fall in love with boys. Dedicated to his art, inhabited by it, he is devoted only to his self-improvement. This self-control explains why Badr 'Awad has been unchallenged for 16 continuous years, whereas other less ascetic *mufaḥḥaṭīn* have been seriously wounded or have died. The discipline required for a career as a "*ṣarbūṭ*" (hooligan) is sometimes justified in a more practical way:

> You are working for a company in which there is an outstanding employee. Of course, you want to be better than him. It is the same in *tafḥīṭ*. There is the love of younger boys (*wir'ānjiyya*). But it is a kind of extra reward you get only if you become the best employee. If you enter *tafḥīṭ* for the boys' eyes, you will be bad in *tafḥīṭ* and lose the boys. You have to get into *tafḥīṭ* for *tafḥīṭ*'s sake. You have to become the best one, because boys love excellence and dedication. (interview, Riyadh, February 2006)

These sentences encapsulate the essence of the movement that is *tafḥīṭ*: giving up oneself to a higher cause to achieve one's ends, putting oneself at risk to prove one's control, forgetting about the boys in order to conquer them. There is such thing as an "ethics of *tafḥīṭ*," and it is an ethics of despair. The words they use to describe their lives tell a lot about the current condition of Saudi youth: *Ṭufush*, according to the origin of the word, means the random movements of a drowning man. *Tafḥīṭ* is all but a provisional and desperate way to stylize these movements, to accelerate them, to magnify them into collective enthusiasm and popular art. One is supposed to drown in the end—death, prison, accident, or unemployment. Salvation is not desirable, because it would mean a long life of social and economic paralysis or marginalization. *Tafḥīṭ* is thus the last burst of the drowning man—a way to express one's rage before being swallowed up and overcome.

Conclusion

It is not so much Islam that defines the way young people are politicized as it is the features of the social and economic situation in which they find themselves. Extensive ethnographic fieldwork in Riyadh reveals that, besides the much-studied expressions of Islamic defiance toward the state and its foreign sponsors, many other acts can be recognized as intelligent political behavior. Even practices that at first sight seem self-destructive and pathological can rightly be described as political protest, although their degree of political consciousness as well as their political impact may be limited. Despite their propagation efforts, Islamic groups are not open to everybody, and remain closed to the majority of young people who lack the social or cultural qualifications to join. In our view, more than Islamic defiance, deviance from the norms imposed by a fast-changing society thus provides a means by which ordinary young people can relate to various, albeit seemingly modest, spheres of power. As a violation of multiple Saudi norms and values, *tafḥīṭ* is no less political for being oblivious to grand schemes of power. On the contrary, for:

> when the poor rebel they . . . often rebel against the overseer of the poor, or the slumlord, or the middling merchant, and not against the banks or the governing elites to whom the overseer, the slumlord, and the merchant also defer. . . . Simply put, people cannot defy institutions to which they have no access, and to which they make no contribution. (Piven and Cloward 1979: 20–23)

Crime, riot, and mob action may well be means to fight a class war; yet, when social institutions are inaccessible, this war sometimes results in the self-destruction of the less powerful members of society. It can also generate radicalization without an ideology, thus providing a rare example of continuity between street protest and global resistance.

Acknowledgments

Special thanks to Dr. Yahya ibn Junayd and Dr. Awadh al-Badi (King Faisal Center for Research and Islamic Studies), and to Dr. Bernard Haykel (Princeton University), who have been very supportive of fieldwork that was deemed by some to be "foolish" and "useless." Many thanks to all those who have agreed to speak with us about their experience in *tafḥīṭ*.

6

The Battle of the Ages: Contests for Religious Authority in The Gambia

Marloes Janson

On our way to visit a local Quranic scholar, my interpreter ran into her cousin. Although normally she was exuberant, she greeted this young man in an almost shy manner.[1] I was surprised not only by my interpreter's attitude, but also by the young man's appearance. When we continued our journey, she told me that because her cousin is a *Mashala*, he wears the "Mashala uniform." This term is derived from the Arabic *ma sha'Allah* (what God wishes), an expression that is frequently exclaimed by people like this young man.[2] My interpreter explained that, following Prophet Muhammad's example, Mashalas don a turban and wear their trousers above the ankles to prevent their feet from burning in hell.[3] After I invited him to talk more about his views of Islam, my interpreter's cousin visited me in the compound in the Gambian town where I was conducting field research. My surprise grew when my host, an elderly Muslim man educated in the local Sufi tradition,[4] received the young man in his home with the following words: "Is your father not at home? Where is your mother? Don't you have a wife? How do you feed these people? It's better to support them than to sit the whole day in the mosque and call people to Islam."[5]

My interpreter's cousin reacted to this offensive greeting by saying that it is his duty to worship God and to "invite people to follow the Prophet's path." When my host left, he sighed and said that he expected to hear such words from the "old grandpa."

This incident illustrates the competing generational perceptions in The Gambia of what a proper Muslim is, the attributes he or she should have, and who holds the power and authority to determine "true" Islam and its principles. These generational differences will be studied here against the backdrop of the proliferation of the Gambian branch of the Tabligh Jamaʻat. This transnational Islamic missionary movement, which originated in the reformist tradition that emerged in India during the 19th century, encourages greater religious devotion and observance. Its founder, Mawlana Ilyas, strove for a purification of Islam as practiced by individual Muslims through following more closely the rules laid down in the *Sunna*, the Prophetic traditions. To make Muslims "true believers," Ilyas insisted that it was the duty of not just a few learned scholars but of all Muslims, men as well as women, to carry out *tabligh*—that is, missionary work aimed at the moral transformation of Muslims. Missionary tours by lay preachers became the hallmark of the Tabligh Jamaʻat, established officially in 1927 in the Indian capital of Delhi.

This chapter explores the intergenerational contests for religious authority, battled via the Tabligh Jamaʻat in The Gambia, a West African country where—in contrast to its neighboring country Senegal—our knowledge of Islamization is largely lacking (see Janson 2009).[6] Before elaborating on these contests, attention should be given to the dimension of generation and power. In Mandinka, the *lingua franca* in The Gambia, the term for *youth* is *fondinkeo*. In addition to an age category, ranging from approximately 15 to about 45 years, *fondinkeo* has the connotation of strength, virility, fearlessness, and mobility. When I asked a young man when a *fondinkeo* becomes a *keebaa*, an "elder," he responded, "When his hair has turned gray." Gray hair is a symbol of old age, wisdom, and authority. Young people can have knowledge of, for example, Islam, but they are not allowed to express this in public. Elders, on the other hand, have the authority to express their knowledge, which must be obeyed unquestioningly by the younger generation. As such, the spheres of action open to the categories of youth and elder are clearly defined, and appropriate behavior kept distinct (see Last 1992: 388–389). Remarkably, although *keebaa* has a female equivalent, *musu keebaa* (referring to a woman who has passed menopause), *fondinkeo* has not. Youth thus appears to be a male category (Wulff 1995).[7]

Age and generation are structuring principles in West African societies, based on gerontocracy. In societies where leadership is of old in the hands of the male elders, the subordination of the young is conceived as a traditional imperative (Diouf 1996: 225–226). As a result of the generational rules of submission and deference, for most "traditionalist" West African

Muslims, showing respect for the older generation is one of the most important cultural obligations. The Gambian Tablighi youth, however, actively question the moral legitimacy of parental authority, through their insistence that a son's primary allegiance is to God rather than to his father (Eickelman and Piscatori 1996: 82). A zealous Tablighi told me: "We must profess Islam in a proper way, because Allah is going to judge us on the Day of Judgment, not our fathers and mothers. I care only about Allah and His Prophet." Once a Tablighi quarreled with his mother because he did not agree with her choice of a wife for him, and he told her: "You don't have the right to talk to me like this since you are not Allah." When I asked his friend whether it is not morally sanctioned in the Quran that a child should obey his or her parents, he responded: "The Prophet incited us to respect our parents, but when they become like a millstone round our neck, we have to be on the alert."

Gambian Tablighi youth are largely dissatisfied with the Islam of the older generation because they are aware that the Islam of their parents was learned in a different sociocultural setting and during a different era. Therefore, they dismiss much of what the elders see as Islam as *aadoo* (tradition) and criticize especially those indigenous elements that have become an integral part of local Islamic life, such as visiting *marabouts* (local Sufi clerics) for healing, practicing divination, wearing amulets, and ostentatious gift giving during the life cycle rituals associated with Islam (Masquelier 1996, 1999). The Tablighi youngsters whom I interviewed argued that instead of paying a *marabout* to make a charm, one should pray to God directly. In their opinion, visiting *marabouts* is similar to idol worshipping (*shirk*). In addition to putting an end to *maraboutage*, their ardent wish is the performance of life cycle rituals according to the *Sunna*. This implies that, for example, the naming ceremony is reduced to its essence: The baby's hair is shaved, it is named, and a ram is sacrificed. All the other activities taking place at naming ceremonies—such as singing, drumming, dancing, spending a lot of money on food, intermingling between the sexes, and the like—are considered to be *bid'a*, deviations from the Prophet's path.

This chapter investigates, on the basis of the Gambisara mosque crisis, Islam's role as a source of identification and a political instrument for Gambian Tablighi youth.[8] This mosque crisis, a conflict that is associated with the proliferation of the Tabligh Jama'at in The Gambia, played a major role in reconfiguring the generational categories youth and elder. Attention is paid to the Tabligh Jama'at as a youth movement. This case study will allow for insights into what it is like to be young and Muslim in the current moment in The Gambia, where many youth are marginalized and have little opportunities.

History of the Tabligh Jama'at

The emergence of the Tabligh Jama'at as a movement for the revival of Islam can be seen as a continuation of a broader trend of Islamic resurgence in India in the wake of the collapse of Muslim power and the consolidation of British rule in the mid 19th century. One manifestation of this trend was the rapid growth of madrasas (Islamic schools). The Jama'at evolved out of the teachings and practices of the founders of the orthodox *Dar-ul 'Ulum madrasa* in Deoband, a town near the Indian capital of Delhi. The scholars affiliated with this school saw themselves as crusaders against popular expressions of Islam, as well as Hindu and Christian conversion movements, and they aspired to bring to life again the days of the Prophet's companions (Ahmad 1995: 165; Masud 2000: 3–5; Metcalf 2002: 4, 8–9; Sikand 2002: 16–17, 66).

Mawlana Ilyas was a disciple of the leading Deobandi scholars, who, after his graduation, taught the Meo peasants—a marginalized group regarded as nominal Muslims—from Mewat in northern India about correct Islamic beliefs and practices at mosque-based schools. However, he soon became disillusioned with this approach, realizing that Islamic schools were producing "religious functionaries" but not zealous preachers who were willing to go from door to door to remind people of the key values of Islam. He then decided to quit his teaching position to begin missionary work through itinerant preaching (Ahmad 1995: 166).

Throughout the years, the Tabligh Jama'at has expanded from its international headquarters in India to numerous other countries around the world, and has grown into what is probably the largest Islamic movement of contemporary times. Despite its worldwide influence on the lives of millions of Muslims, scholars have paid almost no attention to its spread in sub-Saharan Africa. This indifference could be explained by the fact that this region is frequently perceived as the "periphery" of the Muslim world. Here I focus on The Gambia, which, despite its small size, during the past decade has become a booming center of Tablighi activities in West Africa (Janson 2005).

South Asian missionaries, Pakistanis in particular, reached West Africa during the early 1960s (Gaborieau 2000: 129–131), but their ideas did not find a fertile breeding ground in The Gambia until the 1990s. During the country's British colonial rule, which lasted till 1965, English became the national language—a factor that has undoubtedly facilitated the spread of the Tablighi ideology, because the Pakistani preachers were able to disseminate their message in The Gambia in English. The appearance of the Pakistani preachers coincided with the recent political Islamic resurgence in The Gambia. Captain

Yahya Jammeh assumed power in 1994 and invoked Islam to enhance his legitimacy (Darboe 2004). This provided a fresh scope for the creation of a public discourse on Islamic doctrine in The Gambia, as a result of which a growing number of Gambians seemed to be receptive to a new interpretation of their faith, a factor seized upon by the Tablighi preachers (Janson 2006).

The genesis of the Tabligh Jama'at in The Gambia can be traced to Karammoko Dukureh, the son of a respected Islamic scholar from Gambisara, a Serahuli village in eastern Gambia.[9] Karammoko's name reveals that his father, who had given him this name, wanted him to become an Islamic scholar (*karammoo* means "Quranic teacher" or *marabout*). He indeed became a scholar, but another type than his father had hoped for. When Karammoko Dukureh was in his early 30s, he went on a pilgrimage to Mecca and afterward studied Islamic theology in Saudi Arabia. Although he was inspired by Wahhabi Islam, it is wrong, as I explain later, to call Dukureh a *Wahhabi*.[10] In fact, he was the founding father of Tablighi Islam in The Gambia. During the early 1980s, when Dukureh returned to Gambisara, he set out to make the villagers more aware of their religion by denouncing their traditional ways of worship and popular forms of piety. One of his former students told me that Dukureh especially condemned *marabouts*. In his opinion, these Sufi clerics were charlatans who exploit their clients. Aside from a few sympathizers, the villagers—many of whom were *marabouts*—feared that Dukureh wanted to introduce a "new religion" and did not agree with his reformist ideas. Dukureh's sermons became increasingly antagonistic toward the traditions of the village elders and he was eventually exiled. Until his death in 2000 at the age of 80, he continued spreading his ideology in the Gambian city of Serrekunda, in the mosque that later came to be known as *Markaz* (center), where he was appointed imam.

After Dukureh's exile from Gambisara followed a conflict that came to be known as the *Gambisara mosque crisis* (Darboe 2004: 78–79). Because of a lack of firsthand information on this conflict, I decided to set out for Gambisara myself. Remarkably, several villagers did not respond to my greeting "*salam aleikum*" (peace be with you). A Tablighi posted in Gambisara explained to me that in order not to be termed a *Wahhabi*, it is better to greet the Muslim villagers in the local language of Serahuli. It was then that I realized that there is an ongoing conflict between Dukureh's followers and the majority of the villagers, most of whom belong to the Konteh lineage, a renowned family of *marabouts*.

Because Dukureh studied for a long time in Saudi Arabia, his followers are disparagingly called *Wahhabis*. The sign of the so-called Wahhabis' deviant identity in Gambisara was that they, following Imam Dukureh, insisted on praying with their arms folded on the chest rather than, in the Maliki style of praying, with the arms besides the body, which is most common in West Africa. In their opinion, those who prayed with straight arms were not following the *Sunna*, and as such were not "real" Muslims. Because the Wahhabis were beaten when they prayed with folded arms in the central mosque of Gambisara, they decided to build their own mosque. Funds were donated by a Senegalese reformist movement called *Al-Falah*[11] during the early 1990s and a Kuwaiti sheikh, Jarsam Muhammad al-Ai Nait, who was the president of the African Continent Committee of the Revival of Islamic Heritage Society (*Jamiat Ihia Al-Turath Al-Islamiya*) (*Foroyaa*: September 20 – October 5, 1995).[12] Most of the villagers believed it was improper to have two mosques in the same community and sought for state intervention in 1993. The local authorities decided that those in charge of the mosque could continue building it because one is free to construct a mosque in one's own compound.

After the military coup in 1994, the conflict in Gambisara regenerated again to the extent that many feared the outbreak of a civilian war between the alleged Wahhabis and the other villagers. The vice-chairman of the Armed Forces Provisional Ruling Council, the party that had taken over power, personally paid a visit to Gambisara. He called a meeting with the village elders, whom he let sit for hours in the hot sun on the ground. In this way he wanted to make clear to them once and for all that sanction was given for the construction of the mosque. The elders felt insulted by this display of power by the young officer and enlisted the help of the new president, Yahya Jammeh. Jammeh's official intervention in the conflict may be explained by both his age and ethnicity. At the time of his takeover, he was only 29. Being from the Jola ethnic group, which was generally regarded as not being closely affiliated with Islam, did not help his position. To consolidate his power he needed the support of the *marabouts* who had been the most loyal followers of his predecessor Sir Dawda Jawara, and who objected to the idea of a young Jola soldier holding power. In what appears to be a purely politically expedient decision, President Jammeh decided that the mosque should not be built and he arrested his vice-chairman. Eventually, four of Imam Dukureh's most prominent followers were also arrested and their mosque ultimately demolished by decree of the state. Because of this trial of strength, Jammeh was no longer considered a "kid" by the village elders in Gambisara, of whose support he was now ensured.

Shortly after the imprisonment of Dukureh's followers, a number of affluent traders from the Gambian Serahuli community, of whom some had migrated to France and Sierra Leone, bought a plot of land in the city of Serrekunda. They started by building a structure made out of sheets of corrugated iron in which they established a small *madrasa*, and Imam Dukureh was appointed to instruct the neighborhood children in Islamic principles. This structure was later replaced by a brick building and gradually expanded to its current form as a Markaz, a center in which large numbers of young men[13] gather on a daily basis (discussed later). Although the Gambian branch of the Tabligh Jama'at started as a loosely organized rural movement that was not associated with a particular age group, through the years it has grown into a strong urban movement in which young men, in particular, take part, striving vehemently to transform Muslims morally and to implement "true Islam" in The Gambia.

Contests for a Presence at the Local Level

On first analysis, the Gambisara mosque dispute appears as a straightforward competition between Wahhabis as represented in the young men zealously engaged in Islamic missionary work in The Gambia versus the older community of Sufis, belonging to the *Tijani* brotherhood,[14] whose leadership structure is based on a notion of elders. A closer examination reveals, however, that the designation of the young missionaries with *Wahhabi* is misleading. First of all, Wahhabi is a pejorative denomination that is not used by the followers of Karammoko Dukureh themselves. The term was introduced by French colonial administrators who were convinced that *Wahhabiyya* was the new Muslim threat to their presence and policies in West Africa (Brenner 2000). One of Dukureh's followers told me: "Of course we don't call ourselves Wahhabis. People who call us that way sabotage us." Although the majority of the villagers from Gambisara conflate the categories of Wahhabi and Tablighi in that they both attempt to purge Islam from local traditions,[15] they—according to the followers of Imam Dukureh—represent two distinct groups. A leading figure in the Tabligh Jama'at told me vigorously: "We do not have any link with *Wahhabiyya*. Full stop." I noticed that the Tablighis looked down upon Wahhabis, because they are, unlike them, "not willing to sacrifice for their faith by engaging in missionary tours." Although Tablighis focus on preaching, Wahhabis put more emphasis on teaching. A formal Quranic education and a full command of the Islamic scriptures are, in their opinion, indispensable for a career as a preacher (Brenner 2000), whereas the Tablighis with whom I worked took the view that even when one knows just one letter from the Quran, it is one's religious duty to convey it.[16]

In addition to that it is pejorative and not used by the followers of Imam Dukureh themselves, the term *Wahhabi* is also misleading because Dukureh's followers have no direct connection to the historical Wahhabis in Saudi Arabia. Although Imam Dukureh studied in Saudi Arabia, and in this way acquired knowledge of the Wahhabi teachings, for his followers, the Pakistani preachers who visited The Gambia during several missionary tours were more influential. As seen in the next section, many of these followers were not literate in Arabic but only in English, the language through which the Pakistanis preached. It seems that Dukureh's followers strive to "authenticate" Islam in The Gambia not by falling back on the alleged center of the Islamic world (that is, Saudi Arabia), but by involving a conscious assertion of a set of Islamic values that are derived from a South Asian setting.

Instead of *Wahhabi*, Dukureh's followers used the term *Ahl al-Sunna*, "people of the *Sunna*," or simply *Sunnis*, to describe themselves. As mentioned earlier, *Tablighi* was also used as term of self-identification. There is, of course, difficulty in using the general expression *Ahl al-Sunna* to identify the followers of Imam Dukureh. The historical Wahhabis, and even the *marabouts* from Gambisara, also call themselves this way in that their doctrine requires that they assert and demonstrate their ability to enforce the *Sunna* (Brenner 2000: 167). The self-identification of *Tablighi*, which was translated by Dukureh's followers as "conveyer of Allah's words," is more specific. It shows that they indeed consider themselves part of the transnational Tabligh Jama'at.

The Gambisara mosque dispute has not only been described by my informants in terms of a conflict between Wahhabis and Sufis, but also between "youth" and "elders." The president of the Supreme Islamic Council, who acted as mediator between the two parties, explained it to me as "a dispute between the father's generation and that of the sons." At first sight, this description in terms of age and generation seems to be less problematic, because these terms have a more neutral connotation, but appearances are deceptive. Although the actors in the *marabouts'* camp referred to Imam Dukureh's followers as *youngsters*, they turned out to be of the same age, or even older, than the *marabouts*.[17] *Marabouts* stand to lose the most, both economically and socially, from the Tablighis' attempts at purging Islam from local customs, such as divination and wearing amulets. In addition to losing clients, the *marabouts* may lose legitimacy and authority, and this fear may explain the rather insulting tone adopted when talking about Dukureh's followers. The *marabouts* attempt to discredit or undermine the latter by referring to them as *youth*—as people whose Islamic knowledge is incomplete and who are not entitled to speak in public because local power relations are of old, embedded in gerontocracy—seemed to be a strategy used to guarantee their hegemony. The followers of Dukureh, on the other hand, were rather unconcerned about the *marabouts'* insults, equating being "old" with being "ignorant of Islam," rigid and holding on to sinful customary practices. Through their indifference toward the *marabouts*, they placed themselves somewhat above them.[18]

Based on the previous discussion, it may be concluded that identification and naming are part of the generational power struggle in Gambian society. It emerged that *youth* and *elder* are not fixed social categories, indicating a wider meaning than age (De Boeck 2005: 204–205; Durham 2000: 115–116; Massey 1998: 127; Wulff 1995: 6–8) and being reconfigured through Islamic reform in The Gambia. Instead of an age category, Dukureh's followers described youth as a "mentality." In their opinion "youth" should first and foremost be interpreted as having an awareness of what they considered the "real principles" of Islam, and a willingness to live accordingly. These principles enable them to free themselves in part from the traditional sources of religious authority. Similarly, Dukureh's followers used the term *elder* not to refer strictly to age or generation, but rather to refer to a conception of experience with missionary work. It follows that in the relatively young Tablighi movement in The Gambia, an *elder* can refer to someone young in age. The *amir*, the leader of the movement, for example, is a man of 36, but, on account of his experience with *tabligh*, he is termed *an elder*.

Religious Versus Secular Youth Culture

My research assistant, a young man who at one time in his life had wanted to join the Tabligh Jama'at, had a clear view of the situation in The Gambia:

> Nowadays some youth turn towards the hereafter, while others submerge themselves in the material [i.e., secular] world. Listening all day long to hip-hop is a way of submerging oneself in the material world, because the listeners want to have the same kind of clothes as their favorite singers and they also want to have a visa so that they can travel to the West, where these singers live. Turning towards religion or turning towards the material world is all the same; both trace back to poverty. Poverty is a big crime.[19]

In this section I focus on the two categories of youth referred to by my research assistant. I begin with a portrayal of the youth who "turn toward the hereafter," exemplified by the young men involved in Tablighi Islam.

Different from South Asia and other parts of Africa, the striking feature of the Tabligh Jama'at in The Gambia is that it is popular particularly among young, middle class, and lower middle class men between the ages of roughly 15 and 35 (Janson 2009: 143–145).[20] A young man who converted to the Tablighi ideology not long ago explained the Jama'at's appeal among Gambian youth as follows:

> Young people especially are involved in the movement, because the Prophet summoned youth to spread Islam. They are in the position to sacrifice their life for the sake of Allah. In order to disseminate Islam all over the world, the Prophet called upon young people. Most of the Prophet's companions were young. Young people are more energetic and therefore it is easier for them to set out on missionary tours. Allah loves the youth who are willing to spend their life in His path more than the elders.[21]

The other Tablighis agreed that youth are more able and willing to sacrifice for their religion than the older generation. Although Ahmad (1995: 169) claims that in South Asia the Jama'at has minimal influence on college and university campuses, in The Gambia, the majority of Tablighis had a modern, secular education. Because of this type of education, they are referred to as *English students* in local idiom, a designation that highlights that they have not attended formal religious education and are, as such, not literate in Arabic.

Although Tablighis are proliferating in The Gambia, especially among the young student population, it should be noted here that they still form a relatively small group. The Islamic Student's Association estimated that Tablighis constitute about 45% of the student population at the University of The Gambia. Although Tablighis constitute a large part of the student population, the "elders" in the Jama'at estimated they constitute only 1% of the Gambian population of about 1.5 million, but in the absence of membership records it is hard to calculate this number exactly. Just to give an indication of the Jama'at's size, the Tablighis estimated the average number of believers attending the Thursday program in the Tabligh Jama'at's mosque (described later) at about 1,000, and I was told that during the annual congregation last year, 5,000 people—including Tablighis from Mauritania, Pakistan, and even France—participated. According to the Tablighis, it is, however, not quantity but quality that matters. As noted earlier, the Jama'at has been quite successful in bringing about a religious transformation in Gambian society, especially in the performance of the life cycle rituals. Furthermore, the movement has raised religious awareness. A young man who was known as a regular customer of *marabouts*, for example, told me that after having attended Tablighi sermons he decided to remove his charms because he realized that wearing them was a form of superstition, and the only one who could grant his wish of getting a visa for the United Kingdom was Allah.

In addition to a youth movement, the Tabligh Jama'at is also an urban movement in The Gambia. Levtzion (1987: 16–18) argues that modern Islamic reform efforts are usually urban based and that they criticize and seek to eradicate Sufi-oriented Islam, which is generally associated with rural societies. This reasoning holds in the context of The Gambia because a male youth's conversion to the Tablighi ideology often leads to a migration to the city of Ser-rekunda or its vicinity, where the Tabligh Jama'at's mosque, Markaz, is located. This migration usually involves alienation from the family, which stays behind and which often holds more to Sufi conceptions of Islam. Deprived of their traditional social networks, Islam becomes more meaningful to these young men who, confronted with the heterogeneity of urban life, find in Islam a form of identification and a medium of self-expression (Janson 2009; LeBlanc 2000; Masquelier 1999). Bachir, a university student, explained to me:

> We live in an age of chaos and despair. Technology has reached its
> highest level, but we don't have trust in it. A university degree is the
> highest degree one can get, but we don't have trust in it. Therefore
> we engage in *tabligh*, in order to reclaim our lost identity. We derive
> comfort from our religion.[22]

It seems that the infrastructure of the Tabligh Jama'at, with Markaz as its pivot, provides male Tablighi youth with new modes of sociality and support outside traditional family structures. A Tablighi of long standing compared Markaz with a "petrol station," where he meets his "boys" and is "fueled with new ideas and energy." Markaz is the place where large numbers of young men gather daily to perform prayers, immerse themselves in constant remembrance of God, talk about the faith, and sometimes even spend the night. Thursday evenings are set apart for the weekly gathering in Markaz. This congregation starts with a joint prayer, followed by an inspirational talk reciting religious principles, instances from the Quran and *hadith*, delivered by an experienced preacher. The night ends with a call for volunteers for missionary tours both in and outside The Gambia. In addition to the weekly and annual congregations, the Tabligh Jama'at's main form of activity is *khuruj*, or missionary tours, which every Tablighi man is expected to make at least three days per month, 40 days per year, and three months once during his lifetime.[23] Different roles are assigned to the participants in the tour. Prominent among these roles is rendering domestic service (*khidmat*). The Tablighi men with whom I worked talked with great enthusiasm about the tours, elaborating on the mutual support among the members with doctors by profession now engaging in cleaning and the sense of brotherhood existing between them. A young Tablighi man recalls:

When I set out for *khuruj* for the first time I was affected by how kind
the brothers were to me. They hugged me and performed *du'a*
(supplications) for me. On the way I wanted to buy food, but before I
could take out my money a brother had already paid for me. I felt like
a baby who was cared for by everybody. It was a wonderful spiritual
experience.[24]

Despite the Tablighis' withdrawal from traditional family life, the strict rules—
derived from the Quran and *hadith*—imposed by the Jama'at for every conceiv-
able action, from worshipping to dressing, sleeping, eating, and, according to
two Tablighi men, even such a trivial act as "removing a fly from one's food,"
reinforce the movement's cohesiveness to such an extent that it is sometimes
compared with a surrogate family (Sikand 2002: 255). Interestingly, in this context, the Tablighis address each other as *brother* and *sister*. Mamadu, a male
Tablighi who joined the Jama'at a few years ago, noted: "*Tabligh* brings real love.
The brothers in Markaz love each other, care for each other and help each other.
We treat each other as relatives, while our blood relatives sometimes even refuse to participate in our ceremonies."[25] The cohesiveness of the movement is
an important explanation for its successful appeal in The Gambia, a country
that is characterized by socioeconomic and, increasingly, political instability.

    Although the Tablighis have created for themselves an Islamic youth cul-
ture centered around Markaz, their contemporaries hang around in so-called
urban ghettos— that is, meeting places at street corners—spending their time
drinking tea; listening to hip-hop and reggae music; playing football or the
boardgame draughts (see fig. 6.1); meeting their girlfriends; commenting
on local, national, and international news; and dreaming about going to Babylon (i.e., the West).[26] The link between youth culture and locality, the mosque
versus the street, confirms Massey's argument for the spatial construction of
youth cultures. In her opinion, strategies of spatial organization are deeply
bound up with the social production of identities, and she concludes that "the
control of spatiality is part of the process of defining the social category of
'youth' itself" (Massey 1998: 127).

    What this secular and Tablighi youth culture have in common is not only
their link with a particular locality, but the "ghetto boys" and Tablighis also
share what Bourdieu (1992) calls a *habitus*, in that they inhabit an urban space,
belong to the middle class and lower middle class, are acquiring or have
acquired a western-style education, and react against the moral and political
establishment. Furthermore, both groups are characterized by a specific dress
code. The ghetto boys wear baggy trousers, sports shoes, and baseball caps or
grow dreadlocks (depending on their music choice), while the Tablighis wear

FIGURE 6.1. Urban "ghetto" youth in The Gambia playing draughts. (Marloes Janson)

ankle-length trousers and caftans, turbans, and grow beards. Both groups are not only visible in everyday life, but also are audible, with ghetto boys listening to music on their ghetto blasters and Tablighis listening to tape-recorded sermons. Finally, both groups are Muslim, but in distinct ways. The ghetto boys consider their Islamic identity "natural," in that they were born as Muslims, whereas the Tablighis regard it as something they have to prove by observing the *Sunna*. A Tablighi who joined the Jama'at a couple of years ago, expressed it as follows: "Before, I prayed and fasted, but I did not know much about Islam. I conceived Islam as my right and not as a favor from Allah."[27] Paradoxically, although the ghetto boys' parents complain about their sons' religious laxity and their loitering, the Tablighis' parents reject their sons' religious radicalism and their idling in the mosque.

The ghetto boys and Tablighis not only share a habitus, they are also related in other ways. Like my research assistant hinted at in the beginning of this section, both youth cultures spring from what he called *poverty*. The contemporary Gambian economy finds itself in a downward spiral. The rate of unemployment increased and, because of rampant inflation, living costs rose sharply during the late 1990s. Furthermore, the production of peanuts—the only cash crop—fell and the government could not raise the capital to buy what was produced, and tourism—the only other industry—was in an unprecedented decline (Darboe 2004: 81). Youth especially are hit hard by the current socioeconomic crisis. The National Youth Policy Document 1999–2008 shows that the level of youth unemployment is increasing at an alarming rate in The Gambia, and estimates that more than 35,000 youths (out of a total population of about 1.5 million) are now searching for jobs to improve their declining standard of living (The Independent: January 10, 2005). The frustration among youth became highly visible in the demonstrations organized by the Gambian Students Union in 2000.[28] Although the demonstrations were organized to protest the death of a student, reportedly after torture by fire service personnel, and the alleged rape of a schoolgirl by a police officer, they were obviously also an expression of discontent with the rulers, who are held responsible for the socioeconomic hardship.

Biaya (2005: 222) claims that African youth belong to "the sacrificed generation who have no promise of a future." Nonetheless, as Biaya further argues, the African city offers young people a space to escape the disastrous socioeconomic and political conditions, and to affirm their identity. One identity path is what he calls the *syntonic identity*, whereby the youth's behavior is determined by a religious framework. The religious ideology of forgiveness and submission serves to temper the revolt of youth against their inhuman conditions, and it offers them opportunities for rehabilitation (Biaya 2005: 222). For similar reasons, a growing number of Gambian youth invest in *tabligh*. Although the benefit is not material, they are assured—they believe—of a spiritual reward.

Explaining the link between the socioeconomic crisis and the expansion of the Tabligh Jama'at in The Gambia, my research assistant said:

> Many Gambian young people do not have an easy life. They want to work, but there are no jobs, or they want to travel to Babylon [the West], but they don't have papers. It is not easy for them to get what they want. Some start smoking marijuana and go mad,[29] whereas others start praying more regularly. The preachers tell them that they will be rewarded for their prayers. These youth fall in love with the new religion; all they do is follow Allah's commandments and say *"ma sha' Allah."* My old friend is a good example. He worked as a manager for a bank, but lost his job. He got a loan, but, because he couldn't pay the money back, he was arrested. To overcome his problems he became a *Mashala*, a hard-liner.[30]

This narrative suggests that Gambian youth have found in the Jama'at a framework that allows them to cope with social wrongs (see also Khedimellah 2002). The movement's ban on conspicuous consumption and its emphasis on an austere lifestyle fit in with the economic realities of its members.

The previous quote indicates that Tablighi Islam does not provide all youth with a way out of their difficulties and a reassuring sense of their place in Gambian society. Although a number of them do pray (irregularly) and fast during Ramadan, religion does not seem to bring the ghetto boys moral relief. Instead, they spend their days dreaming about traveling to Europe or the United States, whereas for most of them the gates to "Babylon" remain closed. Although Tablighis invest in missionary work as a way of getting rewarded in the hereafter, the ghetto boys do not want to wait; they strive for a better life in this world, but on another continent.

Although the current socioeconomic crisis may be a factor explaining Gambian youth's entry into the Tabligh Jama'at, it does not explain why, under similar circumstances, some youth resort to Islam and others to more secular means for reshaping their lives. From my research assistant's narrative it seems that the choice for religion or the "material world" is rather arbitrary: "Some start smoking marijuana and go mad, whereas others start praying more regularly." The biographies that I recorded during my field research illustrated that before their conversion to the Tablighi ideology, many of my informants had indeed been ghetto boys themselves. Ahmed, a young Tablighi, told me:

> At that time I didn't know the blessings involved in *tabligh*, and I was another person. I was a sportsman, interested in only *dunya* (secular) things such as football, nightclubs, and games, and I didn't pray five times a day. Finally, I decided to talk with the preachers in the mosque and I was so impressed by them that I decided to engage in *tabligh*.[31]

In this case, like in that of many other Tablighis, the meetings with the Tablighi preachers, whether local, from other African countries, or Pakistani, seemed to be the decisive factor in changing their lifestyle. Through these meetings they realized that, in the words of some converts, "drinking tea would not change our situation," and that *tabligh* could bring them self-respect. What turned out to be important in winning the youth over was the preachers' low-key attitude.[32] A Tablighi of long standing, told me that itinerant preachers even visited him in the ghetto. Unlike his parents, they did not tell him to turn down the volume of his ghetto blaster: "Although the music did like boom boom boom, they kept calm and they were so kind to me that in the end I felt embarrassed to decline their invitations to pray with them in the local mosque. I finally went to the mosque and became enlightened."[33]

Once they embrace the Tablighi ideology, the converts become role models for their peers. Lamin explained to me:

My friend and I attended a naming ceremony in the town of
Brikama. During the ceremony we were invited by visiting preachers
to participate in a congregational prayer in the mosque. An old
friend, who I got to know as a very stubborn boy, preached about our
purpose on this earth. I was impressed by his change of behavior and
I decided to be like him. After the congregational prayer, I changed
my life. I joined the preachers for three days in order to learn more
about the *diin* (religion). Even after one day, I noticed a difference: I
was less occupied with worldly affairs. . . . Nowadays even when I am
sleeping I observe the *Sunna*. I worship Allah 24 hours a day.[34]

Although preachers and converted peers may persuade the ghetto boys to
convert to the Tablighi ideology, I also heard examples of converts who later fell
back into their former lifestyle. Because it has grown into a youth movement, a
certain turnover seems to be ingrained in the Tabligh Jama'at in The Gambia.

Conclusion

Although still in a rudimentary state, the Tabligh Jama'at in The Gambia represents a new expression of religiosity among young Muslim men that can be
seen as a form of resistance against the traditional sources of moral and religious authority of the older generation and *marabouts*. These youth are no
longer objects within the religious structures ordained by Muslim elders, but
are religious agents who are bringing about a religious—and indirectly also a
political—transformation in Gambian society (Last 1992: 375).

The Tabligh Jama'at was described in this chapter as a venue to study the
dimensions of generation and power in The Gambia. A frontier between elders
and the young have long characterized West African cultural values, which
favor the authority of elders. Gambian Tablighi youth, however, perceive following the Prophet's traditions as more important than upholding traditions that
simply strengthen the power of the local gerontocracy (see also Masquelier
1996: 246, note 21). By discarding the religion of the established Muslim elders
as "cultural Islam," and by terming their own faith as the only "true religion,"
the Jama'at valorizes youth's quest for religious authority and power. Tablighi
Islam, as a new form of social identification, has become the site through
which young Muslims jockey for space in a web of established power relations
(LeBlanc 2000: 104).

By means of a case study of the Gambisara mosque crisis that underlays
the proliferation of the Tabligh Jama'at in The Gambia, I have reexamined the
concepts of *youth* and *elder*, analytical categories that are usually taken for

granted, and I illustrated that age and generation are linked with other social classifications such as religious and ethnic belonging, as well as authority and power. It emerged that the principles of seniority and gerontocracy have become the basis for a generational conflict in The Gambia, in which the urban young claim for themselves, on the basis of their knowledge of "true" Islam and their "proper" Islamic practices, the position of religious authorities. Through Islamic reform, a reconfiguration of the traditional power system, in which seniority, wisdom, and authority are closely connected, is thus taking place in Gambian society.

It is intriguing that a classic theme of social science literature on youth culture—youth's rebellion against the elderly—is couched here in religious terms. Although the young accuse the older generation of being rigid in their religious views, it could also be said that the Islam propagated by the Tablighi youth is, in fact, more rigid than the Islam professed by their parents and the *marabouts*. It remains to be seen which impact the more rigid social order, which has been implanted by the Tablighi youth, has in the long run on their peers, who are involved in a more secular youth culture. Does it urge them to convert to the Tablighi ideology, or do they invent other ways to negotiate their youthful identity, with "Muslimness" not being a factor? Moreover, how do the Muslim elders react to the situation in which their children try to read them a lecture, now that it seems that age can no longer be used by them as a tool to fight against religious change?

Acknowledgments

This chapter is based on ethnographic fieldwork undertaken between November 2003 and April 2004, April and June 2005, and March and June 2006 in The Gambia. The research between 2003 and 2005 was funded by a grant from the International Institute for the Study of Islam in the Modern World in Leiden (the Netherlands). The research in 2006 was funded by a grant from *Deutsche Forschungsgemeinschaft*, and conducted under the *Zentrum Moderner Orient* research project Urban Youth Cultures in West Africa: Processes of Translocal Appropriation. I thank Linda Herrera, Asef Bayat, Mamadou Diouf, Elisabeth Boesen, Chanfi Ahmed, and Cordula Weisskoeppel for their comments on earlier versions of this chapter. All errors of fact and interpretation are, of course, my own.

7

Cyber Resistance: Palestinian Youth and Emerging Internet Culture

Makram Khoury-Machool

Palestinian Youth and Political Activism

Since the outbreak of the second Palestinian Intifada on September 28, 2000, and despite a significant drop in the average income of Palestinian households living in the 1967 Palestinian Occupied Territories, there has been a sharp increase in the number of Palestinian Internet users—especially youth—through connectivity at home, schools, universities, and youth centers. As a result of the sociopolitical conditions pertaining to Palestinian youth and students under occupation, the Internet now acts as a new medium between teachers, students, and their peers, as well as a tool for intense politicization and peaceful cyber resistance in the public sphere (Palestinian Central Bureau of Statistics, 2006:13).[1]

Palestinian youth have played a key part in the Palestinian national resistance to the Israeli occupation since the *Nakba* in 1948 and particularly since 1967. With the formation of the Palestine Liberation Organization, youth leagues were established to represent the Palestinian cause. The educational system in particular (both universities and schools) has been at the forefront of the national struggle. Student and youth movements, which for the most part have branches attached to the various Palestinian factions, are considered part of a highly politicized sector.

Resistance among Palestinian youth existed long before the introduction of the Internet, and took various forms on the ground. During the first Intifada (1987–1993), the main characteristics of youth activities were community support, demonstrations, and the use of physical force (www.pcbs.gov.ps/Portals/_pcbs/PressRelease/CommTec06e.pdf).1987: 1, 1988). As a result of the Israeli siege, assaults, and restrictions on the Palestinian press, young people resorted to writing political graffiti on the walls of their neighborhoods and other localities as a means of communication and political resistance. However, with the spread of new information and communication technology (ICT), they found more effective ways of communicating.

The emergence of the Palestinian information society began in 1995, the first year of widespread use of the World Wide Web. At that time, there were 16 million users of computer communication networks in the world, based mainly in the United States. This year coincided with the assassination of the Israeli Prime Minister Yitzhak Rabin by an Israeli Jewish activist and consequently the collapse of the short-lived Oslo peace process (Karpin and Friedman 1988). The Palestinian information society has been built within educational institutions and alongside political events; the two have consistently been closely intertwined. Youth skilled in ICT at leading Palestinian universities have been pioneers in positioning post-Oslo Palestine within the newly globalized society.

What follows is an examination of the relationship among Palestinian youth, ICT, and political activism, as it has developed within the formal and informal educational sectors in Palestine. The former is represented by a case study of Bir Zeit University (BZU) in Ramallah, whereas the latter is addressed by reviewing projects and programs devised for Palestinian youth by nongovernmental organizations (NGOs).

Palestinian Students Online

Bir Zeit University, which was established in 1972, has been known for its politically active student body. During the first Palestinian Intifada, it acted as a focal point of resistance to the post-1967 Israeli occupation. One of the most advanced educational centers in Palestine[2] in terms of budgets, learning resources, and curricula, BZU became one of the first Palestinian institutions in the West Bank and Gaza to launch a website in 1994.[3]

The juxtaposition between politicized and information technology (IT)-skilled students led to the first proactive event in September 1996, when students and youth participated in political events using new technology. This was demonstrated by the creation of the "On the Ground in Ramallah" website at BZU, as described here by its webmaster:

Images of Israeli army helicopters hovering threateningly over Ramallah and compelling eyewitness reports provided powerful, daily counterpoints to the international media's version of events. In the two weeks between September 27 and October 12, 1996, the "On the Ground in Ramallah" site received more than 3,000 "hits" (individual visits). Compared to the current 40,000 hits per month on the BZU website, this may seem unimpressive, but given the infancy of the [World Wide Web] in Palestine . . . , it was a significant number. (Hanieh 1999: 41–44; see also: http://www.jstor.org/pss/3013391)

By taking ownership of reporting and attempting to involve themselves in news production processes, in addition to maximizing the use of the possibilities the Internet provides, BZU students launched an online radio station as early as October 1998. Bir Zeit University's "Out Loud" demonstrated an early attempt at convergence between old media (radio) and new media (Internet). Free to anyone with a computer, the student-run radio station was also bilingual. This not only widened access, but also increased the possibility of activating access and sending material to others. This initiative represented a radical breakthrough from the pattern of centralized broadcasting, to one in which "every citizen can broadcast to every citizen" (Rheingold 1994: 14).

There has been a strong correlation between the development of technological skills and the maintenance of a reasonably steady education, despite the reoccupation of Palestinian localities and the paralysis of Palestinian universities after 2002. Having the means to resist the consequences of the occupation has led BZU students and staff to utilize the advantages of the Internet. Bir Zeit University has developed a porters-based method of instruction for students who cannot reach campus because of checkpoints and closures.

A Cisco Regional Academy since September 2000, BZU has attempted to turn the Internet into the technological basis for the organizational form of the Information Age (Castells 2002: 1). As a result of its strong performance, BZU received a Cisco Networking Academy Program Award[4] in 2001. Throughout the first year of the second Intifada, BZU (sponsored by the Welfare Association) completed the Cisco Networking training program for 10 local academies (CCNA Track) in the West Bank and Gaza Strip, and was then able to launch e-learning programs using Cisco's web-based training material, with video conferencing to connect BZU with students in the Gaza Strip.[5]

The scale of projects undertaken by BZU is an indication of the extent to which the university perceives itself as fulfilling a broader social and political role in the lives of Palestinian youth. Bir Zeit University signed the "Across Borders Project" with PalTel one year into the Intifada, in September 2001.[6] Aware of the distribution of the Palestinian population across the globe, and with little possibility of these disparate groups ever meeting, this special project was designed "to empower and improve the situation of Palestinian refugee camps, through the introduction of Internet technology within the Palestinian territories and the diaspora."[7] Information and communication technologies-assisted connectivity between Palestinian youth in the Occupied Territories and their peers, friends, and relatives in the diaspora has empowered those under occupation and given a sense of interconnectedness to all Palestinians across the globe.

Numerous other ICT-based initiatives and projects have taken place during recent decades in this and other Palestinian universities, which have attempted to nurture the concept and practice of a mobilized Palestinian information society resisting or bypassing occupation through its youth. To date, there are 43 higher education institutions in the 1967 Palestinian Territories, 11 of which are traditional universities, whereas the rest are university colleges and community colleges.[8] By 2002, most universities were already using the Internet to communicate with students, and an estimated 8,000 users were using the Internet from university campuses or their satellite offices. In addition, young people were accessing the Internet from other locations, such as Internet cafés or the home.[9]

As part of the endeavor to transform Palestinians into an information society, a government decision was made on May 10, 2005, to adopt the "E-Palestine" initiative, part of which is the Palestine Education Initiative, which was launched in summer 2005. One of the targets of the national strategy is the completion of a project to connect all Palestinian academic institutions and schools. This initiative is designed to maximize the number of pupils acquiring IT skills from humanities subjects, in addition to the existing 30.15% of pupils in high school specializing in a scientific subject (Palestinian Central Bureau of Statistics 2005: 28).

The formal education sector has been a key facilitator of Palestinian youth activism by playing a substantial role in allowing Palestinian youth to develop their ICT skills. This has thus led to transformations in resistance activity, going hand in hand with "the increasing use of [ICT] as enabling technologies for education and learning" (Mansell and When 1998: 66). The Internet has become increasingly central to everyday Palestinian life, acting as a tool for information, commerce, recruitment, social organization and political activism. Universities and schools have played a major role in the support of the community network.

Youth E-Resistance

On September 28, 2000, exactly five years to the day after the signing of the second Oslo Agreement, Palestinians protested at Israeli Prime Minister Ariel Sharon's march on al-Aqsa mosque (*al-haram al-sharif*) in Jerusalem, marking the start of their second uprising against the Israeli occupation. This time, a new facet emerged in the resistance of Palestinian youth: unlike in the first Intifada, when military siege had meant the control of news from an occupied geographical area, Palestinian youth were able to use ICT to bypass so-called "undesirable areas" (Castells 2002: 144).

Since the second Intifada began, Palestinian youth have been at the forefront of the impact of the Israeli occupation and siege, be it in their homes, their neighborhoods, or their educational institutions. As a consequence, connectivity in schools and at home has become a major tool for keeping informed about events, and reporting on matters that affect them personally, or affect their friends, families, neighbors, classmates, teachers, schools, and other youth facilities. In particular, the volume and severity of violent incidents to which Palestinian youth have been exposed in their schools and universities carries a broader significance. Statistics indicate that the total number of Palestinians killed in the occupation from September 28, 2000 to March 31, 2008, is 5,512, with 32,569 injured.[10] Of these, the number of young people killed in the 1967 Occupied Territories between September 29, 2000, and June 30, 2008, is 2,967, of whom 994 were younger than 18 years of age. Between September 2000 and January 2006, among school pupils and other students, 801 youths were killed. As for teaching staff, 32 were killed (Palestinian Central Bureau of Statistics 2006: 64). Furthermore, at least 4,783 people in the educational system (schools and universities) were injured, including 3,471 pupils and 1,245 university students, 54 teaching staff, and 13 other employees. As for detainees, 1,230 were detained (720 university students, 405 pupils, 76 teachers, and 29 other employees). Between September 28, 2000, and May 28, 2004, hundreds of incidents of shellfire and damage caused to schools and universities occurred, along with the transformation of schools into military bases, closures of schools and universities and schools, and vandalizing of colleges and universities. This is in addition to the general disruption of educational activities in 1,125 schools.

Palestinian youth began using the new media as a political tool just 48 hours after the outbreak of the second Intifada, when a Palestinian cameraman working for the French Channel 2 (Antenne 2) filmed a schoolboy, Muhammad al-Durra, being shot while his father tried to protect him. An immense wave of photos and clips of the incident were sent mainly by Palestinian youth to every possible address on the Web. The immediacy of reporting through the Internet via independent youth "journalists" showed the Palestinians the hidden potential of new media for counterhegemony of old bias in the mainstream media. The slain schoolboy's iconic image not only portrayed the conditions under which Palestinians live in general, but the helplessness of Palestinian youth before the occupying machine.

Uncensored access to new media has emerged as a form of empowerment for the traditionally weak, disempowered youth. Equipped with ICT skills and technology they had acquired at school or university, Palestinian youth soon learned that they could resist the Israeli occupation without the use of force alone. Furthermore, the fact that the film of Muhammad al-Durra's death was shot by a Palestinian cameraman opened horizons for Palestinian youths to aspire to become journalists. The utilization of ICT skills by Palestinian youth from the very start of the second Intifada can be divided into two phases. The first phase, which lasted until October 2000, was when Palestinians used all their existing skills and facilities to "tell the world" their story. The second phase, from October 2000 onward, has been characterized by all new-media activism by Palestinian youth.

The Second Intifada and Youth Internet Culture

The second Intifada saw the economically and politically weak rise up against the technologically advanced and militarily powerful other. As pioneers of the IT sector, it was Palestinian youth who carried out the first acts of cyber resistance to the Israeli technological superpower.[11] Although geographically besieged to a greater degree during the second Intifada, the Internet provided a new means of resistance to occupation. One of the most salient extensions of the outbreak of the Intifada was the emergence of the first cyber war within the Middle East conflict, when Palestinian and Israeli/pro-Zionist groups (predominantly youth) engaged in "hacktivism," attacking and, in some cases, paralyzing their opponents' websites (Khoury-Machool 2002). The shift of the Palestinians to the media domain was largely unexpected by the Israelis. By and large, developments in ICT among Palestinians have been influenced or controlled by Israel. Nonetheless, the situation as it now stands has meant the potential for equalization between the two opposing sides, and has since led the Israeli IT sector to seek a "truce" with its Palestinian counterpart, as a result of economic losses arising from hacked and damaged websites.

Since the very outset of the second Intifada, Palestinian resistance has been conducted electronically, and has taken the form, among other things, of mass e-mail calling for demonstrations and meetings, mass e-mail with media value, be it textual or visual (including video), detailed daily press releases, petitions, the countering of misrepresentations, fund-raising, and personal diaries in the form of e-mail (before blogs). This traffic has been channeled to multiple destinations, including relatives, neighbors, and friends in the neighborhood, village, town, or elsewhere in Palestine; media organizations locally and globally; other Palestinians and Arabs in the world; and individuals and organizations across the globe.

Staying Connected from Home

Being physically cut off from one another as a result of the siege, curfew, and checkpoints, and unable to come together physically in the campus or at school, Palestinian youth have been quick to adopt the new technology at home as a way to stay together and to stay connected. Connectivity at home has become a peaceful—and safer—mode of resisting or fighting armed occupation. This explains the increase in the number of landlines in Palestinian households and the sharp increase in personal computers at home. The most recent household survey on ICT carried out by the Palestinian Central Bureau of Statistics shows that, in 2006, 32.8% of households in the Palestinian Occupied Territories owned a computer (with 33.9% in the West Bank and 30.8% in the Gaza Strip), up 24.2% from 2004 figures. In terms of Internet access, the survey shows that of these households, 15.9% have access to the Internet (15.7% in the West Bank and 16.2% in the Gaza Strip), an increase of 72.8% since 2004. The main reason for owning a computer was for educational purposes, with 62.7% of households citing this as their main motivation. Similarly, the purpose of accessing the Internet was mainly for education (19.3%) and knowledge (15%) acquisition purposes (www.pcbs.gov.ps/Portals/_pcbs/PressRelease/CommTec06e.pdf).[12]

Inasmuch as this may be seen to foster geographical isolation, this phenomenon of engaging in cyber communication from the home in fact increases the possibility for communication between youths and their teachers, who are in constant contact with one another on matters relating to their studies. It also allows youth to stay in contact with other unknown virtual friends or opponents, and permits them to express themselves and perhaps report their existence and experiences to the world. Internet connectivity has allowed Palestinian youth to communicate with their fellow youth across the globe as part of a "transnational community,"[13] something that was much more difficult during the first Intifada when the use of facsimiles was restricted by the Israeli occupation, and the postal service was subject to delays and censorship. Finally, it has given them a new channel of peaceful resistance.

Youth Projects and Professionalizing Media Activism

Numerous civil society initiatives have taken place to expand connectivity and access further among youth. International NGOs principally fund nondenominational and nonsectarian Internet education and youth projects. However, these organizations also fund Internet initiatives that have a particular political or social agenda, such as women, democracy, youth, or human rights.[14] Activities of international organizations among Palestinian youth can be seen within a framework that considers the Internet "a fundamental instrument for development in the [T]hird [W]orld" that promotes peaceful, nonviolent activism (Castells 2002: 5). Some projects support youth organizations to develop IT literacy further. For example, the Web Development program caters to refugee children and youth.[15] There are programs such as the IT4Youth, aimed "at enhancing the learning skills and employability of Palestinian youth, ages 11 to 24, through computer-based information technology."[16] Enlighten, based mainly in the Gaza Strip, was established in 1999 to employ and teach residents in the camps computing and Internet skills.[17] Although not overtly stated, these governmental and nongovernmental bodies have been working to promote ICT among Palestinian youth because of the "peaceful" nature of ICT initiatives. Information and communication technology plays a role in raising educational standards, and contributes to producing a more articulate Palestinian youth that is better able to communicate and organize itself. This objective is perhaps most clearly defined in the Palestinian Youth Association for Leadership and Rights Activation (PYALARA).[18]

The Palestinian Youth Association for Leadership and Rights Activation (PYALARA), which appeals to the Palestinian youth leadership, is the only NGO to have made a direct and clear link between the socioeconomic conditions of Palestinian youth and their psychological well-being. With an annual budget of nearly US$500,000 (in the year 2005) generated from various international agencies, NGOs, and the Palestinian Ministry of Finance,[19] its aim is to "prevent young Palestinians from becoming thoroughly frustrated," and to channel their anger arising from the "suffocating atmosphere" toward media activism. *Activation* and *activism* are its main mottos, and it encourages Palestinian youth to voice their experiences through a journalistic method. It has attracted the support of ministries in the Palestinian government, as well as leading international organizations such as UNICEF, which has selected PYALARA as a "major strategic partner." Its young journalists publish a 24-page, bilingual monthly magazine, *The Youth Times*, and a two-hour TV program produced in cooperation with Palestine TV and supported by UNICEF. This program began to be produced three months after the outbreak of the second Intifada, and became weekly in 2002.The Palestinian Youth Association for Leadership and Rights Activation's magazine has more than 100,000 readers, and its TV program is believed to be watched by more than 300,000 Palestinian youths. The program's title, 'Alli Sawtak bears the double meaning "raise your voice/speak up" and "make your voice heard." Working closely with the Ministry of Youth and Sports, PYALARA has chosen a slogan that corresponds with PalTel's slogan "Tell the world" (Haddith al-'Alam).

In line with the strategic national concept "to reinforce and strengthen communication links with Palestinian youth abroad and to integrate them into various youth and sport activities and thereby forge relations with their fellow youth across the globe,"[20] PYALARA develops contacts with international youth organizations. Through their subproject Youth Democracy, PYALARA aims to play a part in citizenship building around concepts of the rights and duties of youth.[21] Through cultural exchanges, PYALARA mobilizes mass participation, which is said to help "in preventing both the marginalization and alienation of youth." (www.pyalara.org). Thus, mediated communication technologies have become one of the primary socializing agents for young people in 1967 occupied Palestine.

A more inclusive youth platform, intended not only for youth leadership but also for all young people, is Multaqayat Nadi al-Shabab (Youth Club Meeting Places). It includes a website and online radio broadcasting from Gaza, FM105. With the logo of al-Aqsa mosque and the slogan "al-qudsu lana" ("Jerusalem is ours"), this website features seven major pages dedicated to youth issues: General Club, Political Club, Literary Club, Entertainment Club, Music Club, Technology Club, and Universities Club. Each one of these boards deals with two to six (or more) threads/topics, and generates a vast number of hits, often reaching 50,000 per topic. Although the political club is exclusively for politics and has two main forums—Shabab dir' filastin (Youth Armor of Palestine) and Shabab filastinuna (Youth of Our Palestine)—most of the other forums relate to political occurrences and to related social and political conditions, be they on the literary, music, ICT, or university "clubs," or otherwise. Nearly all forums feature up-to-the-minute information on social and political events. Multaqayat Nadi al-Shabab sees the digital divide in terms of furthering democracy among Palestinians.

Another website for Palestinian youth is Mawqi' Shabab Filastin (Palestine Youth Website),[22] which deals with matters related to schools and universities, news, chat rooms, and other forums. In addition, it supplies nationalist hymns and songs, and treats women's issues and various types of literature and poems, and has the Palestinian flag as its logo.

Within the context of religion, it is important to note that the only difference among Muslim and non-Muslim Palestinians, is that devout Muslims use religious websites based on confessional features (those that deal with Islam as religion or that are restricted to devout Muslims). These websites can also serve social functions, such as finding a partner for marriage, for example. However, some religious websites can also be political in nature, with particular websites defining or restricting the type of user. For example, Hamas' website is only likely to appeal to a certain type of user—namely, those who share the religious or political ideologies of Hamas. Websites belonging to Palestinian political factions or any other social websites can and are being used by all, because such websites contain common concerns regardless of religious affiliation. For example, although Muslims are the majority in the Palestinian society, an educational website that both Palestinian teachers and students might access would not be restricted to Muslims.

Conclusion

The Internet as a global network has been localized and appropriated to suit the particular conditions of the Palestinian youth as part of a stateless people in 1967 Occupied Territories. This appropriation could not have been as wide without the donations of international bodies to local projects and initiatives, with or without political agendas and interests. It is also highly likely that, in making these donations, these international agencies and NGOs were fully aware of the peaceful and educational potential of activities arising from these projects. The emergence of new youth culture and electronic resistance raises the question of whether the transformation of Palestinian youth toward an information society will assist them in the developmental realms (economic development and its trajectories) in terms of the global economy or the local job market and employability. Given the conditions of the Palestinians under occupation, it will remain fairly difficult to look at ongoing projects in the field of ICT from a purely economic–developmental perspective.

Information and communication technology is being used to empower Palestinian youth in general. The political culture of Palestinian youth may be seen to have increased with the availability of the Internet, and has become more varied in terms of its methods. A large proportion of youth resistance is now nonviolent. New media in the Palestinian context have evolved as a result of the combination of ICT with the local needs of Palestinian youth. New media as used by Palestinian youth have acted as a mobilizer for social movement in resistance to the occupation, and have also generated new opportunities for low-budget and alternative media on the periphery.

The Internet has been the only true boundary breaker under siege conditions in the Palestinian Occupied Territories. Palestinians have turned to telecommunication as an antidote to checkpoints, curfews, and military occupation on the ground. The Internet has widened the participation of Palestinian youth in the resistance movement, whereas various Internet forums foster not only subtle forms of civic participation in the absence of established democratic venues, but also new sociopolitical solidarities. Bands of youth coming from particular classes who did not formerly participate in Palestinian resistance can now participate in online resistance. The Internet has also made Palestinian youth activism wider, speedier, cheaper, less time-consuming, and more focused, in the sense that the so-called "virtual community'" meets for a certain activity at a certain time.

Wittingly or otherwise, the various Internet strategies in Palestine have given space to youth from different backgrounds who, for many reasons, could not or did not previously participate in the physical confrontational struggle against the Israeli occupation, allowing them to channel their resistance via the Internet. Hence, in the short term, passive resistance will continue for as long as the international community continues to allocate funds through the Palestinian government or independent NGOs, during which time Palestinian youth will continue to nurture their ICT skills to full effect. It would also seem, in the short term, that the psychological–educational angle will continue to be given priority over the developmental–economic and employability angles, although these must be considered at a later stage.

Electronic political activism among youth, particularly among the Palestinian student body, has thus far performed a clear function in counter-propagating against the Israeli occupation's media hegemony. For this peaceful resistance to have crystalized as it did, it had to have not only a concept and a medium, but most important a borderless media organization with the financial viability to support the various activities.

In a positive future scenario, ICT-skilled Palestinian youth may emerge as leaders in their field, and in the Arab world in particular. On the other hand, the evolving pattern supporting the establishment of a Palestinian youth information society may serve only to sustain the gap between Palestinians on the periphery and Israel as an information center. Simply put, the budgets that have thus far been allocated by international donors are designed to reduce the use of force against Israel and improve the representation of Palestinians in public opinion.

However, as a result of the particularity of the Palestinian situation, it is very difficult to predict whether the Internet will effect a lasting change on

Palestinian youth culture. It is quite possible that the efforts of some international NGOs to transform Palestinian resistance into a peaceful one will change in the future, resulting in part from the policies of the Palestinian government if the occupation should end. Only then, will we see the extent to which this emerging knowledge society will further its achievements.

PART II

Livelihoods and Lifestyles

8

Young Egyptians' Quest for Jobs and Justice

Linda Herrera

Being Young, Arab, and Muslim in Uncertain Times

In the Muslim Middle East there has been growing concern since the 1980s, but more intensely since September 11, 2001, with Muslim youth. Within a climate of increasing unemployment, repressive regimes, a youth bulge, and an escalation of regional geopolitical conflicts with no resolution in sight, questions and speculation about youth have entered debates about democracy, security/radicalization, citizenship, and economic reform. Much attention has been placed on three general areas of inquiry: the challenges youth face in making the transition from school to work and in contributing to economic growth (United Nations Development Programme 2002, 2003; World Bank 2004); on youth religiosity, especially in light of the burgeoning piety movement (Deeb 2006; Mahmood 2005); and on security and the spread of Islamist politics and youth radicalization (Kepel 2003). Youth tend to be treated either as subjects to stimulate neoliberal development, or as essentially religious and ideological beings with either politically radical or benign tendencies. Youth themselves are rarely consulted about their struggles for a lifestyle and livelihood or about the type of citizens they are or aspire to be. They have been allowed little scope to question, reject, or offer alternative visions, demands, and arrangements for societal change and economic and social justice.

Arab states that are characterized by a youth bulge contain among the highest regional average of young people in the world, with 65% of the population younger than 25 years old, 20% of whom are in the 15- to 24-year age bracket. The Middle East and North Africa region holds the inauspicious distinction of being the fastest growing labor force, which, since the 1990s, has 25% youth unemployment—the highest regional average and almost double the global average, which is 14%. In the coming decade, some 34 million jobs need to be created in the region to absorb the emerging labor force (World Bank 2008). In Egypt, unemployment is highest among the young (youth unemployment accounts for 80% of the country's total unemployed population), and among youth, it is proportionately higher among females and the educated; a staggering 95% of unemployed youth have secondary or university education (Assad and Roudi-Fahimi 2007: 3, 19; World Bank 2004: 92).[1] Of Egyptian youth who find employment, 69% of them labor in insecure circumstances with no formal contract, and nearly half (46%) are in temporary jobs not related to their desired careers (Silver 2007: 9).

It has been pointed out that the youth bulge poses not only a development challenge, but potentially an opportunity, a "demographic dividend" (World Bank 2007: 4) or "demographic gift" (Wolfsensohn Center, The Brookings Institution 2008). A youth bulge becomes an advantage when human capital policies effectively channel the energies of youth for jobs and economic growth. There is evidence, for example, that the economic boom of the Asia tiger countries from 1960 to 1990 was possible, in part, because of education and economic policies that capitalized on its youthful population and turned its human capital to an economic and social advantage (World Bank 2007: 4–5). At the current juncture, there is scant evidence of advantages—economic or otherwise—being reaped from the youth bulge in Egypt, but potentials are clearly there, especially in the realm of youth cultural politics, which allow for new forms of communication and collectivist action.

The economic marginalization of youth has given way to no small degree of concern by the older generation, power holders, and international community that if youthful energies are not harnessed productively, trouble will loom. Part of the concern is economic; without regular work, the young will remain dependent on their families, on the state, on what little remains of welfare programs, and on charity, all of which bode badly for economic growth. A lack of youth economic independence also translates into difficulties with regard to marriage and forming families. With housing costs high and employment low, it can take many years for a couple, usually the man, to save enough to secure housing for a marital home. The age of marriage will likely continue to rise, and youth frustration—sexual and otherwise—may reach new heights (Singerman 2007).

Other exogenous anxieties about youth stem from national and international security concerns having to do with Islamic extremism and terrorism. The post-9/11 "war on terrorism" rhetoric, which ostensibly has been fading since 2009 in the Obama era, is replete with assumptions about how poverty and unemployment can lead Muslim youth on paths of radicalism and violence. As Esposito and Mogahed (2007: 67–68) write in *Who Speaks for Islam? What a Billion Muslims Really Think:* "The conventional wisdom, based on old and deeply held stereotypes and presuppositions about extremists, has often fallen back on an intuitive sense that a combination of religious fanaticism, poverty, and unemployment drive extremism and terrorism." Their analysis of a Gallup World Poll representing 90% of the world's Muslims (1.3 billion people) in 35 countries, call these assumptions into question. They concur that unemployment and poverty are both major social problems, but find that "neither unemployment nor job status differentiate radicals from moderates. No difference exists in the unemployment rate among the politically radicalized and moderates; both are approximately 20%" (Esposito and Mogahed 2007: 71). Clearly, there is a need to look for explanations beyond economic ones to understand the trajectories and choices of youth. There is also an imperative to understand youth not just for their future potential as "human becomings," a perspective that undervalues their lives and influence in the present, but as young social actors, as "beings" in their own right (Qvortrup et al. 1994).

To reach a better understand of the lives, choices, and preoccupations of youth requires going to the source and talking to youth directly. As Honwana and De Boeck (2005: 2) note in reference to youth in Africa, "the voices, views and visions of young people themselves still wait to be heard and considered. We know remarkably little about them. Children and youth . . . have often remained our 'silent others,' our voiceless *enfants terribles.*" Because qualitative and youth-centered research that incorporates the lives and voices of youth themselves is lacking, the methodological approach chosen for this inquiry is the life history method. Unlike a large-scale survey or multicountry poll, life histories cannot claim representativeness or provide the basis for statistical generalization. What the life history approach can offer is a means to arrive at a deeper understanding of the life trajectories of individuals and, in so doing, gain insight into larger social collectivities and conditions. As Cole and Knowles (2001: 11) elucidate in their work *Lives in Context:* "To understand some of the complexities, complications, and confusions within the life of just one member of a community is to gain insights into the collective. . . . [E]very in-depth exploration of an individual life-in-context brings us that much closer to understanding the complexities of lives in communities."

This chapter is organized around the life stories of two "20-something" urban youth from Alexandria, Egypt. They are both from the intermediate social classes (lower middle to middle class) that theoretically constitute the backbone of the modern nation. They have grown up, in fact were born into, the Mubarak regime (1981–present) and have come of age in a globalized, neoliberal era. They represent "ordinary" youth of their age, (see fig. 8.1) insofar as they harbor commonplace aspirations of living their youth, being part of a society in which fairness is the norm, being able to work toward reasonable employment, and gaining the financial means to marry and form a family. However, deficits of jobs and justice make these simple desires difficult to achieve.

FIGURE 8.1. Students at the University of Alexandria. (Linda Herrera, 2006)

"Karim" is a 22-year-old man and seasonal laborer who is waiting for an opportunity that will allow him to "begin" his life. He is what can be called a "youth-in-waiting," and has the classic profile of a potential extremist youth. "Dina," a 21-year-old university student still living at home, wants above all to live an ethical life and to be able to fulfill her desires for a career, love, marriage, and family, but she is highly skeptical that she will be able to realize these commonplace goals. Both these youths are Muslims, but Islam holds a different meaning to each of them in terms of their everyday practices and self-identity. Karim is lax about religious practice but finds some personal comfort in religion, whereas Dina takes pride in her piety and wears her religion on her sleeve. Although the two may differ on their discourse and practice when it comes to Islam, they converge in a markedly similar way about the difficulties of being young in contemporary Egypt and the quest for an alternative order.

Karim: A Transition to Nowhere

Karim, a Muslim male of 22 years, like growing ranks of young men in the country, spends his time in a combination of hanging out, worrying, sometimes working, indulging in drugs, and hoping. He is both living his life in the present, taking pleasure when and where he can, and at the same time hoping for a better future. But he worries that he is embarking on a transition not to adulthood, but a transition to nowhere.[2] Following a long spate of unemployment and a recent breakup by his girlfriend, he sees his chances at a "normal" life of love, marriage, and a family moving further out of reach. He spends much of his time in a coffee shop waiting to get picked up for short-term construction jobs. Wavering between desperation and hope, he says, "They are saying there are opportunities. Where are these opportunities? Where is the starting point, the beginning? If only I could start I could continue my life. But where is the starting point? Tell me; where can I begin?"

As a young boy Karim never imagined he would be in such a rut. He is still trying to understand his family's fall from rapid social mobility and relative prosperity down to poverty in the space of just a decade. He remembers as a child when his family was enjoying mobility from the ranks of the urban poor to the middle classes. His father worked as a low-paid but resourceful construction worker in the 1970s. During the mid 1980s, when Karim was a small child, his father seized the opportunity to travel to Saudi Arabia to work in the country's booming construction sector. He made a good sum of money, much of which he duly invested in property and the education of his children, although he himself had no formal schooling. His father built two houses, one for Karim's paternal grandmother, the other for his family, and enrolled his four sons and one daughter in private schools in Alexandria. He believed in the promise of the education system to raise the social status of the family and to prepare his children for middle class professions. But at the same time, as the family patriarch, he did not want his children to "flaunt" their education in the home where he, the father, was unschooled and unlettered.

Karim's mother, who completed her education through the preparatory stage (grade 8), possessed knowledge of the school system and enjoyed a decent standard of literacy. Karim's father, jealous of his wife's schooling and fearful she would use it to try to exert her superiority over him, put a moratorium on the mother's involvement in their sons' studies. She was only at liberty to assist their daughter with schoolwork, because the girl was not perceived as posing a threat to the father's standing and authority. When the mother so much as asked her sons about school he would shout at and berate her. As Karim recalls, "In our home the father was everything and everyone was expected to obey him."

The brothers all attended an all-boys private school that, before the July 23 revolution of 1952, was the bastion of the elite. It now caters to a social mix of students belonging to the financially strapped middle classes and upwardly mobile working or laboring classes; the latter category is often chided by teachers and students alike as being "uncultured" and the cause of the school's decline. So ingrained is class discrimination that Karim himself—a victim of it—complains that the school's environment has deteriorated and become too "lower class" (bi'a).

Karim displays a keen intelligence and interest in politics and social issues, yet he deeply dislikes school. His memories of school, and especially his teachers, are bitterly painful. "Teachers used to beat students badly and I got a good share of the beatings." He recalls the first day of class in 9th grade when his teacher began the lesson by warning him, "I've heard about you so you better beware." This was "a really black day," he sighs. His school career was spotted with failures and bare passes until finally, sometime during a repeat year in secondary school, he left school for good. Despite his own contentious relationship with schooling, his greatest regret is not having made it to the university and the knowledge that he will go through life as with the labels of an "uncultured" and "uneducated" man.[3]

All three of Karim's brothers also dropped out of school before completing high school. Their low performance at school could be attributed in part to the lack of parental support and their father's policy not to hire private tutors. The vast majority of secondary school students rely on the support of parents—especially mothers—and private tutors to prepare them for their examinations.

Private tutoring in Egypt is so widespread that it makes up a shadow education system; the quality and repute of one's tutor is often considered more important than the quality of the school in ensuring success through the system.[4] As it turns out, Karim's sister was the only one of the five siblings who successfully completed her studies. She went on to work in what the family considers a high-status job in a five star hotel in Alexandria. The fact that the patriarchal family structure served ultimately to disadvantage the male members of the family but not the female member is something outside the scope of this chapter that needs reflection about possible shifting gender relations in the "traditional" family.

By the end of the 1990s, the family's savings were gone, drained from the rising costs of school tuition and health care, raising five children, and free spending. Karim's family eventually fell into extreme poverty, making it imperative for the children to seek employment to support their basic needs. Without not so much as a high school degree and no work experience, Karim initially relied on his father to help him find work in construction, in the subspecializations of tiling and painting. But he has not been offered "good jobs," because of what he believes to be age discrimination. "Society doesn't give any chances to young people to prove themselves" he bemoans. "Young people *can* do some things adults can't do, but no one gives us responsibility. Even my parents still deal with me as a kid. They say youth is not the age of responsibility, but then what is?"

Even though Karim still lives at home, his family can no longer provide him with financial or even moral support, they are so absorbed in their own problems and struggles for survival. Karim measures his life as a series of failures, some of which he recognizes as his own fault, but others he considers are the result of barriers and setbacks out of his control. He explains, "I'm not satisfied with myself at all. How can I be? I failed in everything—in education, in work, in building a family. I don't find my future in anything. I want to have a home and family, succeed in my work, but what will happen only God can decide." He finds some solace in God, and when he is in the right frame of mind he prays, but not on a regular basis.

He is dissatisfied with what he describes as the indifference he encounters from his family, his government, and his society. His friends offer some solidarity, but no real help about how to move forward. His peer group these days is made up of other young unemployed men who, like him, are waiting for an opportunity, a change of fortune, a girl who will love him regardless of his financial situation. Even though some of his old school friends and neighbors call in on him, he avoids the ones who are faring better in the world, the ones with jobs, family support, and girlfriends. Among his current circle of friends are those who fill their time with a combination of drugs, prayer, surfing the Internet for hours upon end, and sitting in a coffee shop waiting for a truck that might pick them up for a short-term construction job.

Feelings of despair mixed with boredom have led him in two directions. Sometimes he turns to the Quran and prays for solace, but more recently his preferred activity is to escape his woes through hashish. He justifies his hashish smoking by explaining that it provides him with some moments of gratification and peace, and, however fleeting, some moments are better than none at all. "I haven't managed to do one thing in my life. I haven't achieved any of my goals, so I got into hashish. The best thing about it is that it kills free time (*al-faragh al-taam*). I burn away six to seven hours in a state of happiness. It takes you away (*biya'azzil*) and I can find myself, achieve everything I ever wanted without moving from my place. Do you understand what I'm saying? You find yourself having done so much when you haven't done anything. It's a way to escape from reality."[5]

When trying to understand and rationalize his situation, Karim returns repeatedly to the question of rights (*haq* or *huquq* [pl.])—the denial of rights, the importance of rights, and the devastating effect the lack of rights and political corruption has on the morale of youth and their ability to earn a livelihood and enjoy a decent lifestyle. He views the twin elements of justice and jobs—or injustice and unemployment—as intricately interwoven. He stresses that opportunity and advancement come primarily through connections, bribes, and dishonesty, not through merit or hard work. Because he does not have the family connections to boost him up, he thinks his best option is to build a future abroad in the West, because, as he understands it, "abroad you can take your rights; here you cannot." But the path of legal emigration is closed to him because he cannot so much as obtain a passport until he completes his military service, something he is categorically opposed to doing as a result of his distrust and abhorrence of the regime. He explains, "I can't serve in the military forces of this country. Why? Because it's just like Adel Iman says in the movie *Terrorism and Kebab* (*al-Irhab wa al-Kabab*), 'I do not serve the country; I serve the respectable Pasha' and this is very bad. I cannot do this."[6]

He describes the Mubarak regime (1981–present) as fundamentally corrupt, squandering the country's human and natural resources and serving the interests of a small inner circle of cronies. He also takes issue with Egypt's most important ally—the United States—and regards its military presence and development aid as highly dubious, divisive, and self-serving. He asks,

Where is this U.S. aid? No one sees or benefits from the aid and it divides us. Why can't Egypt undergo any real development without foreign aid? The US took its opportunities. It had its dreams. But now she's going around starting wars and is driven more and more by [greed] and evil. I can't accept this way of doing things.

Were Egypt to have a regime that operated on some basic principles of fairness, the country could, he believes, enjoy prosperity and pursue a very different course. He explains:

Imagine Egypt's potential if the ruling elite had a consciousness. We would see that in Egypt we have the Suez Canal. This is a great resource! This alone can let people live like Pashas. We have power through our workforce. We have agricultural land and we have a massive desert. We have good things, very good things, but there is no mind!

Despite his strong opposition to the Mubarak regime, Karim is skeptical about formal politics and has no interest in taking part in oppositional political activities. He especially does not want to support Islamist political groups such as the Muslim Brotherhood, which he thinks share the same tendencies toward authoritarianism and corruption as the current government. He disapproves of terrorism and views 9/11 as a reprehensible criminal act. But he explains that terrorism is the offspring of oppression, and although he personally is not pulled toward this path, he understands how others like him could be drawn to it. He cautions that when young people do not have rights, when they lack outlets to express their discontent, when their paths to gainful employment and autonomous adult life are closed, when they face discrimination and observe injustices around them, they could resort to violence or terrorism. He says:

I want to emphasize that the young person who becomes a terrorist sees his life as a closed path. It is closed in its past, its future, its material and moral aspects. This person needs someone to help him, but doesn't find anyone. He doesn't belong to a powerful family that can protect him from failed laws. The social and economic conditions don't provide him with any opportunities. He is angry that all the important things in his life—work and love—have failed. He doesn't believe in the social structure since it's neither just nor legitimate. He considers this system responsible for his own failures and problems of his society. He expresses his anger by attacking Israel and the United States because no act, no matter how enormous, will have an impact on his own life or change the course of his society. This person has nothing to do but to escape.

When young people are unable to secure a livelihood and live a life of dignity, it is often thought they are more susceptible to populist politics or fringe movements that promise them a sense of power and belonging. Although this is the case for some, Karim is categorical that he would not get involved in Islamist or other extremist political movements because he views them as opportunistic and fundamentally corrupt. He is distrustful of Islamist political movements, whether those of the illegal al-Qaeda variety or the more mainstream Muslim Brotherhood, because their leaders tend to misuse the teachings of the Holy Quran for their own political gains. And, more important for him, such groups and parties fail to provide a viable solution or approach to the problems of the youth.

Despite the barriers, Karim lives with a hope that a big change can transpire and his life can take a turn for the better, but he needs to find a way out of his current predicaments and is not sure how to proceed. He says:

> I see constraints everywhere: constraints from the ID card, the army,
> education, many things. I feel if I do something I will do it in a right
> way. If I get interested in something, I will do it 100%. I need to
> succeed in something but I can't find my way. I feel that something
> big will happen. What is it? When? Sometimes you find your heart
> secure. You think something will happen, but you don't know what it
> is. No one can say what will happen tomorrow. Life can turn upside
> down. I will wait.

Dina: Piety and Rights

Dina, a 21-year-old college student majoring in veterinarian science, lives at home in Alexandria with her parents and two sisters. Her father works as a lawyer and her mother, who earned her BA, stays at home and looks after the family. They maintain a modest but comfortable middle class standard of living and enjoy close family relations. Religion plays an important part in the life of the family; they observe daily prayers and read the Quran together. Dina, who wears a *hijab* and has committed the Quran to memory, self-identifies as a pious Muslim youth. Like so many of her generation, Dina aspires to live up to the standards of a virtuous person whom she describes as someone who maintains "high moral standards, preserves [Arab and Islamic] values and traditions, treats her parents well, and follows her ambitions." She believes her outward piety will help her in attracting a compatible life partner. She is currently single, but dreams of finding a love with whom to build a family.

FIGURE 8.2. A couple in Cairo enjoying life's simple pleasures. (Susan Hack, 2006)

The language of religious piety that permeates Dina's life is mixed with a liberal discourse about freedom, rights, and justice. For instance, she depicts her home life as a setting in which freedom and fairness are the norms. She says, "Our parents give us a lot of freedom. They let us express our views freely and ask our opinion." That she refers specifically to freedom of expression and consultation indicates that she has absorbed a particular understanding of freedom rooted in a liberal democratic discourse. Interestingly, when she speaks of restrictions she faces from home, such as the rule that she cannot stay out past sunset, she does not frame this as a lack of freedom. She views her curfew, which sometimes displeases her, as a judgment her parents make about safety and the reputation of girls. Freedom, on the other hand, relates to human respect and dignity.

She juxtaposes her home life, which is built around relations of piety and fairness, to an external environment of corruption and decay. Her principle point of contact with social institutions has so far been through her participation in the education system. From an early age Dina performed at an extremely high level at school, but she does not mince words about the flaws of the education system. She describes it as "broken and sinking," and in dire need of reform, beginning with the need to change the "phantom of the examination system." She views school simply as a gateway to the university and credits her mother—not her teachers—for her good grades and educational success so far. She scored high on the secondary school-leaving exam, which determines university admissions, the *Thanawiyya Amma*, but not high enough to enter the faculty of medicine. She settled for joining the school of veterinary medicine and is currently a second-year student in this highly regarded faculty.

As a university student, her immediate gripes have to do with lack of fair play in the education system and concerns about whether, after years of dedicated study, she would ever have the opportunity to apply her hard work and ambitions to a career. The more awareness she gains of the functioning of the education system, political system, and outlying society, the more she becomes demoralized about the role of connections (*wasta*) in getting ahead. She has been dismayed at the degree of nepotism in higher education as she witnesses the children of professors and those with parents in positions of power get the highest marks and job opportunities (apparently unwarranted), whereas those with no connections go unnoticed, underrewarded, and underemployed.

The lack of fairness in the university parallels what she regards as a more endemic problem—the prevalence of corruption and connections (*wasta*) in the everyday functioning of Egyptian society. "Egyptian society is thoroughly based on connections. It leads to corruption, which spreads like fire from dry leaves." The root of the problem, she argues, emanates from a government that denies citizens even its basic rights as it promotes the interests of the rich and powerful. It uses the entire security apparatus to safeguard the few as it neglects and persecutes the many. She explains:

> The police protect the wealthy people and lock up the poor people
> who fill the state prisons. In the old days we used to say "the police in
> the service in the people" (*as-shorta fi hidmat as-shaab*). Now we say,
> "the police and the people in the service of the nation" (*as-shorta wa
> shaab fi hidmat al-watan*). What I want to know is what, actually, is the
> meaning of the term *nation* (*watan*)? Isn't the nation supposed to be
> the people? Or does *nation* mean something else? Does it mean the
> president?

Mirroring Karim's sentiments about how Egypt has become synonymous with the president, she declares:

> Egypt has become a kingdom of kings. But even in kingdoms the name of the president doesn't become a substitute for the name of the country. In England you don't have people saying "England is Elizabeth." But here we have the expression, "Egypt is Mubarak" (*Misr Mubarak*). We need to change Egypt from the government of a king to a government of the people. Egypt is really going downhill.

The Mubarak regime's close association with the United States further reinforces Dina's judgment that the political elite look out for themselves at the cost of the interests and rights of an entire nation. She strongly criticizes the government's tacit acceptance and complicity in the policies of the "imperial US," which she views as a "thug nation," especially vis-à-vis Iraq, Palestine, and Lebanon. She considers the U.S. interference in national economic policies for liberalization and privatization through the International Monetary Fund and World Bank a central cause of the economic insecurity and unending hardships for the majority of Egyptian youth. Most upsetting to her is how the Egyptian government ignores the plight of its own people and punishes those citizens who agitate for political and economic reform. She stresses: "The government should start trying to listen to the problems of the people, and especially the youth, to give us our rights. We need our rights! Every citizen should have justice and the right to an honorable life." Despite her strong political views, Dina deems Egypt "no place for political ambitions," because on-the-street activism can carry heavy risks like torture and imprisonment.

Youth Cultural Politics and New Media

Given the deep distrust with which Karim, Dina, and presumably scores of Egyptians, young and old, view politics and their government, the question is: How do they respond to their situation? Youth, because of their life stage, particular habitus, and their generational location,[7] respond and pursue strategies that are, in a large measure, grounded in their youthfulness and the cultural politics of their generation.

Throughout the Middle East and North Africa, new information and communication technology has changed the landscape of youth culture, youth sociability, and political engagement (see Bunt 2003; Etling and Palfrey 2009; Maira and Soep 2004; United Nations Department of Economic and Social Affairs 2005). The rate of Internet penetration in the Middle East is 28.3, higher than the world average of 25.5. In Egypt, which has the highest number of

Internet users in the African continent and a penetration rate of nearly 16%, the number of mainly young users continues to rise at a meteoric level. In the year 2000, there were a mere 300,000 Internet users in Egypt, a number that increased to six million by 2006 and to roughly12.6 million in 2009.[8] The Egyptian blogosphere and social networking sites like Facebook (launched in 2004) constitute a veritable cultural revolution mainly as a result of the rapid increase and innovations of youth Internet users. The ways individual youth use new media invariably differs considerably, but it would not be off the mark to suggest that most youth use it for some form or another of subversive activity.

Like growing cadres of youth in the region, Dina views and uses the Internet as an alternative outlet for socializing, academic research, getting information about current affairs, and what can loosely be termed *political involvement*. She has been a dedicated Internet user for the past three years, when she started using it to support her academic work. Being a student in a university with outdated and understocked libraries, the Internet has been an indispensable tool for research. She joins the growing legions of Arab youth who initially turned to the Internet to aid them in their studies (or at least their parents bought or leased computers with the idea that it would serve as a tool in their child's educational advancement), but quickly became adept at the plethora of opportunities and access it offered.

It did not take long after getting a computer for her to discover that she could bypass the local media and access alternative sources—from political blogs to foreign newspapers—about politics, the economy, and world affairs. She considers staying informed a moral duty and a political act, a way to resist being controlled by a government that has historically tried to use the media as an arm of power and suppression. Yet she does not feel entirely at ease using the Internet as a tool for direct political action, as a number of mainly youthful activists have done.[9] She is well aware of state retribution against its citizens who, whether through blogging, online social networking, or other means, agitate for political change.[10] She acknowledges the potential of the Internet for what can loosely be called *civil disobedience*. She herself exercises civil disobedience not by joining organized strikes or political movements, but by deliberately shunning semiofficial news media and spreading information that she deems valuable about national politics, regional politics, and economic development. She confirms the adage that knowledge is power, and feels her generation can use the Internet as a means of empowerment and truth seeking so that justice can prevail.

Yet she acknowledges that the Internet is a double-edge sword. On the one hand, she considers the virtual and uncensored space that provides seeming limitless access to information and communication liberating. On the other hand, she worries that Egyptian and Arab youth misuse the Internet and imitate the "morally bankrupt" (*munharafeen*) aspects of western youth culture. Many young people, she argues, use the Internet purely for salacious means like accessing pornography, lowbrow entertainment, and flirting and forming immoral relations with their peers (gratuitous flirting is distinguished from respectable match-making websites that exist for Muslim singles). Despite her low regard of the morally corrupting influence of western youth culture, she admits that if given the chance she would go to the West to study and work, because these are "open societies" with strong economies where youth can "have their rights" and gain financial independence.

Dina grapples with ways of "doing the right thing," of living a virtuous life while also having her voice heard and her actions count toward some meaningful form of change. She tries in whatever ways she can to inform and influence others, to "transfer her [social and political] consciousness to family and friends" by circulating and forwarding news items and engaging in debates. She is especially keen on interacting with peers, in person and through the social networking sites, because, as she explains, "Once they have consciousness of their rights and their ability to correct social wrongs, they have a duty to act for change."

Conclusion: Big Struggles for Life's Simple Desires

When discussing the ambitions of her generation Dina explains, "The ambitions of young people are modest. We want to live at a decent level (*'ala mustawa karim*), get a job, find love, and get married." Although seemingly simple desires, these goals appear hopelessly out of reach. Arguably the two greatest impediments facing youth in the Arab states are not the spread of Islamist movements or radicalism, but the scarcity of jobs and the absence of justice. Injustice, whether measured as a lack of fair treatment in schools, the role of connections in gaining employment, absence of accountability of the government and international actors in regard to economic and political policies, has a direct bearing on the current lives and future prospects of Arab youth. Although the socioeconomic situations of Karim and Dina differ in significant ways, their stories provide a lens to understand what it is like to be young and Egyptian at the current global moment.

When trying to understand and rationalize his situation, Karim, who suffers from a sometimes incapacitating feeling of "being stuck," returns repeatedly to the question of justice, rights—the denial of rights and the importance of rights—and the devastating effect of corruption on the morale and life chances of youth. Karim alludes to the fact that although he is alive, he does not feel he is living; he does not possess what he considers a *life*. Living would require certain choices, conditions of freedom, opportunity based on fairness, and respect, which he finds generally lacking in society. A system that runs not on merit, but on favors, bribes, and nepotism, can lead youths on a path of radicalism and terrorism, but it can also lead them to withdraw and resort to drugs or apathy. After periods of despair, Karim regains hope and the desire to overcome his difficulties. He maintains belief that his situation will change, that the dysfunctional political and economic order cannot continue indefinitely. He waits for an opportunity to prove himself, to show his worth and to claim his rights.

Dina emphasizes that young people are enormously frustrated by a lack of fairness and ethics in Egyptian institutions and within the government. Her own time in the university has reinforced her already skeptical view about the place of corruption and connections in the everyday functioning of Egyptian society. She believes that youth should strive for a just order, maintain their ethics, and agitate through gaining knowledge and spreading information, against a corrupt regime. Like many youth, she is finding ways of using information and alternative sources of communication to stir a generational consciousness. The Internet and new media have become tools that allow youth to communicate, organize, think, and socialize above and below the radar. Collectively and individually, youth confront and resist a restrictive and unjust order and attempt to construct an alternative to it. In the absence of attaining their goals, they dream of going abroad, where it is believed that young people, even if they might be influenced by morally corrupting elements of western culture, can have a fair chance at success if they are willing to work hard.

The life stories of a young man and woman in Egypt in decidedly differentiated situations both identify the intertwining issues of jobs and justice as the preeminent problems youth face. Both draw in a remarkably similar way on a language of rights and the need to create a situation either to claim or to wait for rights. Whether a new generational consciousness can lead to economic justice and livelihood opportunities is yet to be seen. However, it does appear that rights, more than religion, whether Islam or otherwise, very likely embody the shared values of a generation, and the basis on which it will endeavor to change an unjust order.

Acknowledgments

The life history research on which this chapter is based was initially undertaken as part of a larger comparative study at the International Institute of Social

Studies, coordinated by Ben White, with funding from Plan Netherlands. I coordinated the Egypt component of the research in collaboration with Alexandria University professor Kamal Naguib. For other published accounts drawing on that data, see (Herrera 2006b and Naguib 2008). Many thanks are due to the participants of the study who so generously gave of their time, and to Sanaa Makhlouf who assisted with Arabic to English translations.

9

Reaching a Larger World: Muslim Youth and Expanding Circuits of Operation

AbdouMaliq Simone

The "Right Way" of Being Young

In a world frequently referred to and understood as uncertain and precarious, many youth are preoccupied with conducting themselves in the "right way." With its emphasis on the harmonization of social behavior and the discipline of the body as the material tools for attaining spiritual confidence, Islam provides a map that can guide youth through the ambiguity-filled dilemmas of everyday urban life. As urban economies increasingly depend upon the incessant remaking of space, built environments, and culture, urban Muslim youth must apply this map to experiences and domains that are unfamiliar. As Janet Roitman (2005), in her examination of the transfrontier economies of Cameroon, Chad, and Nigeria—with its reinvented dependence on raiding, smuggling, and theft as a means of ensuring a strangely egalitarian circulation of survival, opportunity, and power—points out, being in "the right way" is less a matter of adhering to principle than an ability to elaborate a narrative that holds together multiple discrepancies and contradictions in a clear sense of how one is situated in relationship to the lives of others.

Ethical action, then, is not so much the persistence of a particular way of acting in face of a complicated world that has many features that must be shut out and avoided; rather, it is increasingly viewed in the contexts I look at here as the ability not to be duped by exposure to seemingly endless new possibilities: for consumption, lifestyles, or achievement. I am particularly interested here in how such applications of Islamic identity operate at the margins of the Islamic world—in other words, when youth do not have recourse to national and social contexts that regulate conformity to faith and practice. What happens when getting a good education, having strong ambition, and staying out of trouble do not necessarily lead to a "good life?" As these conventional parameters of efficacy often become increasingly inaccessible to youth, what does it mean to become an effective individual? Often, family demands are enormous, with parents willing to see their children do anything to make money. Youth often know from an early age that they will be displaced, that they will have to secure some kind of future by themselves in a place they will barely know. Concrete livelihood prospects will increasingly demand an ability to become nothing in particular and to empty oneself of attachments to outmoded family and cultural mores, yet still retain the ability to fashion oneself as available to acting in concert with others. Islam proves potentially useful as a way in which individuals can align themselves and coordinate their lives with each other, because in certain respects there is "nothing to it." Faith and confidence emanate through the self-fashioning of action, of displaying certain manners of speech and behavior, rather than being anchored in weighty theological precepts and institutional orders.

In urban environments full of trickery, reworked imaginaries, and empty images, the bases of social solidarity and cooperation, although often persisting remarkably despite all odds, have been severely weakened. Who can one trust and work when the conventional mediations have dissipated but the need to trust and cooperate remain as strong as ever? How do individuals add others onto their lives? In other words, how do they attach their stories to those of others, when such attachment is likely to be inevitably disruptive, but when one has little choice? The reiteration of an Islamic sensibility then acts as a means of both identifying "a bare minimum" through which such articulations can be considered and a possible frame through which one's life and livelihood can continuously take more and more spaces and factors into consideration as a means for making that life work.

Here I will take into consideration two margins of the Muslim world. They are not intended to be representative of any thing other than themselves, but nevertheless they acts as "bookends." In these contexts I want to look at contrasting ways in which enacting the bare minimum and its relationship to how connections among people and things can be radically transformed are operationalized. In examining a Muslim neighborhood in the overwhelmingly non-Muslim city of Douala, Cameroon, I point to how the apparent reduction of daily life to a set of minimal actions in part compels an emerging practice in which everything everyone does is somehow taken seriously as something potentially useful. In Bangkok, I focus on how the need to find expanded "staging areas" to make individual livelihoods is needed to sustain a notion of Islam as something with efficacy.

It is clear that many cities in the global South face "demographic imperatives"—where a sizable majority of their population is younger than the age of 18. Spaces of the city are increasingly closed off to youth (in terms of finding places of privacy, sex, leisure, or productivity), let alone the space of imagining an existence beyond the present. An important object of the structural adjustment policies of the past 25 years has been temporality itself, such that the prospects for attaining a reasonable future are increasingly difficult to imagine, let alone concretize (Agier 1999; Devisch 1995; Ferrándiz 2004; Masquelier 2001). Larger numbers of youth are unable ever to leave the households of their parents, and are never able to raise sufficient funds to marry and have children of their own, thus prolonging the status of youth often far beyond the ages usually associated with it. Even as youth persists as a somehow bounded object of reflection and analysis, as temporality is being structurally adjusted, the entire "sequencing" of generational categories and distinctions is changed (Argenti 2002; Durham 2000; Honwana and De Boeck 2004).

New Bell Service sociale is the Muslim neighborhood of New Bell—Douala, Cameroon's sprawling historic inner city quarter—that abuts the city's main Nkloun market. Muslims are a clear minority in both this quarter and the city, but they continue to play a dominant role in the market. The neighborhood is a mélange of ethnic origins, reflecting the complex intersections of trade circuits at the regional confluence of Cameroon, Nigeria, and Chad, from where most of the original households have come. The neighborhood has also historically harbored significant numbers of migrants from Mali and Niger. The neighborhood is caught in a downward spiral of impoverishment, particularly as the sectors in which it specialized—livestock, agricultural produce, and leather goods—are subject to heavy competitive pressures from elsewhere.

Many youth have retreated back to regions of northern Cameroon, which they only know nominally, to join militias, raiding parties, and smuggling rings that have become increasingly important to secure inputs of basic commodities throughout the country. Those who remain are badly schooled, see no future in Douala, and view Islam as something that marks a disjuncture with a normal future life in Cameroon—a disjuncture that they understand would most likely happen anyway, despite their religious identification. But because it is largely understood neither as a tradition that must be reproduced, a comprehensive modality of identification, nor a way of life that guarantees anything in particular, Islam in their view becomes an instrument with which one can venture certain risks.

Because making prayer five times a day is a minimal investment—with potentially great rewards—reducing one's life to a minimal series of actions potentially leaves one free to be ready for something else, whatever that might be. Instead of encumbering oneself with cultivating social connections, going from office to office looking for work, of biding one's time waiting for sufficient funds to start a small business, or of making long journeys overseas to jobs that pay next to nothing, the key is not to pay attention, not to let these considerations crowd out what could be a profound reconfiguration of who one is and what value one has. Despite their inability to adhere to all the requirements usually associated with being a Muslim, these youth, nevertheless, seek within Islam a way of attaining self-value, of becoming a real person. But it is a tentative identification. Instead of using it as a platform through which to engage confidently in a wider world of economic activities, family responsibilities, and social exchange, it is almost as if all "the decks are cleared" to live a rudimentary understanding of a "Muslim life." The notion of *tawhid*, for example, is not so much the sense that Allah is what encompasses all that exists, but is rather the ability to find a mechanism that "flattens" out the hierarchies of status and privilege that permeate Cameroon. Here, the assumed minimalism is not so much a way of not only refusing the conventional practices of individual success, but a means of not being intimidated by it, of having to take it seriously, and of making it ordinary and mundane.

For many youth in New Bell now, the interface with the market appears sometimes reduced to the most petty of initiatives. Many youth with no job or trade get up early in the morning to intercept small items from those on their way to the market to sell, or during the early stages of opening their stalls or shops. This prolific but gentle looting never aims to amass large quantities, but is just enough either to make the items taken that which will be consumed for the day or sold for any price available. To do the minimal is what can be guaranteed and anticipated, in a merging of necessity and expectation that puts aside the ever-increasing gaps between these two notions that have characterized so much of urban mentality. After the looting, there is a ritualistic recitation of the items acquired, a roll call where they are then bartered or matched to running lists to which neighbors are the usual contributors: "If you happen to come across a broom [for example], would you let me know?" Without wages or large bankrolls or scams behind them, the "minimalists" are forced to make every opportunity count. In a country like Cameroon, where economic success is largely viewed as a matter of grand theft, the focus on a minimal life is often viewed, then, as a means of keeping theft itself to a minimum. Even as youth acknowledge that Islam strictly forbids stealing, many simply see that these minimal thefts are the closest they are going to come to adhere to such a prescription.

In fact, for the youth who make up the majority of these quarters, there are few apologies for the extent to which theft constitutes a daily living and the way the market itself seems to concede to this thievery as a kind of excise tax. As more players use the market, there are more participants that slip from any effective control. As more items are smuggled from loosely controlled borders and docks or are dumped in large volumes at neoliberalized ports of call, profits are reduced for many entrepreneurs, in turn reducing the ability to maintain adequate control and storage. An indifference to theft escalates; but the more thieves there are, again, the smaller the takings, the lower the expectations. It is not uncommon to see middle-age men still residing in the house of their parents, even subletting out their rooms for a little cash, while sleeping by the side of the house. In a country where barely 2% of school graduates will find formal employment, in these neighborhoods in particular, school attendance is a rarity; the minimal can be attained for minimum effort.

When New Bell was first designated as the primary site for permanent African urban residence by the colonial regime, it was an intense laboratory of entrepreneurship, as the convergence of peoples from different towns and villages of the exterior gave rise to new forms of collaborative effort that largely remained opaque to the scrutiny of the authorities. Artisans, traders, tailors, vulcanicians, and mechanics of all kinds helped secure an economic platform on which many households were able to secure land, build homes, and invest in a so-called modern urban future for their children (Schler 2003). Although Muslims were included in such accumulation, the emphasis on maintaining strong community cohesion meant that few set up operations or residence in other parts of the city, and investment in secular education was not a strong priority. There was almost a symbiotic attachment to the market, as if venturing too far away into other territories and occupations would pull at the entrenched rhythms of publicly visible trade and prayer.

Today, New Bell remains full of entrepreneurship and improvised making-do, but there are simply too many making too many demands on available resources. Physical, built, and social environments are progressively eroded by overuse, the lack of money for repair and rehabilitation, and the incessant shortcuts and improvised uses of objects, tools, and spaces, with little being replenished or renewed, and where the discarded remains in plain sight. In a market area with a protracted history of countless performances, where so many have attempted to make their existence relevant to so many others, a density of actual or potential interference has become a legacy. For everything that is attempted, it is not clear just who the endeavor will implicate, and it is never certain just who has to be looked out for, who will demand a cut of the proceeds, or who will see it as their duty to remind the enterprising individual of his or her obligations.

In economic sectors that have become vastly overcrowded, and thus where the need to come up with something new is incumbent upon anyone who wants to emerge from the crowd and eke out a little bit of profit, the improvisation stands out like an ambulance on a choked highway, where everyone subsequently tries to follow the path-breaking move. Again, under such conditions, it is difficult for youth to make plans, to project into the future, to pace oneself with a series of advancing steps geared to some overarching objective, particularly when the state, at all levels, no longer cares what happens, and where politics is itself the pursuit of parasitism.

Still, in the scores of neighborhood markets that operate with small margins across the rest of the city, the indiscriminate valuation of goods that has emerged from the daily thefts rampant in the central market has generated certain expansive effects. Intended or not, the reduction of livelihoods by youth to a certain bare minimum, undertaken in order not to be cluttered with or boxed in by social mores, institutional norms, or work with little payoff, in a small way accomplishes the very opening up and expansions they say they want to be ready for. If not necessarily directly applicable to their own individual lives, a practice has emerged whereby, in addition to the sale of the usual array of commodities, various items, services, and prospects are bundled together and sold as such. For example, boxes of pasta are bundled with reparations of household water taps as well as with opportunities to acquire aluminum roofing materials that are purportedly on their way to the area after "falling off a truck" at the Nigerian border. Different materials—commodities, information, services, commitments, affiliations—are converged into a single unit of sale and, as such, markets are opened up to the participation of a wider range of actors looking for opportunities, proclaiming skills and insider information, or looking to be that extra person needed to complete transactions when some kind of labor is involved. By removing things from set, privileged positions or removing them from accustomed frameworks of use and regard, there is potentially greater latitude to get whatever exists in the market into more expansive and intensified circulation. Here, things and services try to "piggyback" their way into wider dissemination through their often highly unconventional associations with other things.

Although defying economic common sense, both excess and scarcity are brought together to get what can be marketed—which is now nearly everything—to move. Hoarding and profit taking, of course, continue to exist, yet this dispersion of the minimalist sensibilities of New Bell youth, which results in a freeing up of the conventional relations of value between goods and things, enables, by default, a kind of mediation between two problematic tendencies: on the one hand, the tendency of urban residents to narrow the scope of their social worlds to the familiar tropes of ethnicity and family as the arenas through which some kind of trust can be guaranteed; on the other, the tendency to try and seize chances opportunistically to involve oneself in scenarios, deals, and networks that do not obligate any particular course of action or responsibility. Here, being in the "right way" demands a sense of invention, not just adherence to the rules, but also not simply any kind of invention, but rather one that takes what others are doing into some new kind of consideration, that attempts to find value in what they are doing so that their lives can be "bundled," however momentarily, to one's own.

Whether such a practice may be just a momentary holding pattern, as *Service sociale* faces either implosion by depending too much on too few people and resources, or dissipation altogether as its residents rampantly become small pieces in the games of much more powerful others, remains to be seen.

Bangkok

In New Bell, Islam was popularly referred by some youth as the instrument through which one could risk doing the minimum as a means of keeping oneself available for something big and transformative, even if there were no guarantees that such change would ever come. In the following story from Bangkok, Muslims do something of the inverse; they focus on Islam as the instrument for a collaborative entrepreneurship with expanded scope as an essential feature of the ability to sustain the minimal identification of themselves as Muslims, where such an identification has a semblance of efficacy.

Soi Sukhumvit 3 is at the heart of the Middle East quarter in Bangkok. With its restaurants and *shish* cafés, its mosques lodged across from apartment buildings and profligate telephone bureaus, the quarter anchors the intersection of Arabs and Africans from all over the world. From young men filling the 550 rooms at the Grace Hotel, in both temporary and prolonged respites from the sexual constrictions of home, to the black *chador*-clad women with a passion for shopping, the area harbors a plethora of agendas and proclivities. The quarter is firmly ensconced in the Sukhumvit district—a large area of tourists, multistory condominium developments, upscale and nondescript hotels, commercial sex zones, and a vibrant street economy that shifts character daily, depending on the time of day. Although retaining some basic segmentation according to commercial activity and residential capacity, the main thoroughfares are a mélange of diversities, of the covered and the uncovered, the religious and the hedonistic, families and singles.

Small Arab *commerçants* specializing in jewelry, textiles, and leather goods were able to consolidate territory in a district that largely grew without systematic planning or regulation—a process facilitated by the gaps created through competing trajectories of infrastructural developments, wildly fluctuating land valuation, and political expediency. The close proximity of the Middle East quarter to the sex and tourist businesses provided it both a measure of stability and invisibility. Muslims have been an intrinsic part of the city for a long time, constituting the bulk of the crews that built the major canals eastward from the royal center under Rama III during the mid 19th century. In return, Muslims were ceded land along the banks of the canals, where to this day are lined scores of mosques (Boontharm 2005). The current Middle East quarter is located just below a major node in this canal system, along which runs Petchaburi Road, which at the time of the quarter's initial settlement was a rambunctious avenue of various illicit trades.

Given the difficulties Arabs and Muslims face in securing visas, Bangkok has become a favored vacation destination, particularly because its competitive retail prices and flexible customs policies support acquisitions of all kinds. Although the incessant low-intensity warfare waged by Muslims in southern Thailand has raised some concerns about the influx of visitors from the Arab world, these "troubles" are largely apprehended in very local and national terms. Although Bangkok remains a critical locus for the intersection of multiple illicit economies, and for even confounding clear distinctions between the licit and illicit, these are opportunities seized upon by many different nationalities, and so there is nothing particularly problematic about the status of Arabs within the largely urban economy.

What is then striking about the visible complexion of the quarter is the close proximity of actors from various positions across the Muslim world enacting often highly divergent agendas. Although comments and criticisms may be made, no one agenda or orientation dominates, as space for the expression of a wide range of particularities is somehow found. Scores of different venues for prayer are found in light of different backgrounds and inclinations. There are small cafés for Arab men to hang out with their Thai girlfriends next to restaurants for religiously highly disciplined families and these are next to businesses that adhere obsessively to what they say they do, next to those who make no effort to do what they claim. Whatever is done is undertaken largely because it wants to be done. In a context of such heterogeneity, no one could hope to impose their will, and in a city that guarantees little security amid incessant change, there is little basis from which to determine who is being threatened or excluded. Although there are no places that make room for all, Sukhumvit remains a district where almost any identity can find a room.

This brief exposition is offered to situate what is to come: On the night of the Qana massacre in Lebanon, July 2006, a large crowd gathers at the glittery Egyptian al-Nasir restaurant—which wraps itself boldly around a key passageway on Soi Sukhumvit 3—and is glued to one or more of the four large television screens tuned to Al Arabiyya and Al Jazeera. The grisly images dampen the usually festive atmosphere that prevails, as people seethe in yet another reminder of humiliation and helplessness. Black plastic nose and mouth coverings are dropped to permit some of the older women to bleat out their anguish, pipes are inhaled more deeply as in an act of fortification, and hands shaped as pistols are pointed to Condoleezza Rice and the assortment of Israeli officials paraded in front of the cameras.

I am sitting at a large table to which individual customers are often directed, with two Jordanians, a Togolese, Somalian, Nigerian, two Indonesians, and three from Bahrain, all men. Because the place is open until five o'clock in the morning, it is a convenient place to be out in public. The only language everyone at the table has in common is English and a little bit of Arabic, mostly derived from Quranic studies for those not originating in the Middle East. The conversation began awkwardly, a few stray comments stemming from the obligation of the entire restaurant to pay attention to the images being screened. I am clearly the eldest at the table—no one else older than 30, I initially surmised (and later confirmed). The obligation to speak in face of what was being shown, coupled with the rapid exhaustion of the obvious expressions of anger and cynicism, led to several mundane queries regarding what people were doing in Bangkok—a process always subject, itself, to a kind of obligatory dissimulation. Even if one is engaged in the most boring of forthright formal work, the reputation of the city as a smuggler's paradise (not really deserved) usually means that individuals want to lend some sense of excitement and possibility to their existence in the city.

The discussion quickly picks up a sense of urgency, punctuated with invocations of the need for something to be done. But here the something to be done is not in the form of revenge or the customary litanies of the need for the *umma* to come together to exert its power, or to overcome sectarian differences. Rather, it is how those gathered at the table could use this opportunity that a particular city provided—as one concretization of its "cityness"—to do something that would enable them to keep going. The aspiration at times assumed strong overtones, such as, "Fuck this shit; we always have to be bothered by what is done to us, well let's do something that shows that we are not bothered."

During the course of several hours, it was evident that each person had moved a great deal through various cities and that Bangkok was not a necessary haven, intended or final destination, nor preferred outpost of opportunity. For most, it was an almost accidental arrival, a chance taken for cheap commodities or a job as an accountant. For others, the stories were highly peculiar. For one, it was a place to wait out clearance for "refugee placement"; for another, a familial enforced apprenticeship with an uncle following a mishap with the law in Jordan; and for still another, the absconding of funds intended as a scholarship for a university far away.

Almost all had arrived in the city via places other than home, as if passed on by the uncertainties of other circumstances. Each claimed a range of small troubles—being too or insufficiently religious, refusing the imposition of prospective spouses, familial jealousies, and intractable problems with more powerful elders. Nothing had specifically prepared them for what they were currently doing, and, with few exceptions, livelihoods were completely opportunistic. A brief liaison with a woman had left a more enduring friendship with a brother who worked in a travel agency that often needed freelance photographers to take shoots of resorts for Arabic magazines, a third party was needed to hold different consignments of gems being hedged against other transactions outside Thailand for which these consignments were a kind of collateral, and an uncle had come to Thailand in the 1970s to invest in a factory that produced waxed cloth and had left a few commercial and residential properties to be managed when he moved on to China. Instead of identifying and consolidating particular occupational specializations, each had used initial footholds as ways of speculating on other activities.

New coworkers, settings, patrons, neighborhoods, or cities did not offer necessarily more money, but different opportunities and networks. To expand the circumference of possibilities, any modicum of security in the present had to be relinquished and forgotten, even if the speculation was directed to what could be gained by articulating disparate jobs, identities, and locations. In other words, each conveyed a curiosity and determination not to stay put, to see what else they could do, where else they could go. Such maneuvers were not to substitute a more promising life for one perceived as lacking, but rather to extend experiences and skills outward into new "neighborhoods" and uses. Their perception was that this objective could not be a matter of explicit planning, but of a willingness to eject themselves out of whatever constituted their current conditions.

Of course, such transitions were not often so smooth. Some were waiting for money to be sent from elsewhere; almost all had some debts to pay and obligations to get out of. Yet in all of this, there remained in our discussions during the course of the next several weeks a willingness to incur new responsibilities and to intensify a sense of being implicated in the lives of others. This was the case even when it came to an abstract offering of friends and relatives as possible resources for those who, before this night, were complete strangers. Someone knew of a shipping company who had "special" relationships with various customs authorities, someone else had contacts with agents adept at acquiring highly cut-rate airline tickets, someone had a warehouse of auto parts with nowhere to go, and still someone else had a sister in Rome looking for flat-mates. The Somali guy had once worked as a janitor in Dubai and would find unused and underregulated spaces for Senegalese money merchants to set up shop, in turn financing Nigerian electronics transactions, which brought in Nandi merchants from Bunia who did mineral concession deals with Malaysian holding companies, which in turn brought in other Somalians to drive trucks from Mombassa to the Great Lakes. Someone else had ideas about how to set up a Web order cut-rate provisioning system for migrant construction crews across the Middle East. In this inventory of "possessions," the mundane, sinister, and singular are collapsed in a running list looking for a frame that could cohere a means in which everyone gathered could somehow be enrolled in some conjoint project.

After several weeks, preexisting travel plans and other responsibilities made it difficult to sustain these conversations in their prior form. The Blackberries and address books of each participant increased significantly in volume, and agreements were made to try out a small number of different trading transactions involving Lagos, Dubai, Rayong (Thailand), and Udjung Padang (Indonesia) among small clusters of the participants, eventually to see how these could be concretely broadened to involve the interests and resources of others. Because I was really the odd one out in this grouping, in terms of age, profession, and place of residence, I could really only offer limited support to the number of ventures to be tried, and so do not know how the subsequent mechanics will unfold. But the point here is not in the details of the deals, but in the sentiments that underline them, and the motivations professed for their undertaking.

Because the participants wanted to be "smart" about what they did—not only in terms of getting away with shortcuts or working in risky commercial environments—but to exude to some larger abstract audience that being Muslims was itself something "smart." That being Muslim was neither the embodiment of a history of commercial proficiency or an impediment to be overcome, but an opportunity to do business in a way that was creative, daring, and successful. It was being smart at a game that did not necessarily belong to Muslims, to the exclusion of others, but whose practices and efficacy could be felt as an extension of the practice and efficacy of Islam itself. As one Jordanian participant liked to say, "I have to make the right moves five times a day, and the right time is always right on time." Still, the game necessitated, unlike those "minimal" youth in Douala, a need to be further out into the larger world as a means of being able to "hold oneself together."

The Practice of Islam as the Practice of the Emergent

Islam has long been a locus of business—a means of cohering disparate localities and actors into collaborations that sought expanded reach for the activities in which they were engaged (Ho 2004). Local specificities—in language, social practice, and geopolitical positioning—could be articulated through the elaboration of a series of practices and discourses that could be shared across various divides, constituting a platform of mutual recognition. What such a commonality could do—in other words, its generative possibilities—would far outweigh any experience of rootedness or a need for a definitive reference of belonging (Abaza 2002; Hassan 2002). Although the concrete possibilities and supports for disparate localities being able to have this something in common had to be fought for when threatened, such commonality was to be deployed as a means of extending the reach of localities into territories where they would be inevitably compelled to come up with revised versions of themselves—in other words, that held in common was deployed to generate difference. Efforts on the part of others to sum up, apprehend, and confine the capacities of Muslims would always be "one step behind," always partial in their understandings and anticipations. In a not dissimilar set of sentiments, the urgency of this group to do something was motivated by a desire not to succumb to the images others might have of them, not to do what was expected, and to undermine the plans and apprehensions of those others through the intricacy of dealings that had no clear outcome other than to keep things open.

It is hard to predict just what skills and performances will be necessary to eke some kind of advantage from territories that are both under more proficient surveillance yet, at the same time, often off the maps of policy makers and developers. Yet, if long-term change of lives and creative engagement are to be viable, these singular local operations must be articulated across platforms of mobilization and belonging that value these singularities, and at the same time network them in coordinated actions and investments (AlSayyad and Castells 2002; Saint-Blancat 2002). In this way, Islam operates as a gestational form of urban correspondence—relating the initiatives, styles, interpretations, and experiences of different kinds of Muslims; opening up circumscribed resource bases onto a wider range of opportunities, even under conditions of intense scrutiny and fear (Haenni 2005).

Although the practice of Islam embodies a series of seemingly clear coordinates where it is evident what Muslims must do to perform their religious identity concretely, the increasingly complex challenges posed by "being Muslim" in a larger world exceed the conventional grammars of practice. For faith for many is not simply a matter of having an anchor in turbulent political and economic times, but to be a Muslim "for something"—to make one's position as a Muslim count in trying both to adapt to and to change the circumstances within which a persons finds him- or herself. For these youth in Bangkok (as well as for many others with whom I have worked in Dakar, Phnom Penh, Abidjan, and Douala), various forms of a militant assertion of religious identity, although seemingly emotionally gratifying, does little in terms of enabling Islam actually to do something different in the world.

This insufficiency and the need to enhance the seepage of the religion—both as an intact framework of guidelines for living and as a means of dealing with matters of concern—is incisively expressed by the Marseilles–based hip-hop crew IAM. Five Muslim men are at its core plus associates—Muslims from Sicily, Tunisia, Gambia, and Algeria, with pre-Islamic names like Akehnaton, Shurik'n, and Menelik, who claim Marseilles as an extraterrestrial place—taking the growing sense of Muslims being confined to a new spatial arena. Marseilles becomes Mars—more than the abbreviated nickname for the city, but a city that belongs nowhere, on which one suspects life but it is not clear what life has existed or could exist. At the same time, the realities in IAM's songs of the concrete zones of HLM (habitation á loyer modéré) projects built on the almost lunar landscape to the north of the city are conveyed as intergalactic video games that render the wounds of the street, the emptiness of unemployed futures, and the territorial constrictions exerted by competing gangs and political Mafia like a cartoon, disembodied from history, denied politics, but at the same time extricating the icons of nonwestern civilization from the obligation to conventional historical narratives.

Akhenaton thus can be an imam in the hood, whose sister's head is properly covered even if her ass isn't. It is this willingness to face one's situation with the determination of ethics even if one knows one lives in nothing more than a prison where no discourse, no violence can really cover one's back. Like the *Beurs* movement that initially promoted a prointegrationist strategy, IAM could have announced, as one of their tracks is entitled, "*J'aurais pu croire en l'Occident ("I could have believed in the West")*." But they have refused, because it would have rendered the notion of belief impossible. In other words, the precariousness in the relationship of French Arabs and Africans with Europe is not because of the impediments to belief. They were prepared to believe; they wanted to believe, but they were "sliced" out of the picture, instructed as to what could be made visible, what could be talked about and how. As a result, Freeman of IAM raps, "take all that which is visible and visualized—lives, targets, mirages. Defend with fervor all this which is mistargeted and bizarre, spent casings and face emaciated, visible features, heritages, missiles, and trails, missive and visa, illegible epitaph."

In tens of thousands of *jum'a khutba* heard around the world, the imam will make reference to the situation of Muslims in Afghanistan, Chechnya, Iraq, and especially Palestine. Many of the tracks in IAM albums also deal with these topics, but with a twist. Thus, one member of the group Shurik'n would say that Palestine is not waiting to be a state, but rather is something for "all of those which survive, mothers Muslim or Jewish who do not dream of power; all of those without affection, people without aversion who keep the history as if a furious and deforming version of it. A limpid strategy, not the apology of emptiness."

Unlike those who apologize for the emptiness of the HLM Solidarité, that huge expanse of concrete barriers, squatted flats, vacancy, and regimentation—either those who are sorry about the conditions in which African and Arabs, French or non-French are condemned to live or those who are apologists for the styles of emptiness, the drugs, the rape, the bitterness—IAM speak as Muslims to the abandoned industrial parks and wasted infrastructure as spaces waiting to happen, as gifts to the process of bringing into play various influences, logic, moral sensibilities, and ways of making money and lives.

IAM are the offspring of a generation that had to delink themselves from tradition to immigrate and to reinvent a truncated, disembodied tradition to compensate for the inability really to participate in a modernity responsible for the very inadequacy of that tradition. Muslim youth are caught in a space where family cannot be denied, but neither can a partial sense of connection to a past that is unable to connect be embodied. At all costs one cannot be an instrument or occasion for French "moderns" to criticize Islam, so most Muslim youth of Marseilles have little but their individual initiatives to consider in making life better.

In a not dissimilar way, the group in Bangkok talks about the still intact ports of decaying secondary cities, the old commercial districts of Dubai and Karachi, or the seemingly endless expanses of the periurban areas of Ho Chi Minh City and Jakarta with their jumbled up landscapes of failed and new industrial and commercial projects as places "waiting to happen." Given all the places that Muslims are either under threat, scrutiny, or denied access to, the world still makes available many places of opportunity—not clearly discernible and requiring piecing together particular forms of collaboration, exchange, and movement. As economic gamesmanship becomes increasingly cutthroat and consuming of an expanse of human energies, the question becomes how religion can be put to work to facilitate the kinds of collaborations needed to cultivate the opportunities that lie in waiting.

No one in the group assembled in Bangkok is a genius at anything; there are no big entrepreneurs, academics, theologians, or even criminals. Everyone is looking for an angle, a way out of either self-deprecation or collective humiliation, as well as some relative autonomy and money to make their own lives. So nothing is well thought out. These are not sophisticated conceptual formulations; they are going more on instinct, believing that the way forward is about using what little they have in common, among themselves and other Muslims that they do and could know, to do more for themselves by virtue of doing more for the religion. Not in rededicating themselves to being "good Muslims" in the way this notion is usually associated, but in the sense that being "a good Muslim" means working with other Muslims to do something that no one thought could be pulled off in areas of entrepreneurship and in sites where few are paying attention.

In some respects these discussions were hardly that different from the thousands that take place on a daily basis among all kinds of partners trying to do deals. Yet, here there was a self-consciousness about generating a new sense of religious responsibility that addressed the exigency to take risks. The working assumption here is that a faith under threat requires risk. But risk needs a sense of the subversive in that it mustconnect places and economic activities and actors that, on the surface don't go together, yet still maintain the desire to produce viable livelihoods. Several aspirations are then conjoined, and the very possibility that they could be conjoined is attributed to their very existence as Muslims.

10

Being Young, Muslim, and American in Brooklyn

Moustafa Bayoumi

Rami is reciting in Arabic. The 19-year-old Palestinian American is quoting one of his favorite verses in the Quran, from Surah *At-Tawbah* (Repentance):

> Say: If your fathers, and your sons and your brothers and your spouses and your clan and the worldly goods which you have acquired, and the commerce whereof you fear a decline, and the dwellings in which you take pleasure—[if all of these] are dearer to you than God and His Apostle and the struggle in His cause, then wait until God makes manifest His will; and [know that] God does not grace iniquitous folk with His guidance. (9:24)

He sits back on his plastic chair and, under the glare of the doughnut shop lights, the smile on his face is obvious. For the last four years, the young man has been trying something quite new to him: a proper Muslim life. This way of living, which offers him guidance, solace, and community, has become especially important now because Rami no longer lives with his father, who was picked up for immigration violations in Brooklyn under the law enforcement dragnet directed at Arabs and Muslims in the United States following the September 11, 2001, terrorist attacks.

Rami's own circumstances then help explain why the young man finds this verse particularly meaningful. Worldly goods, worldly pleasures, and the comforts of family have been disrupted. On Mondays, for example, he drives three hours each way to visit his father in a New Jersey detention center. His family has spent thousands of dollars on lawyers, trying to get his father out of jail. After the latest round in immigration court, they believe the saga will finally end soon, but not well. The lawyers have told them to expect that the father will be deported back to Jordan. Since his father's incarceration, Rami has turned more deliberately to Islam.

When Rami recited this verse to me, it was a Sunday night in July 2006. I was in a Dunkin' Donuts with him in Bay Ridge, Brooklyn, home to one of New York City's largest Arab American communities. Israel had just begun bombing Lebanon a few days earlier. With us was Rami's friend Ezzat, a portly young Lebanese American who was born in the port city of Tripoli and who is one of several informal mentors to Rami. Ezzat is well informed about Islam and about Middle Eastern politics, and Rami looks to him for knowledge and guidance. We were joined later by three more young Lebanese American men and an Egyptian American, and the night's discussions swung easily around Hezbollah and Lebanon, around Israel and politics, and around cars, work, and school (but not women). Islam, however, remained central, especially for Rami and Ezzat. Our evening, as is often the case, didn't end until after 2 AM.

Rami's recitation from *At-Tawbah* didn't come out of nowhere. Ezzat and he had been telling me about his and Rami's devotion to Islam, and he related how he had been studying *aqeedah* (theology) for a year and a half now. He then told us about the time that his more secular father had screamed at him in anger. The devout son had been reading the Quran when the time for prayer descended. Ezzat prepared for his prostrations and asked his father, as he often did, if he would join him in prayer. This time he was finally successful. But his father told him that, with Ezzat's superior knowledge of Quran, Ezzat should lead the prayer, and so he did. Aloud, he read the ninth sura, which includes this key verse: "O you who have attained to faith! Do not take your fathers and brothers for allies if a denial of the truth is dearer to them than faith; for those of you who ally themselves with them—it is they, they who are evildoers" (9:23).

The men finished their prayers. Ezzat's father silently turned his head from side to side and then exploded. "Are you saying I'm a *kaffir* [nonbeliever]?!" he yelled at Ezzat, who defensively replied that he was just reciting the Quran.

When he told us the story, Ezzat laughed, and this prompted Rami to remember how much he admires the next verse. The conversation led me to ask them if they believe their generation is more pious than the last. Ezzat answered, but with the air that I had asked an obvious question. Of course, he replied, but not because of the faith of individuals. This is a historical trend, he explained. Each generation for the past 50 years has been getting more religious, he said, but still they aren't religious enough. Satellite television provided him with his evidence. "Look at all those Egyptian movies from the 1950s," he said, explaining how "everyone is drinking whisky" in them, and how the characters all look like they're trying hard to mimic westerners. He described the progression for me. His generation's parents are more religious than their grandparents, and today's generation is more religious than its forerunner. But still it's not enough, according to the young man. "There are a lot of Muslims," Ezzat says, "but there is no Islam."

Brooklyn's Arab Muslim Youth

Since 2005, I have been spending time with people like Rami and Ezzat while researching a book I had been writing on Arab American youth (defined for my project as those between 18–29 years of age) from Brooklyn, New York (Bayoumi 2008).[1] I spent three years in regular contact with scores of young Arab Americans, especially young Arab Muslim Americans, in an attempt to understand their lives. (My access was facilitated by the fact that I, too, come from an Arab and Muslim background, although I am older by at least a decade than those I spent time with.) I chose Brooklyn as the location for several reasons. For one, New York City has the largest Arab population in the United States according to the 2000 U.S. Census (de la Cruz and Brittingham 2003: 7). The city has approximately 70,000 Arab Americans (de la Cruz and Brittingham 2005: 7), and more live in Brooklyn (approximately 35,000) than in any other borough (U.S. Census Bureau 2000).[2] The U.S. Census does not tally religious affiliation, but one study puts New York City's Muslim population at 600,000 (with Brooklyn and Queens having the largest Muslim populations) (Beshkin 2001).

Brooklyn's Arab and Muslim populations also tend to be made up of newer arrivals to the country. According to the 2000 Census, for example, 46% of Arab Americans nationally arrived between 1990 and 2000 (de la Cruz and Brittingham 2005: 9).

As with most immigrant populations, both Arab and Muslim Americans are younger than the general population. Twenty-one percent of the American public is between 18 and 30 years of age; 30% of American Muslims are (Pew Research Center 2007: 16).

The median age of Arab Americans is 31 years, compared with 35 years for the whole of the United States (Samhan 2003).[3] What this means is that many young Arabs and Muslims have no significant adult experience of the world prior to September 11, 2001. And, although nationally Arabs and Muslims are generally more affluent than average Americans, many in Brooklyn come from working-class backgrounds. In this chapter, I focus primarily on second-generation college-age and college-attending (or college-educated) Arab Muslim American men that I encountered through my study. (The vast majority of men I encountered fell into this category. Women would be another study.)

Rami and Ezzat are in many ways typical of this new generation of male Muslim youth in Brooklyn, New York. Many of today's young Muslim men who have been raised in the United States and entered adulthood after the terrorist attacks of September 11, 2001, see themselves as substantially more pious than their parents' generation, which was largely made up of immigrants to the nation. Moreover, they often separate themselves spatially and socially from the wider society, achieving a kind of group solidarity with other young Muslim males. From this group sensibility, they then reintegrate collectively into larger society, but often with the express purpose of propagating the faith.

Survey data bear out the observation that the younger generation is more pious, and this trend is found not just in Brooklyn, but also across the United States. According to a 2007 Pew Research Study on Muslim Americans, 50% of American Muslims age 18 to 29 report attending a mosque weekly or more often, compared with 35% of American Muslims older than 30. Sixty percent of these young American Muslims (age 18–29 years), moreover, consider themselves "Muslim first" (as opposed to "American first"). That percentage drops to 41% for American Muslims older than 30 years of age. As a point of comparison, 59% of Christian Americans, according to another study, report identifying as Christian first, American second (Cable News Network 2007).

This growing religious affiliation and identification should be considered, at least in part, in the context of the "war on terror." Since the attacks of September 11, 2001, state repression aimed at Muslims has increased markedly, and generalized hostility against Muslims has grown significantly. Hate crimes against Arabs, Muslims, and those assumed to be Arab or Muslim shot up 1,700% during the first six months after September 11, 2001, and have never returned to pre-2001 levels (Human Rights Watch 2002: 4; Victims of Crime 2003). Specific policing strategies have also been aimed specifically at Muslim populations. Special registration, for example, required nonimmigrant males from 24 Muslim majority countries to register with the government, and that program led to the initiation of deportation proceedings against almost 14,000 people (Bayoumi 2006b). The government also began what *The Washington Post* called "a sprawling inquiry" into hundreds of Arab- or Muslim-owned small businesses for any financial irregularities, in the event that these "small scams" were possibly funding terrorist activity (Mintz and Farah 2002). Such inquiries frequently swept up people who had no connection to terrorism, but had some unresolved immigration issues, such as

Rami's father. And racial profiling against Arabs and Muslims was essentially legalized in 2003, when President Bush ordered a ban on the practice but included "exceptions permitting use of race and ethnicity to combat potential terrorist attacks".[4]

The degree of animosity against Muslims in the general culture has also been studied. A 2004 Cornell University study found that 44% of Americans believe that some restrictions of civil liberties by the government is necessary for Muslim Americans (Nisbet and Shanahan 2004: 6). A USA/Today Gallup Poll from August 2006 discovered that 39% of Americans admit to holding "at least some prejudice" against Muslims. And the 2007 Pew study found such prejudice affects Muslims younger than 30 more than those older than 30.[5] Forty-two percent of American Muslims age 18 to 29 (compared with 29% of older Muslims) report having experienced "verbal taunts, been treated with suspicion, been physically threatened or attacked, or been targeted by police because they are Muslims" during the past year (Pew Research Center 2003: 38). Notably, 40% of younger American Muslims also report that they received expressions of support because they were Muslim (Pew Research Center 2003: 37–38).

For many American Muslim youth, the new landscape is daunting and defining. They are in the eye of today's security storm. The state apparatus increasingly encroaches on their lives and lays suspicion on the most mundane of their activities. The New York City Police Department, for example, released a report in August 2007 titled "Radicalization in the West: The Homegrown Threat," which claimed that the "emerging threat" to law enforcement resides with "unremarkable" Muslim men younger than 35 years of age who visit what the reports dubs "terrorism incubators": mosques, "cafés, cab driver hangouts, flophouses, prisons, student associations, nongovernmental organizations, hookah (water pipe) bars, butcher shops and book stores" (Silber and Bhatt 2007: 20). By focusing not on probable cause of criminal activity, but on ordinary and unremarkable behavior, the report essentially criminalizes any and all young Muslim males who congregate together.

How have Brooklyn's young Muslims responded to this inhospitable environment? There have been several reactions that I witnessed during my research. Some young people have downplayed their ethnicity and their religion, and have sought to "pass" as non-Muslim and non-Arab.[6] In Brooklyn, that often meant assuming a Spanish-sounding name and passing oneself off as Latino (Bayoumi 2006a: 23). (Some Muslims have gone so far as to seek legal name changes to escape discrimination.) Others have already left the country or are considering leaving the country when the opportunity arises (Bayoumi 2008). Because the U.S. government does not tally migration out of the country, we do not know how many people this includes, although one community leader told me in 2006 that he believes the Arab American community in Bay Ridge, Brooklyn, has dwindled by about 20% since 2001 (Bayoumi 2006a: 23).

But the most evident reaction among Brooklyn's young Muslim men to the current inhospitable environment has been to develop a strong sense of group solidarity, turning the harsh spotlight that currently shines on Islam and Muslims around, and in so doing engaging in efforts to propagate the faith. In this way, these young people seek to reinforce their sense of an Islamic identity while they educate themselves and others in what they understand to be the true message of Islam. One could express the situation in another way: Rather than allowing the culture to define them, today's young Muslims exhibit a determination to define themselves. These self-definitions, moreover, acknowledge and enhance both their western and Muslim backgrounds simultaneously, finding no contradiction (because there really is none) between the two.

This sense of strong solidarity is further emphasized by the places where they congregate. Young male Muslims currently tend to associate with each other in specific geographies in the city, including doughnut shops, *shisha* cafés, and club rooms on university campuses, where they discuss religion and, to a lesser extent, politics (but never to plot terrorist violence, as alleged by the New York City Police Department report). What many people told me throughout the course of my research was that such geographies are preferable to young Muslim Americans in part because they offer some respite from the cultural, religious, and financial pressures of the outside world. Although in a place like Lebanon, Dunkin' Donuts symbolizes the (often destructive) penetration of American capital into the local economy, in Brooklyn it is almost the opposite. These shops are usually owned by other Muslims, who counsel their Muslim customers on what products they can eat or drink (i.e., don't contain pork by-products). For the young working-class Muslim men of Bay Ridge, doughnut shops are advantageous. With just a few dollars, they can sit around for hours and, with no alcohol served, resist the temptations to engage in anything forbidden or contrary to Islamic law and custom.

Similar arguments are made by the youth who hang out in the *shisha* cafés. Since 2001, the presence of *shisha* cafés has expanded significantly in Bay Ridge, Brooklyn. (In 2001, there were three or four in Bay Ridge, which now counts approximately eight.) Unlike the *shisha* clubs in Manhattan, which serve a mixed (largely non-Arab non-Muslim) population and trade in exoticism, these cafés have a very simple decor and an overwhelmingly Arab clientele, including many second-generation young men who spend many hours there.

(Arab and Muslim women can be found there as well, but in much smaller numbers, and the very pious tend to avoid the *shisha* cafés. Their absence, however, is not absolute. Rami, for example, occasionally visits a *shisha* café if some extended friends are there.) When I ask the young people why they come to the *shisha* cafés, the answer is almost always the same. They report that it is much better to be there than in a typical American club, as they (or their older brothers, if they are too young) used to do before 9/11. In a *shisha* café, they also spend only $5 or $6 for the evening (compared with the $40 or so that a dance club requires). Moreover, they aren't breaking any religious precepts by being there, and they are learning about themselves through conversations with other Arabs and Muslims.

This is what Fadi, a young Palestinian American, told me one night at Meena House, one of the popular *shisha* cafés in Bay Ridge, Brooklyn. He also described to me the conflicts he has in his day-to-day college student life and offered his explanation as to why he identifies now more forcefully with his Arab identity and his religion. "We get into arguments all the time with people who say all kinds of things against Islam and Arabs," he said, "so we have to know where we come from." At Meena House, the young men talk about how to frame their debates with their schoolmate interlocutors.

And university campuses, as in years past, are also central locations where young Muslims congregate (each campus in New York City has a Muslim Students Association [MSA].) There are other locations as well. In Brooklyn, the Muslim Youth Center, in the neighborhood of Bensonhurst, offers a similar space, as do the mosques of Brooklyn and the various conferences and lectures hosted around the city on an almost weekly basis. In all of these locations, college-age Muslims play a dominant role, from organizing to participating in various functions, as they create a platform from which to understand themselves as Muslims and from which they exhibit and project their ideas of Islam onto American society.

More important than geography, however, is the function that these spaces enable. Largely away from the older, immigrant generation, these locations are where young American Muslims are coming together and finding solidarity with each other. In this context, young American Muslims are separating themselves for the purposes of taking charge of their own definitions of their faith and identity, and forging their own individual and collective futures. Through their efforts at solidarity and community building, they are producing leaders among their own, where leadership is based primarily on one's ability to demonstrate a command of Islam and its scholarly traditions and one's ability to communicate successfully in an American Muslim idiom.[7] (And although an earlier generation, namely my own, generally measured social success and status by one's ability to achieve a reputable career and earn a high income, this specific generation of young people often emphasizes levels of piety as a measure of individual achievement.)

Most important, these young people are *self-consciously* young, American, and Muslim. They understand that they have advantages that their parents didn't have, that they live in a period of heightened stereotyping against Islam, and that they are forming and leading a multiethnic and multicultural Muslim community in the West. They do not see their youth as a by-product of their circumstance. Rather, they understand their youth as a responsibility. Young Muslim Americans, in other words, constantly and self-consciously *create* and *recreate* their youth by seeing themselves and by functioning as a vanguard generation.

A Vanguard Generation

One can hear this sense of a vanguard position in their own words. Rami explained it to me this way on another occasion:

> Thirty years ago the Muslims were more cultural. They were new to the country and it was their way of fitting in. The *masajid* [mosques] didn't do anything. When [the earlier generation] first came, they just stayed in the *masjid*. But now [with] the second generation, the kids have grown up here, their English is good, and they interact with people as Muslims. . . . the generation before us wasn't into the *deen* [religion] at all. They were more cultural. But now, my generation is coming up, it has a sense of pride, a sense of a big movement.

The youth understand themselves, in other words, not just as Muslims, but as young Muslims with "pride" and with the responsibility inherent to being part of a religious "movement."

Rami and many in his generation explicitly see their participation in this movement as being part of a growing global revival of Islam (see also Cainkar 2004). They pay some attention to Muslim communities in the Middle East and South Asia and, as Ezzat stated, they believe that Muslims across the world in their generation are increasingly raising their *deen* (becoming more religious). They attribute the global revival to the fact that "people are asking questions now, more than ever before," as Rami put it. (He was including both Muslims and non-Muslims in his category of people asking questions.) For Muslims in the United States, he told me, a major reason stems from the current inhospitable environment:

When you're being attacked and you don't understand why. . . . And
you don't know what Islam says about terrorism, [then] you go to the
masjid and ask, and you sit down and hear, and [discover] you like the
masjid, and you come the next day and the next day, and all of a
sudden, you're like, oh! You're learning and you're into it.

This kind of group solidarity also reinforces several aspects of young
American Muslim identity, which in Brooklyn is generally suspicious of contemporary reformers and apologias that appear to collapse "Islamic" and "western" values into essentially the same thing. "A lot of modern scholars today will
tell you crazy stuff," Rami told me. (And I heard similar responses from many
others along the way.) "The secularist kind of Muslims tell you that homosexuality is okay, that *hijab*, don't wear it, whatever." He reported that most Muslims
he knows will not accept such arguments. Instead, he said, "people are swinging
the other way, the way the *deen* [religion] was, and that's the way it should be."

That these young American Muslims have little patience for self-described
"progressive Muslims" should not be interpreted as indicating opposition to all
aspects of American culture, however. In fact, many young Muslims repeatedly
emphasized to me their acknowledgment and appreciation for American multiculturalism, because it mirrors the diversity of the *umma*, the global Muslim
community. This generation feels bound far less by the ethnic and national
divisions that they feel limits the older, immigrant generation. National origin
matters little to the young Muslims, and race and ethnicity even less. Although
doughnut shops and *shisha* cafés are found primarily in ethnic enclave neighborhoods and thus draw a largely ethnically homogenous crowd, campus MSAs and
citywide Muslim events tend to be extremely multiethnic and very multiracial.
Moreover, many young Muslims explained to me (after I asked about their
futures) that marrying a good Muslim of any background was more important to
them than marrying someone from their own ethnic or national background. (It
is likely that cross-ethnic marriages among American Muslims will only increase
in the years to come.) Young Muslim Americans repeatedly refer positively to the
multiculturalism of their faith, interpreting it as evidence of Islam's universal
appeal within all contours of American society. Thus, although easily rejecting
what they see as western-style innovations or apologetics for Islam, young
American Muslims are defining their Islam within an American context even
while accepting and rejecting specific aspects of their American society.

Their self-consciously western Muslim identity is further emphasized
through their own educational endeavors. Many young Muslims in Brooklyn
today are seeking an Islamic education that speaks to their experiences. They
constantly reported to me that the immigrant generation preceding them
could not speak to the young people in a language and idiom that spoke to

their lives. The ability to speak Arabic well, and English fluently and idiomatically has become highly prized. Because leadership roles are also often assigned to peers who are judged more knowledgeable than others, a formal Islamic education is increasingly seen as an essential component of participating in the Muslim community.

What has become increasingly popular in recent years, then, are seminars by burgeoning Islamic educational organizations. One such initiative is AlMaghrib, an Islamic studies institute that "has dedicated itself to providing courses on Islam in a six-day, two-weekend, intensive seminar format."[8] AlMaghrib is directed precisely at these young, western-born and educated Muslims (hence the name, meaning "the West," in Arabic). Founded by Muhammad Alshareef, a 32-year-old Egyptian Canadian and staffed largely by younger Islamic scholars who have been educated at least partly in the West, AlMaghrib has a growing following among New York's young Muslims. The institute offers seminars and full courses in more traditional topics such as theology, ethics, *hadith*, law, legal theory, *tafseer* (exegesis), Islamic history, and *dawah* (propagation of the faith). They also run a seminar series. Popular seminars include "The Light of Guidance: Fundamentals of Faith 101," "Fiqh of Love: Marriage in Islam," and "Rules of Engagement: The Islamic Code of Ethics" (Smith 2007). AlMaghrib describes its approach as a way "to help the average [w]estern-raised Muslim to appreciate the complexities of the classical sciences of Islam in a practical and pragmatic way," explaining that its "methodology of fiqh [Islamic law], respect[s] . . . all of the classical madhabs of Islam (primarily the Hanafis, Shafi'ees, Malikis, and Hanbalis [i.e., the classic sources of Sunni Islamic law]) . . . [and] wishes to instill in its students the spirit of tolerance regarding legitimate differences of opinion. Recognizing that AlMaghrib Institute will not produce mujtahids [renewers of the faith], and appreciating the dynamic and multi-cultural milieu of the Western Muslim situation, it shall try to combine traditional madhab-based fiqh with comparative fiqh."[9] This recognition of Islamic scholarship within the framework of the "multicultural milieu of the western Muslim situation" goes a far way in explaining AlMaghrib's popularity with the young Muslim Americans I have encountered.

Dawah, or propagation of the faith, also plays a central role in the way young American Muslims construct themselves as the vanguard of Islam in the United States. Many connect dressing along Islamic lines with efforts to call others (nonpracticing Muslims and non-Muslims) to the faith. In this, too, they find a difference from the older generation to the younger. Consider Muhammad, for example. A friend of Rami's, he is a 22-year-old Egyptian American who is very knowledgeable about Islam and *aqeedah* (theology). Muhammad has assumed one such leadership role among young American

Muslims. He is in heavy demand to lecture at various mosques around the city and increasingly around the country (meanwhile, he does not having a specific mosque he calls home). Muhammad's travels are all part of his *dawah*, as he understands it. (In fact, many young people are now frequent *khateebs* [Friday prayers leaders] around the city, and the opportunity to lecture at a Friday prayer is considered by many of this generation as a desirable goal. It indicates a kind of rite of passage, illustrating that one has moved from belief in Islam to knowledge of the faith and, ultimately, to transmitting that knowledge.)

Muhammad also sports a thick beard and is always wearing a flowing *galabiyya* and *kufi* on his head. He explained to me one day the advantages of appearing different from mainstream American society, drawing first a comparison with the older generation, which rarely donned Islamic dress. "People think hiding their Islam will protect them." He then said, "It's exactly the other way around." He said that his appearance regularly prompts people to ask him about Islam. His dress, too, has become a part of his *dawah*.

Jeannette Jouili, a sociologist of Islam in France, has made a similar point. Jouili explains that many pious French Muslim women are attempting to render themselves visible to the world at large by donning *hijabs* or praying out in the open while at work or school. They do so in an attempt to mark and claim a presence in the public sphere. "This hints at a typical feature of the struggle for recognition by minority and stigmatized groups," Jouili writes. "Visibility is considered a source of power whereas its opposite, invisibility, becomes a sign of oppression" (Jouili 2007: 32–33).

Dawah, she explains, thus takes on a newly invigorated urgency, the struggle to represent Islam positively to non-Muslims to counter its negative image. Because *dawah*, according to Jouili, is "now perceived to be the precondition for the (social, political, and spiritual) well-being of the Muslim *umma* [community] in the West, it has thereby been elevated to the status of religious obligation" (Jouili 2007: 32). (Some Muslims would argue that *dawah* has always been a religious obligation.)

Such a drive for visibility can be seen on many college and university campuses in Brooklyn and throughout the United States today. On my campus of Brooklyn College, for example, the MSA hosted in March 2008 its first Islam Awareness Week, an event gaining popularity with MSAs across the country. During Islam Awareness Week, the MSA set up two tables outside and in the center of campus, each with pamphlets and literature about Islam. The pamphlets included "What Does Islam Say about Terrorism," and "Unveiling the Mystery Hijab," both published by the Islamic Circle of North America. (One table was manned by men, the other by women.) The space where the Muslims had set up is outdoors and is commonly used by different clubs to advertise their activities. When the time for prayer came, the Muslim men transformed the space by performing their prostrations out in the open air (the women meanwhile tended to both tables). Similar to how Jouili (2007) describes the situation of French Muslim women, visibility here may also be understood as a way of claiming one's rightful space among the many groups that make up the culture of the college.

During Islam Awareness Week, the college's MSA also hosted a week of lectures. With titles such as "Terrorism, Fundamentalism, Extremism: Fact and Fiction," and "Islam: Is It Too Great to Believe?" the lectures again illustrate the ways that young Muslims are responding to the demands established by the culture at large (namely, discussing terrorism), but nevertheless seek to establish the discourse around Islam on their terms ("Too Great to Believe?"). Members of the association were asked to bring at least one guest to the events for *dawah* purposes. During the lectures, the audience was separated by gender, with a physical divider running down half the room. One lecture focused on why Islam is a religion attracting many new followers, and the lecturer explained to the assembled group that non-Muslims carry "a right" to know about Islam and that "the Muslims have an obligation" to let non-Muslims know about the faith.

Dawah is not limited to campus activities. Muhammad and a few others host a website called FreeQuran.org, which, as the name promises, is an organization that sends Qurans to anyone, Muslim or non-Muslim, who wants one. Housed in a small office on Staten Island, the organization is supported by private donations (including the collections Muhammad receives for his Friday lectures) and sends approximately 3,000 Qurans a month to people. New Muslims who visit the website are asked to fill out a brief questionnaire, after which they will receive their free Islamic literature package. The website naturally also receives its fair share of hate mail, but what mostly arrives are inquiries from individuals who are thinking of converting to Islam (or who have converted) and from various prisons around the country seeking Qurans for their own libraries. The organization also distributes Qurans and literature at various lectures on Islam held around the city. During the warmer months, it also commonly sets up a table on the street or in a park to reach the American masses.

Rami and Muhammad often spend several hours a week here. When I was with them, they would leave the office energized by the work, and enthusiastic about the possibilities of *dawah* in the United States. Their optimism is further buoyed by an appreciation for the postal service and for technology. The work of the organization is predicated on the mail, and Muhammad frequently illustrated to me his understanding of mechanics of the postal system and his admiration for it smooth functioning. (He's a known customer there by now.)

Technology, likewise, facilities many aspects of Muslim life today. This organization, FreeQuran.org, would not exist were it not for the Internet. Technology further enables young Muslims to connect with each other around the world. They read websites such as Islamway.com, use YouTube.com to exchange videotaped lectures, and belong to various chat rooms and list-servs that enable them to keep abreast of global Islamic trends. Muhammad, for example, uses the Internet to follow the life and rulings of Abu Ishaq Al Heweny, an Egyptian Muslim scholar he admires.

Conclusion

Prior to September 11, 2001, young American Muslims certainly had already established networks across the country. College campuses frequently hosted lectures by Muslim scholars, and organizations such as the Islamic Society of North America held national conferences annually. However, today's young American Muslims, based on my research in New York City, understand their role differently than young Muslims did prior to September 11, 2001. This is true in the way today's generation has drawn a difference between themselves and the older generation, seeing themselves as part of a narrative of progress in the spread of Islam globally.

But the difference is not limited to the progress narrative. Today's young American Muslims in fact understand themselves as the vanguard of Islam in the United States, and in their vanguard role, they do not live in opposition to the larger American society, nor do they see themselves as being opposed to American society in general. (They do oppose its foreign policy, however, and feel the brunt of the surveillance arms of the state.) To the contrary, they frequently take advantage of specific elements of American culture that can further the aims and expansion of the Muslim community. Young Muslims in Brooklyn do, however, often separate from the mainstream, and this separation enables them to seek out and support each other, endowing this generation of young American Muslims with a strong sense of group solidarity that appears to be, at least in part, born out of hostility from the general culture that have they encountered since September 11, 2001.

But 9/11 also energized these young American Muslims, who feel a newly invigorated sense of obligation to represent Islam properly to both Muslims and non-Muslims alike. They are self-consciously creating a Muslim community, a community that places young people at the center of that experience and that understands youth as being a bearer of responsibility for an Islamic revival. *Dawah* plays a central role in their lives, and they affirm their own sense of being

Muslim when they invite non-Muslims to Islam. Global and national politics may have specifically caused today's hostility to and interest in Islam, but the youth are not interested in arguing politics with non-Muslims. Rather, they are dedicated to capitalizing on the current attention given to the religion and in producing a version of Islam that is consistent with their multicultural and globalized vision of the faith.

PART III

Strivings for Citizenship

II

"Also the School Is a Temple": Republicanism, Imagined Transnational Spaces, and the Schooling of Muslim Youth in France

André Elias Mazawi

The schooling of Muslim youth in France does not cease to capture the public imagination.[1] How Muslim youth are schooled, how and where they are educated, and how they are clothed when they show up for school choreograph competing media narratives of France as a nation-state. For some French politicians, officials and activists (including some Muslim ones), the establishment of Muslim schools is perceived as promoting *communautarisme*—that is, the ghettoization of ethnic communities and the fragmentation of the Republic's social fabric and political ethos. For others, protests by Muslim activists who seek the licensing of a Muslim school are perceived as a threat and a "plot against the Republic" (see Morvan 2008: 205, 208).

The current chapter addresses four intersecting aspects associated with the debates concerned with the schooling of Muslim youth in France. First, it positions these debates in relation to the shifting bases of political power that operate under the Fifth Republic. Second, it examines how the (hyper) mediatization of Muslims and those of immigrant background constructs the schooling of Muslim youth as a fulcrum in approaching issues of integration, social diversity, and multiculturalism. Third, it examines initiatives to establish Muslim schools against the backdrop of shifting class stratification and spatial segregation of cities and their *banlieues* (suburbs). Fourth, it positions the schooling of Muslim youth against the larger backdrop of European political integration and the emergence of a "European space" of praxis in relation to which new forms of citizenship and political action are possible. The concluding discussion offers a reflection on the role schooling plays in the construction of competing notions of Muslim youth within the wider context of a transnational "European" space.

"*Laïcité*" and the French Republican School

Laïcité represents a "founding myth of the French Republic" (Gunn 2004: 428), "perhaps the strongest normative pillar of French political philosophy" (Limage 2000: 79).[2] *Laïcité* refers to the struggle over separation of church and state since the early 19th century with the introduction of free, compulsory, and public primary education operated by the state. In the field of education, this separation is enshrined in laws, notably in a 1905 legislation that banned all religious orders in France and introduced the principle of "freedom of instruction" from clerical intervention along the lines of secular humanism (Wykes 1967: 219–220). According to Gresh and Tubiana (2005: 7), to the extent that the values of Catholicism and *laïcité* were perceived as incompatible in France of 1905, the same would apply with regard to public perceptions of Islam in relation to education in France of 2005. French public opinion has come to construct Islam as a new "threat" to long-standing republican traditions (Bowen 2007b: 31–32).

In debating the schooling of Muslim youth, the notion of *laïcité* is deployed as an immutable attribute of French political philosophy. Little is said about the fact that French governments have continued actively to fund and support Catholic schools overseas, in what was at the time France's colonies or zones of influence. Within France, following the 1905 legislation, the gradual *rapprochement* between the state and Catholic schools means, as Limage (2000: 80) points out, that "further advantages were granted to Catholic schools without a demand for reciprocal responsibilities."[3] A series of laws enacted during the 1950s through the 1970s, and referred to by some as "*lois anti-laïques*" (anti-secular laws), consolidated the operation of private (church) schools and confirmed the state's commitment to their existence and to their teaching staff alongside their public counterparts.[4] For instance, the *Debré* law (1959) frames the reciprocal relations between the state and private (mainly Catholic church) schools as part of a *contrat* (contract). The latter recognizes the autonomy of private schools while securing the implementation of state-mandated curricula and the granting of public funding.[5] The *Guermeur* law (1977) affirms the responsibility of the state toward teachers in private schools. Legislation also facilitates the operation of school chaplaincies, effectively extending their operation into secondary public schools (Beriss 1996: 379; Massignon 2000: 355–356). Four decades ago, Wykes (1967: 227) concluded that because of considerations associated with parliamentary coalition building, "[t]he legislation of the Fifth Republic, granting such substantial direct financial aid to the private schools, constitutes a major victory for the Church, and the measures appear to be continuing." The legislation resulted in arrangements that recognize *un pluralisme scolaire* in which the state "assists the private sector to maintain its services" as part of "a continuing reconciliation" (Wykes 1967: 232). Moreover, the Concordat of 1801, signed between France and the Catholic Church, and which still applies in the Alsace-Moselle region, institutionalizes religious teaching and endorses the display of religious signs in public schools (Willaime 2000). More recently, President Sarkozy's statements on the role religion plays in public life, and their presentation as "complementary" with regard to the education of youth, illustrate the continuously shifting political terrain of state–church relations in France (Refer to the commentaries by Tincq [2008] and by Etchegoin and Askolovitch [2008]).

The notion of *laïcité* stands out as a contested construction when approached over the backdrop of parliamentary power politics between the French Left and Right. Gunn (2004: 428) points out that "[d]espite the lack of certainty about what *laïcité* actually means, officials, politicians, scholars, and citizens are often effusive in their praise of the term." Nevertheless, deployed as a unitary political philosophy when it comes to the schooling of Muslim youth, its proponents disregard the involvement of the French state in the provision of private education within France.[6] Its deployment "racializes" Muslim youth, as the different and excluded "other." Taken from this perspective, *laïcité* undergirds a putatively "integrative" mode of educational organization that effectively recasts public education as a performative ritual of allegiance to a particularistic political and cultural order. The "integrative" claim of public education represents, therefore, an assimilation agenda, in which the school casts particularistic constructions of *francité* (Frenchness) as universal foundations of citizenship and political participation. In previous decades, the "melting pot" function of the republican school was instrumental in assimilating regional groups within France and immigrant workers originating from other parts of Europe. Yet, for van Zanten (1997: 353, 357), it remains unclear "how long it will be possible for state institutions to succeed in acculturating immigrant populations that are increasingly diverse and distant from French culture."

Within public schools, it is not clear what exactly *laïcité* is supposed to help achieve or prevent from happening. Whereas *laïcité* is articulated in relation to the institutionalized separation of state and church, as distinct organizational jurisdictions, much less clarity prevails when the discussion turns to issues of social and cultural diversity. The confusion becomes more daunting when one realizes that *laïcité* is rhetorically used in such broad terms that any custom or norm—from the wearing of a headscarf, to girls' nonparticipation in sports classes, to the consumption of particular kinds of foods in school (e.g., *halal* meat)—is perceived by many politicians, policy makers, teachers, and school administrators as the expression of organized religion and "proselytization," rather than as an expression of culturally embedded practices. One of the outcomes of this conflation is that sociocultural diversity is conceived of in terms of religious faith rather than in terms of ethnicity or culture, as would be the case, for instance, in the United Kingdom (Liederman 2000: 112). Thus, Muslim youth attending the republican school are often perceived as bearers of a collective agenda seated within organized "planetary" religious movements that extend beyond their families and communities.

It is over the backdrop outlined here that Kilani (2005) calls for the effective *déconfessionnalisation* of the notion of *laïcité* and for a "new model of integration" (Kilani 2002: 84), in which religion could be approached as a subset of culture, thus rendering the notion of *laïcité* sensitive to dynamics associated with multiculturalism (Kilani 2002: 83).

For the observer, what stands out in the debates is an overemphasis placed on the symbolic dimensions of *laïcité* within the school. The inordinate attention given to the *affaire des foulards* (affair of the headscarves) is indicative of this overemphasis. According to Chérifi (2005), the *affaire* "has shaken the school and triggered polemics among intellectuals." The "hypermediatization" of headscarf-wearing girls, "forcing" themselves on the public school, epitomizes the prevalent perception of Islam as "invading" the public sphere. Windle (2004: 109) points out that media reports have "symbolically invested [headscarves] as representations of counterstate allegiances," which operate as "a site for the playing out of anxieties over ethnically and religiously coded 'social exclusion'" of Muslim migrants who "occupy the bottom rung" of social stratification (Windle 2004: 101). For Keaton (2006: 4–5), media representations have also fashioned Muslim adolescent girls "as quintessential other vis-à-vis French culture and the national representations in the courts of public and private opinion."

The articulation of the symbolic aspects associated with the enactment of *laïcité* within the republican school find their rarefied enunciation perhaps best expressed by philosopher Alain Finkielkraut, who addressed a parliamentary round table on "*Ecole et laïcité aujourd'hui,*" held by the Commission on Cultural, Family and Social Affairs in May 2003: (The quote is in the original French with English translation).

J'irai jusqu'à dire que l'école aussi est un temple.
Ce n'est pas seulement un sanctuaire, c'est
aussi un temple. Et on enlève son foulard dans
ce temple, précisément pour se rendre disponible
aux grandes œuvres de la culture, aux œuvres qui
font l'humanité. Si l'instituteur, le professeur est le
représentant des poètes, des artistes, de la culture,
rien ne doit s'entremettre entre sa représentation
et la réception par l'élève. Or le foulard est quelque
chose qui s'entremet, il s'agit même d'un rideau
que l'on tend devant la culture. Voilà ce que l'école,
en tant que temple, se doit de refuser. L'école est un
espace séparé qui obéit à ses propres règles :
la laïcité (Finkielkraut 2003).

I would go as far as to say that also the school
is a temple. It is not only a sanctuary, it is also
a temple. And one takes off one's headscarf
in that temple, precisely to become available
to the great works of culture, to the works that
make humanity. If the instructor, the teacher
is the representative of the poets, the artists,
of culture, nothing must come in between his
representation and the student's receptivity.
Yet the headscarf is something that comes in
between, it is even a curtain that one pulls in
front of culture. This is what the school, as a
temple, must refuse. The school is a separate
space that obeys its own rules: laity.

Finkielkraut's narrative erects the public school into a "sanctuary" cum "temple" in relation to cultural production. Underpinning his narrative is the distinction between what stands for "culture" and what lies outside of it. The republican school's mission revolves around bringing the different "other"— here, Muslim young girls—into that sanctuary–temple that makes their humanity possible. The teacher is construed as a guardian of culture, by virtue of *his* role as vicar of sorts of the muses of modernity associated primarily with the project of Enlightenment. As part of this vision, it may be argued that Muslim youth— particularly girls—lose their individual agency. Their bodies become a site of political struggle between, on the one hand, young males who are constructed as members of "planetary" Islamic movements or as despotic siblings and patriarchs—these "new principal enemies" (Guénif-Souilamas and Macé 2004)—and, on the other hand, humanist republican vigilantes who seek to emancipate Muslim girls and adolescents. This *bricolage* of essentialized identities effectively racializes the bodies of Muslim youth, constructed as a site over which competing political forces struggle for control (Guénif-Souilamas and Macé 2004). The approach of the Stasi commission[7] is particularly indicative in this regard. According to Gunn (2005: 101), it proposes to French schoolchildren "the 'freedom' to be schooled in the statist system that has already decided what is best for them because they cannot be trusted to decide for themselves".

School, Ethnicity, and Spatial Exclusion

In France, the overwhelming emphasis placed on the symbolic dimensions of social integration is paralleled by much less attention granted to the actual social and institutional cleavages associated with the marginalization and exclusion of youth on the basis of their ethnicity, gender, sexuality, locality of residence, and disability. This imbalance contrasts sharply with advances in the sociology of education, one of the most thriving and productive critical fields of research in France since the 1960s (Vasconcellos 2003: 554). Duru-Bellat and Kieffer (2000: 334) observe that "empirical studies on equity issues have remained scarce in France." More particularly, research on the public school's catchment area map (*la carte scolaire*), and the extent of its effectiveness in ensuring equality of educational opportunities by "mixing" students from various geographic locations, still face serious challenges when it comes to exploring the schooling of Muslim youth. Data that account for students' ethnicity—not just citizenship—are not available, because of legal and other constraints imposed on their collection. This leads some researchers to account for ethnicity, for instance, by inferring it from students' first names (Felouzis 2003). Felouzis et al. (2003: 128) report that, for instance, in the Académie of Bordeaux,[8] 10% of the middle schools (*collèges*) enroll 40% of all youth found in families who have immigrated from the Maghreb, sub-Saharan Africa, and Turkey, and who are among the most disadvantaged socioeconomic groups. In popular parlance, these educational settings are referred to as *collèges ghetto*. Felouzis et al. (2003) estimate that to achieve an equal distribution of these students across all *collèges* in the Académie de Bordeaux, 89% would have to transfer to another institution. These authors conclude that "the ethnic segregation observed in the *collèges* is tightly linked to urban segregation" (Felouzis et al. 2003: 129) as well as to strategies practiced by the more powerful parents to circumvent catchment areas by obtaining special "derogations" (Felouzis et al. 2003: 130–134). Catchment areas are thus seen as reinforcing spatial ethnic segregation associated with the emergence of the *banlieues*—or suburbs—as ghettos (Giblin 2006; Oberti 2007).

Some critics on the conservative Right capitalize on these spatial dynamics in order to legitimize and promote an agenda of educational deregulation, decentralization, and ultimately privatization. They point out that the logic underpinning catchment areas exacerbates spatial *sectoralization* and operates as "an instrument of segregation".[9] They call for the revocation of the catchment area map and its replacement with parental choice and competition between schools. This position was expressed, several months ahead of the 2007 presidential elections, in an opinion piece authored by the then French Minister of the Interior and currently France's president, Nicolas Sarkozy:

[La carte scolaire] est contraire aux principes les plus essentiels de l'école républicaine, laïque, gratuite et égalitaire. La carte scolaire se voulait un instrument de justice. Elle est devenue le symbole

[The catchment area map] contradicts the most essential principles of the republican school, lay, free, and egalitarian. The catchment area map was intended to be an instrument of justice.

d'une société qui ne parvient plus à réduire ses injustices parce qu'elle n'ose pas s'interroger sur ses outils. . . . Certains demandent: 'Si l'on supprime la carte scolaire, par quoi la remplacera-t-on?' Je leur réponds: 'Mais par rien! Ou par un système d'inscription dans, par exemple, trois établissements au choix.' (Sarkozy 2006).

It has become the symbol of a society unable to reduce its injustices because it does not dare question itself on its instruments. . . . Some ask: 'If the catchment area map is canceled, by what will it be replaced?' I answer them: 'But by nothing! Or by a system of registration to, for example, three institutions of choice.'

Sarkozy's call to revoke catchment areas, and his support for competition between schools, aims to promote parental choice as the penultimate expression of a reclaimed sense of social "justice," which he considers to stand fully in line with republican egalitarian heritage.[10] This position also opens up the possibility of operating private schools, and by implication Muslim schools as well, funded directly by parents and communities rather than by the state, following the charter school model, for instance.

Deregulation is opposed by the far Right and the socialist Left, albeit for different reasons. The far Right considers educational deregulation, and the endorsement of "confessional" schools, as signaling the disengagement of the state from its commitment to "Frenchness." It also fears that private Muslim schools would eventually challenge the hegemonic position held by Catholic schools, of which they are supporters (Deltombe 2005: 102). In contradistinction, as Laronche and Rollot write in *Le Monde*, the Left and its allied professional unions perceive a deregulatory policy as *irréaliste* and *dangereuse*, and as a blow to the social democratic underpinnings of a unitary republican system, ultimately leading to "a competitive system similar to the one practiced by the English.[11] Cornered, some activists on the Left admit that the catchment area is "generating inequalities." Yet, they oppose its complete revocation because they believe it will introduce "a savage liberalization of the system, with, as a consequence, a two-tiered education".[12] Instead, politicians and union leaders on the Left suggest a contained reform, or *"assouplissement"* (relaxation) of catchment areas. Such reforms would commit greater state investments in "centers of excellence" in schools operating within socioeconomically weaker communities, alongside some constrains that limit parental flight.

Muslim Schools and the Question of Citizenship

Between 2001 and 2007, three secondary Muslim-run schools were launched within metropolitan France: the Collège La Réussite in Aubervilliers (founded in 2001 in the district of Seine-Saint-Denis, Académie de Créteil), the Collège-Lycée Averroès in Lille (founded in 2003, Académie de Lille),[13] and the Collège Al-Kindi in Décines-Charpieu (launched in 2007 in the district of the Rhône, Académie de Lyon). The three Muslim schools are located within regional academic jurisdictions that included more than one fifth of all zones of priority education (*zone d'éducation prioritaire* aka ZEP) in 2004.[14] Some of these schools were initially launched within mosques.[15] Activists affiliated with the *Union des organisations islamiques de France* (UOIF) were involved in the launching of the Collège-Lycée Averroès and the Collège Al-Kindi.[16] Some commentators present Muslim schools as an outcome of the restrictive legislation introduced in 2004 following the Stasi report. It is worth observing, however, that Muslim school initiatives predate that particular legislation. Nevertheless, Bowen (2007b: 151) does report the claim that, after the 2004 legislation, "several hundred [Muslim] girls had never showed up at school," thus motivating the UOIF and its allies to seek "more funds to start private Muslim schools" (Bowen 2007b: 151).

The launching of private schools for Muslim youth gives rise to arguments in support and opposition among Muslim writers, activists, social movements, and associations. Muslim activists associated with the UOIF consider community-run schools as institutional leverages that counter the reproductive power of public education and the "iron cage" imposed by spatial segregation. For them, such schools provide an institutional platform for political mobilization and community transformation. According to UOIF officials, Muslim schools aim to "train cadres with a Muslim reference, with a triple culture: French, Arab and Muslim".[17] Rejecting the perception that these schools represent "communitarian" and socially regressive projects, they further state that Muslim schools express "*une réelle ouverture sur la société*" ("a real openness on society"); places where "*Nathalie, Jacques ou David sont les bienvenus*" (Associated Press 2006), in reference to their readiness to enroll youth of different religious backgrounds.

In contrast, Muslim activists associated with the *Collectif des Musulmans de France* (CMF), are rather opposed to such ventures.[18] They perceive these schools as "confessional" institutions that will ultimately enclave Muslim youth in segregated educational settings, thus deepening their social exclusion (Chaambi 2007). Such schools are also perceived as "creating a ghetto within the ghetto" (Roman-Amat 2007), and as exacerbating economic hardships on Muslim communities given their economic precariousness. Instead, CMF activists (many of whom self-identify as "secular Muslims"), call for a "political struggle for a tolerant and inclusive public education and against the banning of the headscarf" (Roman-Amat, 2007).

Within the wider French political spectrum, vocal opposition to the operation of Muslim schools is more vehemently heard on the far Right. The latter considers that these institutions contradict France's republican ethos. Explicit or implicit support for Muslim schools is voiced from other quarters within the French political system, although for different reasons. For some of those aligned with the conservative Right, private schools are perceived as an opportunity to bring Muslim organizations under the aegis of state influence and co-optation through the *contrat* system. For others, more often situated at the center of the political map, the operation of Muslim schools is perceived as facilitating a market-driven and voluntary model of social and economic integration. Still, those who support economic liberalization and educational privatization do not perceive private schools as reflecting communitarian initiatives. Rather, they point out that private school initiatives are also taking place, for instance, among Sikh communities whose children have also been affected by the 2004 legislation on the banning of overt displays of religious signs in public schools. A report published in *Le Parisien* (Saint Sauveur 2007), and which reflects this position, disputes the assertion that the rise of "confessional schools" signals "the grand return of God into the schools of France." It presents Muslim schools within the wider context of increasing parental involvement in education against the backdrop of a profound dissatisfaction with the state's coping with the challenges posed by immigration, shifting class inequalities, economic deregulation, and protracted hopes for social and economic mobility.

Transnational Spaces and the Schooling of Muslim Youth

The schooling of Muslim youth enrolled in public and private schools is subject to a myriad of institutional and constitutional arrangements that vary considerably across the European Union (EU) (Shadid and van Koningsveld 2005). The emergence of a European educational "space" transcends the territorial bounds of a particular nation-state, in this case France, raising new issues and challenges. As a "transnational" or "supranational community" (Soysal 2002: 55), "Europeanness" "is presumed to be what naturally united and makes Europeans and what distinguishes them from others" (Soysal 2002: 56). Yet, on the one hand, constructions of Europeanness are largely based on what Nóvoa (2002) calls "geographical forms of citizenship." These emphasize the locality and the nation-state and do not account for citizenship in terms of "new journeys and itineraries (by refugees, exiles, illegal aliens, migrant workers, intellectuals, etc.) that encourag[e] non-territorial forms of affiliation and solidarity" (Nóvoa 2002: 139). Current conceptions of citizenship promoted in school textbooks remain concerned with the "replicat[ion] of national endeavours at a European level" without allowing "an accurate understanding of a situation that needs to be analysed in its own terms" (Nóvoa 2002: 139).

On the other hand, the political construction of the EU opens up new horizons for political and social action, in relation to which Muslim activists seek, in the words of Soysal (2000: 1), to "recalibrate" their narratives around schooling, constructing their discourses in ways that institute "new forms of making claims, mobilizing identity and practising citizenship, . . . beyond the limiting dominion of ethnically informed diasporic arrangements, transactions and belongings." These processes reflect dynamics of cultural production that transcend the merely diasporic. They rather reflect what Bowen (2002: 9) refers to as the "predicament of locating oneself in multiple networks of movement, communication, and imagination." These new horizons engage (what Bowen calls) a "translocal" space of reference that negotiates the location of Muslim youth in society, not only as citizens of the French Republic, but also as "European" members of the Islamic *umma* and as members of a cultural and ethnic heritage. Salih (2004: 997) points out that a "new European public sphere is emerging where young Muslims are actively seeking to promote new and changing frontiers of identity and political activity." In this sphere, she further argues, education stands out as one of the aspects of social and political organization (Salih 2004: 1008) through which Muslim youth seek to transcend their "minority standpoint, [by] articulating the Islamic identity with universal values, rather than just claiming respect for 'difference'" (Salih 2004: 1009), thus "embod[ying] the emergence of a post-national generation of European Muslims" (Salih 2004: 1010). According to Salvatore (2004: 1024), this process moves schooling away from a vision of education as "disciplining instruments" through which "the nation-state forcefully integrates cultural and religious minorities" to the articulation of a "democratic and dialogic public sphere" that benefits "the lives of Muslim citizens" and "the long-term vitality of European polities."

Conclusion

The heated debates over the schooling of Muslim youth reflect not only power relations between and within the Right and the Left in France. They are also indicative of representations that transcend the territorial bounds of the nation-state (France) and its transnational articulations (EU). These debates are symptomatic of the multilayered discursive ruptures operating between what may be labeled as two "European" transnational "scripts." The first is associated with EU institutions and their political elites. It seeks to "Europeanize" identities within the framework of a secularized Judeo-Christian tradition and harmonized nation-state relations (Soysal 2002). The second is associated with social movements that invoke conceptions of Islamic and other sociocultural traditions, imagined by opponents as being located "beyond" the European continent. This second dynamic expresses standpoints of voices that seek to articulate visions of Europe, and visions of schooling, in which one is not perceived as an "other" outsider but as an "authentic" and "indigenous" insider. Hence, debates over the schooling of Muslim youth may be seen as part of attempts to localize or "indigenize" transnational "imagined communities."

The schooling of Muslim youth in France also revolves around the role schools play in constructing alternative "interconnections" of power relations in which the production of civic and political identities takes place. The media debates surrounding the schooling of Muslim youth in France—and more particularly those concerned with catchment areas and their "ghettoizing" effects—are part of the contestation of the geographies of power that underpin the violence (symbolic or effective) involved in the colonization and territorialization of spatial power relations within which schools operate. Seen from this perspective, the heated debates over Muslim schools, and over what "republican" education stands for within France, operate as "a foundational ritual," embedded within the "transformation of spaces into places" (Appadurai 1996: 183). In this sense, it is worth emphasizing that the power wrestling over the schooling of Muslim youth in France operates, simultaneously, both *within* Muslim communities and *among* social groups and movements positioned across the political spectrum. As such, it reflects a struggle among competing social forces that powerfully intersect along spatial, ethnic, class, and gender lines.

Approached from this particular vantage point, the question at stake is not whether the republican school should tolerate the display of religious symbols, nor is it about the limits of deregulation and the retrenchment of the state in terms of educational provision. The question, rather, hinges on the role that the school—as a political *ritual*—is allowed to play in rethinking and envisioning the structural and sociocultural disjunctures of a much transformed French (and European) "public" sphere in relation to which Europeanness, state, community, and individual could be imagined and positioned in their diversities and differences.

12

Avoiding "Youthfulness?": Young Muslims Negotiating Gender and Citizenship in France and Germany

Schirin Amir-Moazami

The rise of a young generation of Muslims born and raised in European societies has put new questions onto the public agenda that differ from the problems specific to immigration of the first generation. These young Muslims raise claims for participation as citizens and representatives of a religious tradition, which is not (yet) part of the European imaginary. The questions that arise are, for the time being, specific to the young generation, even if they do not, per se, characterize Muslim "youthfulness." Considering that the subject's relation to Islam is shaped, constructed, and modified differently within different generational patterns and within different contexts, my major concern is to tackle the issue of being "young and Muslim" from the perspective of members of this generation whose life center is non-Muslim majority societies. The phrase *young generation of Muslims* would obviously require a closer specification of what "young generation" means in this context, a temporal clarification of where the generation starts and where it ends. I can only provide a loose approximation here. I am speaking about a generation of Muslims that has grown up in European contexts as an effect of their parent's immigration to these countries. They are recurrently labeled as the *second generation*—a term that I do not find convincing, because it attributes them the status of immigrants, which is in fact inadequate. In my own fieldwork, these people range in age between 16 and 30 years.

It goes without saying that the label *young Muslims* can mean many different things. It can imply identifying oneself with Islam without practicing it in a day-to-day manner. Islam, for both young and old, can even signify a loose reference to a background that only implicitly influences daily life practices. Such versions of Islam might even comply with what has problematically been labeled the "silent majority" (Broder 2007) of young Muslims living in Europe today. In this chapter I focus on versions of belonging to Islam that assert particular forms of piety,[1] and in which Islam serves the believer as a guideline for daily life practices and moral conduct. Moreover, the subject's relationship to Islam extends an individual relationship to God and fashions a sense of belonging to a wider community, however plural and fragile this might be. More specifically, I focus on young women, participants in Islamic organizations, who have opted to don the Islamic headscarf in two European settings: France and Germany.[2] This is, I claim, the issue that has caught the most public attention because it challenges a gradual acculturation of forms of religiosity through generational shifts.

I structure my arguments around two interrelated questions. First, I analyze the ways in which Muslimness is shaped by the young generation of Muslims through a particular focus on dominant notions of youthfulness and its challenges for and by young Muslims. I use the term *youthfulness* here as conceptualized by Asef Bayat (2007b). There are two main aspects of his work that I consider important to retain. The first concerns his distinction between being young as an age category and youth or youthfulness as a social category (Bayat 2007b: 64), the latter implying a self-consciousness about being young. The second and related aspect concerns the common denominators that youthfulness as a social category comprises: idealism, individuality, spontaneity, joy, and fun, to cite only a few (Bayat 2007b: 59, 63). Although not necessarily neglecting these "youthful dispositions," the young women I talked to seem to challenge or redefine some of them by confining themselves to forms of piety that consciously attempt to overcome certain youthful temptations.

Second, I argue that these emerging forms of pious youthfulness among young Muslim women are intertwined with a particular way of situating themselves within a non-Muslim secular[3] context. In other words, they do not stem from an Islamic tradition alone or in any isolated way, but have to be related to a broader secular context. Through the comparative focus on France and Germany, I illuminate that this engagement takes different forms in different national settings, and is shaped by dominant narratives on citizenship and the management of (religious) plurality.

Muslim Piety as One Version of Youthfulness

In the summer of 2004, *Künsterhaus Bethanien* in Berlin hosted and curated an exhibition with large photographs of young covered women. On the occasion of the opening, a round table was convened, and a scholar of cultural anthropology (Nanna Heidenreich) discussed with journalist, who specialized on Algeria, gender, and Islam (Sabine Kebir). Kebir, in brief, emphasized the blurring of public and private and religious and political domains through veiling, warned about Islamist activism exposed through the headscarf and its dangers for the secular norm, and lastly noted the oppressive character of veiling for women. So far, nothing spectacular, in that Kebir's arguments basically reproduced the dominant discourse on veiling in Germany or elsewhere in Europe.

Some of the young women portrayed in the photographs sat in the audience and after Kebir's discussion contradicted her point by point. They primarily stressed that, for them, the headscarf was, in the first place, an expression of personal belief, that it would not deprive them from fully participating in society, and that they did not feel disrespected by male Muslims because of being covered. Again, such conversations are not necessarily exceptional, because controversies among covered women sitting in an audience or on panels and speakers at roundtables, public talks, and so forth have become quite common both in Germany and in France. What was more interesting was Kebir's reaction to what the young women had told her. She stressed that even if the women did not know it themselves, being covered and thereby asserting modesty and reluctance in their interaction with young men would sooner or later cause mental and physical illness to them. That is because experiencing and experimenting with sexuality during adolescence is, according to Kebir, a necessary step in the process of becoming a psychologically and physically healthy young adult.

Such statements reveal in a symptomatic way the contradictory character of the public discourse on veiling in European countries. It recurrently denounces veiling as a form of social control of the body and, more generally, female sexuality. However, by intervening into a very intimate sphere of the female body and imposing (permissive) sexuality norms, this discourse seeks to regulate and control sexuality. It is driven by a missionary goal to liberate Muslim women from their oppressive communities, or in this case, even from themselves. What I find more important is the logic behind Kebir's concern of the well-being of these young covered women. Being a healthy young woman in this assessment means to experience sexuality and to adjust to dominant standards of youthfulness. My aim here is not to denounce such assumptions, because I assume that they probably emerge from a serious concern about the oppressive character of patriarchal systems, even if they, too, often result in a problematic goal of obsessively liberating the oppressed by imposing one's own norms (Guénif-Soulimas and Macé 2004; Scott 2005). What I find more relevant to focus on here is the specific conception of youthfulness that statements like Kebir's reveal. Or, to put it another way, what is relevant here are the divergent rationalities behind the conceptions of youthfulness exemplified in the conversation between the young covered women and the journalist.

Similarly, the proponents of secularism and opponents of the headscarf in various heated debates on the Islamic headscarf (Amir-Moazami 2005; Bowen 2007) not only seem to be generally ill at ease with the forms of public religiosity that this particular Islamic dress asserts, but they are especially irritated about the fact that, in particular, the *young* generation of Muslim women, who have been socialized in secular educational institutions deliberately choose to cover themselves. In other words, the wearing of headscarves by the older generation of immigrants was not even considered problematic because it was socially more or less invisible and fell under the category of "folklore". However, when young women born in Europe cover their hair it disturbs public opinion to the extent that political authorities feel obliged to codify legal regulations to ban them from state schools (Mazawi, chapter 11, this volume).[4] I argue that the student veiling, a "voluntary adoption of stigma symbols," as Nilüfer Göle (2003) puts it, is so contested because it presumably deprives these women from what is considered, according to the dominant understanding, an adequate and legitimate "youthfulness."

In this respect, I do not see any major differences between France and Germany. Also, in France, scenes like the one I witnessed at *Künstlerhaus Bethanien* are common. If we look, for example, at the arguments put forward by a number of commentators in the controversies on the headscarf, a similar understanding of freedom and autonomy associated with sexual permissiveness is prevalent (Scott 2007). Many French authors associated the unveiled body with women's liberation and equality, while at the same time revealing the limitations of the underlying notion of freedom, which required specific dress codes and norms detached from any religious affiliation. The French discourses on the headscarf reproduced a logic that equates external appearances with particular (i.e., Muslim) identities, while associating the visibility of feminine sexuality superficially with belonging to French society. The indicator for Muslim girls' integration into French society was, accordingly, to lie "at the beach with naked breasts", as anthropologist Emmanuel Tood put it (cited in L'Express 2004). Also in the French mainstream discourse, the purported submissiveness of women with headscarves is mainly based on the fact that these women are perceived as completely lacking personality and autonomy.

Similar to the women in the audience of the round table, the covered women whom I interviewed put forward a quite different understanding from what the mainstream discourse on youthfulness seeks to make normative. For them, searching to please God, fulfilling religious duties, and cultivating piety are the touchstones of their way to adulthood. Although these women simultaneously negotiate freedoms within intergenerational conflicts with their parents or the extended family, it is not sexual liberation that is meaningful for them; on the contrary, the avoidance of the temptations of dominant sexuality norms outside of the framework of matrimony is important. I illustrate this in the following pages by focusing on the implications of veiling for these women as one important element of the creation and externalization of a particular kind of youthfulness as Muslim piety.

Looking at veiling of the young generation of Muslims in France and Germany from an intergenerational perspective, what I consider important to stress is that, for most of the women, being covered does not result, in the first place, from a family tradition that has been transmitted to them regardless of the new setting. Often their mothers were not initially—and still are not—covered. Consider, for example, the statement of Nura [name changed], the director of an informal group for young Muslim women in Marseille: "[My mother] put on the headscarf after me. By the way, when I started to practice Islam, people said to me: 'Oh, your parents made you do it.' And I said: 'Why do you want them to make me do it? My mother doesn't even wear the headscarf. My parents don't even practice.'" Such statements not only illustrate differences in the versions of religiosity between different generations of Muslims, they also elucidate that the transmission of religious traditions and knowledge does not seem to work in a unidirectional, linear way from one generation to the next. It can also work the other way around, meaning that the children encourage their parents to reinforce religiosity and to accumulate religious knowledge—and to don the headscarf.

Even if they similarly negotiate spaces of freedom, these women do not seek to distance and emancipate themselves from their parents by struggling for freedoms in the name of being young, and also not in domains "typical" for young people (like going out at night, experimenting alcohol, experiencing sexuality, and so forth). The intergenerational struggle in their case rather works according to different notions of Islam. That is to say that they often consider the version of their parents as "traditional," anchored in prohibitive norms and actually "un-Islamic". Meanwhile, they regard their own version to be the "true Islam," based on religious sources (Jacobson 2004; Jouili and Amir-Moazami 2006). This is also translated into the different versions of veiling—their own "correct form," and the wrong way of their mothers (i.e., leaving some hair visible), which they consider an unreflected reproduction of custom.

The choice to wear the headscarf for these women is not only an external marker, which displays their belonging to Islam, nor is it a mere inherited custom. It also signifies their attempt to abstain from seduction. Referring to the Quranic meaning of veiling, the women interviewed commonly stressed that a Muslim woman should preserve modesty toward unknown males. The headscarf is a tool for hiding female sexuality and attraction in public domains, because women's hair is considered particularly seductive. Moreover, donning the headscarf for these young women is also a matter of "distinction" in the sense of Bourdieu, in that it comprises a whole set of cultivating virtues that distinguishes them from other (i.e., uncovered) women. Although these women naturally interact with both covered and uncovered peers, for them, exposing (female) sexuality is a sign of weakness, which they try to overcome through a continuous work on the self.

Especially the women enrolled in higher education emphasized how important it was for them to be regarded as "intellectual beings," detached from external beauty and from the body. Contrary to the public discourse that especially in France considers sexual liberation and the freedom to be "naked" as one of the most important achievements of women's emancipation (Guénif-Soulimas and Macé 2004), the women I interviewed reversed it into a sign of female oppression. Moreover, they turned their own choice to cultivate and externalize modesty into a sign of female liberation. Even if the interviewees did not necessarily put forward a discourse of superiority toward non-Muslim women, sometimes a quite black-and-white image of them, as reduced to the visible body, emerged. The following comment by Farida [name changed], a woman active in *Jeunes Musulmans de France*, demonstrates this:

> [W]e are not obliged to follow the media, we are not obliged to be like
> Claudia Schiffer, for example, because our husbands don't see this. . . .
> In the moment in which you are a Muslim woman, what does he
> see? He sees that I practice my religion well, he sees that I educate
> my children well according to Islam . . . that's all."

Cultivating and displaying modesty for them is a sign of one's strength, whereas exposing femininity in public domains is regarded as an abusive reduction to the female body.[5] The women not only distinguish between the "sacred" and the "aesthetic" body (Göle 1996); But, for them, the headscarf becomes a means of making visible invisible characteristics (i.e., inner virtues) that they oppose to external beauty.

Although the public discourse constantly puts pressure on them to be young like "everybody else," and to fit into dominant sexuality norms, these women consciously and deliberately impose limits on themselves, adjusting to their ideal of cultivating modesty and overcoming the temptations of liberal majority societies. This might also constitute an interesting difference to Muslim majority contexts, in particular those in which public religiosity is prescribed and imposed by political authorities, and in which external signs of piety are mandatory, like veiling in Iran, for example. Although imposed piety seems to encourage young people to overcome religious affiliations and to long for a globalized (i.e., American-influenced [Massey 1998]) version of youthfulness (Bayat, chapter 2, this volume), these young women attempt to reemphasize and stage manage piety in public domains, maybe precisely because it is so contested according to the dominant secular understanding. It even seems that the more they interact in spaces in which particular kinds of religiosity are considered illegitimate and in which homogeneity is compelled, the more this staging of Muslim virtues becomes a form of resistance. The search for recognition might then go hand in hand with a search for a stable "otherness." The cultivation of modesty should thus not be misunderstood as fashioning a "pious self" in any sense, isolated from power structures and techniques, but should always be interpreted against the backdrop of the (liberal–secular) context in which it is shaped and performed. What results from this is, quite often, a sort of mirror image of the images commonly projected within the French or German public spheres of the unequal and oppressive character of veiling for women. The counterimage is that of the exploited and obsessively sexualized "Occidental" woman. As a result of the intensity of the public debates on the headscarf, this attitude seems to be more frequent among the interviewees in France. There occurs some kind of *duplication* effect that leads to a sort of "hyperdiscourse" (Salvatore 2001) of Islam created from stereotypes channeled through the mass media, as the debates on veiling succinctly bear witness.

The constraints of the secular order are paralleled by other, somehow reversed constraints within the women's families. These young women are often tied to more social control than their male peers and are central for the maintenance of norms, that their families consider as being in danger of extinction in western European societies. In these contexts, the women seem to negotiate spaces for liberty and individuality, which in contention with liberal– secular constraints they seem to neglect or at least put into question. A recurrent argument in this intergenerational struggle for gender equality and female participation in public domains is their parent's lack of adequate religious knowledge that they juxtapose to their own inquiry into religious sources. Often the women uncovered their parent's "wrong reference" to Islam and replaced it with their own "correct" version, based on a (re)reading and a (re)interpretation of the sacred texts. In this sense, continuing and transforming a religious conduct becomes a source in the struggle for greater equality in those contexts in which the parents' generation increases the scope of the *haram* for women. Here, the stage of adolescence, in which these women are confronted most heavily with restrictions and constraints, seems to be crucial. Most of the women to whom I talked, indeed marked adolescence (which is again not a fixed category) as the period during which they started to question and at the same time challenge certain gender norms transmitted and/or imposed by their parents or by the extended family. The effects of this conflict are, of course, multiple and can also lead to a complete neglecting of normative religious ties. However, the women I interviewed were encouraged to search for a alternative approach to Islam than the one that was transmitted to them, without denying normative components of Islamic sources but ascribing different values to it, as the statement by Bahia (name changed) most tellingly shows:

> In the practice I told myself, honestly, if this is Islam it doesn't interest me. I know that I am of Maghrebi origin, I know that the Qur'an is the word of God, I believe in the existence of a unique God, as in other monotheist religions. Afterwards, in the practice there was something which didn't satisfy me. I told myself, you hear everywhere that Islam is a tolerant religion, and me, in daily life I don't see this. . . . And then by growing up, by being adolescent, and by being able to read, to see the texts, and so forth, I became aware that everything was in this religion, all these aspects are there, which the people could not concretize in their daily actions.

The women's discourses point to their complex relationship to the former generations that experienced the process of migration. On the one hand they criticize the unequal gender norms, imposed by their families; on the other hand, they base their self-esteem on female "modesty," as one element in their search for piety, and thereby adjust to imposed principles like honor, highly contested within mainstream society and also by themselves. They turn this stigma into a positive capital, and declare virginity and modesty, displayed through the headscarf, as elements of free choice and self-respect. The women thus seem to be confronted with an ongoing tension between the neglect of youthfulness within the extended family on the one hand and the pressure to adjust to certain youthful standards in the wider public sphere on the other.

It should be pointed out the women are not necessarily unanimous in their ways of using the headscarf or of generally following Islamic dress codes. In other words, the clear-cut distinction between the "pure" covered and the "impure" open woman can lose certain credibility among some of the women

I interviewed who embrace commodified aspects of sexuality, combining makeup and high heels with veiling. These women are often blamed by those who consider being modestly dressed and denounced as "playing with religion, which in fact is not allowed," as a high school student in Berlin put it. Through the boundary drawn between the "licit" and the "illicit" way of covering, the "community" of veiled women is becoming much more fragmented than is often represented in public discourses and by the women themselves. Yet, the women who combine high heels or tight jeans with veiling seem to perceive themselves as being on the edge of "wrong" and "right" wearers of the head-scarf, and are sometimes also quite aware of the ambivalence that their external appearance reveals. A high school student who had recently started to don the headscarf admitted:

> I know myself that it is a mistake how I am dressed . . . . Once a
> guy said to me—I was about to tell to my friend: "Shit, I am too
> skinny," and then the guy said, "No hey, you have a smashing body!"
> And this was really embarrassing, because . . . I was dressed in a
> way that this guy was able to see what kind of a body I have.

Such statements mark the ambiguity with which, in particular, unmarried young women seem to be confronted. In some cases this seems to lead to a number of compromises, which, however, do not compensate ambivalences, even if the ideal of modesty and the attempt to increase coherence are opera-tive. I would therefore not qualify these tensions as ultimately leading to an adjustment to dominant norms or as processes of a devaluation of religious meanings of bodily practices such as veiling as mere identity markers. I would rather argue that these women attempt to overcome age-related temptations to expose femininity, to flirt, or to adjust to fashion norms through a constant work on themselves. Saba Mahmood (2005) aptly put it with regard to her interviewees:

> [W]hat is also significant in this program of self-cultivation is that bodily
> acts—like wearing the veil or conducting oneself modestly in interaction
> with people (especially men)—do not serve as [manipulatable] masks
> in a game of public presentation, detachable from an essential
> interiorized self. Rather they are the critical markers of piety as well as
> the *ineluctable* [emphasis by the author] means by which one trains
> oneself to be pious. (Mahmood 2005: 158)

Moreover, self-imposed modesty does not prevent the women from actively participating in public domains, just as it also does not prevent them from enjoying youthfulness in domains specific to youth (dancing, listening to music, meeting peers, and so forth). Instead of limiting contacts between the two sexes, the women commonly emphasized, for example, that the headscarf facilitated their encounters with young men, because these relationships occurred within certain preestablished rules and within the limitations imposed by their own understanding of modesty and sexual restraint. What arises from this is an understanding of female sexuality, and in particular a notion of freedom that lies in blatant contradiction with the public discourse, as exemplified by the statements of the journalist Kebir.

The experience of youthfulness, for them, occurs within certain limits of what they consider *halal*. In this regard, also the organizational life plays an important role, because it provides and strengthens a sense of belief *and* belonging to a wider community beyond the level of the individual Muslims. Islamic organizations in both countries increasingly provide activities targeted specifically to youth within a legitimate Islamic framework to guide young people in an "Islamicly" correct life and often with a religious touch (in leisure, gender separated sports, Islamic music festivals, coffee shops where no alcohol is served, and so forth). Rather than necessarily expressing "ghettoization" or the rise of "parallel societies," as is most often assumed in public discourses, one could simply interpret this creation of Muslim youth spaces as one among many other forms of youth domains, or even as one among many other forms of youth subculture—at least if we understand subculture in terms of creating spaces outside of mainstream culture. Although the women clearly do not confine to the standards of what is predominantly associated with youthfulness (especially with regard to sexual norms and bodily practices), they nonetheless create their own version of youthfulness within a normative Islamic framework.

Claims for Muslim Piety in the Mirror of French and German Citizenship Traditions

Looking more closely at the ways in which these emerging forms of piety are reclaimed in the public spheres of France and Germany, we can detect some major differences that reflect, from the perspective of the believing subject, the different citizenship traditions, as much as different modalities of dealing with religious plurality. Although we can clearly see convergences between the French and the German women with regard to their relationship to Islamic traditions, their self-positioning within these societies as full citizens (France) or not-yet-citizens (Germany) reveals signs for their self-understanding being shaped by dominant discursive patterns, which are characteristic for the respective national frameworks and their conceptualizations of citizenship and nationhood.

Let me illustrate this more thoroughly by, first, focusing on the German situation and, later, on the French. What is important to stress for the women I talked to in Germany is their common self-reference as non-Germans. The young women did not—at least explicitly—identify with the German polity and therefore rarely perceived themselves as full members of German society. More frequently, they spoke about themselves as "Turks" or as *Ausländer* (foreigner) (Jessen and von Wilamowitz-Moellendorff 2006), although not necessarily connoting these self-references negatively. The label *Ausländer* seems to be incorporated to the extent that it is not even considered problematic anymore. Thus, young Muslims in German virtually reproduce the image of the everlasting foreigner, which dominates the German public sphere, although there is a trend toward naturalization among the generation of Muslims who were born and raised in Germany, which turns notions like *Ausländer*, Turk, and so forth, juristically inadequate.

The women thereby confirm the recent shift from the "political–legal" to the "symbolic" *Ausländer*, which still predominates the perception even of German-born children of immigrants. They consider their ethnic background as some kind of destiny—quite similar to the dominant discourse in Germany, which still confines to notions like *deutsche Schicksalsgemeinschaft* (German common destiny). The belonging to a national community here resembles a blood relationship that one cannot choose or freely define, "because in the end one is always in a foreign country as a foreigner," as high school student Esra (name changed) and member of the Islamic organization *Milli Görüs* put it. One can denote, here, an incorporation of the discourse on incommensurable cultural differences of Turks or immigrants, and the adoption of the stigma of otherness as theorized by Erwin Goffman (1967; see also Jenkins 1994: 206).

Accordingly, young pious Muslims like the women with whom I spoke raise demands for participation as committed Muslims in Germany much less offensively than in France. This is obviously related to different debate cultures that both societies have traditionally shaped. I argue, however, that the fact that Muslims have only recently started to raise demands for recognition of religious practices on a broader public level is to be interpreted as a result of Germany's restrictive citizenship tradition and ethnicized understanding of nationhood (Brubaker 1992; Mandel 2008), which has not encouraged immigrants or descendants of immigrants to consider themselves full members of German society, attributed with full political rights.

Yet, one can simultaneously observe that these young Muslims identify in important domains with "German" (or rather supranational) norms and values, even if they do not associate this identification with their status as citizens. Many of the women admired, for example, the principle of religious freedom and—related to that—the tradition of "tolerance." A sizeable number of my interviewees spoke about the "tolerant" and "liberal" character of German society, emphasizing the openness in regard to the ways in which Germany deals with religious plurality and diversity in more general terms. In France, on the other hand, public piety is offensively rejected. The women with whom I talked in Germany stressed their positive assessment toward the fact that "here everybody can live as she wants" (Sabiha [name changed], member of the largest Turkish-Islamic organization in Germany, *Türkisch-Islamische Union der Anstalt für Religion e.V.*). Although some of the women had encountered difficulties because of their headscarves, they generally expressed sympathy for the possibilities to show religious confessionalism in public spaces in Germany. The relatively privileged status that the Christian churches maintain in Germany and the tradition of a strong cooperation between religious and political domains seems to have opened paths for Muslims to institutionalize Islam in more visible ways than in France.

The women's positive assessment of the tolerant character of German society should, of course, be problematized, in that it simultaneously confirms their self-understanding as outsiders. Here we are confronted with a more general problem of tolerance as a frequent positive self-referential virtue of liberal societies. Political theorist Wendy Brown (2006) is one of the most outspoken critics of "tolerance discourses" and, indeed, points to some problems inherent in this concept in contemporary liberal democracies. Brown (2006) continues, most notably, a line of thought that Michael Walzer (1997: 52) already traced with his assumption that "to tolerate someone means to be in the position of power, to be tolerated implies a position of weakness." In other words, tolerance always has to be related to questions of power and authority. It is less of an innocent act or virtue pointing to any neutral stance, but more often a practice "concerned with managing a dangerous, foreign, toxic, or threatening difference from an entity that also demands to be incorporated" (Brown 2006: 27).

This assumption can indeed be concretized through a cursory look at approaches on the tolerability of religious (i.e., Islamic) practices in Germany, where tolerance has worked as a paternalistic gesture openly revealing the power position of those who set the normative lines according to which tolerance is regulated. The recurrent markers of the limits of the tolerable, often articulated in terms of "wrong tolerance" or "false tolerance" (e.g., in the debates on the Islamic headscarf [Amir-Moazami 2005]), indicate the hegemonic power positions with which the implications of the tolerable are produced. This has recently also expanded the level of public discourse and reached the domain of governmental and legal practice, considering, for example, the regional laws banning headscarves at state schools or the attempts to "test" Muslim's adaptability to German norms, before being entitled to German citizenship. In light of this, the recourse to tolerance discourses by these women can be interpreted as a sign for them having arranged themselves with their position to be the ones who to ask for toleration, exactly in this sense of being "suffered" or tacitly ignored.

With or despite this conception of tolerance, and with their reliance on the state under the rule of law, Muslims in Germany have been quite efficient in achieving rights, particularly rights of young people. Back in 1992, the Supreme Administrative Courts in Münster and Lüneburg decided, for example, in favor of Muslim girls abstaining from coeducational sports lessons. Similarly, young students' absence from swimming courses in state schools has frequently been accepted by teachers on the basis of religious freedom. This confirms a general phenomenon of Muslim's claims making in Germany, which has so far predominantly been carried out in the courts and thereby indicates a "juridification" of questions related to religious plurality questions (Reuter 2007). Only recently have such cases started to be discussed on broader public and political levels. As a matter of fact, recently the courts have treated Muslim's claims for particular rights much more reluctantly and less liberally than before.[6] More generally, the processes of "juridification" has more recently been paralleled by processes of "governmentalization" of Islam, in which both the state and civil society attempt to regulate and control religious practices of Muslims. The field of gender is of particular importance in this regard (Ismail 2008).

If we now take a look at France, a quite different picture emerges. There, the women I interviewed articulated a much more outspoken critique on the modalities in which Islam has been managed so far. These women all defined themselves as "French" citizens and often rejected any affiliation to the countries from which their parents emigrated. At the same time, they did not confine themselves to the dominant request to privatize their religious ties, and thereby went beyond the dominant notion of citizenship as a religiously neutralized category. Their discourse reveals clear signs of their incorporation of dominant principles, even though they put forward interpretations outside the mainstream discourse. What these women are doing could be described as "politics of redescription," which is, in particular, translated into a redefinition of the premises of citizenship.

The most interesting example for this is their recourse to the notion of *laicité*. The *laic* principle can have many different meanings, ranging from a strict separation between political and religious spheres to a more open interpretation, which understands it as a metaphor for religious pluralism, implicated in the spirit of freedom of consciousness. More recently, and in particular as a result of the increasing public visibility of Muslims, *laïcité* has turned into a tool of controlling religiosity in the public sphere (Asad 2005; Bowen 2007). The most telling example for this is, of course, the "law on *laïcité*" which targets specific religious signs (i.e., headscarves) adopted in 2004.

Referring to the more pluralistic understanding of the notion, my interlocutors in France interpreted this concept in terms of a principle that favors the pluralization of religious expressions in public domains, rather than as a means for the restriction or control of public religiosity. The statements by Khadija (name changed), a student of psychology, and Nura (quoted before) both from Marseille give a taste of this tendency: "In the texts today, the texts about *laïcité*, there is nothing in France that prohibits us to wear the veil. Hence, why do they speak all the time about *laïcité, laïcité, laïcité*?"

Nura added:

> They have dramatized this concept of *laïcité;* they have really
> dramatized it because France has lived throughout its history this
> battle for *laïcité*. This has nothing to do with the headscarves. The
> headscarf of a girl at school, where is the relationship? For me the
> headscarf and the cross and the *kippa* were only the pretext for
> pointing the finger: "Look! These people are dangerous. We don't
> want these people." *Laïcité* was a pretext for me because, on the
> contrary, a *laic* state is something good for us, . . . *laïcité* implies the
> freedom of religions.

This politics of redescription challenges the dominant understanding of *laïcité* as a means to transform Muslims into "culturally neutral" citizens (Asad 2005). The women with whom I spoke complained in particular about the asymmetrical effects of the implementation of *laïcité*, and more generally of abstract universalism, by pointing to the contradictions inherent in the notions of equality or freedom, which still represent largely unfulfilled norms and often serve as instruments to legitimize hegemonic politics vis-à-vis minorities (Amir-Moazami and Salvatore 2002). Moreover, this strategy does not seem to be a phenomenon limited to the women I interviewed. In a comparative study on Muslims' claims making in four European countries (Britain, France, Germany, and the Netherlands), Paul Stratham and Ruud Koopmans (2004: 30) observe with regard to their data gathered in France "several examples of this kind, where the claim reaffirms the principle of *laïcité*, but in doing requests more space for the expression of cultural difference within it, often making clear, however, that this is an expression of culture not politics."

The emerging understanding of citizenship is characteristic for the young generation of Muslims who, through their embeddedness in and familiarity with French society, are empowered to speak from "within," while simultaneously criticizing and challenging dominant normative standards. Faith-based citizenship clearly differs from the guidelines implied in the recent shift from "Islam in France" (*Islam en France*) to "Islam from France" (*Islam de France*), as proposed by French politicians, which ultimately confirms the French assimilation policy of the past decades (Bowen 2004; Caeiro 2005; Kastoryano 2003). Religion, instead of its declared absence from matters of civic life, becomes an integral element of citizenship. This is, furthermore, something that irritates public opinion, because it contradicts the hope for a gradual assimilation of young Muslims into dominant norms, inviting them to "become French citizens," as anthropologist Emanuel Todd (*L'Express* 1994) put it during the second phase of the headscarf debate.

The young generation of pious Muslims thus advocates an interpretation of *laïcité*, that contradicts the dominant discourse while still relying on an existing discursive tradition—namely, an understanding of the *laic* principle as a tool for religious plurality and freedom of consciousness (Baubérot 2000). They ask to adapt certain principles to the transformed religious landscape through immigration, while neither following the common demand of their one-sided assimilation into dominant norms nor necessarily establishing "separate units" detached from mainstream society. On a symbolic level, this was made visible, for example, in the demonstrations against the law banning headscarves in French state schools, where a number of young women were covered with headscarves colored in the French flag.

Contrary to the women with whom I spoke in Germany, the interviewees in France did not signify in any sense to be willing to leave things as they are, but rather emphasized their capacity and even their duty to fight for their rights: "We are in a republican state—liberty, fraternity, equality; there was the French Revolution, and everyone can do whatever he wants. This is not me who says that; the French people themselves say it. Well, or they have to change the constitution" (Zeynab [name changed], secretary of a mosque in Marseille).

Their claims for more representation as publicly visible Muslims in the name of their belonging to France should therefore be interpreted as an expression of their awareness to be legally members of French society. The demands for equality and participation are articulated in the name of French norms and less in the name of a distinctive religious community (as mostly criticized in the polemics on "Islamic communitarianism"). This must be emphasized, because it shows that, in particular, young Muslims have adopted dominant norms that are usually turned against their public visibility, while filling them with contents that promise to enhance their status as Muslims within society. Accordingly, women's demand to be accepted as full members of French society could be interpreted as a request to fulfill the promise of a politically defined concept of citizenship.

Yet, these women are clearly confronted with barriers in their struggle for recognition as publicly committed and pious Muslims *and* French citizens. Such limitations become obvious in the revitalization of republicanism (Leruth 1998) and the rejection of public forms of Islamic piety, more recently also translated into legal norms. The French tradition of controlling religiosity in public domains and France's assimilative policy confronts these women much more offensively with imposed restrictions on recognition than in the German case. Put differently, even if they consider themselves as full members of French society, they are not necessarily perceived as such by mainstream society. They attempt to become French, while the public discourse constantly reminds them that they are not French enough unless they give up what is sacred to them. Moreover, looking retrospectively at the dynamics of the public discourse and recent legislation on Muslims and secularism, their adoption of a discourse of rights almost seems to have caused backlashes. As Wendy Brown (2005) compellingly reminds us, the adoption of rights discourse by morally injured minorities should not simply be interpreted as an act of empowerment. Relying on the legal principles of dominant political orders can even reify these injuries, as it does not break out from the thick discursive texture and power structures and positions from which rights can never be immune.

Conclusions

The snapshots from the discourses of young covered women in France and Germany are only a few among many other examples of a wider phenomenon that can be observed in other European countries. Accordingly, young pious Muslims in European settings increasingly demand space for religious practice by referring to norms anchored in the "recipient" societies in which they live and interact, and thereby adopt notions of membership that are shaped by national or supranational European traditions.

Although in both cases (in France and Germany) young Muslims confirm their anchorage in the respective citizenship traditions, their discourses simultaneously reveal clear challenges to the management of religious plurality and the policies of integration. Even in Germany, where the women did not explicitly define themselves as full members of society, their self-perception as outsiders and their comparatively silent efforts to transform their role and status as Muslim citizens in Germany constitute no less of a challenge for German society and for its self-understanding vis-à-vis Islam. These women's discourses simultaneously generate an implicit critique of the dominant tools and mechanisms for dealing with (Muslim) immigration into Germany, reflecting the often-propagated version of toleration as a tacit ignoring of the "Other." Moreover, the struggle for recognition on a legal and publicly less visible level has started to convince the public opinion that the young Muslim *Ausländers* are increasingly speaking from within.

This tendency should not be understood as a move toward "Euro-Islam," meant in the sense of a gradual submergence of Muslim forms of social life into dominant forms of religion, as also anticipated in the academic literature through notions like "secularization," "individualization," or "hybridization" of Muslims (for a critique see Salvatore and Amir-Moazami 2002; Teczan 2003). Especially young female Muslims have often been regarded as pioneers of a "Euro-Islam," presumably adopting dominant gender norms with an Islamic touch (Klinkhammer 2000; Venel 1999). Although this might suit a large number of Muslims in both countries, those who reclaim public piety reveal more complex forms of religiosity and, related to this, also divergent understandings of youthfulness.

What the women are looking for cannot simply be subsumed under categories that the majority societies or, more generally, western liberal discourses (Mahmood 2005) understand as elementary for the formation of viable subjects, such as autonomy or equality, relevant also in steps to adulthood. The forms of piety, displayed, for example, by young covered women and primarily directed toward the "inside" of the subjects, simultaneously gain a public dimension and seem to provoke such strong reactions precisely because they do not correspond to what mainstream discourses consider being a "healthy" or "normal" youth. These subject positions also illustrate that there seems to be no universal modality of being young and youthful, and that various versions of youthfulness largely depend on the contexts in which they are molded, articulated, and claimed.

13

Struggles over Defining the Moral City: The Problem Called "Youth" in Urban Iran

Azam Khatam

Creating an Islamic society has been the cornerstone of the project of the Islamic Republic since 1979. Iran's regime has been successful in implementing fundamental changes in a number of key institutions over which it has held monopoly control—such as the legal system, the educational and school systems, and the national radio and television. Nevertheless, 30 years after the revolution, the project of shaping a monolithic Islamic society according to the proclaimed ideological vision of the regime has been a failure. Present-day Iran is de facto a post-Islamist society, despite sustained efforts, often coercive, of the political regime to mold public culture and especially the young generations in its desired image. I use the concept of post-Islamism as deployed by Asef Bayat (2005: 5), who describes it as a "political and social condition where, following a phase of experimentation, the appeal, energy and sources of legitimacy of Islamism get exhausted even among its once-ardent supporters. Islamists become aware of their system's anomalies and inadequacies as they attempt to normalize and institutionalize their rule." The aim of this chapter is to analyze the successive Islamization policies of the Iranian state, and the causes and dynamics of its failures. In particular, it focuses on the successive attempts to police moral behavior by young people in public places in urban areas. To do this, I concentrate on the project of *Amr-e be Ma'ruf va Nahy-e az Monkar*, a quranic verse meaning "Commanding what is just and forbidding what is wrong." For the past 30 years, this moral policing project has been in charge of enforcing Islamic codes in urban public space. Its performance is an indication of the effectiveness of officially sanctioned Islamization policies of the Islamic Republic.

A Problem Called "Youth"

Since the early 1990s, the issue of the booming young generation has been placed at the top of the public agenda of the Iranian state. A national center, The Youth Organization, was created for the analysis and the forecasting of problems of concern to the youth. In part, the topic has been cast as a crisis. By the end of the 1980s, much of the Iranian economy was in ruins following a decade of international sanctions and a devastating war with Iraq. Poverty was up and standards of living had plummeted well below the prerevolution years. Furthermore, Iran had experienced a demographic revolution. With estimated population growth rates of around 3.8%, the number of Iranians had increased from 34 million in 1976 to 49 million in 1986 and 70 million in 2006(Markaz Amar Iran 1387/2009). However, the most significant increase had been among the demographic category of young adults between 15 and 24 years of age. (Throughout the rest of this chapter, my reference to "the young generation" refers to this age group.) By definition, this young generation is in a state of transition to adulthood, entering the labor market and forming independent families. With the voting age set at 15 years of age, and with relatively high electoral participation rates in Iran, this population group is also of great political significance. Furthermore, by the end of the 1980s, this young generation had been completely socialized under the Islamic Republic, during the fervent and trying first decade of the revolution and the war with Iraq.

Technocratic authorities at the time cast the issue as a looming crisis, arguing that the baby boom of the early eighties had significantly increased the young population, from 6.5 million in 1976 to 14.3 million in 1996 or 24% of the total population. In large part, the crisis was framed in terms of the enormous burden of providing social services for this group which increased to 17.7 million in 2006, nearly triple the amount prior to the revolution.

Education was the more challenging problem. As a result of postrevolution grassroots developmental efforts, literacy rates among this age group increased from 56% in 1976 to 93% in 1996. Although education had expanded after the Revolution, the gains were most noticeable at the primary and secondary levels. According to the Public Census, in 1996, about 50% of male and 66% of female youth were out of school and a majority of them had a primary or secondary

FIGURE 13.1. Girls roller-skating in a Tehran park. (Nazi Neivandi, 2003)

certificate. At a critical time in their lives, when they needed to acquire skills and work experience, 33% of youth (9% of males and 58% of females), were neither in school nor at work.

Higher education has become a prestigious path by which urban youth aspire to establish their future economic status and lifestyles. However, the gap between supply and demand for higher education is daunting: Of the roughly 70% of youth who graduated from high school in 1996 and took the general university exam, only 20% gained acceptance.[1] Only 12% of 19- to 24-year-old urban youth were university students or graduates in 1996. Student migration to the West and, more recently, to Turkey, Cyprus, Malaysia, and Dubai, is an alternative choice for upper middle class youth who can afford migration. Others look for scarce, low-paying jobs available in the unstable economy.

In a country like Iran, where the state dominates much of the economy, the main factors shaping the life opportunities of this age group, such as access to training and education; employment; social and leisure services such as recreation, sports, and cultural facilities; health and insurance services; and, finally, obligatory military service, are fundamentally affected by government policies and state resources. In 1996, the official rate of unemployment for those between 15 and 24 years of age was 19%, and has reached 24% in recent years. Before the revolution, the unemployment rate was 13%. The unstable economic situation has constrained opportunities for job creation. During the second decade of the Revolution, the public sector provided only 23% of new employment opportunities, compared with 80% during the first decade. Youth in lower classes are pressed to look for jobs in family-owned business where they find temporary low-paying work.

By the mid 1990s, the vast majority of young adults were literate, urban, and had professional and middle class aspirations, but were highly frustrated by the scarce resources available to them. Youth blamed the government for its exclusionary policies such as admission policies based on Islamic/non-Islamic criteria. Many view the government's Islamic cultural policies as responsible for their social marginalization.

Public Morals: Text and Context

Since the revolution, public cultural policies of the Islamic Republic have affected young Iranians, forming the image of the Islamic state in their minds through everyday confrontations, resistance, and negotiation on codes of conduct in public life, especially in urban areas. Since the early 1990s, young people have played a major role in the resistance against official attempts to reshape the cultural and even the physical space of urban areas along monolithic moral guidelines.

The increasing obsession of the political elite with the *youth crisis* was not the result of youth socioeconomic needs only, but also a matter of visible sociocultural trends among the young population. During the postwar years of 1989 to 2000, the young generation, who had been brought up and socialized under the Islamic Republic, displayed and expressed distinctly non-Islamic ideals, aspirations, and representations. Young urbanites created new, customary, public, cultural codes (*urf*) to resist officially imposed, and often coercive, moral codes of conduct. This cultural agency manifested the power of the *urf* as one of the sources of legitimizing the public moral codes and challenged the fundamentalist homogenized approach toward sin and crime in social life.

Debate on the legal connotation of "sin" has been one of the controversial debates among different Islamic trends since the Revolution. Different interpretations of social codes in Islam have been involved in the debate of limits of government intervention in public morals. Some of the reformist figures define "crime" on a societal base, as the violation of social order and security, and call for limits on forceful government interventions on crime. They suggest that sin should not be criminalized but treated as a personal or spiritual shortcoming. The conservatives tend to make sin and crime equal, referring to the negative implications of "apparent sin" for public morals and extending the sphere of "moral crimes."[2]

The cultural agency of youth intensified this debate because of widespread legitimacy of *urf*-based norms among them and the creation of new social imaginarics about moral codes. Comparative national research on religious faith among Iranian youth before and after the Revolution indicates a drastic decline in religion as a collective identity and commitment to a set of public obligations and norms. However, there is a high degree of personal religious beliefs, with religious practices performed in individualized ways (Kazamipour 2003: 35). Youth cultural agency, the power of *urf*, was the main barrier to the imposition of the monolithic cultural policies of the 1980s.

It is important to note that since 1979, there have been at least two distinct and parallel cultural projects within the Islamic Republic. The first project was concerned with the public life of the general population, whereas the second project focused on shaping the intellectual, educational, and cultural elite of the country. The executive mechanism of the former was the *Amr-e be Ma'rufva Nahy-e az Monkar* project (which I henceforth refer to as *Amr-e be Ma'ruf*). (Translated, this means "Commanding what is just and forbidding what is wrong" one of the basic tenets of Islamic jurisprudence and the moral task of any Muslim). The second project was institutionalized as the Islamic Republic's Cultural Revolution, launched in 1980, which closed the universities for three years, only to be reopened after extensive purges and Islamization of the faculty, administration, and student body. The Cultural Revolution was later extended to all cultural centers and activities.[3] Because of limited space, this chapter does not address the Cultural Revolution, the project directed toward the activities of the cultural elite. This chapter focuses on youth and public cultural policies of the Islamic Republic.

Looking at the trend of activities of *Amr-e be Ma'ruf* from its beginning, three distinct phases of varying intensity can be distinguished. The first and formative phase was linked to Ayatollah Khomeini's directive to the Revolutionary Council in April 1979 to create a morality bureau (*Dayere Amr-e be Ma'ruf*) to uproot prerevolutionary corrupt cultural habits. The second phase was initiated with volunteer militiamen (the *Basij*) returning from the war with Iraq, directing their revolutionary zeal toward the domestic battle front. This second phase of *Amr-e be Ma'ruf*'s activity, from 1988 to 1996, was a long, repressive, and intense period that peaked in 1993 with the command of Ayatollah Ali Khamenehei, Khomeini's successor as Supreme Leader, to confront the "cultural invasion" of western, secular, nonrevolutionary, and non-Islamic influences. The target groups changed from the antirevolutionary and secular groups of the 1980s, to the masses of urban middle class youth and women. Patrolling units of *Amr-e be Ma'ruf* would harass, humiliate, and arrest young men and women in the streets, workplace, universities, and other public places, accusing them of moral misconduct. Even private homes were raided to punish partygoers, alcohol drinkers, illegal video watchers, the owners of satellite televisions or sex workers and drug users. The social backlash against the cultural oppression of the postwar years was a main factor contributing to the reformist movement. From 1996 to 2005, there has been a marked decline in attempts at moral policing of public urban space. This relative relaxation has been correlated with a markedly greater access of young people of diverse class and cultural backgrounds to the public arena; their increased resistance against enforced, rigid religious codes; and, at the same time, a growing discord and fragmentation among government factions over cultural control and state intervention in public/private life. Finally, the third phase of *Amr-e be Ma'ruf* activity was launched by new conservative groups after their takeover of Tehran's city council elections in 2003, the national Parliament in 2004, and the presidency in 2005. During the third phase, regular urban police (*Niroie Entezami*) took the main responsibility of implementing the project, as opposed to the *Basij*. Special patrolling units of police (*gasht vijeh ershad*) would pursue and arrest young men and women in the streets, shopping malls, and other public places.

During each of these stages, radical calls for imposing rigid Islamic ethics have been raised against the claim for a more flexible interpretation of Islam. Although the reformists and moderates never entered into an open confrontation on *Amr-e be Ma'ruf*, they have created a distinct cultural discourse by making references to more moderate Quranic verses and *hadiths* concerning ethics, the tolerance and mercifulness of God, and the Islamic safeguards for the sanctity of the private sphere.

The Islamic Revolutionary Ideal: The First Stage
of *Amr-e be Ma'ruf*

The first phase of activities to discipline the public culture in the Islamic Republic lasted from 1979 to 1982, when the *Dayereh Mobarezeh ba Monkarat* (the Department to Combat Immoral Behavior) was established in Tehran. At the time, there was a high degree of consensus among revolutionary leaders on cultural policies aimed primarily at creating a moral society and eliminating sinful practices affiliated with the prerevolutionary era. The first activity of the *Dayereh* was to demolish the *Qal'eh*, the old red-light district of Tehran, removing 2,700 prostitutes. In a single month, some 160 brothels were shut down in Tehran, and an average of 800 to 1,500 people were arrested every month for moral crimes, with a few being imprisoned and many receiving corporal punishment by being lashed.[4] The offenders' average age is not known, but it seems they came from different age groups. About one in every four arrested was female. The punishment for some female crimes, like prostitution, could be very strict. Of the 650 persons who went to court in March 1982, only one was sentenced to death, and she was a prostitute. Crimes mainly consisted of illegitimate sexual relationships, rape, alcohol consumption, gambling, and pederasty. The head of the *Dayereh* announced, "We want a spotless society and people should help us to realize it."[5] These remarks are reminiscent of Crane Brinton's (1965) comments on the puritanical streak within modern social revolutions:

> All revolutions adhere to a devout quality in their critical periods.
> Those who have power truly strive to uproot even the most minor
> offenses and thus they destroy some of the most basic joys of life. . . .
> In the years 1793 and 1794 there was a serious attempt to cleanse
> Paris, shut down pleasure houses, casinos and to stop intoxication. . . .
> Righteousness was the rule of the day. One could not even be lazy.
> The righteousness of the Bolsheviks might even be more paradoxical
> but it undeniably existed. (Brinton 1965: 212)

The eighth article of the Islamic Republic's constitution designates *Arm-e be Ma'ruf* as one of the bases of social relations, and as a mutual obligation of ordinary citizens and government. This institutionalization was an indication of the revolutionary puritanism of the time and its populist potential. In a speech in May 1979, Ayatollah Khomeini hinted at this populist potential: "*Dayereh Mobarezeh ba Monkarat* will be independent from the state, in order to supervise it and no one, not even the highest authorities, will be free of its supervision."[6] In practice, enforcement of *Amr-e be Ma'ruf* has been directed overwhelmingly at the citizenry—and at women, in particular.

The more liberal members of the Revolution Council, who disapproved of the project but could not deny its religious legitimacy, opposed it on legal grounds, arguing it would undermine the due legal process. Sadegh Qotbzadeh, a member of the Revolution Council, objected to the formation of the *Dayereh Mobarezeh ba Monkarat*, independent of the Revolution Council, and solely answerable to the Revolution Court: "If the Revolution Court makes the law, implements it, and then judges infractions, then there is no need for any of the other bodies of the government."[7] These objections led to the disbanding of the *Dayereh* for a while.

The *Dayereh* was reestablished as a special court (*Dadgah Zede-Monkarat*, the Court of Antiforbidden Activities) in 1981.The obligatory veiling for women was enforced that same year. The new wave of *Amr-e be ma'ruf* activities, nourished by the political tensions with the *Mojahedin-e Khalq*, the militia opposition group of the time, led to the first attempt to pass a law by Parliament to implement *Amr-e be Ma'ruf* in 1981, The cabinet of Ali Khameneie also ratified a bill for the struggle against immoral behavior in November 1982, and an Islamic dress code for women was formally legalized.

For two years, *Amr-e be Ma'ruf* was basically implemented in Tehran. During this first stage, the boundaries of public political rhetoric revolved around a dichotomy between *Eslami–Taghuti* designations (*Taghuti* means idol worshipping, a term for those sympathetic or affiliated with the Pahlavi regime). The *taghuti* were not only the anti-Islamists, the secularists, and the feminists, but also those affiliated with imperialism, and, as a result, unworthy of acceptance in an Islamic society. Through a combination of sanctions and incentives, the revolutionary Islamist state sought to construct young Islamic personas.

Spaces, as well as citizens, were the subjects of this cultural project. Symbols of martyrdom and self-sacrifice were used to signify sacredness of the public spaces. The transformation of urban public spaces into a sacred scene happened during the first years of the Iran–Iraq war by posting pictures of martyrs in the streets, constantly broadcasting revolutionary songs, and organizing large funeral ceremonies through the city to show and create national solidarity for the war effort. *Amr-e be ma'ruf was part of the attempts.* These symbolic performances along with formulated discourses on the role of the Islamic state, on moral guidance of individuals and society (*Ershad-e Eslami*) created a formal Islamic public sphere, which excluded any emanation of perceived non-Islamic life styles.

At first, the power of the morality court was absolute. Then, in 1982, the first Islamic penal law was ratified by Parliament. The law codified the prohibition of "non-Islamic" dress for women. Article 102 declared that women dressed "improperly" in public would receive up to 74 lashes. This clause of the penal law remains the only legal instrument for implementing *Amr-e be Ma'ruf*. With codification, the bureaucratic state sought not only to restrain judicial autonomy, but also to construct an Islamic identity through threat of sanction. The activities of *Amr-e be Ma'ruf* and moral court, even at this stage were looming and threatening. Authoritarian enforcement of *Amr-e be Ma'ruf* created what Roxanne Varzi (2000) has called a "public secret," by which many urbanites hid their "non-Islamic" beliefs and habits at home, while appearing to be properly Islamic in public.

Youth in the Post War Era

The second phase of *Amr-e be Ma'ruf* is marked by the end of the Iran–Iraq war in 1988, and the return of thousands of *Basij* activists (voluntary militia) from the front. Even during the final stages of the war, prominent conservative figures took the line that the struggle over moral issues should not take backstage to the war. In 1986, a new plan was formulated to make *Amr-e be Ma'ruf* a greater priority. This call was embraced by rallies following Friday prayers in many cities, demanding greater government attention to moral issues, and was accompanied by a pervasive surveillance program. The peak of this period was the leader's public decree of July 1990, calling for the struggle against "cultural invasion," and demanding the support of the *Basij* forces.

This second phase had two particular characteristics. First, it was supported and implemented by a large organization like the *Basij*, with 3.5 million members. The *Basij*, initially created to shield the Islamic Republic from internal security threats, was now assigned the role of ensuring that Islamic ethics were observed. Many *Basij* volunteers, mostly young people from lower income urban groups, had joined the organization for the war effort. Some of them left the organization to find a job. Those who didn't, were involved in new task of policing the streets. *Basij* checkpoints in the streets gradually turned from security issues to imposing Islamic codes. In March 1993, the commander of the *Basij* stated that "from now on, the mission of the *Basij* is to implement *Amr e be Ma'ruf va Nahi az Monkar*"

Second, the target groups of the project had changed during this second stage, from combating affiliates and sympathizers of the previous regime to young people who were born and raised under the Islamic Republic, and supposedly had internalized and been shaped by revolutionary Islamic ideals. During this second phase, the discourse of *Amr e be Ma'ruf* was articulated as an attempt to forestall the dangers of external "cultural invasion" through new communication technology and mass media, and also as a reaction to the resistance of middle class youth to the dominant cultural ideology.

This is a period of fragmentation in public opinion on cultural values, with the families of the martyrs of the war and the revolution on one side, willing to fight to maintain the moral promise of the Revolution, what was supposed to be the cause of their sacrifice; whereas on the other side were the modern middle class and professionals, eager to make a clean break with the "Republic of Piety." Furthermore, the gap within the government, between pragmatists and conservatives had been enlarged.

The discourse of cultural invasion was used by conservatives to confront pragmatic leaders who were accused of being indifferent to the ethical promise of the Revolution. Indeed the new postrevolutionary technocratic elite (e.g., the managerial class and the emerging private sector), who made fortunes using their political power or benefiting from the closed economy, which created enormous profits for those with rare commercial licenses and subsidized foreign currency, was eager to cast aside the "Republic of Piety." Karbaschi, the pragmatist mayor of Tehran, symbolized these efforts in his modernizing projects for the capital and in his revitalization of Tehran's public spaces (Khattam 2005). The conservatives' attacks on the newly established cultural centers in Tehran illustrated growing disagreements on cultural policies between different fractions. Challenges continued, with constant back and forth during Rafsanjani's second presidential period without much noticeable change. Nevertheless, one clear outcome was that the *Basij* had been transformed from an informal organization of volunteers dedicated to defending the Revolution and the country to an organized cultural police.

Voicing the Public Secret: Youth Social Visibility

During the 1990s, breaking the "public secret" turned out to be an important element of joint experience of the young generation from different classes. A generation becomes a significant social force if its members share a common habitus (Bourdieu 1993: 95). Although the upper class youth has more openly challenged the restraints and rigid moral values denying their perception of freedom as personal autonomy in access to amenities of modernity, the middle and lower classes who are eager but unable to simulate an upper class lifestyle, disappointed from a proper economic and social life, show more aggressive indirect reactions. Soccer games have been one of the reflected scenes of this social anger. A research on riots in Azadi stadiums in 2001 indicates around 70% of spectators show their dissatisfaction of the game result through some kind of destructive behavior like breaking seats and damaging buses (Safabakhsh 1382/2003: 10). Gerhardt (1383/2004: 50) points to the "stadium discourse" as it has emerged as a venue for foul language and a kind of protest against the obsession with discipline and moral order: "The attractiveness of the stadium for some men lies in the fact that it is the only place where foul words can be used relatively freely in public." Celebrating for victories of national soccer teams in the street is another example of popular youth's contribution to breaking the "public secret."

The initial 1997 celebration represented a turning point in the
development of Iranian civil society. In fact celebration in the street is
a new phenomenon. It started with the draw in the Australian game,
then there were more demonstrations for the America–Iran game
and now people celebrate in public for the smallest thing. These
emotions were expressed in public effectively for the first time since
the revolution. (Gerhardt 2002: 51)

Cultural Reform under Khatami

The long challenges between conservatives and pragmatists entered a new
stage following the unexpected victory of Khatami, a reformist figure with
strong cultural affiliations, in the presidential election of 1997. One of the main
cultural policy changes during Khatami's presidency was a distinctly more
moderate approach toward increasing modernist cultural tendencies, and
markedly greater intellectual freedom and tolerance. These policies facilitated
the greater social integration of the Iranian society through the diversification
and the relative pluralization of Iran's formal public sphere.

As Minister of Culture and Islamic Guidance, Khatami ratified *Osul-e
Siasat-e Farhangi* (Principles of Cultural Policy), which became the reformist charter of cultural reform. Although *Amr-e be Ma'ruf* is a main article of
the Constitution, the Principles of Cultural Policy contains no such reference. On the contrary, it calls for government institutions to restrict the
selective imposition of severe religious views upon the public, for fear of
negative social consequences (Vezaarat Farhang va Ershad: 1371/1992). The
Survey on Values and Norms of Iranians(*Arzeshha va Bavarhaie Iranian*)
conducted by the Ministry of Culture in the late 1990s, was one of the
important national surveys of the time, which became a reference point for
reformists in their challenges with conservatives to document the obvious
weakening popularity of religious practices among the young generation, as
a result of state enforcement. An appraisal research on *Amr-e be Ma'ruf*,
commissioned in 1999 by Jahad-e Daneshgahi at Tehran University,
proposed that

the political system should avoid imposing too much ideological
pressure and restrictive codes on people, as well as exaggerated
propaganda on religious principals. Our society should experience
the state of *raha shodegi* [libertarianism]. Of course, this does not
imply giving up the law, but giving up the pressures which are not

within the context of the law, but which we implement and pursue as
if they were part of the law. (Jahad-e Daneshgahi 1378/1999: 138)

Indeed, there was not any collated law for *Amr-e be Ma'ruf*. Reformists had
ignored the pressures for passing new laws to support *Amr-e be Ma'ruf* and at
the same time did not enter in an open legal or political challenge to decon-
struct semi- military para-state forces who were behind the project. In his last
days, Khatami proposed *Layehe Hefazat az Harime Khososi* (The bill to protect
private fringe) to Parliament. The bill was mainly focused on political rights
and was distinguished as a late response to the chaotic situation of individual
rights in the Islamic Republic.Yet the ascendancy of the reformist bloc in
Parliament, and the associated intellectual and cultural ferment, effectively
ended the second stage of moral policing in the name of *Amr-e be Ma'ruf*.
From 1996 to 2005 the *Basij* checkpoints were fewer and further between,
the government told the *setad* it lacked legal authority for its indiscriminate
patrols. *Amr-e be Ma'ruf* authorities also lost their control over believers in
faraway cities. The discourse of "cultural invasion" through communications
technology and mass media was replaced by Khatami's talk of the "dialogue
of civilizations." People expressed their will for cultural change through
street celebrations, starting with the victory of the national soccer team over
Australia in the 1997 World Cup qualifying match. These celebrations were
a cultural turning point, since such 'non-Islamic' emotions of jubilation had
not been expressed in public since the revolution. Yet the hardliners did not
simply acquiesce in their marginalization. Renegade 'operational teams' of
the *Amr-e be Ma'ruf* meted out 'Islamic punishment' in such instances as the
serial killings of women accused of being prostitutes in the cities of Mashhad
and Kerman in 2002 and 2003.

Youth and the New Puritanism

The conservative victory in the Tehran city council elections of 2003 led to
increasingly vocal demands for greater governmental intervention in cultural
public codes, reaching its zenith after Ahmadinejad's presidential victory two
years later. The hardliners consolidated themselves in a coalition of more than
18 groups, some of which had been active since the 1990s, and others of which
were new associations organized by clerics and officials. Although the coalition
had ties to traditional conservatives in the bazaar and among clergy in Qom
and Tehran, it aimed primarily to give voice to the less privileged among Islamist ranks, including the radicals marginalized under Khatami and the urban
low-income strata. The hardliners turned *Amr-e be Ma'ruf* into a mobilizing

slogan for radical Islamist forces as the reformists' moment waned. Eventually, the unprecedented political ground for finally approving strict regulation and the full implementation of article 8 of the Constitution was laid.

From their first move back into power, they upped the volume of their demands for aggressive policies to control public life. The judiciary announced another initiative to create a force responsible for policing "moral crimes in November 2004. Committees answering the force's national command were to be formed in each mosque, neighborhood, factory, school and government office, with the task of implementing *Amr-e be Ma'ruf*. Independent lawyers who criticized the plan pointed to the clear conflict of interest, as well as the lack of parliamentary approval for it. However, this plan established the idea of shifting moral policing from the *Basij* to a regular police.

As the 2005 presidential campaign got underway, the leader of the hard-line coalition, Ahmadinejad, promised his followers a new age of economic justice and Islamic piety. The two components of his populist platform were harmonious, even if they aimed at different political targets. With his denunciations of corruption and promises to put the fruits of oil wealth on the humblest of dinner tables, Ahmadinejad cast himself in subtle, but clear opposition to Islamist power brokers such as former President Ali Akbar Hashemi Rafsanjani, a founder of the Islamic Republic who wound up as his rival in the presidential runoff. At the same time, he stoked resentment of the reformists among the more ideological sectors of his base, such as war martyrs' families and *Basij* members families, by decrying reformist disregard for *Amr-e be Ma'ruf* and vowing as well to crack down on conspicuous consumption. This was the first presidential election after the revolution which candidates had to announce a 'mild' position on veiling. Wary of being labeled a fundamentalist, Ahmadinejad promised that he would not "interfere with the choice of hairstyle of young people." But after he won, and all the branches of government were back in conservative hands, the conservatives resumed attempts to discipline public behavior with the language of *Amr-e be Ma'ruf*.

In May 2005, Tehran's conservative city council called in the police commander and blasted him for excessive tolerance of "inappropriately veiled" women in public. A few days later, special morality patrols reappeared in the streets, for the first time employing women officers. In August of that year, the arch-conservative newspaper *Keyhan* demanded that the government step up its efforts to enforce *Amr-e be Ma'ruf*: "Why do secular states expend such great effort to protect their youth from moral decadence while our Islamic state is painfully indifferent and silent toward the degradation of ethics among our youth?"

The same month, the city council ratified a document called *Rahborhaye Gostaresh Efaf* (Strategies to extend chastity) mandating still more bureaucratic organs, including a coordination committee drawn from various ministries and executive bodies, that would cooperate with police to punish violators of moral codes. By the spring of 2006, the morality police were once again ubiquitous, arresting or intimidating young women and men for their dress and conduct, confiscating satellite dishes and punishing shop owners who were selling 'inappropriate' articles of clothing. At the same time, several cultural institutes formed during the reformist period were closed. Others were severely restricted; the budgets of cultural centers in Tehran were cut by half, while more funding was provided to religious institutions. Within the conservative coalition, there were disagreements over *Amr-e be Ma'ruf*. The director of the parliamentary cultural commission mounted what he called a "fundamentalist critique of fundamentalism," pointing the inefficacy of past attempts to police morality. Another conservative said enforcement efforts should be "soft, not hard." As conservative intellectuals left the coalition in protest at the morality campaign, more power accrued to the radicals.

In the spring of 2007, the most extreme conservatives in the Tehran courts designed *Tarh-e Amnit-e Ejtemaee* (public safety program) aimed at soothing public fears about increased consumption of drugs, thuggish behavior among youth, rape and burglary—but also at enforcing *Amr-e be Ma'ruf*. As it was nominally a normal anti-crime initiative, the program was assigned to the regular municipal police by the president. The move was in keeping with Ahmadinejad "stealthy radicalism" during the campaign, for he sought to assure Tehranis that the regular police, not the notorious *Basij*, would be the enforcers. As a police commander told the Fars News Agency, "We didn't use *Basij* forces, because we assumed there would be more resistance on side of people."

The *Basij*, however, criticized police for their "mild" methods. By August, the *Basij* had been invited to take over operations targeting drug dealers and gangs of robbers. *Basij* commanders, embedded in the state bureaucracy, used the chance to proclaim themselves the saviors of political stability of the Islamic Republic in the cities. They inveighed against a "cultural NATO" and a "conspiracy of foreign forces" seeking to overthrow the Islamic Republic through the propagation of "non-Islamic" behavior among youth and women. The mix of cooperation and competition between the *Basij* and police ended in a kind of military occupation of cities in the spring of 2008. Patrols crisscrossed each of Tehran's 23 main thoroughfares, where confrontations between police and citizens over "moral issues" were a daily occurrence.

The fresh campaign was vicious in its treatment of young people dressed in "non-Islamic" fashion and its harassment of alleged *arazel va obash*, a derogatory phrase meaning drug dealers, addicts and thieves. In the first four months, nearly 1 million people were publicly humiliated, or "instructed," in the streets and 40,000 were arrested. Of those detained in 2007, 85 percent were youths aged 16 to 26, and 10 percent were accused drug dealers and thieves, 35 of whom were executed within a month of their arrest. Reports on the program's progress were released to the press as a warning to all. Investigative reporters revealed that "instruction" center for addicts in Kahrizak, on the southern fringe of Tehran, was turned into a temporary prison, where "criminals" were severely tortured for one or two months, without trial, to terrorize them prior to their release. This is the notorious place where some of the youth active in presidential election of 2009 would be tortured and killed.

In the summer of 2008, human rights lawyers and women's rights and student activists started a round of protests against the *Tarh-e Amnit-e Ejtemaee*. At the same time 20 independent lawyers took a complaint against police to the highest supervising court on governmental bodies (*divan e edalat edari*) claiming the 'public safety program' is illegal because it is not included in routine police tasks and it lacks any other legal instruction or sanction by parliament. In the summer of 2008, the main independent student organization, '*tahkim vahdat*' initiated a series of public meetings on violations of human rights by *Tarh-e Amnit-e Ejtemaee* in Tehran and other cities. In most of these activities, there were references to the principles of human rights and the protections of personal freedom outlined in the constitution. At the same time, *Basij* commanders and others among the arch-conservatives dream of institutionalizing the agencies enforcing A*mr-e be Ma'ruf* as a separate ministry and turning it to the basis of the penal system. Already, toward the end of 2008, the *Basij* had declared that its enforcement activities would intensify as a result of the "retreat" of the regular police.

The constant failure of the *Amr-e be Ma'ruf* project is only one piece of evidence for the proposition that present-day Iran is de facto a post-Islamist society, a place "where, following a phase of experimentation, the appeal, energy and sources of legitimacy of Islamism get exhausted even among its once ardent supporters"(Bayat, 2007). The campaigns for the tenth presidential elections and the events after the election mark both the beginning of an important phase of youth political activism in post revolution Iran and an unprecedented degree of political fragmentation within power centers of the Islamic Republic.

PART IV

Navigating Identities

14

Securing Futures: Youth, Generation, and Muslim Identities in Niger

Adeline Masquelier

Since the 1990s, a wave of Islamic revivalism has swept through Niger. Against the backdrop of intensified global flows, liberalization of national politics, and deepening economic crisis, a state-controlled, ostensibly monolithic Islamic tradition has given way to multiple (and often competing) modes of Muslim religiosity, leading to the development of a "heightened self-consciousness" of Islam as a religious system (Eickelman and Piscatori 1996: 39). This trend is particularly noticeable among youth. Claiming expertise in religious matters, some Nigérien youths reject secularism, denounce the practices of elders as un-Islamic, and decry the erosion of moral values. Arguing that moral corruption leads to God's wrath being visited upon human communities in the form of poverty, AIDS, and political mismanagement, they exhort Muslims of all ages to leave behind sinful practices and commit to a life of piety.

For the large majority of youth, however, "being Muslim" is not about engaging in pious acts (daily prayers, fasting, and so on) so much as it is about seeing the world through the lens of Islam. This does not mean that these youths do not consider themselves Muslim. Socialized in an overwhelmingly Muslim society, they make choices about the role that Islam plays in their lives, and their self-definition is strongly shaped by a sense of belonging to the *umma*—the global Muslim community. Yet because they do not express their commitment to Islam through the performance of religious duties, it is often assumed that they are less Muslim than religiously inclined

Nigériens and, particularly, elders. Although it is largely true that many Nigérien youth do not exemplify virtuous Muslim conduct, it is nonetheless problematic to state uncritically that youth are not "real" Muslims because they neglect prayers and would rather go dancing than attend a *wa'azi* (sermon). Such a statement implies that because they do not visibly express piety, youth do not concern themselves with Islam. Heeding the warning of those who have cautioned against privileging religion as the primary foundation for Muslim identity (Abu-Lughod 1989; Silverstein 2004), this chapter aims to complicate the equation of Nigérien youth with irreverence for Islam by exploring the place of Muslim identity in the lives of young men in the provincial town of Dogondoutchi. Dogondoutchi is a town of about 38,000 Hausa-speaking people, the overwhelming majority of whom identify as Muslims.[1] In discussing what it is like to be both young and Muslim in rural Niger, I find it useful to distinguish religious identity (a sense of belonging to a religious community) from religiosity (the performance of religious acts). As Roy (2004) points out, the two do not necessarily go hand in hand. Some people perceive religion to be an integral part of their cultural identity even though they do not regularly engage in acts of religiosity. For others, conversely, religiosity is more important than religion. A significant proportion of the Nigérien male youths whose values and vision of society I discuss here belong to the former category; that is to say, they identify as Muslim despite the fact that they do not engage in the explicitly pious actions that, in the eyes of their more religiously inclined counterparts, mark people as Muslim. As I hope to show, this shared sense of Muslimhood has important implications for the way that young men relate to both the Nigérien state and the West as they struggle to gain a purchase on the newly emerging sociomoral as well as economic realities of the post-9/11 world.

As they negotiate their youthfulness through the adoption of distinct styles and practices, young men are often at odd with elders who complain that youth should listen to religious sermons instead of rap music and exchange their foreign-made T-shirts and jeans for the less expensive *jaba*, the modest tunic of devout Muslims. To such admonitions, unrepentant young men generally reply that being Muslim has little to do with one's choice of radio program or wardrobe. In exploring the generational basis of emerging disagreements about what Islam is or is not, I focus on youth as a "social shifter" (Durham 2004)—a category that exists independently of the particular environment in which it is used at the same time that it is understood anew in relation to each specific situation in which it is invoked. Summoning the notion of social shifter helps us recognize not just the transitional nature of youth in structural terms, but also the ways in which youth as a category is "always in the process of being remade in sociopolitical practice" (Durham 2004: 601).

On the African continent, youth has emerged as a salient category for addressing issues of agency, authority, and consciousness (Comaroff and Comaroff 1999; Diouf 2003; Honwana and de Boeck 2005; Reynolds 1995; Weiss 2004). Nigérien youth, for instance, have much to say about what it means to be Muslim and what such understandings of being Muslim entail for matters of common interest. To make sense of Islam and Muslim practices in contemporary Niger, it is therefore crucial to trace the new forms of Muslim religiosity that emerge in tandem with youthful models of personhood and public life, and new understandings of power and political action. Generations are not homogenous entities, however, and analytical categories such as "Islamists" versus "lax" or "liberal" Muslims do not adequately capture the range of ethical orientations adopted by diversely situated Muslim youths. In what follows, I underscore the fluidity of Muslim identities and highlight the role that struggle, ambivalence, and contradictions play in the fashioning of these identities.

Reforms in Late 20th-Century Niger

During the past two decades, an anti-Sufi movement of Nigérian origin, the Society for the Removal of Innovation and the Restoration of Tradition,[2] commonly referred to as Izala, has gained prominence in Niger through its ability to channel discontent and oppose both the state and existing Muslim traditions (Grégoire 1993; Loimeier 1997; Masquelier 1996, 2009b; Niandou-Souley and Alzouma 1996; Umar 1993). Believing that the ills of the present are a consequence of the failure to follow properly Quranic teachings, Izala reformists urge all Muslims to return to what they believe is authentic Islam, devoid of heathenism and innovations.[3] They frown on the vain pursuit of pleasure, the westernization of local values, and the display of ostentatious consumption, promoting instead moral discipline, self-restraint, and frugality.

In the face of recession and downsizing, many young men hoping to secure a future embraced Izala's vision of a new moral order. They agreed with Izala that Sufi scholars were greedy, questioned the ascendancy that fathers held over sons, and criticized the practices of supposedly unenlightened Muslims. Overall, the 1990s saw a significant rise in young Nigérien men's participation in Islamic associations, a process that produced a key moral discourse by which youth challenged the authority of both government and elders.[4] In a country that was, until then, ostensibly oriented toward Sufism (Meunier 1998), those who opposed Izala reformism have become loosely identified as 'yan darika (members of a Sufi order) despite the fact that few of them are actually

Sufi.[5] Because of their religious divergences, those who reject Izala cannot be defined as a collectivity, however. As a largely heterogeneous population that includes both Muslims who pray and nonreligious observant Muslims, they acquire coherence as a group largely by defining themselves in opposition to Izala.[6]

During the past decade, Niger's already troubled economy has worsened. Seventy-five percent of the population is under 25 years of age, a situation that has resulted in severe shortages of educational and employment opportunities. The massive reforms brought about by structural adjustments, the dismantling of the state as provider of public services, and the collapse of patronage and other social institutions that had ensured resource redistribution have further curtailed job opportunities and access to marriage[7] (Masquelier 2005). Literate or not, few young men in Dogondoutchi can hope to make a living through farming as their fathers had, and yet fewer, among those who graduate from high school or university, will find permanent employment as civil servants. Unable to find work and marry, a growing number of them spend their lives as "social cadets" (Argenti 2002).

Dynamics of Inclusion and Exclusion

Although economically marginalized, male youths have nonetheless been granted unprecedented emancipation thanks to the global flows of commodities, information, and images that they can access almost anywhere in Niger. The emergence of private radios and televisions—media in which Islam is discussed outside the control of religious authorities or the state—has enabled young Nigériens to participate in debates on what it means to be a Muslim, a citizen, or simply a youth with moral convictions. It has also encouraged the spread of youth-oriented forms of musical and political expression.[8] Through the paradox of their structural position—connected to the world, yet excluded from it—youths are well situated to confront problems of power, abuse, violence, and social dislocation, something that they do primarily, although not exclusively, through the medium of rap music. Many of them have also adopted the dress of hip-hop artists: Baggy pants, oversized T-shirts, ankle-high shoes, and baseball caps are now must-haves for any fashion-conscious young man (figure 14.1). Predictably, rap music and the clothing trends it has fostered among young men have been condemned as anti-Islamic by Muslim elders. Youths (and young men in particular) nonetheless justify their adoption of rap musical and sartorial styles by claiming that they are informed by new ethics and motivated by the existence of previously unknown crises, such as

government corruption and the AIDS pandemic—themes that feature prominently in the lyrics of local rap songs.

Countering Muslim clerics' claims that listening to rappers and looking
like one are sure ways to experience the fiery tortures of hell, young men insist
that hip-hop is educational. It is a medium of consciousness raising—a platform for questioning the status quo in a country where widespread social inequities, corruption, and job scarcity are the norm. Aside from exposing the
social problems, such as poverty and unemployment, rap songs supposedly
teach young people how to survive the specific dangers (such as STDs and early

FIGURE 14.1. Male youths in their best hip-hop gear attending a dance party
in Dogondoutchi, Niger. (Adeline Masquelier, 2004)

marriage) they face in today's unforgiving world. More so than other forms of popular culture that have become ubiquitous dimensions of everyday life in Niger, rap music is for and about youth. Thus, although parents bemoan their children's choice of entertainment, many of them nevertheless leave youths to their own devices, hoping that they will eventually move on.[9] On this issue, young men partially agree with elders, noting that when they grow up—and produce children of their own—they will leave rap culture behind to focus on more "serious" things. Like Islam.

Situational Ethics

If parents worry that rap-centered practices might threaten their sons' spiritual future, youth, on the other hand, are more worried about their material prospects. As awareness of their bleak predicament sinks in, they look for means to take charge of their future. Islam figures prominently in these strategies of identity making and empowerment, even among those who are not religiously inclined. Muslim youth see themselves as belonging to a worldwide community whose members are united by their submission to God. For Izala members, the notion of global Islam implies the emergence of a "new universal community that can bypass and transcend the failure of past models" (Roy 2004: 13) and provide an alternative to the West's morally bankrupt values. Other Muslim youths, too, emphasize the unity of Islam rather than its fractious nature, pointing out that all Muslims are inspired by the same Quranic message. Yet few, among the older generation, have forgotten the terrible clashes of the 1990s, provoked by Izala's efforts to discredit local Muslim traditions. Today, past verbal assaults and physical confrontations have nevertheless given way to more civil interactions and a recognition that people must coexist peacefully despite religious differences. Although Izala-led riots have broken out elsewhere to denounce, for instance, the immorality of western dress (Cooper 2003; Masquelier 2009a), in Dogondoutchi intra-Muslim disputes remain confined to the "aurally saturated" (Hirschkind 2006: 21) environment within which mass-mediated sermons are delivered, circulated, and listened to.

Having come of age at a time when tolerance is the order of the day, male youths want nothing to do with the "petty" sectarian disputes that once absorbed their elders' attention. Their own recognition of Islam's transcendental unity is more literal and assertive. In the previous generation, the swift rise of Izala and the concomitant emergence of public debates regarding the authenticity of certain religious practices (such as the celebration of the Prophet's birthday) confused those who were unprepared to question previously immutable Islamic truths; but today, youthful Muslims are confident in their identities. The violence that once engulfed Niger is for them a thing of the past. Youth see the criticisms that preachers on both sides still occasionally level at each other as frivolous and of no consequence. As well as insisting that they had better things to do than argue about praying styles, university students periodically reminded me that Niger was a secular state where everyone was free to practice their religion. Nigériens, I was repeatedly told, are tolerant people.

What this means, concretely, is that although they retain a self-conscious sense of doctrine, young Muslim men no longer feel the need to legitimize the sectarian roots of their faith as visibly as their parents did. If the older generation of reform-minded 'yan Izala have retained their turbans, their ankle-length pants, and their beards, their young successors are less eager to don so visibly the mantle of piety. Few wear beards or turbans. If they put on a *jaba* to pray, so do countless other male youths who do not claim to be part of Izala. As a result, it is difficult to identify Izala members from other Muslims who do not embrace the reformist message based on their appearance. Male youth, in my experience, rarely argue about religious issues. Nor do they challenge each other over the superiority of one style or schedule of prayer over another. Indifferent to the sectarian distinctions that once provoked deep enmity among their elders, they forge friendships, professional ties, and even political alliances across religious affiliations on the basis that Islam should unite, rather than divide, Muslims. This is not to say, of course, that young members of Izala no longer attempt to rally every Muslim to their association or that the piety minded among them have stopped condemning music listening as a sinful, Satan-inspired activity. Rather, mindful of how earlier disagreements over what constituted "true" Islam tore the town apart, young Dogondoutchi residents are consciously opting not to focus on what separates them religiously, sartorially, or even socially.

Some young men interrupt their activities to take part in the performance of daily prayers, but many others are widely suspected of forgetting their religious duties. Local clerics routinely berate young men for ignoring the call to prayer when their favorite television shows or musical programs are on. I was often told that if prayer coincided with a popular television series, young people would opt to turn on the television. The issue of the timing of prayer flared up when 'yan Izala insisted that the prayer schedule adopted by their Muslim opponents was incorrect. They created a prayer schedule of their own, in which daily prayers took place roughly 15 minutes before the conventional times of worship, and warned followers and foes alike that exactitude in worship was a good way of ensuring one's place in paradise. For those for whom punctuality now determined one's eternal fate, young men's reluctance to pray on time, or at all, was a distressing sign of their characteristic impiety.

Male youth themselves admit to living with significant compromise. Yet most do not want to give up rap music for the sake of looking "more Muslim." They insist that wearing baggy jeans does not prevent one from praying. Several of them described piety to me as an intensely personal attitude that was not motivated by one's external appearance; it did not matter what clothes one wore at prayer time as long as they were clean. For many of them, adapting to changing socioeconomic realities has meant satisfying their needs and aspirations as consumers—even if such strategies are perceived as symptomatic of a lack of piety and seriousness. Mindful of the limitations of cultural models that equate consumption with triviality (Miller 1994), I see youth's ostentatious consumption of hip-hop culture in an age of economic collapse as a strategy of identity making that roots consumers in an imaginary, better elsewhere. Like other African youth who have embraced hip-hop styles and attitudes to redefine their relation to the wider world (Weiss 2002), young Nigérien men do not so much express a prior identity so much as they create it through the performance of a "cultural style" (Ferguson 1999).

Young Muslims may continually engage in makeshift compromises but they do not perceive any contradiction in their casual invocation of different levels of self-identity to justify their actions. As they see it, the world is increasingly devoid of opportunities; therefore, one must be open-minded enough to consider—and occasionally grab—whatever comes one's way for the sake of survival. Those who are hampered by an excessively dogmatic vision of Islam will not make it in today's world. *Flexibility*, then, is key to securing the often contradictory and increasingly tenuous promises of the current neoliberal moment when one lives in the world's poorest nation. By waiting for their favorite radio shows or soap operas to be over before making their way to the prayer grounds, young men restrict Islamic practices to specific spaces and temporalities, apart from the realm of secular, western-inspired practices, and they carefully negotiate their way between these two domains. They have become pragmatic Muslims.

For pragmatic Muslims, there is a time to demonstrate one's devotion to God and a time to fulfill other imperatives, such as the mundane concerns of modern existence. From this perspective, ethical behavior is *situational* rather than immutable. I once asked a young man who wore a baseball cap how he felt about local clerics' injunction that youthful Muslims stop wearing "American" hats because they were anti-Islamic. He first looked offended by the question before answering curtly, "This is my *maganin rana!*" (protection against the sun). Whether he was parodying those who invoke practical rules of pietistic conduct for everything they do or simply stating the truth, what is significant is that he denied any hint of impropriety on his part by resolutely summoning the

most pragmatic of reasons for wearing such "wicked" headgear. Muslims routinely invoke their health to justify what might otherwise seem to be a violation
of some Quranic principle. Thus, breaking one's fast is not a sin if one does it
to preserve one's health, and drinking alcohol can similarly be justified if it is
done for medicinal purposes. By cleverly invoking the need to protect his face
from the sun, the young enthusiast of western fashion was eschewing any
suggestion that the baseball cap he wore could be construed as un-Islamic.
His choice of words was not fortuitous; *maganin* literally means "medicine
for." Like his contemporaries who routinely pointed out to me that the Latin
American teledramas they watched on television were often more useful than
Islamic sermons because they were educational (Masquelier 2009a) and more
in tune with the concerns of contemporary youth, he provided an eloquent
demonstration of how Muslim youths combine piety with pragmatism in their
struggle to participate in the definition of Islamic modernity. If he remained
unconditionally committed to Islam at one level, at another, more practical
level, his participation in Islam, like that of many Nigérien youths I met in
2004, was largely situational, informed by a pragmatic knowledge of the exi-
gencies of life on the margins of the Islamic world.

For Islam and against the West

Among male youths who pray regularly, some, rather than remaining faithful
to a particular mosque, regularly attend *salla* (prayer) at the mosque that is
nearest to where they find themselves when they are summoned by the call to
prayer—regardless of which religion faction claims that mosque. They generally justify themselves by invoking convenience; it is easier simply to walk
to the nearest mosque. Yet it would be a mistake not to see this practice as an
explicit effort to demonstrate the extent to which the youthful Muslim community has transcended internal divisions.[10] Because the mosque is the place of
God, I was often told, it matters little what affiliation one has. What matters is
the actual act of prayer, not the place where that prayer takes place.[11] That a
number of male youths consciously opt to transcend factional boundaries
through their choice of prayer sites as well as friends speaks to the compromises they have made as they negotiate their participation in what they hope
will be a renewed moral order.

For a majority of male youths, the notion of a common Islamic identity
also means that, regardless of whether they engage in pious activities, they are
"for Islam." More often than not, they are unconditionally so. Thus, at a time
when the Israeli–Palestinian conflict and the invasion of Iraq have crystallized

anti-U.S. sentiments among many Muslim youths, young Nigériens find themselves loudly cheering for Osama bin Laden, who has become the hero of the Muslim world. After September 11, many in Dogondoutchi celebrated the end of the "evil empire," and T-shirts bearing pictures of the infamous terrorist sold quickly. Boys and girls enthusiastically purchased flip-flops whose upper soles were adorned with a picture of the World Trade Center's burning towers, so that they could stamp on the graphic symbol of America's financial hegemony a thousand times a day. Today, numerous male children born since 9/11 bear the name of Osama—a name that, although not in use before, sounds very Hausa.

By providing (through its dual role as the global bully and the victim of retaliation) a blatant confirmation that the world is starkly divided into Muslims and their enemies, the United States has emerged as a new focus of Muslim anger—something it was not before the events of 9/11, except in the moralizing discourses of Izala reformists who have long perceived the West as a cradle of impiety and decadence. Being "for Islam" sometimes has little to do with faith and religiosity, and everything to do with solidarity, as this comment by an 18-year-old shows: "When bin Laden attacked America, all the Muslims of Niger were happy. They think that all Americans are pagans, and since bin Laden is a Muslim, they like him; they like everything he does. They support him."

From this perspective, joining the al-Qaeda movement, even if only in spirit, has become the duty of every Muslim, for Muslims must unite against their aggressors. Predictably, young men routinely justified their support of bin Laden by an appeal to Islam. It was all, they said, because of Islam.

In the eyes of many Nigérien youths, 9/11 is the well-deserved punishment the United States received for its tyrannical domination of Muslim lands. At the practical level, the jihadist cause promoted by al-Qaeda is largely irrelevant to the struggles of ordinary Muslims for a better life. Yet, as De Waal (2004: 50) notes, jihadism's "failures as a positive political project do not undermine its appeal as a banner of resistance." This is why some young men assured me that if bin Laden ever called on them to fight for the Muslim cause, they would follow him. However, even if bin Laden's spectacular terrorist acts and his "rhetoric that pits the dispossessed Muslim world against America and its puppets" (De Waal 2004: 19) have captured the political imagination of Muslims the world over, they have not, at least in Dogondoutchi, provoked a widespread emigration to Afghanistan, Pakistan, or Iraq. Ironically, among the young men I met in 2004, those who most vocally articulated their hatred of the United States on the grounds that Americans were "against Muslims" were often the first to express a desire to emigrate to America. How, then, do we reconcile this manifest loathing for U.S. moral and political values with the widespread aspiration to emigrate to America?

What seems like a contradiction may not be one if we focus once more on the concept of "situational ethics." For young Nigériens, emigrating to America has nothing to do with expressing moral convictions and everything to do with economic survival. Now that the Nigérien state can no longer guarantee economic security to its citizens, it behooves them to try to make a future for themselves, even if that means temporarily living in a country of alleged unbelievers. For a generation of young Muslims who have grown up in the shadows of America's growing dominance over world affairs, such a strategy may require adjustments, but it should not compromise their moral integrity. Although every young man dreams of finding prosperity in the United States, few have thought of what such a move might entail at the practical level. They are nonetheless profoundly ambivalent about what the West, and the United States in particular, has come to represent. Although they hope to emigrate to the "land where everyone is rich" and see America as a vital source of cultural capital, they are also keenly aware that, as Muslims, they belong to the *umma*, and must therefore unconditionally oppose the hegemony of the morally bankrupt United States. In the end, as they consider the choices they must make, practicality prevails. There is a time to express Muslim solidarity and denounce the American oppressors, and then there is a time when economic survival and a chance of earning a social position become more important than moral solidarity.

Muslim Youth and the State

To make sense of the surge of enthusiasm that Osama bin Laden and his attacks on U.S. soil generated among Nigérien male youth, one must situate it in the context of youthful discontent with the national policies of a secular government that is widely blamed for the crisis in which the younger generation finds itself. Regardless of religious affiliations, young Nigériens are thoroughly frustrated with the state's failure to improve the country's troubled educational system and to provide jobs for the emerging cohorts of high school and university graduates; the civil service sector is facing drastic budgetary cuts. Hoping to have an impact on the political orientation of their country, a substantial number of Dogondoutchi youths became involved in the presidential campaign of 2004.[12] Youthful members of Izala rallied around Mahamadou Issoufou, the Socialist candidate and leader of the PNDS (*Parti nigérien pour la démocratie et le socialisme*), whom they saw as more concerned with the predicament of youth.

Given Izala's decidedly populist orientation, it is not surprising that so many of its members voted for Issoufou. The PNDS was widely believed to be closely associated with Muslim reformists.

If members of Izala's youth wing actively participated in Issoufou's presidential campaign, they did so alongside other young Muslims who shared their problems and their preoccupations. Thus, although Izala overwhelmingly supported the PNDS party, nonmembers of Izala, equally worried about their future and eager to do away with a government they perceived as corrupt and irresponsible, also voted for and, in some cases, campaigned for the Socialist candidate. In the end, Issoufou lost the election and the incumbent, Mamadou Tandja of the MNSD (*Mouvement national pour la société de développement*), was reelected. Despite the defeat of the candidate favored by the younger generation, the election confirmed the emergence of youths as social actors in the public sphere. It also demonstrated to what remarkable degree they were united by a common struggle against poverty and unemployment. Although not all of them display, like members of Izala, an overriding concern with revitalizing Muslim practices by encouraging a stronger commitment to the teaching of the Quran, they nonetheless share a vision of a more fiscally responsible, kinder society attentive to the needs of the underprivileged and the younger generation.

A number of youths see being actively engaged in politics not just as a way of contributing to the political life of the country, but also as a means of developing themselves—and ultimately of enhancing their chance of escaping poverty. In the context of widespread debates about *l'avenir de la jeunesse* (the future of youth), notions of progress and development are gaining widespread currency, and a number of youth have become involved in politics. The desire to be politically active is motivated by a conviction that the government is misappropriating national resources for its own fraudulent use, and that it must be held in check and its agents punished. Through their scathing critiques of the government, Nigériens, young and old, provide a moralizing discourse in which corruption is assimilated to a sin perpetrated by "bad" Muslims.

In a post-9/11 world where the experience of poverty and crisis is routinely articulated—most notably by preachers—in terms of Manichaean sentiments, Islam actively shapes the emerging Nigérien public sphere by providing a moral framework for scrutinizing, not just social arrangements, but also the public conduct of elected officials. Just as it allows disenfranchised youth to feel connected to bin Laden and sympathize with the cause of jihadists everywhere on the grounds that, because they oppose the United States, they must be "good" Muslims, Islam also provides a means of assessing the moral worth of public officials—who, as puppets of foreign administrations, supposedly rarely act in the best interest of their constituency. Because the government is widely

perceived to flout basic Quranic principles, young men feel justified in opposing the state. With the state largely unable to enforce legislation and provide for
its citizens, Islam is an ever more central source of moral order and political
engagement for Nigérien youth.

Conclusion

For male Nigérien youths confronted with the state's failure to provide employment and educational services, the quest for a prosperous future has been
increasingly imperiled despite Muslim reformists' concerted efforts to purify
society of its allegedly wasteful practices, promote resource conservation, and
generate new forms of social services. As they struggle to make something of
themselves, some young men end up breaking moral rules and circumventing
conventional circuits of exchange to ensure economic survival (selling drugs,
stealing, and so on), whereas others opt for political activism to enhance their
economic prospects. Regardless of how they capitalize on new possibilities,
many have made significant social and moral compromises that rarely meet
with elders' approval, especially when they are perceived to threaten Islamic
values. Yet, even as they selectively adhere to some tenets of Islam while rejecting others (or ignore most of them altogether), their search for a viable identity
is inescapably rooted in a sense of Muslimhood. Besides pointing to the complexities and contradictions involved in Muslim self-fashioning, these trends
illustrate how Islam provides a moral framework for scrutinizing contemporary society. They also show the extent to which, through a process of objectification (Eickelman and Piscatori 1996), religion has become an object of
individual scrutiny. At a time when the state no longer controls the definition
of public interests, and the production of a Nigérien citizenry has become
fraught with ambiguity, Islam emerges as an important source of identification
for young Dogondoutchi residents struggling to redefine themselves.

   For male youth, the shared experience of crisis has created perceptions of
a radical disjuncture between inherited traditions and lived reality, heightening
generational tensions. By focusing on generation as the new axis of difference
that has replaced class as a principle of consciousness, I have highlighted the
pivotal role of youth in processes of social transformation. Through their
embrace of hip-hop style and values, young Nigérien men invoke the right to be
different from their elders. Although elders often lament these permissive sartorial, musical, and social practices, youths contend that they do not contradict
the basic tenets of Islam. What this means, as we focus on the imaginative
ways in which young Nigériens avidly "consume" (Appadurai 1996) modernity

to reinvent themselves as Muslims, youth, and citizens, is that there is no consensus on how to define Islamic attire, Islamic entertainment, or even Islamic activity. As Huq (1999) notes in her discussion of Bangladeshi literature, "Islamic" in this context becomes a volatile signifier, but one that is nonetheless indispensable to the public performance of identity.

In making sense of these new posturings toward Islam, we can no longer ignore the impact of the attack on the World Trade Center on Muslim subjectivities. The events of 9/11 helped focus what had been relatively dispersed recriminations about unemployment, poverty, and marginality. Youths who maintained no connections to the Izala association, and even professed to be against it, now read their experience of crisis through the lens of 9/11 and the Manichaean world that has emerged in its wake. They express their Muslim identity not by observing prayer, but by professing to be on the side of bin Laden and the global Muslim community. Aside from demonstrating that the "very nature of Islam itself as a religion . . . depends as much on 'non-Muslims' as it does on Muslims themselves" (Launay 1992: 76), these strategic positionings encourage us to think beyond essentialist (and often distorting) models of Muslim identity to explore more fully how "being Muslim" in contexts of economic and political uncertainty can be fraught with challenges, ambivalence, and inconsistencies.

In this chapter, I have examined the production of modern Muslim subjects by focusing on generation and generational change. Demographically, politically, and religiously speaking, youth is a force to contend with in Niger. Battle lines over issues ranging from fashion to education to the performance of piety tend to be generational, with young men's activities being understood by their seniors as un-Islamic and revolutionary. Because youth is technically a stage of life, one is expected to outgrow one's youthful tendencies. Indeed, youths told me that their current "impiety" was only temporary and that, come 40, they would become better Muslims as much to provide proper role models for their future children as to ensure their entry into paradise. Although this suggests that we should not lose sight of the continuities, it hardly implies that the futures of young Nigériens are predictable—or, for that matter, viable. In the end, the development of Islam in Niger is intimately connected to the ways in which and the extent to which youths will be able to shape their future.

Acknowledgments

This chapter is an abbreviated version of a previously published chapter by the author, "Negotiating Futures: Islam, Youth, and the State in Niger," which appeared in *Islam and Muslim Politics in Africa*, edited by Benjamin F. Soares and Rene Otayek (2007: 243–262). The article has been reproduced with the permission of Palgrave Macmillan. This chapter was originally written as part of the African Studies Centre, Leiden/Centre d'Étude d'Afrique Noire, Bordeaux project "Islam, the Disengagement of the State, and Globalization in Sub-Saharan Africa," which was funded by the Netherlands Ministry of Foreign Affairs, The Hague. Research in Niger was carried out in November and December 2004. A rudimentary draft was presented at a workshop held in Bordeaux in March 2005 under the aegis of ASC-Leiden and CEAN-Bordeaux.

I thank all the project participants for their tolerant comments on my early attempts to grapple with this material. I am grateful to Benjamin Soares and René Otayek for their useful suggestions for improvement. Thanks as well to Salifou Hamidou for his generous help during field research. My greatest debt, as always, is to the people of Dogondoutchi for their hospitality, their guidance, and their willingness to share their lives with me.

15

"Rasta" Sufis and Muslim Youth Culture in Mali

Benjamin F. Soares

Islam in Mali

Mali is a country of approximately 12 million inhabitants who are
overwhelmingly Muslim; indeed, the population is estimated to be as
much as 90 percent Muslim. A very small percentage of Mali's
non-Muslims are Christians, predominantly Roman Catholic,
whereas the rest engage in a range of "traditional" religious practices
that their detractors usually gloss as "paganism" or "animism." In
the country's social and historical imagination, Islam and Islamic
religious practice both feature quite prominently (Soares 2005,
2006), although the non-Islamic (and non-Christian) also remains
an important reference point. However, Islam has been a dominant
feature of the sphere of public discourse in Mali, a *laïc* or secular
state in which the political class has frequently and actively associated
itself with Islam and various Muslim religious leaders. In recent
years, there have been significant changes in the practice of Islam—
and by Muslim youth in particular—that have accompanied political,
economic, and media liberalization and the expansion of the public
sphere. In addition to the creation of new Islamic associations,
including Muslim youth associations, Mali has witnessed the rise and
sometimes fall of various charismatic Muslim and non-Muslim
("pagan"/"animist") religious figures who sometimes feature
prominently in the public sphere. These public figures include
various Muslim preachers, Sufis, healers, and non-Muslim ritual

specialists, many of whom promise good health, wealth, and success to their followers, clients, and sometimes even the nation-state. My focus here is on a group of self-styled Sufis, a young charismatic Muslim religious leader and his followers in urban Mali. They are new social actors who provide valuable insight into changing modalities of religious expression among youth in Mali in the current era of liberalization and increased global interconnections.

By the late 1990s, groups of young Muslims who had a rather distinctive appearance came to have a much more visible presence in Bamako, the capital of Mali and its largest city. Most notably, many of these young men sported dreadlocks or they wore their hair in braids, sometimes shoulder length. Although young male urbanites, especially those who have studied in state schools, including the university, and those employed or seeking employment in modern sectors of the economy, usually wear some sort of western-style clothing, the young men sporting braids or dreadlocks tend to wear attire that is not considered western, but is rather unambiguously Muslim, African, "traditional," or some combination of these. Instead of the western-style trousers with a shirt or T-shirt or even the professional man's two-piece garment with three pockets made of matching fabric (commonly referred to as the *trois poches*—literally, three pockets) worn by many male urbanites, these young men wore long flowing robes—that is, the African *boubou*—over the "traditional" draw-string trousers, a caftan, or a burnoose. Their headgear also set them apart from most of their peers and included turbans, the *keffiyeh*, and, in the case of a leader of one of the new groups, a fez—something Malians do not ordinarily wear. While in public, these young men also usually wear around their necks large, conspicuous prayer beads adorned with bright, colorful tassels. In addition, some of them wear badges of various sizes, which feature laminated color photos of their "Sufi" leaders with the name of that person and his organization spelled out in French, the official language of Mali. These young men refer to themselves as Sufis. Many Malians associate the wearing of braids and dreadlocks by young and adult men either with non-Muslims (who sometimes historically had long hair, which they invariably shaved off upon conversion to Islam) or Rastafarians, who are present in small numbers in West Africa (Savishinsky 1994). Given these young men's braided hair and dreadlocks, which Malians frequently call "Rasta hair," many eventually referred jokingly and sometimes even mockingly to these young men as "Rasta Sufis." Although "Rasta Sufi" is not ordinarily a term of self-designation for the young men in question, they do not seem to find it disparaging. During the past decade, some of these new Sufis and their youth culture have come to assume a rather prominent place within the social and religious landscape of urban Mali.

The Recent Historical Conjuncture

To understand the development of Muslim youth culture in contemporary Mali, and so-called Rasta Sufis in particular, it is absolutely imperative to consider the broader recent socioeconomic and political context, which has been characterized by dramatic changes as well as upheavals.[1] In 1991, there were mass demonstrations against the authoritarian rule of President Moussa Traoré. Many young people, including student activists, played an important role in these demonstrations, which led to the overthrow of the regime. After leading a coup d'état to remove the military dictator President Traoré from power, army officer Amadou Toumani Touré (and Mali's current elected president in his second term) headed a transitional government before multiparty elections in 1992, after which the country's first democratically elected president took office. In the immediate aftermath of the coup d'état, and with subsequent political liberalization, there was much optimism about the future in Mali, a country consistently ranked among the poorest in the world. In addition to rising economic growth and considerable outside investment, for example, in the gold-mining sector, there was rapid and visible development of the urban infrastructure in a country that had seen only minimal investment in previous decades.

After the end of the Traoré regime, the sphere of public debate in Mali expanded considerably. Given the government's new commitment to freedom of expression and freedom of association, new political parties were formed, and new secular and religious associations were organized and proliferated. With media liberalization, the country's media landscape, especially in the capital Bamako, was dramatically transformed. A rather lively press developed, and numerous private radio stations were opened throughout the country. Malian national television reception, which had previously been limited to the capital and other large towns, was made available nearly everywhere in the country.

After the coup, many Malians had rather high expectations about the future. This was particularly the case for youth in a country in which more than half the total population is younger than the age of 18. Although the economic liberalization accompanying political liberalization helped to facilitate economic growth after long periods of stagnation, economic reforms and austerity measures also had some rather deleterious effects. Not enough jobs have been created for the many un- and underemployed job seekers, and regular salaried employment is well out of reach for most Malians. The devaluation of the currency (the West African franc) by half in 1994 created enormous additional burdens for the vast majority of Malians, who saw their purchasing power dramatically reduced. Under considerable pressure from donors and multilateral lending agencies not to increase state expenditure, the Malian government found it increasingly difficult to accede to all the demands placed on it, not least from the restless and impatient youth who had helped to end the much-despised rule of Moussa Traoré.

Although education has been a high priority for both the Malian government and the country's major donors, the educational system of secular schools and institutions of higher learning has been severely disrupted and even at times barely able to function since the 1990s. As many Malians will readily explain, for nearly a decade after Moussa Traoré was removed from power, state schools failed to function properly. In fact, in the years following the coup, the government has faced a series of student and teachers' strikes over state funding of schools, among other matters.[2] This has led to the cancelation of several entire school years and recurrent disruption of the operation of the country's schools. At the time of writing, the overcrowding of schools, inadequate infrastructure, teacher shortages, outright corruption, and the threat of strikes cast a long shadow over the Malian educational system. Throughout the years, students have suffered terribly, with their studies frequently interrupted or simply cut short. Many students and entire cohorts have had to repeat years. Many youth in their late teens and 20s with few job prospects have sought to extend their studies indefinitely or they have simply dropped out. In recent years, there have been some improvements, particularly in primary education, as international donors have focused heavily on such early education. Although primary school enrollment and attendance rates have increased, secondary school rates of attendance are estimated to be as low as 15% for males and 11% for females.[3]

With the economic liberalization that accelerated during the 1990s and the opening up of the Malian market to greater imports, all sorts of new possibilities for consumption suddenly became a reality. Malians now saw many new desirable consumer goods on national television, on satellite television (increasingly important since the 1990s), in films viewed on videocassette (and now DVD), in the market, and in the many new European–style shops constructed in the era of economic liberalization. Malians also saw such desirable consumer goods on the street and with visiting or returned migrants—Malian relatives and acquaintances living in Europe, North America, and elsewhere on the African continent. The new Malian economic and political elites who were prospering in this era of liberalization and reforms also usually became conspicuous and ostentatious consumers. A new culture of consumerism was spreading throughout the society, but especially in urban areas where there was a greater impetus to consume newly available imported goods. Many urban youth hoped their parents would be able to provide them with the money to purchase the latest fashions in clothing, wristwatches, *accoutrements*, scooters, motorcycles, electronic goods, and, eventually, mobile phones, all of which had become even more expensive with the worsening exchange rate. Indeed, the difficult economic circumstances the vast majority of Malians face almost seemed to guarantee that the new consumerism would put great pressure on most families and exacerbate generational tensions. Many parents clearly resented their children's sense of entitlement. That is, parents chafed at their children's desire for the new consumer goods without having to work to be able to purchase them for themselves. Faced with the deteriorating educational system and bleak employment prospects, many youth longed to emigrate to Europe, North America, elsewhere in Africa, or beyond where they might have access to the wealth to be able to acquire such alluring consumer goods.

It was around this same time that the social phenomenon of the *thé-chômeur* (literally, "the unemployed tea") or unemployed tea drinker became the subject of much discussion in Mali (see de Noray and Maïga [2002: 12]; for neighboring Senegal, see Ralph [2008]). *Thé-chômeur* is a term used to designate young unemployed men who sit around all day preparing and drinking tea—the sweetened Chinese green tea that is a popular drink served throughout the country when Malians socialize. Many Malians will tell you that the *thé-chômeur* is a largely urban phenomenon in a country where approximately two thirds of the population remains rural. In fact, just about anywhere in Bamako one encounters young men gathered together in small groups around portable charcoal stoves with enamel teapots and sets of tiny glasses, making tea, and passing the time. As many Malians note, if such young men were living in rural areas, they would undoubtedly be expected to engage in agricultural labor, as the vast majority of rural dwelling Malians must. Such unemployed habitual tea-drinking young men have usually engaged in formal schooling, but they have not been able to obtain the kind of work, not involving physical labor, for which their schooling has ostensibly prepared them.

The phenomenon of the idle *thé-chômeur* signals a significant social and generational change and is a particularly poignant sign of the recent era. Most of those of the two generations preceding today's urban youth would not have had such difficulties finding employment. In fact, after completing their schooling, many, if not most, would have taken up government posts of one sort or another or they would possibly have migrated in search of work to more prosperous countries in the region such as Côte d'Ivoire or farther afield to Central Africa or France. The era of the providential state is, of course, now gone. With more school leavers and graduates than in the past and reductions in the number of posts in the civil service, there are simply not enough jobs that these men find desirable or suitable. Moreover, much of the secondary educational training available in Mali ill-equips most graduates with the skills to manage in a liberalizing economy where the state in accordance with neoliberal prescriptions is not supposed to be the country's main economic actor. At the same time, there are greater and greater obstacles to migration to Europe as well as to some other favored countries of migration in Africa—most notably, Côte d'Ivoire, where hostility against foreigners has been a feature of the ongoing recent conflict (Marshall-Fratani [2006]). In recent years, numerous Malian youth have been among the thousands of Africans who have been making often desperate attempts to cross the Sahara and eventually the Mediterranean to make their way to Europe and beyond.

Youth Politics

In the years following the coup and the era of multiparty elections, Bamako, the main center of economic activities in the country, has continued to draw in young people in search of a better life. During the period of hopefulness immediately after the overthrow of Moussa Traoré, migration to Bamako from rural areas and smaller towns and cities elsewhere in the country surged. Such migration to Bamako continues apace. As elsewhere in Africa, many of the young people moving to Bamako face considerable difficulties, including limited possibilities of gainful employment. Many are students who have dropped out of school or failed to pass examinations, which would have allowed them to continue with their studies. Faced with so many disappointments and failed expectations, many youth are indeed restless. But not all young Malian men living in urban areas are, of course, idle tea drinkers. It is clear, however, that many youth have become disillusioned with formal politics and multiparty elections, which many hoped might help bring an end to the economic malaise of the Traoré years. All reports seem to suggest that most young Malians do not even bother to vote in elections. This seems to have led two otherwise astute observers of Malian society to make the following claim:

> Evidently, more individualist, the attitude of Bamako youth does not
> really lend itself, for the moment, to group enthusiasm for shared
> ideas, utopias, dreams of a better world. The notion of citizenship is
> not called into question, nor are support for the democratic system
> and democratic values. . . . It is rather disappointment with the
> leaders about the state of collective well-being. (de Noray and Maïga
> 2002: 97)

However, such a view of Malian youths' purported lack of enthusiasm for collective action and utopian ideals simply does not square with recent history.

Although it might be true that few Malian youth are actively engaged in political activities, conventionally understood as secular politics, this does not mean
that they are not enthusiastically working toward what they see as a better
future. Like many other young Africans, many Malians are actively involved in
creative cultural production in areas such as rap music, which frequently offers
a social critique of the injustices that many youth face.[4] However, it is in the
realm of religion where many young Malians have been involved in building
new communities and dreaming of a better world than the one in which they
find themselves.

The youthful turn to religion has been both broad and much discussed in
Mali. The same parents who might decry youths' avid consumerism frequently
remark that Malian youth today often take their religion much more seriously
than they did when they were young. One can see many youths' attention to
the practice of the religion in regular ritual prayer, frequent visits to the
mosque, assiduous fasting during Ramadan, and other signs of public piety
(Soares 2004). One can also see this turn to religion in the way many Malian
youth invoke Islam in their collective actions, particularly through activism in
some of the various new Islamic associations. If many young Malian students
have been involved in formal student organizations such as the Association of
Students and Pupils of Mali or AEEM (*Association des élèves et étudiants du
Mali*) that has planned demonstrations, organized strikes, and lobbied the
government on behalf of students, other students have shifted their attention
from such secular to more religious organizations. During the 1990s, many
young Malians got involved in Ançar Dine, which was to become the country's
largest modern Islamic association. Chérif Ousmane Madani Haïdara, the
founder of Ançar Dine, inspired many Malians, including many youth, to
practice Islam with greater commitment. In his view, this requires more than
the simple outward signs of religious practice such as regular ritual daily
prayer.[5] A modern-style preacher and media star whose sermons circulate on
cassette, video, and DVD, Haïdara's highly successful career has been dependent upon his skill as a media-savvy orator who frequently broaches such
controversial topics in his sermons as pre- and extramarital sex, artificial
contraception, and drug use, all of which are of great interest to youth.
Haïdara's rise to prominence has also been dependent upon his use of the
model of the "traditional" charismatic Muslim religious leaders and leaders of
Sufi orders who are often seen as closer than ordinary Muslims to God, as well
as potential intermediaries with God. Born in 1955, Haïdara is no longer considered a youth, although he himself has clearly been a model for younger
Muslim activists, including some of the new Sufis, who, following him, have
also sought mass appeal.

Beginning in the 1990s, with greater freedom of association some youth founded their own specifically Islamic youth organizations. One of the largest of these, the Malian Association of Muslim Youth (*Association malienne des jeunes musulmans* or AMJM) was founded in April 1991—that is, in the month following the coup. It is effectively a modernist organization that practices *da'wa*, the call to Islam, seeking to teach people to practice what Dale Eickelman (1989) has called a "generic" Islam of assumed universals (see also Soares 2005, chapter 8).[6] For example, the members often remark that many Malian Muslims (and not just youth) do not know how to perform regular ritual prayer or even how to perform the ablutions required for prayer. As some of the members of the AMJM have explained to me, they teach Muslims the "correct" way to pray and such other basic information as what verses in Arabic one should recite, for example, before entering a mosque, the toilet, or a car. They also teach people about the importance of morality and truthfulness, and tell people to work and to conduct themselves as upstanding Muslims. In keeping with its modernist objectives, this organization has also been particularly active in areas of health, working at times with UNFPA, the United Nations Population Fund, and it has helped to organize blood drives (Dicko 2005). Some of the leaders of the organization have also been involved in UNESCO-sponsored activities for "the dialogue of civilizations."

Although some Muslim youth have been involved in this kind of activism, which combines Islamic religious activities and *da'wa* with such civic activities as blood drives and interreligious and/or "civilizational" dialogue, other Muslim youth were radicalized during the same period. Most Malians agree, however, that radical Muslim youth are actually a very small minority in the country.[7] In 2002, during the month of Ramadan, a group of Muslim youth leaving prayers at a mosque physically attacked an adjacent bar and assaulted its male and female patrons in a Bamako neighborhood. The perpetrators allegedly attacked the bar because they objected to the playing of music during Ramadan (Diarra 2002). Some Muslim youth activists from some of the new Islamic associations were accused of involvement in the attack, and they were subsequently arrested and detained. However, on the whole, Malians were very surprised that such an act of violence was committed. Indeed, such violent acts by Muslim youth in Mali are quite rare.

The New Sufis

Despite the long presence of Sufism and organized Sufi orders in this region of Africa, most Malian Muslims today are not formally initiated into any Sufi order.

In fact, the number of young Malians seeking formal initiation into a Sufi order had been on the decline for decades (Soares 2005). This does not mean that Sufism has become any less important or that reformist Islam or Islamism for that matter has become any more appealing to Malian Muslims. Among ordinary Malian Muslims, including many youth, there is great interest in Sufism, as well as in some of the past and present charismatic Muslim religious leaders with reputations for exemplary piety and miracles who have been invariably associated with Sufi orders. As indicated earlier, in the late 1990s, groups of young Muslims calling themselves Sufis, with their distinctive hairstyles and clothing, started to have a much more visible presence in Bamako. One of these was Bilal Diallo, who now refers to himself as Cheick Soufi [pronounced Shaykh Sufi] Bilal (see figure 15.1). Born in 1974 to a rather modest family, Bilal attended state schools until early in 1992, when at the age of 17, while in his ninth year of school, he did not continue with his studies. This was around the time of the coup when such an interrupted educational trajectory became typical for many young Malians. After ending his studies, Bilal lived in his hometown of Ségou, Mali's third largest city and an important Islamic religious center.

Unlike many youth who were to join the ranks of the urban unemployed or even become *thé-chômeurs*, Bilal, like many of his generation, developed a particular interest in religion. The city of Ségou, where Bilal was living, has a special place in the social and historical imagination in Mali, not least for its particularly important role in the region's Islamic history as a capital of the large precolonial polity founded by al-Hajj Umar Tall in the wake of his *jihad* in the 19th century. In addition to being a major Islamic religious center with some of the country's oldest and most prestigious private *madrasas*, where students combine an Islamic religious education with the study of modern subjects using western pedagogical styles, Ségou has historically been an important center for Sufism. In fact, the most widespread Sufi order in Mali (and in West Africa more generally), the Tijaniyya, has long been associated with some of Ségou's leading Muslim religious figures, including the descendants of al-Hajj Umar Tall and some of his entourage. Several different, rival branches of the Tijaniyya are present here and in the broader region. Since the mid 20th century, Ségou has also been an important hub for the branch of the Tijaniyya that Ibrahim Niasse (d. 1975), the *shaykh* from Kaolack in Senegal, propagated in large parts of Africa. In fact, Ségou is one of the few places in Mali with significant numbers of followers of Ibrahim Niasse, including some who are rather high in profile. There are also adherents of the Qadiriyya in Ségou and the broader region.

While in Ségou, Bilal apparently did not frequent any of the city's *madrasas*, where some of the country's most prominent and respected Muslim religious leaders, including Haïdara, have studied. Instead, Bilal began to

FIGURE 15.1. Cover of book by Soufi Bilal. (Soufi Bilal Diallo, n.d.)

associate with some of the young men involved in more "traditional" forms of Islamic education, as well as Sufism.[8] In the 1990s, Ségou had become known as a place where some young men who were engaging in "traditional" Islamic education had started to sport dreadlocks or braided hair. Some Malians called these men "the Ségou Rastas," even though their direct ties to Rastafarianism were tenuous at best. Since the 1980s, reggae music and the images of such reggae stars as Bob Marley and Alpha Blondy from Côte d'Ivoire have been enormously influential among Malian youth and West Africans more generally. Many youth, especially those in urban centers such as Ségou, integrated certain Rastafarian elements of style, particularly the idea of long hair, into their youth culture.[9] Although some youth also took up the smoking of canna-bis, which is associated with Rastafarianism, most young Muslims in the circles in which Bilal moved did not. Bilal began to wear his hair long like other Muslim students nicknamed the Ségou Rastas. It is important to note that Bilal and his peers specifically associated this element of style with Sufism and youth culture, not with Rastafarianism. In this way, Bilal was exhibiting his affinities with contemporary urban youth culture, but also with the new fashion in Sufi style. As suggested earlier, this new style indexed a shift in what was considered acceptable appearance for Muslim men, as well as Muslim youth.

While in Ségou, Bilal came into contact with Lassana, a charismatic Muslim religious leader who is best known as Soufi Lassana. Although Lassana was also young, he is quite a bit older than Bilal. Over time, Lassana has developed a reputation as a Sufi and is known for the many astonishing things or miracles associated with him. In Ségou, Lassana had become a prominent Muslim religious leader to whom many Malians have turned to ensure wealth, success, and good health. He has many followers who have gathered around him in Ségou. Those who go to see Lassana to have a problem of love, marriage, health, or money resolved range from ordinary Malians to the country's political and economic elites, including former government ministers. Some claim that Lassana is the person who initiated Bilal into Sufism while he was in Ségou, and that their relationship was that of Sufi master and disciple or teacher and protégé. Although Bilal denies the existence of any such relationship, the exact nature of their relationship remains unclear. After moving to Bamako, Bilal seems to have cut all ties with Lassana and his circle and he subsequently started to position himself as a religious entrepreneur in his own right.

In Bamako, Bilal moved to a modest home in a neighborhood not far from the city center. While he was still relatively unknown, Bilal apparently attempted to associate with some influential Muslim religious leaders in Bamako. Indeed, the preacher Haïdara has told me how Bilal used to pay visits to him at his Bamako home. In 1999, Bilal published a short pamphlet (in French and Arabic) about the Qadiriyya, in which it is claimed that he was "a sure source of knowledge, a luminous source of divine energy" (Bilal n.d.a: 5). It is unclear how well Bilal was known or how widely accepted such lofty views about him were at the time of publication of this first pamphlet. Be that as it may, in the decade since Bilal moved to Bamako, he has developed a reputation as a Sufi, and for exemplary piety and numerous followers.

In addition, Bilal has become particularly known for hosting large celebrations of the *mawlid*, the birthday of the Prophet Muhammad, in Bamako. Although historically the Prophet Muhammad's birthday has been celebrated in various places in Mali and with much fanfare in certain parts of the country, especially in some of the long-established Islamic religious centers, there have, in recent years, been rather heated debates about the legitimacy of doing so.

Muslim reformists—frequently called "Wahhabis" in local parlance—who are present in considerable numbers in Bamako strenuously object to *mawlid* celebrations, saying that they are unlawful innovation (Arabic, *bid'a*) (see Brenner 2000; Soares 2005). It almost goes without saying that such Muslim reformists also condemn Sufism and its associated practices as unlawful innovation. In one of his other published pamphlets, *La célébration du Maouloud* (The Celebration of the Mawlid), Bilal defends the licitness of the *mawlid* (Bilal n.d.b). He even includes a poem in the pamphlet that is a rejoinder to critics of the *mawlid*, whom he dismisses—in terms that are derisive and occasionally humorous—as "corrupt," "deviant," "manipulated," and "shipwrecked" (Bilal n.d.b: 36–37).

Libyan leader Muammar al-Gaddafi has long been a proponent of pan-African objectives and a staunch opponent of Islamism. In December 2004, the Libyan government sponsored a large conference on Sufism in Bamako. The conference was apparently designed, in part, to showcase Sufism following the attacks of September 11, 2001, when there was considerable attention to the possible rising influence of Islamists in sub-Saharan Africa and elsewhere in the world. The Malian government endorsed and sent representatives to the Libyan-sponsored conference, which featured both academics and members of Sufi orders from Mali and some of the neighboring countries. Although most of Mali's most esteemed leaders of Sufi orders stayed away from the conference, Bilal and some of his followers attended and actively participated in the conference. Bilal's presence was much remarked upon by attendees and in press reports (see, for example, Dicko [2004]). If Bilal had been receiving some favorable attention in Bamako's press and on private radio stations leading up to this conference, this seems to be the point at which members of Mali's political elite, the media, and the general public started to pay more serious attention to him and his activities.

Early in his career, Bilal claimed to have reached the highest stage of Sufism, and he had taken to calling himself "Sufi." Before Bilal and his generation, this was something virtually unheard of in Mali. Indeed, many older Muslims found openly calling oneself a Sufi terribly immodest, even outright preposterous. After all, many remarked that no "real" Sufi in Mali had ever before deigned to designate himself publicly as such. Bilal had also adopted the honorific title of *shaykh* that is usually reserved for the country's most esteemed Muslim religious leaders. During the past few years, Bilal seems to have joined the ranks of prominent Muslim religious leaders—like Lassana in Ségou—to whom many Malians turn to ensure wealth, success, and good health. He has become a charismatic religious leader who attracts numerous followers, many of whom look to him as an intermediary with God. In addition to his ordinary followers, he also has many deputies—*muqaddams* and *khalifas*, all of whom have long hair—in Bamako but also elsewhere in the country. In addition to his main *zawiya* (or Sufi center) in his Bamako home, he has named deputies who run smaller *zawiya*s in different neighborhoods of the city and in some regional towns and even villages where they are claiming public space. Bilal and his deputies organize regular gatherings at his many *zawiya*s for recitations of *dhikr*, the special litanies of prayers associated with Sufi orders, and they are involved in helping to spread Bilal's reputation and Sufism. However, Bilal's version of Sufism seems to borrow for its practices from the various Sufi orders present here, all the while he claims to remain autonomous from any other Sufi leader or order in the country.

Although there are several other well-known young Sufis with long hair and/or dreadlocks in Bamako (Soares 2007b), Bilal stands out from his peers and other prominent Muslim religious leaders in Bamako in several important ways. As I have noted, Bilal is known for the series of pamphlets written primarily in French, mostly primers about Sufism and ritual practice, which he has authored.[10] With these pamphlets, at least eight in total, which some allege must have been ghost written, Bilal seems to be positioning himself as a learned Sufi. In this way, he is following in a long line of Muslim scholars from this region of West Africa who have been known for a body of written work, which is usually in Arabic (Hunwick 2003). However, Bilal is perhaps the only new Sufi to found a formal Islamic association that has gone on to be so highly successful. His association is called the Muslim Community of Sufis of Mali (*Communauté musulmane des soufis du Mali* or CMS-Mali), and it has achieved widespread recognition in Mali's crowded field of new and often ephemeral Islamic associations, attracting considerable interest and attention, much of which is focused on Bilal.

Like many of his peers, Bilal has actively sought public attention for his activities and those of his followers. Unlike most young religious entrepreneurs in Mali, Bilal has managed to attract considerable attention. Arguably, the sophisticated religious marketing that he and his followers have actively deployed has been key to the spread of his reputation and fame. Early on, Bilal actively embraced and sought to engage with the media, including the print and audiovisual media and new media. Interestingly, Bilal was Mali's first Muslim religious leader to have his own website, which featured his photo, a short biography, and contact details, along with photos of some of his closest followers.[11] In addition to his publications, the religious marketing around Bilal includes regular paid advertising about him on the radio and in the press, extensive media coverage of his activities (such as the *mawlid* celebrations), billboards with his name and mobile telephone number, as well as the use of his image on promotional materials ranging from posters, lapel buttons, print-ed fabric, and banners to wall clocks. In this religious marketing, Bilal is offered as a potential key to attaining success in both this world and the next. Such religious marketing is directed to his existing followers, as well as to the broader general public—potential new followers and clients—in Mali's increasingly competitive but also diversified religious market.

Equally significant perhaps is Bilal's attempt to speak directly to his own generation. Bilal has told me that he wants to spread Sufism quickly, and his main target audience seems to be youth, many of whom are avidly interested in Islam and Sufism. In contrast with the main Sufi orders in Mali, which have had numerous and often intractable succession and leadership disputes between the sons of the deceased head of a branch of a Sufi order and the deceased's brothers, Bilal presents himself as independent of all main Sufi groups in the country and, therefore, more autonomous to act and to innovate. Unlike most Sufi leaders who usually make their followers wait for years before advancing in Sufism and getting closer to God, Bilal claims he is able to help people progress very quickly along the stages of Sufism.[12] In conversations with Bilal, he has suggested that the Sufi way he offers is much faster and more expedient than other available Sufi ways. As he explains, although each person who becomes a follower is different, some might be able to advance very quickly. He has, indeed, named many deputies, *muqaddams* and *khalifas*, estimated in the many dozens, most of whom are his peers or younger in age than him and ostensibly able to progress quickly as Sufis. This is all in sharp contrast with the existing Sufi orders in Mali in which there seem to be few and limited possibil-ities to be formally named a deputy. Many Malians Muslims actually do com-plain that it is very difficult to advance within the established branches of the Tijaniyya and the Qadiriyya in the country. This allegedly quick path to advancement within Sufism that Bilal offers is very appealing to many Muslim youth, many of whom have been eager to associate with him and his deputies.

In addition to drawing youth into the Sufi order by directly naming them his deputies and giving them such leadership positions, it is striking—indeed remarkable—how Bilal has been actively incorporating elements of youth cul-ture into religious practice, which is most apparent in the distinctive way he celebrates the *mawlid*. This seems to stem from Bilal's idea that religion is not to be limited to readings of the Quran, sermons, and devotional acts—that is, the kinds of activities associated with most celebrations of Islamic holidays such as the *mawlid* in Mali. In fact, during the celebration of the *mawlid*, Bilal has inaugurated a week of activities clearly targeted toward youth. During the *mawlid*, there is actually a soccer tournament called *la Coupe Maouloud*—the *Mawlid* Cup—as well as displays of juggling and martial arts, such as Kung Fu, which are very popular among West African youth. When Mali hosted the Africa Cup of Nations in 2002, some Malian Muslim religious leaders actively condemned the state's involvement in the soccer tournament on religious grounds. In contrast to such Muslim religious leaders of a more conservative outlook for whom sport is suspect if not explicitly illicit, Bilal eagerly embraces and even celebrates sport and such youth culture as martial arts, as well as the long hair and colorful dress of his peers.

Many of Bilal's initial followers were clearly socially marginal youth— dropouts from public schools, university, and "traditional" Islamic education (although not modern-style *madrasas*), low-ranking temporary clerical workers in offices, and poorly paid casual laborers. Indeed, when I first came in contact with Bilal's followers in 2003, the overwhelming majority of those around him seemed to be members of the young, urban poor, many of whom were recently urbanized. These are the Malian youth who are trying to make ends meet under very difficult conditions. There are, of course, exceptions. One of Bilal's closest deputies has a degree in economics, but this person never managed to land a job before meeting Bilal in 2000.

In joining Bilal, Muslim youth actively devote themselves to religious practice and Sufism, and, in doing so, they are also able to make a living—often a much better and secure one than before. Drawn by Bilal's charisma, Muslim youth have worked to build a movement and his Islamic association, CMS-Mali. Bilal's fame has spread quite rapidly, not least by way of the sophisticated religious marketing that has developed around him. During the past few years, as Bilal has become much more well known and indeed even influential, the powerful now seem to want to associate with him. Bilal has recently constructed a large multistory compound in Bamako, the kind of urban housing that requires large sums of capital. He has also acquired some of the other outward trappings of success, such as new cars. As his resources have increased, he seems to provide for the many more people who have gravitated around him. Indeed, following the model of a charismatic Muslim religious leader, Bilal redistributes some of what he receives as gifts from followers or those seeking to have a problem resolved. According to press reports, the wife of Mali's current president, Amadou Toumani, runs a charity that has given large gifts to Bilal (Haïdara 2008). But there are also widespread rumors that the first lady is one of his main patrons.

Like most of the other young Sufis, his anti-"Wahhabi" statements notwithstanding, Bilal generally does not make public pronouncements about politics. This is possibly part of his appeal for some Malians among segments of the political class who prefer religious leaders not be involved directly in politics. With youthful exuberance, Bilal remains committed to Islam and

Sufism, but also to such pleasures as football, as well as such alluring elements of urban youth culture as fashionable hairstyles and dress. This helps us to understand why more and more people—and not just youth—are paying attention to Bilal. Interestingly, the former president Moussa Traoré, who was released from prison a few years ago, is reported both to eschew politics and to devote himself to Islam. Traoré has been publicly associated with Bilal, and, he has actually been the guest of honor at Bilal's celebration of the *mawlid* in Bamako (Haïdara 2007). Although this might seem surprising, there has recently been an increase in nostalgia for Mali's authoritarian past and even the formerly much despised Traoré regime. In fact, at the time of writing, many Malians openly long for some of the certainties of that period, which are so obviously lacking today.

Conclusion

As I have suggested, the young Muslims in Mali who are self-styled Sufis are in certain respects rather similar to the "traditional" charismatic Muslim religious leaders and leaders of Sufi orders in the country. In numerous cases, certain Muslim religious leaders in Mali, through gifts of inherited charisma, have been able to draw people to them, and they have been able to exhibit the signs of fame and success: wealth and many followers.

However, the rise of a figure like Bilal and his marked presence in the public sphere allow us an opportunity to reflect upon the changing cultural politics of Muslim youth in a place like Mali, which has experienced momentous changes since the early 1990s. During this period of political, economic, and media liberalization as well as increased global interconnections, new unconventional figures like Bilal have been able to operate and flourish in ways that have defied the expectations of commentators in and outside of Mali (cf. Soares 2007b). At a time when many are talking about post-Islamism (Bayat 2007b; cf. Osella and Osella 2008; Otayek and Soares 2007; Soares and Osella 2009), Bilal and the movement around him show some of the complexity of the ways some Muslim youth are refashioning how to be young and Muslim that challenge conventional understandings of Muslim youth and their assumed proclivities toward Islamism. Some Muslim youth in Mali who are disillusioned with or uninterested in secular politics or activism have been turning to religion. Many of those who have gathered around Bilal are social marginals. With youthful enthusiasm, they have embraced a new Sufi movement in which they have ostensibly been able to progress very quickly, but also share in some of the signs of success that Bilal and his movement seem to hold out to them. Although not completely *sui generis*, Bilal is actually quite an original religious entrepreneur in contemporary Mali. He has been able to take advantage of and flourish during the current neoliberal era. This success comes despite the fact that many in the older generation have been disparaging about what these youthful Muslims know and are doing, as so clearly indexed in the moniker "Rasta Sufis." Not unlike post-Islamists, Bilal and some of his followers are pragmatic; they advocate the importance of ethical behavior without necessarily being secular in outlook or orientation. In this way, Bilal is rather similar to many similar budding religious leaders in contemporary Mali. Like other Muslim media stars in Mali, such as Haïdara and elsewhere, Bilal has been particularly adept at employing the media to spread his message and fame. In addition, his active incorporation of youth culture into religious practice has been quite innovative and has been a key factor in the making of success of this religious personality and his fellow Sufis, particularly among Mali's youth who have been consistently marginalized politically, economically, and religiously.

16

Performance, Politics, and Visceral Transformation: Post-Islamist Youth in Turkey

Ayşe Saktanber

Introduction: Being Young and Muslim in Modern Turkey

Every Friday afternoon just after prayer time, in one of the far corners of the expansive Middle East Technical University (METU), a beautifully designed green campus university located in Ankara, the capital of Turkey, a fairly large group of male students coming from somewhere that does not appear to be a mosque is a common sight. It is not possible to see even the point of a minaret from any corner of the university, as the mosque that the students unassumingly attend is actually located in a small village annexed to the campus. These young male students—in their regular outfits of colorful shirts, shabby jeans, and casual haircuts with heavy school bags on their shoulders—seem to be coming from a crowded engineering class from one of the several popular engineering departments, which are mostly comprised of male students. Whether male or female, these students who have managed to attend METU are the most successful among the many who pass a highly competitive general university entrance exam that must be taken by every high school graduate in Turkey for admission to both state and private universities. The students come from almost every geographical region of the country, especially from the well-developed urban centers of the different provinces, but not necessarily from the largest metropolises. There is no doubt that their families invest a considerable amount of emotional labor and financial capital in them to allow them to receive a better education and, hence, a better career.

For many, especially those who either belong to secular, westernized sections of society or call themselves Muslim in name only, it is quite unusual to think of these students giving precedence to their Muslim identity. It is even harder to imagine them as observant Muslims who perform their ritual prayers and/or go to a mosque for Friday prayers, because they do not seem related to the Islamist students who were active at METU throughout the 1990s. As students at one of the most prestigious international universities in Turkey, METU students are expected to be rational, enlightened young individuals who put scientific thinking above all else. Therefore, they are also assumed to be closer to western and/or universal/secular values and norms than local ones, including all kinds of religious persuasions.

Regarding this particular example, it is worth asking from a broader perspective why it is so unusual to think that high-achieving university youth would consider themselves as Muslims first in a country such as Turkey, in which 90% of the population is said to be Muslim and 50% of the whole population is younger than the age of 25. Furthermore, the age group between 14 and 24 constitutes 31% of the whole population.[1] What is the meaning of being a Muslim in Turkey? More specifically, what does it mean to be both young and Muslim when these two terms—*young* and *Muslim*, as distinct from young and *Islamist*—together create such a paradoxical effect? Can such "paradoxical" situations be explained only by envisioning Turkey as a unique case (Hermann 2003)? The case of Turkey in general, and the case of youth in Turkey in particular, deserve a critical analysis that focuses on the complex relationships between the specific modalities of youth, the changing interpretations of both religion and secularism, and the rapidly globalizing Turkish social context.

Turkey has a longer history of secularism than any other Muslim country, and religious politics contained in the parliamentarian democratic system are carefully controlled by state forces. Even the head of the pro-Islamic Justice and Development Party (*Adalet ve Kalkınma Partisi*, AKP), Tayyip Erdoğan, promptly declared himself and his party to be thoroughly loyal to the principles of the secular republican regime. During the subsequent years of the AKP's rule, some other prominent members of Islamist circles, once known as Muslim intellectuals who had been ideal role models for youth with Islamic leanings, started to reassess their Islamist identities and issue self-criticisms.[2]

The emergence of self-confident Muslim intellectuals who were strongly against justifying Islamic principles from a western perspective, and who attempted to create a sense of authenticity for Muslims in Turkey, set the model for Muslim youth throughout the 1980s and '90s. Yet during the 2000s, not only did everybody start talking about a process of change that could be observed among Islamists, but the agents of such change have also been designated as "post-Islamist" intellectuals who no longer argue that Islam and western democracy are incompatible. On the contrary, as some observers have pointed out, they have started to demand a genuinely liberal democratic regime in which principles of a just and egalitarian society will no longer be grounded in Islam and Islamic values, but also will be embraced by the universalistic values of modernity (Daği 2004: 136–139). How, then, can this process of change be connected to the situation of youth in Turkey, particularly to the condition of the pious youth? Today, even the most religious activist young do not want to be referred to as Islamist, which would have been perfectly acceptable before; instead, they prefer to call themselves and to be called *dindar* (that is, pious or devout) as opposed to *dinci* (religionist), which is usually used interchangeably with *Islamist*. In addition to these terms, a third one, *mütedeyyin*, stands between the two in colloquial Turkish, denoting elderly, wise, and apolitical pious Muslims. Religious or not, being labeled both young and Muslim still presents a difficult situation in Turkey because of the ways in which both secularism and modernity have been understood by large sections of polity and society, despite emerging trends of reconciliation between the two.

Turkey's New Generation of Muslim Individuals

Questions about what it means to be a Muslim have not been common in republican Turkish society until the rise of Islamic revivalism during the 1980s. Islam and Muslimness, rather, have referred to an Islamist political current. When it comes to thinking about the Muslim identity of urban youth in contemporary Turkish society, certain classifications about youth identity are needed. One such classification could be between those who have been raised with local and religious values rather than secular and western ones. However, a clear-cut distinction between these two systems of thought is becoming almost impossible in recent Turkish society because of ongoing efforts of reconciliation between the two. Another classification includes those who were taught religion as a matter of other-worldliness, which might be recalled at difficult, troubling times when divine help is needed, or as something with which to deal during the later stages of life, particularly at a time when one starts to feel him- or herself getting closer to the other world. A third classification—and call it Islamist or *dindar*—comprises those who have been either trained by their families to be religious from childhood under the tutorship of different religious institutions, orders, or associations, or became religious during their youth, mostly by getting involved with either religious politics or Islamic intellectualism, or both. In all three of these cases, religion turns out to be a matter of negotiation rather than an inviolable set of normative rules when being young is at stake, despite the fact that different youth groups tend to interpret religion and incorporate it into their ordinary lives in their own ways, with considerable similarities among them.

Muslim youth in Turkey, as in many other Muslim societies, no longer rely solely on religious authorities to understand and make sense of their religion. But, there can be little doubt that religiosity and identification of Turkish youth with Islam is widespread. A rare representative survey published in 1999, which aimed to explore the place of religious values in the process of shaping the worldviews of youth in Turkey, found that 27% of all respondents use "Islamic faith" to define themselves (Konrad Adanauer Foundation 1999).[3] Religion seems to form the main axis through which youth construct an identity outside the modernist project of Turkey (Konrad Adanauer Foundation 1999:80). A total of 21.1% of the respondents indicate "religion and faith" to be among the top three values that impart meaning to life. The highest percentage of respondents who associate religion and faith with the meaning of life is found in the clusters that are concentrated by the cities located in the southeastern and central Anatolia regions, which constitute, respectively, economically less developed and moderately developed regions of Turkey. This percentage drops below average in Istanbul (the largest and most developed metropolitan city in the country), declines sharply in Izmir (the biggest port city on the Aegean Coast), and in the cities that are in the third cluster of this survey—that is, Antalya and Edirne. The former is located on the Mediterranean coast, one of the most famous cities in Turkey among foreign tourists, and the latter is in the northwest of Turkey, at the gate to Europe. Moreover, a similar pattern is observed in the distribution of references to religion as a virtue acquired from the family (Konrad Adanauer Foundation 1999: 45). What is the significance of such findings for understanding youth, religiosity, and generation in Turkey?

In her essay on changing conceptualizations of youth, Linda Herrera argues that the term *youth* simultaneously refers to a cultural group, an age cohort, and a sociopolitical category (Herrera 2006a). For the Islamist youth in Turkey, the emphasis has always been on the last categorization, and their emergence as a social collectivity has been associated with those episodic instances of Islamic revivalism. On the other hand, young people are regarded as "youth" as long as they develop and express a consciousness of themselves and act upon this consciousness across various lines of divisions (United Nations Department of Economic and Social Affairs 2005: 117). Envisioning youth as a collective identity that bears a collective consciousness fits well with Karl Mannheim's classic work on generations, in which he suggests that members of a generation are held together by the experience of historical events from the same or similar vantage points. For Mannheim (1997), generations can transform society by challenging customary thoughts and by offering new political and cultural visions when radicalized by traumatic experiences.[4] To explain how generations act strategically to bring about change, June Edmunds and Bryan S. Turner (2005) suggest that the way in which generations shift from being a passive age cohort into a politically active and self-conscious one must be understood. For them, this can only be possible when generations are able to exploit political, economic, and educational resources to innovate cultural, intellectual, and political spheres (Edmunds and Turner 2005).

Although all of these discussions can provide a productive perspective with which to study how Islamist youth have developed a collective identity and consciousness that also forms the basis of their collective action, this chapter argues that, in addition, self-criticisms and reassessments of Islamist youth regarding their collective identity can constitute a very important aspect of the orientation of the sociopolitical and cultural change that they can cause. Cultural dilemmas and paradoxes that Islamist youth have experienced throughout one or two generations caused them to break with their collective identity and allowed at least some of them to develop a new discourse of reflexive subjectivity.

To see the ways in which the boundaries of the identity of Islamist youth in Turkey have shifted from a thoroughly communal identity to an individual one via self-reflexivity in a constantly changing political and cultural Turkish social context, some of the textual and audiovisual literary and factual autobiographical accounts of the once Islamist young activists who now identify either as *dindar* democrats or as liberated individuals will be examined.

Literary Muslim Identities: Between Communal Identity and Self-Reflexivity

The first novel under review, *The Saint of Incipient Insanities* (Shafak 2004), is written in English by Elif Safak, a young female writer and a rising literary star, particularly among Turkish youth.[5] It is based on the stories of three young male and three young female graduate students whose lives cross paths in Boston. Considering the differences of the place of religious values in the worldviews of Turkish youth depending on the socioeconomic level of their place of origin, it is not at all surprising to see that all the male characters have some religious cultural repertoire except for the Turkish one who has been raised in a secular, highly modern, upper middle class urban family originating from Istanbul.

The three young men share the same apartment. One is a peaceful, good-natured Spaniard with deep Catholic leanings, obsessed with cleanliness and sharp objects. One is a Moroccan with considerably well-developed Islamic cultural capital, deeply attached to his local cultural values yet quite modern; he is a highly conscientious character with slightly paranoid tendencies. The third one is a Turk with many sharply drawn characteristics, such as his heavy addiction to coffee and alcohol; he is a sophisticated music freak, a fast womanizer, a witty intellectual, and a charming friend with no religious identity whatsoever. In terms of religion, this Turkish character, Ömer, is depicted—deliberately or not—as if he comes from a planet whose inhabitants are not even aware of religion or religious cultural codes. This very accurately reflects the essence of one segment of youth in Turkey, sketched out in the earlier classification about the ways in which they acquire religious identity in modern Turkish society. The fictional identity embodied in Ömer can also shed light on another situation related to those observing METU students described earlier and the reasons for the bewilderment these students create among the secular Turkish elite. The fact is that "the Ömer type" has been construed by the secular elite as almost "the way it should be." For them, characters such as Ömer represent normalcy; types like some of the METU students who are practicing Muslims and also have an elite university education background, do not.

As always, there is another side to the story. The new Islamist youth in Turkey put great effort into the reconciliation of Islamic intellectualism with popular culture, through which they can find different ways to express themselves and their subjectivities in all walks of life in a secular, highly fragmented postmodern context. In this respect, since the 1990s, new radio stations, television channels, newspapers, magazines, music groups, novelists, and filmmakers that cater to Muslim youth have become ordinary players in the market for popular culture, as well as the publishers of Islamic cartoons and comic strips, and all kinds of "small media" such as postcards, stickers, and posters (Saktanber 2002a: 262–269). Public spaces and performances such as fashion shows, concert halls, fancy restaurants, coffee shops, tea gardens, and summer resorts are no longer merely construed as the domains of modern secular public life in Turkey.[6]

Similarly, by the end of the 1990s, with the advent of computer-mediated communication technologies, the construction of new websites and web blogs, and thus communication through the Internet, had become quite widespread among Muslim youth in Turkey, as has been the case in the entire Muslim world (Anderson 2003; Eickelman and Anderson 1999). Thus, as a result of these developments, debates on the blurring of boundaries between the public and the private spheres regarding religion have also become one of the most favored discussion topics of both academia and the mainstream media in countries such as Turkey, where religion has been essentially confined to the private realm as a matter of individual conscience. In this context, the "headscarf dispute" and its several cultural and political connotations not only created a heated discussion, but brought Muslim women, if not the critique of Islamic patriarchy, into the heart of public debate (Saktanber 2006). This also created a remarkable situation regarding the gendered aspects of Muslim women's identities, to the extent that Muslim women are almost only taken into account as long as they participate in public life with their heads covered (Saktanber 2002a). This particular issue has been singled out among many others without opening a meaningful discussion on their gender identities as a whole. Similarly, the covered women themselves did not seem to be willing to open up such a public discussion. They mostly remained satisfied with raising their immediate problem of being unable to use their rights to attend institutions of higher education while wearing their headscarves, and hence became the object of debates on Islamism in Turkey.

The question of becoming either an "object" or a "subject" is not a new problem for the many generations of youth in Turkish society (Neyzi 2001). However, when Muslim identity is at stake, the tension between the imperatives of communal identity and the desire for reflexive self-expression can best be observed from the self-narratives in the 1990s of young men and women who eventually transformed themselves from being militant Islamists into "dindar Muslims."

One such example of an autobiographical exposition on the transformation of political identity is by Metin Metiner, once a fervent advocate of Islamism. In his autobiographical book titled Yemyeşil Şeriat, Bembeyaz Demokrasi (All Green Shari'a, All White Democracy), Metiner, as a young Muslim Kurdish man in the 1970s and 1980s, relates the ways in which he struggled to develop an intellectual identity within the very limited economic and cultural capital of his own sphere. It is his great conviction that the Islamic cause is the only one with which one could impart meaning to this unjust world of inequality. Although political activism filled almost his entire life, he also got married at quite an early age (in an arranged marriage), had children, received a higher education, and became a writer.

After all those tough years, the only resentment he felt toward his private life was about his behavior in his marriage. He criticized himself for how he had forced his wife to have an extremely modest wedding ceremony, how he had denied her wish to walk with him on the streets hand in hand, how he had forced her to cover her head, and how he left her and his first daughter alone for years back home while he pursued his own political career and education by traveling between different towns in Turkey. Nevertheless, it can be understood in between the lines of his narrative that during those lonely days, especially when pursuing a life in Istanbul surrounded by his young Islamist fellows to whom he almost became a mentor, he could not prevent himself from the dictates of sentimentalism. He listened to the sad love songs of the most famous and popular female music star in Turkey, Sezen Aksu. But, he hid this from his roommates, who would probably have thought of listening to such music, and particularly the songs of a liberal woman like her, as almost an infidelity. It seems that romantic love and sentimentalism as a transformative force did not played a significant role in the self-development process and the questioning of subjectivity of this young Muslim man of cause.

In his prize-winning and best selling novel, *Kar* (Snow), the 2006 Nobel prize winner Orhan Pamuk also points out the ways in which the conflicting nature of falling in love can make everything much more complicated for Islamist young men and women, forcing them to take unusual steps in their lives both in political and personal terms, particularly within the limited cultural confines of a provincial town (Pamuk 2000). Actually, in this town, Kars, which is located in northeastern Turkey and often cut off from the outside world by blizzards, neither Islamists nor atheists take a clear-cut side against anything, including belief in God, but lead their lives as being caught up in passions, politics, and groupings.

Among the emerging voices of self-criticism and reflexivity, the novel *Mızraksız İmihal* (Book of Manners without a Lance) by Mehmet Efe (1993) has been particularly popular among various circles of Muslim youth. The novel, usually considered autobiographical, is based on the story of the transformation of a young Islamist university student into a moderate young Muslim man by the power of love (Efe 1993).[7] Being a child of a small town with a modest family background, he is the first in his family who has access to higher education and urban life. In Istanbul, where he attends university, he not only becomes an Islamic activist, but also has the opportunity to mingle with the "opposite sex," although he is careful not to lose his sobriety. He is convinced that a Muslim does not fall in love with a woman, but only with Allah. Then, quite unexpectedly and immediately, he falls in love with a covered girl—a fellow university student—who is critical toward the roles assigned to covered female university students not only by the secular authorities, but also by the male Islamist students who seemed to support those girls mainly for their own political purposes.

Although she is quite strong in refusing the politicization of her subjectivity, her compliance with the prevailing patriarchal role of femininity is striking, for she considers herself first and foremost a "small" and "weak" girl who wants to lead her life in peace and harmony. Falling in love with such a girl, however, who is actually in perfect harmony with her Islamic *fitrat* (believed to be the innate characteristics attributed to men and women by God) is not surprising at all for an Islamist young man, despite her reluctance to participate in political matters. Thus, Irfan, the hero of the novel, also starts to yearn for "small things" as well, such as searching for a job, marrying this small yet strong girl, buying her some presents (such as a colorful dress and a silk headscarf), cooking together, reading, laughing, and the like. In other words, he starts to search for the road that can lead him to heaven on his own terms, as a challenge to militant Islamism. If not the whole story, then the title of his novel attests to this. With it the author makes an allegory to one of the oldest and most popular Islamic books of manners, written by Muhammed İzniki (d. 1480) and used as a standard elementary school book for centuries. The original meaning of the title of Izniki's book is "the key to heaven's door" (*Miftah-ul Cennet*), although it is widely known and read as *Mızraklı Ilmihal* (Book of Manners with a Lance).[8]

The novel that was published in 2005 by Barış Müstecaplıoğlu, *Şakird* [Disciple], a name that stands for a novice in the hierarchical ranks of the youth who rallied around the teachings of Fethullah Gülen, constitutes another good example for the trend of self-criticism and reflection that has started to find echoes among young Islamists of various kinds. This novel is a rather radical account about the way in which the material and moral comfort of communal life can turn out to be a cage for a young university student who is constantly exposed to the realities of everyday urban life, which entails the disenchantment of the comfort of a strictly disciplined brotherhood. Thus eventually, among those highly restrictive activities of this brotherhood, one starts to appear much more unrealistic—that is, the avoidance of any contact, including merely in a friendly manner, with the opposite sex. The hero of the novel, Murat, breaks with his old communal bonding and professional life when he leaves his successful position in a corporate marketing company and ventures onto the unpredictable paths of his own destiny. In doing so, he not only finds the true love of his life, Elif, but also manages to develop an unconditional, true friendship with a woman with whom he shares not only the details of his daily life, but also the very existential questions that he contemplates. His relationships with two quite open-minded women were not the only reward of Murat's freeing of himself from his communal ties and choosing the uncomfortable paths of independence of mind and of critical thinking. In tracking down his own destiny, he finds the testament of his late best friend, who had inspired him to take a more critical stance toward the conformity of the brotherhood with which he had been affiliated throughout his university years. He also manages to assure himself that there can be different answers to the questions of life and death, as well as different patterns of sacrifice and dignity for the human cause other than the ones that were once suggested to him by the religious community in which he had sought the meaning of life.

The struggle of youth in acquiring a coherent subjectivity by freeing themselves from the dictates of restrictive religious ties does not always end with the acquisition of a confident self and a peaceful state of mind that also signifies a transformation into moderate Muslim practice. It is especially difficult for those who actually challenge the overall gender role that has been assigned to them as young Muslim women by society. Notwithstanding the rhetoric of freedom and equality among educated Muslim youth, covered female university students are severely criticized, especially by their male fellows, if they, for instance, insistently frequent newly established coffee houses that cater to Muslim youth and show "loose" behavior there, such as smoking, laughing and talking loudly, playing backgammon, using its jargon and cursing while playing it, and getting physically too close to male friends, as has been clearly indicated by a newspaper article published in a Turkish daily on the changing cultural meanings of coffee shops in Istanbul (Çizmeci 2005).

Much more sophisticated and philosophical sufferings can be observed among some young Muslim women as a result of the social pressures they experienced in their family lives and close environments. The frustrations may have gone so far as to make them lose their faith in God and religion. A short 1995 documentary shot and produced by Jeanne C. Finley in Istanbul entitled *Conversations Across the Bosphorus*, is a rare example of an attempt to explore how women's relationship to religion might influence their identities. It also focuses on the narrative of the radical transformation of a young woman who has decided to uncover her head during her late teens, although she has been brought up in a highly devout family.[9] Her parents migrated to Istanbul at the beginning of the 1960s from a southeastern Turkish town and settled at Fatih, one of the oldest districts of Istanbul, which was populated mostly by highly devout, conservative families and Islamists, facilitating her father's becoming an extreme religionist. The reasons behind her radical change were not unpredictable, but the action she takes to this end is not so common at all.

At quite an early age she started to question the secondary role that was assigned to her not only by her family, but also, according to her own conviction, by her religion. Although she did not stray from any code of modesty and became a mindful child and a successful student while attending an Imam Hatip School (schools for secondary education with a religious curriculum along with the compulsory one), her cravings never ceased because of the way she was treated as a young girl in her close environment. She kept asking herself, referring to the tradesmen and artisans of her childhood neighborhood: "Why do all these men continue to harass me even though I am a covered girl from head to toe and do not show me any respect at all?" Moreover, she eventually started to ask herself some further questions that could have been quite self-destructive, particularly for a devout Muslim young girl, such as: "Why does God punish me only because I am a woman although I love Him so much and obey Him with all my heart?"

Consequently, after suffering through a series of psychosomatic illnesses and receiving several medical treatments, her family set her free with her rebellious decision and allowed her to live on her own as an uncovered woman. At the time when this film was shot, she was an undergraduate student in the Department of Arabic Language at Istanbul University, and she continued to visit her brother and mother but not her father. The audience is not informed, however, about whether she earns a living on her own or receives financial aid from her family. However, what is shown throughout this documentary is a beautiful, modern, and self-confident but deeply sad and lonely young woman who thinks that she has no one to trust but herself, ever since losing her faith in God.

In his discussion of how the positioning of the self is central to the construction of the self-narrative, Michael Bamberg (2004: 153) argues that whether fictional or biographical, narratives are not transparent windows into narrators' minds, their subjectivities, or their lived experiences, but are interactively accomplished situated actions. This reflects, in part, what Anthony Giddens (1991: 243) suggests when he argues that self-identity is the extension of the "narrative of the self"—that is, the "story or stories by means of which self-identity is reflexively understood both by the individual concerned and by the others." The stories of the self-narratives that are highlighted here are the reflections of how young men and women situated themselves or were situated by their narrators vis-à-vis their religious identities, which are in constant interaction with the social conditions, political ideals, cultural norms, and moral values that are available to them in the social context in which they have been living as young individuals. Thus, the critical discourse that they have created throughout that struggle of positioning themselves as interactive yet autonomous individuals by breaking with their religiously determined collective identities carries the potential of opening new avenues for other young Muslim men and women in their search for constructing independent self-identities.

Conclusion

To be both young and Muslim has never been an easy condition in the Turkish context, regardless of whether these two states of being taken together have been politicized. Furthermore, Turkish youth have always had some difficulties in sharing their experiences with youth from other parts of the Muslim world at the global level because of Turkey's highly secularized background. However, following the emergence of a global youth culture, which has enabled youth to share their experiences in many different ways regardless of their national origins, this situation has started to change. It seems particularly so for the Muslim youth who started to be exposed to similar kinds of social and political pressures all over the world, particularly after September 11, 2001, despite the differences they carry in their cultural baggage.[10] In this context, further elaboration needs to be made regarding the extent to which not the national but the subjective identities that have been pieced together from various sources of communal ties, ideals, and worldviews will overlap with the subjectivities of the Muslim youth at the global level, compared with the ones who, despite living in the same society, may have completely different experiences as young Muslims. So far, the cultural dilemma faced by Muslim youth in the Turkish context mainly stems from the ways in which secularism has been handled in this society, through which the relationship between the two has been seen as if they were inevitably irreconcilable. This situation seems to have started to change, however, as secularism and democracy are open to public discussion more efficiently than ever before and are proliferating through the participation of various social actors coming from different ethnic, religious, and class backgrounds with different political affiliations.

What has to be asked now is to what extent the new experiences of Muslim youth will contribute to the development of individual freedoms, tolerance, and mutual understanding. Only that enhancement can help solve the youth's cultural dilemma, which stems from the tension between the imperatives of communal identity and the urge felt for reflexive self-expression. Although the shifting of Muslim identity from the highly politicized "Universal Muslims" (Zubaida 2003: 95) to mainstream Muslims of various lifestyles seems to be the growing trend among Muslim youth in Turkey, the fact that new generations may tend toward new forms of religiosity distinct from that of their parents and religious authorities as well as from their earlier generations should not be disregarded. Thus, they are constantly open to producing new forms of cultural dilemmas and visceral transformations. After all, trying to understand the problems, expectations, and aspirations of youth at one moment in history means no more than to suggest making social and political investments to develop a further understanding of the cultural dilemmas of future generations of youth.

Acknowledgments

A longer version of this chapter was previously published by the author by the title, "Cultural Dilemmas of Muslim Youth: Negotiating Muslim Identities and Being Young in Turkey" (*Turkish Studies*, 8(3): 417–434, 2007).

17

Negotiating with Modernity: Young Women and Sexuality in Iran

Fatemeh Sadeghi

Iran has undergone dramatic changes since the revolution of 1979. Although these changes are mostly visible in the appearance of the people and cities, less visible changes have happened in traditional family norms and private life, especially where young people are concerned. When acknowledged, these changes are referred to as a "generation gap."[1] Among young women, changes in behavior and identity are evident not only among the "misveiled" (*badhijab*) girls (those who wear *hijab* to accommodate themselves to Iranian legal requirements yet intentionally disregard the spirit if not precisely the letter of the law), but also among "veiled" girls (often referred to as *chadori*, regardless of whether they actually wear the *chador*). Based on research done in 2005 through 2006 through in-depth interviews with young, urban Iranian women about their private and public lives, this chapter examines whether as these girls are becoming less overtly traditional they are claiming their own subjectivity. The analysis indicates that although these young women are not as docile to traditional norms as previous generations, they can hardly be considered a radically modern generation in terms of breaking with the deeper social conventions of the past.

The surprising inner conservatism of the youth, in comparison with their public claims to modern styles of identity, reveals the misperception of two common interpretations of youth behavior. The first is that misveiling is a kind of political resistance against the Islamic regime; young women themselves characterize their style of dress as a personal choice and an indication of social rather than political identity. Therefore, although misveiling has some implications of political resistance, one can hardly interpret these new kinds of behaviors as directly oppositional. The second misperception is that removal of the veil is equal to the free expression of female sexual desire and agency; although young Iranian women (both misveiled and *chadori*) may be engaging more freely in premarital sexual relationships, they do so in a social context, which is still very much structured by the privileging of male desire over female sexual expression. Given the surprising contradictions and continuities revealed by the research, this chapter looks at ways to interpret the changes that have occurred among the younger generations, especially young women, in Iran.

A New Generation in a Changing Society

Since the Islamic revolution of 1979, many changes have occurred in the political, social, and cultural, as well as the private and public, aspects of life in Iranian society. These changes so deeply reshaped the face of the country that except for some explicit manifestations such as women's veiling, today Iran seems less Islamic than it used to. More than any other aspects, these changes are visible within youth culture and the younger generations' attitudes and behaviors. In practicing new lifestyles, which are different in many ways from the previous generations,' the new generation by and large does not seem as Islamic as the ideological government had expected it to be (Kurzman 2005).

Iranian youth culture is a heterogeneous phenomenon, consisting of different dimensions, including new styles of dress, makeup, language, music, *weltanschauungs* (world view), beliefs, and identification; longer life expectancy; different heterosocial relationships; drug use; and leisure time. Despite this heterogeneity, the differences between the generations are so big as to be referred to as a *generation gap* (Ministry of Islamic Guidance 2001). The generation gap includes the misveiled girls as much as it does the *chadori* girls (Moruzzi and Sadeghi 2006). Although in most youth studies, *chadori* girls are excluded and are assumed to be religious and loyal to the Islamic Republic, it is worth considering their experiences and the differences that exist between them and their parents regarding private and public aspects of life.

To understand the significance of the changes in contemporary young Iranian women's lives, it is necessary to put their generation's experiences within the historical national context. The consistencies and social transformations within more than two decades of postrevolutionary formal political policies have resulted in a younger generation that is cynical toward formal politics as well as organized social responses to their current situation, and they tend to regard their privatized individualism as a sign of their adamant modernity. But to the extent that the behaviors of today's youth are generationally distinct, they react as much against the models of the previous generations as they innovate their own social–political and cultural models (Mannheim 1952).

A major difference is that rather than ideological devotions, sexuality is the ideological and practical construct around which youth social identity is being shaped. This is true among not only misveiled girls but also *chadori* girls. As a misveiled girl noted, "Being misveiled generally means to feel more relaxed in relationships with boys." For *chadori* girls, refusing to be sexually molested is one of the main reasons to wear the *chador*. In their choices, both groups are separating themselves from the ideological typologies of the older generations. For both groups, the instrumental means for making feminine personal identity is the male gaze, to which they are reacting differently.

In any case, sexuality is not, therefore, just a certain set of physical relationships among individuals. As a discourse, it has to be regarded as bodily reproduction and the construction/reconstruction of power relations in public as well as private spheres (Foucault 1976). Therefore, without considering the social and political changes that have occurred in many areas of life and the youth culture as a whole, any understanding of the challenges girls face and the ways they are socially and sexually representing themselves would be incomplete.

Young people are, to some extent, independent subjects, but they are also socially and politically constructed. As Pierre Bourdieu (1977) argued, orientations toward actions are "structuring structures" and "structured structures." They shape and are shaped by social practices. Thus a practice does not necessarily signify actions on the basis of rational strategies but can simply be a "learned" or internalized way of doing things. That is why the younger generations' attitudes are, to some extent, the consequences of the new postrevolutionary political arrangements, which mostly demand that the subject/people be atomized individuals incapable of collective actions. In addition, the political arrangements cause youth to be disappointed in the revolutionary ideals, such as a just society.

Younger generations are dependent on family structures and internalized actions, which are practiced within different intimate spaces. This is also why youth culture, despite being much more apparently tolerant, also contains some strong, exclusive, undemocratic aspects that reinforce the power relations of class, gender, ethnicity, and religion.

Government Politics and Policies: Social Implications

Women's participating in the Islamic revolution provided opportunities for them to feel for the first time that they were equal to men. Following the encouragement of Ayatollah Khomeini, huge numbers of women actively participated in the street protests. They felt at the time that their presence was needed for overthrowing the corrupt Pahlavi regime (1941–1979), which was trying to make women depoliticized "western dolls" (*arusak Farangi*), as the contemporary Islamist intellectual Ali Shari'ati (1983: 78) described. Ayatollah Khomeini appreciated women's participation within the revolution (Khomeini 1991: 134).

The moment of revolution was liberating for women in the sense that being appropriately feminine did not mean having to avoid political activities. Unlike during the period of the Pahlavis, in which women's perfect femininity was defined as their being sexually desirable, the revolution made women feel they were not sexual objects but political agents. Having been inspired by Shariati's criticism of the Pahlavi regime's policy of sexualizing and depoliticizing women, many women wore *hijab*, poured into the streets, and shouted against the shah. Even secular women, while not believing in *hijab*, wore it in solidarity with other women to be part of that moment.[2]

However, soon after the revolution, the family code, ratified through long years of women's struggles during the first and second Pahlavi monarchies, was canceled by Ayatollah Khomeini, who ordered it to be replaced by a very reactionary religious code. Despite his support for women's revolutionary participation, the ayatollah's hostility toward the Pahlavi regimes and their perspective toward women led him to reject their legal and juridical reforms. Thus, although the Islamic revolution welcomed women's participation as a key element for the revolution's victory, in postrevolutionary Iran women's rights were mostly ignored and the government forced women to go back to their traditional domestic roles. Such policies were partly successful, but not exactly in the way the government wished.

During the years of the Iran–Iraq war, which began immediately after the establishment of the new government, women were expected to be at the service of the country, performing their tasks as loyal wives and mothers. During the war, *hijab* became another flag for the Islamic country (Moruzzi and Sadeghi 2006). The government indefatigably reminded the zealous Muslim of the task of defending his honor not only from the external enemies but also from the internal ones. These two concepts—namely, *jihad* against external and internal enemies—overlapped and legitimatized each other. A misveiled woman was likened to the Baathist enemy in the sense that both threatened (male) Muslim honor.

Along with all these changes was a shifting in the feminine symbolic models of the Islamic Republic, which has encouraged women to be domesticated objects rather than political agents. In this shift the model of Zeinab, the Prophet's granddaughter and a female warrior figure, was gradually replaced by the model of Fatima, Zeinab's mother, whose image as represented on Islamic Republic television, in religious books, in speeches, and so on, is of an utterly domesticated woman, completely docile under the demands of her husband and father. Fatima's position as a model of tradition, as reproduced by the Islamic Republic, is totally different from the position of today's young women, and she seems incapable of offering something progressive to them. Despite this, there are some strong similarities between Fatima and the young women of today's Iran. Both the traditional and the contemporary reinforce a sexualized femininity and the domestication of women.

It was during the postwar era, during Hashemi Rafsanjani's presidency (1989–1997), that women began to wear more fashionable, colored dresses rather than *chadors*, long dark mantels, formal head scarves, and *maghna'ahs* (dark-colored head and neck coverings). In Iranian historical memory, these years are linked with the sudden reappearance of romantic love and the importation of some Japanese (nonwestern) sentimental series on state television, all of which constituted a breakthrough for a society that had just come out of a war. The license for temporary marriage, a controversial issue during this period, was also among the major reforms promoted by Rafsanjani. He raised the issue in a Friday prayer ceremony as a solution for the psychosocial problems of youth, who nonetheless mostly continued to regard it as legal prostitution. Temporary marriage continues to be a legitimized, if unpopular, option to solve the sexual needs of young people, and every once in a while it is still encouraged by the bravest officials.[3]

The support for temporary marriage was also a recognition of the class distinctions that appeared during the postwar era, because it was supposed to be a solution for poor people—both men and women—who faced economic obstacles in making a family through a formal marriage (Haeri 1993). Apart from all those policies, Rafsanjani's neoliberal policies have been criticized for providing the economic foundations for the prevailing ethics of consumerism, self-interest, and increasing individualism that seem to constitute the younger generations' major attitudes toward life. For instance, the revolutionary slogans on public spaces gradually disappeared and were replaced mostly by new commercial advertisements. The elimination of the slogans from public spaces also meant a distancing from the revolutionary period's desexualization of public spaces. In the meantime, Tehran and other major cities were changing rapidly as they became major draws for employment and educational opportunities for a youthful population of former peasants and residents of more provincial towns. This retreat of ideology and the commodification of many aspects of life are said to have resulted in a low interest in collective goals, especially among the younger generations, who have been most affected by the economic liberalization during the postwar era and who have become disappointed in the revolution and the promised Islamic utopia. Therefore, compared with the morality of the generations of the revolution and war, and their willingness to sacrifice their lives for the people and for what they believed in, the new generation is assumed to be more individualist and hedonist.

Women's responses toward all these changes were different, ranging from public oppositions to informal politics. The important reactions of the younger generations were mostly individual strategies, among which misveiling and women's university enrollment, which exceeded the rate of men during the reform era (1997–2005) and for the first time in Iranian history, are worth mentioning (The Iranian Presidency and the Management and Planning Organization 2004). Both phenomena have been indirectly and directly encouraged by the government. Misveiling was an unwanted result of the Islamic government's shifting of its gender role models for Iranian women, from Zeinab the revolutionary to Fatima the housewife.[4]

Although education was tremendously encouraged by the Islamic government, women's push for higher education was mostly the result of limited job offerings and few opportunities for women's social and political participation (Mehran 1991). Women's responses, however, have not been welcomed by the new conservatives and Ahmadinejad's government, whose reactions are stronger against misveiling and whose plan is to restrict women's presence in university disciplines up to 40% (Daftere Motale'ate Farhangi 2007: 13.) In the midst of these contradictory policies and ambivalent social changes, the expectations of young women reflect these paradoxes.

Public Versus Private: The Politics of Sexuality

The Islamic discourse in Iran has been a response to the cultural aspects of the modern world, challenging certain facets of modernity while at the same time wittingly and unwittingly engaging in some of the essential elements of the modern culture.

—Vahdat 2005: 650

New intrusions into family and private affairs tended to take people's affairs out of traditional private or familial supervision and subjugate them to governmental discipline.[5] The Islamist project has been also inclined to homogenize and discipline sexuality on the basis of what is legitimate and illegitimate in the Sharia. This in turn has had some major impacts, including the domestication of heterosocial relations, meaning the moving of courtship from public spaces, like cinemas, restaurants, parks, and universities, into the private spaces of homes, apartments, and cars.

Domestication of heterosocial affairs appeared in postrevolutionary Iran as a result of the politicization of sexuality. What was mostly controlled by society and *urf* (social convention) before the project of Islamization became a matter of legal control and political scrutiny after the revolution. Instead of the traditional familial control that was part of social life in Iran before and after the revolution, the morality police (*gashte Amre be ma'ruf va nahy az monkar*) was launched soon after the founding of the Islamic Republic, and its task was to sweep away all nonreligious behaviors like unveiling and, later, *badhijabi* (veiling badly), drinking and selling alcohol, and illegitimate heterosocial and homosexual relationships.

The politicization of sexuality also resulted in a major change within Iranian families, transforming them from the traditional controlling apparatus of young people's behavior into a relatively tolerant place, where a youth could take refuge. This change also can be regarded as relocating modern social life in the conventional (as opposed to formal or legal) domain. Despite the Islamization of public spaces and the formal sphere, private and familial spaces remained relatively open and may have become even more so as a response to the closure of public alternatives. Therefore, the public prohibition of so-called illegitimate relationships led many young people to privatize their relationships and pursue their freedom in private spaces. Such a transformation was a unique phenomenon when compared with other Islamic societies, in which the legal state apparatus may sponsor greater social opportunities for youth, while conventional family spaces remain more traditional.

Shifting from public into private spaces also seems to have resulted in a more precocious sexuality among the new generations. It seems that the younger generations may experience sexual affairs much sooner than the previous ones did, although such a conclusion cannot be confirmed statistically thus far. Despite the deep-seated belief of the younger generations (and also their parents) that they are socially repressed by the postrevolutionary government, it seems that the youths' claim to their own spaces and identities is much more tolerated within the household space and the conventions of family life.

The postrevolutionary politicization of the public sphere created a contrasting duality of public versus private spheres, in which people's self-representation is very much different. This difference is especially true for the less religious, who learned to accommodate the newly imposed Islamic behaviors in public but often continued conventional practices (non-related heterosexual mixing, playing music, dancing, consuming alcohol, and so forth) in private. The overwhelming Islamic agenda thus led to the withdrawal of less Islamic behaviors from the public into the private. As a result, many Iranians live more or less a double standard as a result of the different atmospheres in the different spheres and spaces of their lives. They have more freedom in the private sphere, whereas the public is surrounded by Islamic norms of behavior. Although in recent years many things have changed and society seems much more open than before, and despite many young people feeling relatively free to publicize their private affairs, there is still a sense of fear among the youth that does not allow them to behave freely within public spaces.

Yet the double standard of gender relations, both conventional and legal, has continued in both spheres. Whether defined as "modern" or "Islamic," attitudes that privilege men's desire and sexual agency at women's expense are held by most members of society: women and men, young and old. According to a questionnaire conducted by an Iranian researcher in 1997 on sexual behaviors among 60 Iranian men and women age 20 to 40, 55% of Iranian men believe that in a time of sexual needs, their partner is expected to respond, regardless of whether she favors it. The same report holds that 81% of Iranian men and women believe that women must be virgins before getting married. And although only 15% of men of this questionnaire were against the idea that a man is allowed to have premarital sexual relationships, 60% of Iranian women completely disagreed that women or men are allowed to have premarital sexual relationships (Kahen 1997). Thus, although virginity still matters seriously among Iranians, the majority of Iranian men believe that a man is allowed to have premarital relationships.

As is indicated by this research, most people believe men are less capable of controlling desire and that, in the realm of sexuality, a woman is much more responsible than a man, whereas men are allowed to be more sexually expressive than women. These beliefs are maintained regardless of whether they are placed within an Islamic legal framework. That is why, among the younger generations, virginity is still, by definition, an indication of women's modesty, even though the concern for its preservation is decreasing practically. Some girls are not so worried about it, viewing it as an obstacle to be managed in their relationships with boys. Anal sex, for instance, is one of the widespread ways to preserve technical virginity. However, within such relationships, the men benefit more than the women, as even within a sexual relationship, both partners may still place high ideological value on the woman's modesty, no matter what their practical relations. In addition, the domestication of sexual affairs within private spaces and the household actually increases the risks for young women, including the possibility of sexual violations, unwanted pregnancies, and unhealthy precarious abortions (given the legal restrictions on its medical practice).

The loss of virginity in a premarital relationship is not irretrievable, however, thanks to underground clinics that repair the hymen. For people with higher economic and modern social capital, virginity seems to be less problematic than it is for people with little economic capital and/or with traditional social capital. However, on this issue, there is more pressure from Iranian social conventions than from the government, which encourages temporary marriage as a solution for the sexual needs of youths. The result is a complicated situation, which is the outcome of a threefold phenomenon: the surveillance and limits placed on public spaces, which in turn have led to domesticated and precocious affairs among the youth, putting pressure on traditional family values.

Many young men, who are capable of having their own private space, tend to privatize their affairs, keeping their relationships entirely within the confines of their own spaces. In any case, the male members of both secular and religious families are free enough to have their own affairs within the family boundaries or in their private apartments. Compared with boys, girls from both secular and religious families are less capable of hosting boys, either because they are economically less independent or because they are worried about losing their reputation and honor.

The internal realities of these relationships indicate that although many contemporary young women seem to be more liberated and modern in their behavior than the traditional ones or the previous generations, they may also experience more dishonoring violent behaviors, given the fact that private spaces are mostly masculine and that these spaces are much less controllable either by the girls or by conventional social norms (Hoodfar 2000). The domestication of affairs therefore seems to be more costly for young women, who are socially and economically less privileged than young men. Such intimate relationships are nonetheless power relations, in which the male members are active sexual partners, expressing their sexual desires, whereas female members are mostly passive and respond to their male partner's demands. This is the paradoxical duality that many modern Iranian girls face. On the one hand, the male-oriented society expects them to be sexually more open than traditional girls. On the other hand, this more open female sexuality is not treated by the same society as an appropriate form of feminine behavior. Being a modern girl in Iran means being trapped between tradition, which keeps them uncritical and acquiescent toward the norms and attitudes of a discriminative society, and a patriarchal modernity, which makes them more bodily expressive. The youth culture, therefore, has been shaped as a result of this conflicting situation.

Thus, the younger generations' discourse of sexuality cannot be detached from their own embodied social representation. Although mis-veiled girls are, to some extent, behaving and representing themselves as modern in relation to the context and conditions in which Iranian girls live, they are not necessarily critical toward the traditional norms of that society, whether those norms are represented as Islamic or conventional. Therefore, on the basis of what the younger generation articulates, being misveiled does not necessarily lead to a more liberated female role in heterosocial relation-ships. Although many of the misveiled girls seem to offer a more eroticized public self-presentation, most of them are also hesitant to challenge discriminative gender attitudes within their own experience of public and private affairs.

Having been asked why some girls dress this way, a misveiled girl answered:

> Some of them want to attract attention.
>
> *Then what is the difference between you and them?*
>
> In my opinion, the way one behaves is important. Even if I go outside like this, I don't think the people will look at me like that.
>
> *Have you ever attracted attention when you go outside like this?*
>
> Yes.
>
> *Then what is your reaction?*
>
> I don't care.

Few misveiled girls describe this kind of dressing as being in direct opposition to the Islamic government. Rather, they stress taste and personal choice, in-cluding competition with their peers, as their real motivation.

Some of the girls believe, however, that misveiling is not an appropriate means of self-presentation in public spaces, saying: "In my opinion, this kind of dressing is worse than wearing nothing. I don't want to dress like this, because of attracting attention. When I dress so, I feel bad. Everybody has to have the rights of being veiled or not veiled." In phrases like this, misveiled girls make the government responsible for making them do something they otherwise would not do.

Strategies of Security Combined with Doubt: Being *Chadori*

Being a *chadori* in such an atmosphere is another sexual identity taken by more religious girls. It is necessary to mention, however, that the *chador* is losing the ideological implications it had before and after the revolution. This change has happened especially since the invention in 2002 of the so-called *chador melli* (national *chador*) as a solution for preventing *chadori* girls from removing their *chadors*. The national *chador*, although black, is more practically comfortable and aesthetically favored by many *chadori* girls. As a result, the ideological revolutionary ground for wearing the *chador* is gradually fading out.

For many *chadori* girls of the younger generation, being veiled or misveiled has more to do with "personal choice" and the insecurity of public spaces than it does with political devotion to the Islamic Republic's official ideology. Throughout the years after the revolution, women have been told by the government that *hijab* is necessary because of the insecurity of public spaces. Despite *hijab*, the threat of public insecurity has not decreased. Rather, it has been produced and reproduced by the intentional and unintentional policies of the various governments. Although every generation of women complains about the insecurity of public spaces, the government has done little in this regard in terms of the practical problems of making women more comfortable and secure in public spaces. Even the government plan under Ahmadinejad to increase feelings of public security, and called a "social security program," took the form of fighting against misveiling and street thugs, thus characterizing the social security of public space as dependent on the control of women's (and some young men's) behavior in public, rather than ensuring that public space is available and socially secure for all citizens.

Many *chadori* girls prefer to wear more modest dress because, according to them, it protects them from sexual molestation in public spaces. Many of them complain of the insecurity of public spaces, which are male dominated. By wearing the *chador*, they can be publicly present while actually resisting the male domination of public spaces, where a woman's perceived sexuality matters greatly in how she is treated. These *chadori* girls describe their wearing of the *chador* as a matter more of feeling sexually secure in public spaces and social activities than of religiosity:

> Because being involved in such [university social] activities means
> that you have a wide contact with boys, who are not capable enough
> to sexually control themselves. They may allow themselves to say
> anything to you and behave as they wish. Wearing *chador* means that
> they don't allow themselves to do whatever they wish.

According to many of these girls, the *chador* makes them feel secure, although for many of them, wearing the *chador* is completely conditional. Having been asked what she would do if she were forced to choose between *hijab* and personal progress, a veiled girl answered: "In that case, I would choose my progress, not veiling." Having been asked what they would do if they were someplace where nobody cares about veiling, many *chadori* girls answered that they would remove their *chador* and would choose a more comfortable *hijab*.

Unlike their parents, who regarded veiling as the obvious sign of recognizing a good woman from a bad one, *chadori* girls express doubt and believe that according to God, being a good or a bad woman has little to do with *hijab*. Many who have misveiled friends also criticize the compulsory veiling mandated by the government, noting that it is "the worst way to force people to believe in Islam, because it will result in the contrary." According to one *chadori* girl who believes in *hijab* but not especially the *chador*:

> I've been thinking about this for a while. If *hijab* is important, then why is there no punishment for that in the Quran? In the Quran there is no verse saying that when a woman doesn't preserve *hijab* she has to be forced to do it. Nothing says that in that case she has to be isolated.

Although *chadori* girls are vague about whether they, themselves, have chosen to be veiled, they recognize the difference between the way their mothers wear the *chador* and the way they do:

> *What is the difference between you and your mother in wearing the* chador?
>
> She believes in it. I do not. She has to do that; I do not.
>
> *So, why do you wear the* chador?
>
> For girls it is a matter of being forced. Girls do not believe in it, but they're forced to do that . . . because they're in religious families. They're known as religious, so it's not easy to break the rules. People's judgment matters. My mother can't decide to put aside her *chador*. My father was capable of breaking norms. My mother never was.

Without recognizing the government's responsibility in creating this situation, or criticizing male domination and patriarchy, this group actually more clearly acknowledges the cultural weaknesses of Iranian gender norms. Despite this position, they still blame (misveiled) women, who (according to them) are responsible for the "bad situation."

Like the misveiled girls, the *chadori* girls are also trapped between traditional and modern norms. They are caught between the conventions of society on the one hand and the more individualized ambitions of self-expression on the other. Yet, although they wear *hijab* because of the male gaze and avoid pre-marital sexual relationships for fear of being exploited by boys' conflicted sexual desires, they also fail to claim their own subjectivity. Thus, both groups of girls mirror each other within a limited frame of youthful feminine possibility.

Furthermore, for many *chadori* girls, wearing the *chador* does not necessarily mean avoiding sexual relationships. For religious *chadori* girls, what is of utmost importance is to be sure that a girl is not used by a boy. Although they are reluctant to speak about their intimate relationships, according to a few of them temporary marriage is an available means for women to have legitimate affairs. As long as they remain within the Islamic structures of legitimacy, it seems a few *chadori* girls do not care about their virginity as much as the mis-veiled girls do, for whom it remains the chief sign of feminine virtue. Despite this apparent flexibility, it is unclear how, exactly, the more religious girls deal with the practical implications of a more active feminine sexuality.

Wearing the *chador* for *chadori* girls is a strategy to be respected and may even provide them with a protofeminist means of pushing back against both the conventions and Islamic norms of masculine domination (Moruzzi 2006). It does, however, have its own inevitable costs. The *chador* is a public marker that provides some girls with increased security from male harassment, but it also imposes an obligation on the wearer. That is why many *chadori* girls are concerned not to do something demeaning to the *chador;* the garment carries its own sense of honor and vulnerability to its shaming.

Neither Islamist nor Secular: Youth as a Third Way

Regarding the social and political changes of Iranian society and the differences between younger and older generations, one may expect the youth to put a political alternative on the table. The younger generations' reaction toward the unwanted consequences of the Islamization of society, including compulsory veiling, however, is mostly the day-to-day "quiet encroachment" by individuals within the public and private spheres (Bayat 1997: 7). This quiet encroachment includes individual behaviors that are breaking the limitations and rules of traditional familial spaces while also defying the desexualization of public spaces imposed by the Islamic government. Such individual informal actions have been resorted to after many struggles between society and the state. Hidden language (slang or jargon), dress, makeup, hairstyles, music, and the body and sexuality have been shaped as a response to an intransigent political atmosphere.

Similarly, political jokes are the main instrument of criticism and are popularly disseminated throughout the virtual spaces of the Web, on mobile phones, and in ordinary public conversation. Like the youth culture, such exchanges are mixed with ordinary pleasantries, including banal dirty jokes poking fun at provincial and ethnic groups as well as women.

The "third way" is neither secular nor traditional. It tends to mix all traditional and modern aspects of Iranian life in a more pleasant, accessible way. A good example is the appropriation in Iran of the *Ashura* street ceremonies, which were traditionally commemorated by religious (male) participants. In recent years, many boys and girls, wearing fashionable dresses and makeup, attend different public *Ashura* celebrations in Tehran. During these "Hussein parties," as the ceremonies are called, the boys act as the ritual participants, whereas the girls are involved as spectators (Yaghmaian 2002: 62).

Practicing not only different styles of language, dress, and behavior, while also using different political instruments, they blur the borders of belief and disbelief, which were so apparent for the previous generations—that is, for the main supporters of Ayatollah Khomeini and for his dissidents. Yet the question of whether this kind of informal practice is able to change the unwanted structures of society remains open. In the current situation, one may doubt whether the private practices without formal strategy are really enough.

Conclusion: Modern Choices, Old Problems

Compared with previous generations, the current younger generation in Iran seems by and large more ardent and audacious in pursuing its own interests and rights. This position is, in part, the consequence of the social and political developments of the postrevolutionary period and the popular experiences of and reaction to the government's programs of Islamization. Despite the external prestige of the country, the majority of Iranian people are less interested in the government's goals than in following their own individualistic interests.

The Iranian younger generation is made up of individuals who have not experienced collective political actions but have been socially constructed by the aftereffects of those actions. They have been born and raised within a national context frustrated by war, political suppression, and disappointment at the failures of a revolutionary Islamic utopia. This experience has led them to be less political than their parents and to prefer to follow their personal interests. Even though young people tend to be detached from traditional rules of behavior, they are still shaped by conventional norms, and their pressures on the social limitations they experience tend to be haphazard and erratic. Most of them are not interested in pushing for more formal individual rights, mostly because of a lack of interest in organized or collective actions.

Contrary to Islamic discourse, which aimed to desexualize bodies in public spaces, bodily representation matters very much to girls. Young women struggle to construct their bodies through dieting, dress style, and makeup. In so doing, many spend a good deal of time and effort managing their bodies to make them socially presentable. More so than the older generations, many Iranian girls are by and large shaping their identity through negating or accepting conventional and legal sexual discourses mixed with some modern representations. Therefore, although Iranian youth have been quite successful in the ongoing battle over the appropriation of public space, their presence has been accepted at the expense of reinforcing certain traditional power relationships within both the public and private spheres. In particular, conventional gender relations have maintained their inequality, especially in sexual relationships, despite the apparent ability of some boys and girls to engage freely but unequally in premarital affairs.

Acknowledgments

This chapter was originally published as an article in *Comparative Studies of South Asia, Africa and the Middle East* in 2008 (28(2): 250–259). Many thanks to the journal for permission to reprint the article.

PART V

Musical Politics

18

Fun^Da^Mental's "Jihad Rap"

Ted Swedenburg

> Reject your polluting oil guzzling cars
> Reject your morality that's fallen down
> Reject your flag, it's a crusader cross
> Reject your army that murders civilians
> I reject your pork. I reject your beer
> Reject your wealth as a sign of status
> Reject your miniskirt liberation
> Reject your racists and the ones who hate us
> Reject your concept of integration
> Reject your beauty and Barbie doll figure
> Reject your thieving foreign polices
> Reject war on terror, it's a war on Islam
> Reject your democracy, it's all a big sham
> Reject your proof and American pie

The lines (reproduced here in a different sequence than in the original) are from the opening song, "I Reject," of the British music group Fun^Da^Mental's album *All Is War: The Benefits of G-had*, released to a firestorm of controversy in August 2006. Originally scheduled to appear on July 17, the album's production was initially held up when two directors of Nation Records, which is run by Fun^Da^Mental's "leader," British Asian Muslim Aki Nawaz, threatened to resign if Nation released the album. When the album went out for prerelease reviews, Aki Nawaz and the group were subjected to withering media attacks, especially from the tabloid press. A headline in *The Sun* declared, "The Jihad Rap." The article's first line read, "Album's sick suicide bomb and Laden [i.e., bin L.] rants," and it went on to claim that the album "promotes the 'benefits' of *jihad*, or holy war".[1] An *Evening Standard* headline proclaimed, "Muslim rapper defends his suicide bomber lyrics," but the article contained no defense by Aki and instead quoted some lines from the song "DIY Cookbook," which appeared to evoke 7/7: "I'm strapped up, cross my chest bomb belt attached/Deeply satisfied with the plan I hatched/Electrodes connected to a gas cooker lighter" (Singh 2006). The *Sunday Star* labeled the album a "hate-filled rant that glorifies suicide bombers" (Chandler 2006). Such articles also typically raised objections to another song, "Che Bin Pt. 2," which features spoken words by Osama bin Laden. Labor Member of Parliament Andrew Dismore called for police to investigate Fun^Da^Mental and to consider prosecuting them under Britain's antiterrorism laws passed in 2005, which make it an offense to "glorify" an "act of terrorism" that has occurred anywhere in the world, if this encourages others to emulate the act (Bhattacharyya 2006). The commotion forced Fun^Da^Mental to create a new company to put out *All Is War* and to have the CD pressed at a "secret location" outside Europe.

The uproar eventually subsided by late August, after the publication of some serious reviews that discussed the actual content of *All Is War* (see, for example, Campion 2006), and after the media moved on to other matters. The hubbub about the album is symptomatic, however, of larger fears in Britain surrounding British Muslims, and particularly Muslim youth.

BrAsian Muslims

Who are Britain's Muslims and what are the sources of the worries about them? About 1.6 million Muslims reside in Britain today, of whom one million are BrAsians, as I will call them here, following Sayyid (2005: 7),[2] or British of South Asian origin, mostly from rural areas of Pakistan and Bangladesh. These immigrants and their offspring are the products of Britain's post-World War II decision to import a labor force from its colonies and ex-colonies to man industrial sectors that were in decline. South Asian Muslims entered at the bottom tier of the British labor market, and have mostly remained there. Living chiefly in deindustrializing mill towns in the North, like Bradford, as well as London (Abbas 2005: 9–10), BrAsian Muslims are the most economically marginal of all ethnic minorities in the country, with unemployment rates for BrAsian Muslim males nearly three times that for white men, and high rates of residential segregation (mostly enforced), in the most dilapidated housing (Kundnani 2001: 107; Peach 2005: 28).

The background of Fun^Da^Mental leader Aki Nawaz (given name Haq Nawaz Qureishi) is rather typical for a BrAsian Muslim of his generation. Born in a small village in Punjab province, Pakistan, in 1964, Aki's parents brought him, at the age of three, to Bradford, where his father worked as a bus conductor.

BrAsian and especially BrAsian Muslim working-class communities were, for decades, an invisible ethnic minority in Britain. In part, this was a product of how race has been constructed in Britain during the past three decades. Understandings of race in Britain have very much been informed by hegemonic U.S. analyses, according to which race is a matter of skin color and revolves, in particular, around black/white differences. Within the British antiracist movements, especially in their heyday during the 1980s, activists and radical intellectuals attempted to mobilize Afro-Caribbeans and South Asians together under the category "black." Although many progressive South Asians embraced the designation, in practice, this politics of naming served to marginalize South Asians. According to "black" movement logic, South Asians shared *political* blackness with British Afro-Caribbeans but not *cultural* blackness, which was defined by Afro-Caribbean culture (Hyder 2004: 19). Moreover, according to conventional racial understandings of the time, Afro-Caribbeans (the stereotypical "blacks") were the "problem" minority who bore the brunt of racist and anti-immigrant assaults. South Asians were, by contrast, seen as largely passive and law abiding, and possessors of an exotic and alien "culture," in contrast to black Britons, who were considered lacking in culture. This skin color model of racism does not account for *cultural* racism and has been unable to explain why racial prejudice has tended to be greater, sometimes *much* greater, against South Asians, and especially Muslims, than against Afro-Caribbeans— especially of late (Modood 2005b: 67). The antiracist mobilization's effort at black unity was ultimately unsuccessful, and since the late 1980s, South Asians have mostly abandon the "black" label in favor of mobilizing and self-identifying as Asians or as Muslims or both.

Aki Nawaz, however, is a product of the era of joint mobilization of Afro-Caribbeans and South Asians as "blacks," and in certain senses remains loyal to it. His cultural–political formation, however, cannot be reduced to this manifestation of blackness. The first band Aki saw in concert was the Sex Pistols, and this was by his account a formative experience. It is important to recall that even though the primarily punk subculture was largely white, it did include progressive elements who played leading roles in the antiracist mobilization connected with the Rock Against Racism organization of the late 1970s (Hebdige 1981). From 1982 to 1983, Aki (using the name Haq Qureshi) played drums for the post-punk proto-Goth band Southern Death Cult, whose leader, Ian Astbury, later formed the legendary Goth band The Cult.

It was only in 1989, when working-class BrAsian Muslims organized demonstrations, and a couple of highly publicized book burnings, to protest what
they considered the blasphemous character of Salman Rushdie's *The Satanic
Verses*, that Muslim communities really become visible in England. Aki got
embroiled in the controversy, too, when press reports appeared claiming that he
supported Ayatollah Khomeini's *fatwa* (formal legal opinion) calling for Rushdie's death. Aki eventually clarified that the press had misquoted him, that he
opposed efforts to silence or kill Rushdie, but that he also understood "why Muslims are upset with the writer" (Lewis 1994: 180). Meanwhile, Aki had cofound-
ed Nation Records with his Afro-Caribbean friend Katherine Canoville in 1988,
and the label rapidly became a trendsetter in the emerging "world dance music"
scene, characterized by the fusion of dance beats and world music sounds.

Fun^Da^Mental Seizes the Time

Aki organized Fun^Da^Mental in 1991, and the band was very involved in the antiracist campaigns launched during the early 1990s in response both to an upsurge
of racist attacks orchestrated by the British National Party (BNP) and to expanded
BNP electoral activity. Along with other progressive Asian bands like Asian Dub
Foundation, The Kaliphz, and Hustlers HC, Fun^Da^Mental performed and delivered speeches at various antiracist benefits, carnivals, and rallies. The political–
cultural work of Asian bands and grassroots organizations helped push BrAsian
issues to the forefront of antiracist organizing during the mid 1990s.

During this same period, "Muslims" (taken to mean, in conventional understandings, South Asian Muslims) came to replace Afro-Caribbeans as the
"problem" minority in Britain, and young BrAsian Muslim males came to
assume the new role of "folk devil" (Cohen 2002/1972). The media and police
increasingly highlighted the "dangers" that young inner-city Asian Muslim
males posed. They were "pathologized," racialized, stigmatized, depicted as
gang members, and held responsible for ostensibly rising rates of inner-city
violence, crime, and illegal drug usage and dealing. Alternatively, Asian
Muslim youth were represented as dangerous and criminal "fundamentalists"
(Alexander 2000, 2005: 258, 266).

At the same time as they were being vilified as Public Enemy Number One,
Asian Muslim youth were left vulnerable to racist attack. As a result of the hegemony of the color racism model, when antiracism legislation was passed in
Britain it failed to include protections against physical attacks, discrimination,
or libel against Muslims based on their religion. By contrast, Sikhs and Jews are
so protected. The legislation did, however, offer legal protection against racist

attacks visited upon them as South Asians. The extreme Right has exploited this loophole, and during the past several years the BNP in particular has repeatedly published incendiary attacks on Muslims, which would be liable to legal prosecution as racist incitement if leveled against blacks or Asians.

It is in this context of increased visibility and notoriety for BrAsian Muslims, of moral panics over Muslim youth, of an upsurge in racist violence, and of anti-racist mobilizations, that Fun^Da^Mental released its first album, *Seize the Time*, in 1994, whose title "samples" that of Bobby Seale's (1970) famous account of the rise of the Black Panther Party. The album, mostly composed of rap numbers, conveys a "state of emergency" by means of an aggressive and dense sound mix. It blends, in a very striking fashion, the musical sounds and beats of the Asian subcontinent with the funk of the Black Atlantic, seasoned with samples of speeches from Malcolm X and Louis Farrakhan, dialogue from the film *Gandhi*, a recorded hate message from a British neo-Nazi group, and so on. The album's atmospherics, urgency, and militancy recall Public Enemy's celebrated rap releases of the late 1980s and early '90s. *Seize the Time*'s lyrics promote militant antiracism and community self-defense, pride in (South Asian-based) Islam, race consciousness, anti-imperialist sentiments, connections between black and Asian struggles, and the teachings of the Nation of Islam (considered heretical by many Orthodox Muslims), mixed with a strong dose of punk provocation. The song "Meera Mazab" ("My Religion") includes the following lines:

> You go for yours cuz I'm in jihad
> Allahu samad [*"God the eternal," from the Quran*] . . .
> So I'll be comin' around the mountain[3] With my
>   Islamic warriors
> Nubians[4] wid jihad in my mind.

The song also includes a comment on the Israeli army's slaughter of 17 Palestinians in October 1990 at Jerusalem's Haram al-Sharif: "Massacre in the mosque, suicidal frame of mind/Take a look, can't you see, look at Palestine."

Seize the Time, therefore, articulates a complex array of political and cultural concerns having to do with the religious, racial, and postcolonial dimensions of BrAsian Muslim experience, the upsurge of racist attacks and Islamophobia; transnational Islamic attachments; anti-imperialist politics; and Asian–Afro-Caribbean solidarities. Its sound and messages, moreover, reflect the band's multiethnic character. Afro-Caribbean Dave Watts, who is not a Muslim, joined Fun^Da^Mental in 1993 and served as the band's other core member until moving to Spain in 2007. The band's revolving personnel over the years, moreover, has included BrAsian Sikhs and Hindus and white Britons, in addition to Afro-Caribbeans and BrAsian Muslims. It should also be underscored that it is a mistake to stereotype or pigeonhole the band as simply "Asian" and "political," for its music has significant aesthetic and pleasure dimensions. Fun^Da^Mental aims for audiences to dance to its soundtrack, an intention inscribed into the band's name and its multivalent meanings. *Fundamental* means "basic" and "essential," while at the same time evoking so-called Islamic fundamentalism. In fact, Aki has said, it represents a reclaiming of a word that was being used against Muslims (Anonymous 1998). The punctuation of Fun^Da^Mental "breaks down" the name, hip-hop style, into its basic elements, thereby highlighting both the "fun" and the serious or "mental" sides of the band and its music. The "fun" and the "mental" interpenetrate, given that this music promises multiple pleasures: the fun of celebrating Asian, black, and Muslim identity; the fun of participating in cultural–political events that express collective and intercultural solidarity; and the "punk" fun of provocation, of venting spleen at authority, and of breaking taboos. The "fun" includes, for the band, the "shaking up" of young whites, who compose an important constituent of its audience. As Aki remarked in 1995: "[W]e kind of look forward to going up on the stage to hordes of drunk and drugged-out indie kids and almost terrifying the shit out of them. We're like the ultimate coming down pill" (Yellow Peril 1995).

Fun^Da^Mental's participation in the early 1990s antiracist campaigns won it the endorsement and publicity of the popular music press (particular *Melody Maker* and *New Musical Express*), which increased the band's visibility on both the political and the pop culture fronts. Meanwhile, Nation Records, cohelmed by Aki, played a major role throughout the 1990s in the burgeoning, multicultural "world dance music" phenomenon, by producing and promoting recordings by a wide array of acts. Besides Fun^Da^Mental, Nation's stable has included artists like world dance fusion group Transglobal Underground; politically activist Asian Dub Foundation, ethnoambient Loop Guru; Asian dance artists T.J. Rehmi, Joi, and Swami; South African rappers Prophets of da City; and Arab dance diva Natacha Atlas. All these artists produced very different sound fusions, which variously incorporated ragga, dub, bhangra, gamelan, Egyptian pop, hip-hop, classical Indian, jazz, and so on. With the significant exception of Asian Dub Foundation, most were not explicitly political, and other than Fun^Da^Mental, the only Muslim-identified Nation artist was Natacha Atlas, whose religious sensibility is more spiritual than militant.

Cool Asians, Criminal Asians

Nation Records also helped create and foster the cultural phenomenon known as Asian Cool. During the mid 1990s, somewhat paradoxically, even as antipathy toward BrAsian Muslims was on the increase, things "Asian" (food, fashion, music, and film) suddenly became very trendy—after decades of invisibility during the mid 1990s. In the music scene, blacks (meaning Afro-Caribbeans) have been regarded as far back as the 1950s as the epitome of cool by hip white habitués of the British club and music scene, whereas Asians, in contrast, were viewed as the essence of *un*cool—nerdy, unfunky, and culturally conservative. Asian men were seen as decidedly nonmacho in contrast to the aggressively masculine and rebellious black man so admired by white bohemians. Asians, therefore, were regarded as essentially incompatible with the glamorous world of pop and rock music (Hyder 2004). Such stereotypes began to be undermined in the mid to late 1990s as BrAsian musicians like Cornershop, Asian Dub Foundation, Bally Sagoo, Talvin Singh, Apache Indian, Black Star Liner, and Fun^Da^Mental began to enjoy a certain amount of mainstream popularity and to gain critical acclaim.[5] (The musical phenomenon was known variously as the Asian Underground, Asian Dance, or Asian Massive.) The Asian Cool moment also coincided with the Blair government's "Cool Britannia" project, an attempt to rebrand Britain by emphasizing its multiethnic composition. The last third of the 1990s, therefore, witnessed *both* a surge in racist attacks and racist policies aimed at BrAsians and particularly Muslims, and, say Hesse and Sayid (2005: 27), a "mainstream passion for all things culturally diverse." Hesse and Sayyid go on to call this phenomenon a kind of "ethnic love and hate fest" (Ibid). Hutnyk (2005: 77) notes a parallel tendency in recent monographs on BrAsians, which, he observes, do an "'exotica–fanatica' two-step," depicting Asians as either or both a people of curious culture and/or a people of fanaticism.

During this period, Fun^Da^Mental moved away from rap, and its music evolved in exciting and provocative ways. The band's 1998 release *Erotic Terrorism*, on the one hand, includes songs featuring vocal tracks from Pakistani *qawwali* singers like Nawazish Ali Khan set to hip-hop beats (*qawwali* is the Sufi devotional music of the subcontinent). It also includes screamingly explosive and abrasive metal/industrial numbers that are reminiscent of the work of Nine Inch Nails and Napalm Death. The lyrics, often hard to make out, rail against oppression, but the emphasis is more on sound than words. A hostile review of *Erotic Terrorism* in *Melody Maker* called the industrial noise tracks "aural torture" (Roland 1998)—which, arguably, was precisely the point. 2001 saw the release of *There Shall Be Love*, which (as the title suggests) has a more positive and upbeat feel than earlier recordings, less focused on militant politics. As products of Fun^Da^Mental's extensive global travels, most of the tracks involve collaborations with artists from outside England. Some tracks were recorded with *qawwali*, classical, and Baul (Sufi mystic) musicians in Pakistan; others with a Zulu choir (Zamo Mbuto and comrades) in Johannesburg; and one with Huun Huur

Tu, throat singers from the Tuvan Republic (Russia). The overall emphasis of *There Shall Be Love* is on exploring and promoting traditional musical genres of Pakistan as well as forging Asian–black global musical connections and solidarities, particularly involving South Africans.

Contrary to what has frequently been claimed, Fun^Da^Mental was not a "Muslim rap band," but rather a kind of mobile political–cultural coalition, whose members, according to Aki, were united musically and politically by a "hatred of inequality" rather than a common religious faith. "We ain't pushing no Islamic ideology," says Aki. "Our message is more, 'Man, lose your ignorance'" (Chu 2001). Aki calls Fun^Da^Mental's genre of music "global chaos," endorsing a kind of tear-down-the-boundaries globalism that is the antithesis of western-driven globalization. Dave Watts, meanwhile, has labeled what Fun^Da^Mental does as "political folk music" (Hyder 2004: 111).

More recently, the moment of Asian Cool has peaked, but has left British Asian music, cinema, fashion, and food with a higher profile than before. Meanwhile, local antipathy toward BrAsian Muslims has continued to intensify, as illustrated by the events of July 2001, when a series of so-called "riots" broke out in several northern mill towns with Asian communities. Essentially, these were battles between Muslim youths and police, provoked by attacks from gangs of extreme Right hooligans, and police responses that came too late and that targeted Muslims, the victims of aggression, rather than the white perpetrators. Media and government commentary tended to blame the Muslims for these events and to ignore the underlying causes—in particular, racist structures and racist provocations (Allen 2003; Kalra 2005; Kundnani 2001).

The terror attacks of September 11, 2001, and more recently of July 7, 2004, have further raised public fears in Britain that Muslims in the country not only possess an alien culture, but also pose a serious security threat as well. More than ever, Muslims are subject to racial profiling and community repression, with police using measures from newly passed antiterror legislation—legislation with a legitimacy among the general public that has been enabled by all the successive "moral panics" surrounding Muslims. Far Right extremist organizations, in particular the BNP, now make Muslims their special targets. Far Right propaganda invariably describes British Muslims as "immigrants," despite the fact that about half are born in England (Peach 2005: 169), and it takes pains to distinguish them from other ethnic/religious minorities, including Afro-Caribbeans and Hindus, who far Right organizations now consider legitimate British citizens who are more readily assimilable than Muslims. (The antiterrorism act passed after 9/11, however, now affords Muslims protection against physical harassment based on religion, but still does not protect against incitement to religious hatred [Modood 2005a: 130].)

Muslimophobic positions, meanwhile, which previously were identified, for the most part, with the extreme Right, have increasingly come to be respectable and mainstream. Journalists, commentators, and politicians from across the political spectrum assert with growing fervor that Islam is essentially incompatible with European values, and that Muslims are inherently hostile to those "tolerant" values that the English hold so dearly, such as free speech, equal rights for women, and tolerance for gays and lesbians. Muslims, it is claimed, self-segregate, refuse to assimilate, insist on arranging marriages for their sons with young brides imported from Pakistan, fail to learn English (Kundnani 2001: 110), and cling to "intolerant" and backward values, besides being responsible for endemic gang violence and drug use (Alexander 2005: 266).

One of the most fundamental objections to Muslims is that Islam is a politicized religious identity—that is, that Muslims are incapable of separating between religion and politics, of making distinctions between politics as public, religion as private, the way one expects in a liberal, secular society (Modood 2005a: 141, 167). Fun^Da^Mental calls attention to the hypocrisies of British secularism when they state, "reject your flag; it's a crusader flag" ("I Reject"). They refer to the St. George's Cross—red on a white background—which was worn by English crusaders from the 11th to 13th centuries and became the flag of England in 1277, and forms part of the Union Jack.

The veil, a term used rather loosely to refer to any kind of Islamic head covering worn by women, functions as a symbolic condensation of the "problems" posed by BrAsian Muslims, and commentators widely read it as a signifier of Muslims' illiberal values—that is, as an index of Muslims' repression of women, of their refusal to keep religion a "private" matter, their insistence on inserting it into the public sphere, and of their assertion of separateness and essential cultural difference. In October 2006, the prominent Labor Party politician and then-Leader of the House of Commons Jack Straw wrote an article in which he revealed that when Muslim women constituents wearing a *niqab* (a full veil with a slit for the eyes) visit his office for consultations, he asks them to raise the veil so that he can see their eyes. The veil, Straw stated, is a "visible statement of separation and difference" (Coburn 2006). The claim raised protests from many Muslims, but both then-Prime Minister Tony Blair and his successor Gordon Brown chimed in to support their colleague. Fun^Da^Mental comments, "reject your beauty and Barbie doll figure; reject your miniskirt liberation" ("I Reject"). An opinion poll conducted shortly after Straw's remarks found widespread public agreement with these views. Only 22% of Britons surveyed thought Muslims had done enough to integrate, and 57% thought that Muslims should do more to fit in.[6] Commentators who agree with the likes of Straw also assert that Britain's multicultural policies have been a failure, that they have given Muslims too much cultural freedom, and that if Muslims are to be accepted as legitimate British subjects (and if the terrorist threat that they embody is to be eliminated), they need to integrate with British society and embrace its values rather than insisting on cultural difference. (Fun^Da^Mental comments: "Reject your concept of integration.") Sivanandan (2006: 3) notes that such policies and sentiments, originating from political leaders and mainstream opinion makers, have exacerbated Muslims' feelings of being besieged and thereby reinforced the sorts of self-segregation that the government says it wants to prevent.

All Is War

The title of the latest Fun^Da^Mental's 2006 album, *All Is War* (fig. 18.1), refers not just to the heavy policing, surveillance, and crackdowns on Muslim communities in Europe, but to the post-9/11 *global* environment, where it's war everywhere—the war on terror, the invasion of Afghanistan, Israeli offensives against Palestinians, the occupation of Iraq, Russia's repression of Chechnya, and so on. The album's political orientation is shared by many Muslims as well as non-Muslims, in Britain and abroad (Krastev and McPherson 2007), and responds directly to widespread feelings in the West, orchestrated by agencies of public meaning, that it is Europeans and North Americans who are especially threatened by assault from a global network of Islamic terrorists, based not just overseas but also within, inside western minority communities.

All Is War intervenes in characteristically complicated and multidimensional ways. It makes no effort to "reassure" the western audiences at whom its messages are aimed and it declines to adopt the sort of "moderate" posture that mainstream commentators so insistently demand of Britain's Muslims (Meer 2006: 50–51). Instead, Fun^Da^Mental responds to the global war atmosphere aggressively, hurling accusations with characteristic punk bravado. Here I will examine the most arresting and effective tracks, beginning with the one that sparked much of the furor in summer 2006, "DIY [do it yourself] Cookbook." Media attacks on "DIY Cookbook" limited their discussion to the first part of a song that has three parts: to the part that presents a suicide bomber who makes his device on the cheap with everyday materials, with the aim of "hitting back at the vice." "DIY Cookbook," however, in no way endorses his actions, but simply presents his point of view along with those of two other bomb producers. Part two describes a PhD holder who produces a dirty bomb with black market materials, which he will sell to the highest bidder. Part three presents a "legitimate" bomb maker, a U.S. government employee, working on a neutron

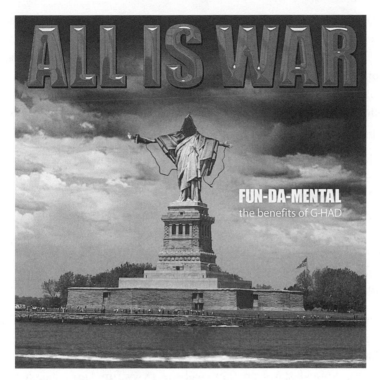

FIGURE 18.1. CD cover of Fun^Da^Mental's *All Is War*. (Fundamental, 2007)

bomb that will kill people but leave buildings intact. He has all the resources he needs at his disposal, paid for by U.S. taxpayers. The song deliberately delivers an incendiary message, particularly in evoking the July 7, 2004, bombings that killed 52 London commuters and four terrorists. Its true purpose is to *relativize* the July 7 (colloquially known as 7/7) attackers rather than in any way sanction their actions, a goal that is arguably more subversive than the "crime" the media originally charged Fun^Da^Mental with (endorsing suicide bombing). Should we regard the actions of the July 7 terrorists as pure evil, "DIY Cookbook" suggests, although we consider innocent the states that finance the making of bombs that have been responsible for the deaths of tens of thousands of civilians in the ongoing wars in Afghanistan and Iraq and the Israeli assaults on Lebanon in summer 2006 and Gaza in winter 2008–2009, and so on?[7]

Then there is "Che Bin" parts one and two. Part one features a speech by Che Guevara, set to an understated accompaniment of flute and acoustic guitar. Here Che explains the difference between sabotage and terrorism in the course of revolutionary struggle, calling sabotage a "revolutionary" and "highly effective method of warfare," and describing terrorism as generally "ineffective and

indiscriminate in its results, since it often makes victims of innocent people."
But, Che adds, terrorism may sometimes be useful for the insurgency when it
involves killing an oppressive leader (Guevara 1998). Part two presents the
voice of Osama bin Laden, from an interview a reporter for *al-Jazeera* conducted
with him on October 21, 2001.[8] Bin Laden speaks passionately, eloquently, and
wickedly over an intense musical track with electric guitar and feedback, set to
a sharp, martial beat. He asks rhetorically:

> Who said that our children and civilians are not innocent and that
> shedding their blood is justified? That it is lesser in degree? When we
> kill their innocents, the entire world from East to West screams at us,
> and America rallies its allies, agents, and the sons of its agents. Who
> said that our blood is not blood, but theirs is? . . . More than one
> million children died in Iraq and others are still dying.[9] . . . They
> react *only* if we kill American civilians, and every day we are being
> killed, children are being killed in Palestine.

Bin Laden concludes: "We kill the kings of the infidels, kings of the crusaders,
and civilian infidels in exchange for those of our children they kill. This is permissible in law and intellectually."[10]

Fun^Da^Mental states on their website (www.fun-da-mental.co.uk/) that
the purpose of "Che Bin" parts one and two is to provoke discussion. "What
makes one a symbol of resistance and the other a terrorist?" they ask. "What do
they have, if anything, in common?" Aki suggests elsewhere that although Che
is a "revered cultural icon" in the West, bin Laden is "vilified as a monster."[11]
But is bin Laden entirely wrong, Fun^Da^Mental seems to ask, to say that
Americans care very little about the shedding of Iraqi and Palestinian blood
and only mourn American casualties?[12]

"786: All Is War" is a sci-fi revenge fantasy, in which the war on terror ends
with Muslims liberating the United States, the Statue of Liberty falling prostrate
before Allah, and "citizens build[ing] . . . a mosque on Ground Zero." Futuristic,
counter-Hollywood images of Islamic warriors and weapons abound in this lyri-
cally clever song: "Sufi surfing on boards of steel" (Silver Surfer mystic?); "Jihadi
jet-skis Hudson River"; "*Deen* (religion) machines replicant Sufis"; "Sunnah
troopers"; "Ibrahim tanks"; "cyborg *mujahids*"; "AI (artificial intelligence) imams,"
and so on, all part of the Dream Team Salahuddin, a supremely hip-hop-esque
formulation (Salahuddin is Saladin, the Muslim hero of the struggle against the
Crusaders). These *mujahideen*, unlike bin Laden's, don't attack "infidel" citizens,
but liberate them from the oppressors, from the *riba* (usury or usurers), "the mon-
eylenders, the bank elite," and "the Pharaoh's sons," in a futuristic *jihadi* apocalypse
that puts end to a United States held guilty of genocide, theft, and mass murder.

The track "Electro G-Had (Punjabi Style)" is composed and sung by 19-year-old British-Asian musician Subiag Singh Kandola, in the style of a Punjabi folk song put to electronic beats. It is in the vein of a BrAsian tradition of "'revolutionary' poetry recitation[s]," held periodically to commemorate the heroes of India's anti-colonial struggle (Brah 2005: 61). This is the album's one song that explicitly deals with jihad, which here is spelled G-had, so as to break it down and defamiliarize its usual meanings. The meaning of G-had is open to interpretation. The "G" here might be the "G" of hip-hop, as in "sup, G?", where "G" stands for gangsta, but originally meant God, for the Five Per-centers, who believe in the divinity of the black man (see Knight 2007). Or it might be the Urdu "ji" for friend. The "had" could be the "hadd" of Urdu (and Arabic) for "limit," and it also refers to the "hadd" offences of shari'a law. The four anti-colonial martyr heroes of the song are Udham Singh, a Sikh nation-alist, Bhagat Singh (d. 1931), a Sikh socialist, Tipu Sultan (d. 1799), the late 18th-century Muslim king of Mysore and a member of the local French Jacobin club, and the Babbar Akali movement, an anti-colonial Sikh movement active in 1921-25, composed mostly of returned emigrants from Canada. There is only space here to discuss Udham Singh, whose tale has been retold in numer-ous bhangra tracks since the early seventies (Kalra 2000: 90). Udham Singh was an eyewitness to the notorious 1919 Amritsar massacre when British sol-diers killed over 1000 Indian civilians. In 1940 Singh took his people's revenge in London when he assassinated Michael O'Dwyer, former Lieutenant-Governor of the Punjab and the purported architect of the massacre. After be-ing arrested by police, Singh reportedly signed his name Ram Mohammed Singh Azad, signifying joint Muslim-Sikh-Hindu participation in the freedom struggle ("Azad" means freedom in Punjabi, Ram is a Hindu god, hero of the Ramayana epic). Singh was subsequently hanged for his crime (Hutnyk 2005: 85; Kalra 2000: 93).

Although Aki Nawaz often uses the stage name Propa-Gandhi, the tradi-tions of anti-colonial struggle remembered in "Electro G-Had" are far from Gandhianism, and instead involve the use of violence and terror against British colonial officials and their native collaborators. The song celebrates the mem-ory of the so-called "terrorists" of the colonial period, fighters against the impe-rial power of the day (Aki Nawaz, personal communication, September 2007). Such traditions have strong roots in the BrAsian community, especially among the organized working class and the left. It is significant, moreover, that the song evokes traditions of inter-sectarian solidarity, a history that is clearly at odds with contemporary efforts in Britain to promote essential differences between "unassimilable" Muslims and "assimilable" Sikhs and Hindus, not to mention contemporary sectarian-based conflicts in the subcontinent.

Three additional songs, which feature mostly female voices, express other important concerns of Fun^Da^Mental. "Bark like a Dog," recorded with the Mighty Zulu Nation, a South African Zulu choir, is probably the album's most joyful dance track, and opens with a guitar riff from the Sex Pistols' punk anthem, "Anarchy in the UK," played over breakbeats. According to Campion (2006), the title "refers to a peaceful protest through joyful noise prevalent in apartheid-era South Africa".[13] "5 Prayers of Afghani Women," a mournful narration by Shivani set to classical Afghani music and the whir of helicopters, raises the overlooked issue of Afghani civilian casualties at the hands of US and NATO forces.[14] "Srebrenica Massacre" is a Serbo-Croation dirge authored and sung by Alma Ferovic, a classically-trained vocalist from Sarajevo, who is now based in London. The song laments the 1995 massacre of over 8000 Bosnian Muslims by Bosnian Serb forces, the largest mass murder to occur in Europe since World War II, and ruled an act of genocide by the International Criminal Tribunal for the former Yugoslavia.[15] "5 Prayers of Afghani Women" and "Srebrenica Massacre" recall instances of violence against Muslims that are largely forgotten or ignored in the West but are vividly remembered in the Middle East and Islamic communities throughout the world. These songs also pose the questions: did 9/11 "change everything," as is often claimed in the West? Are the genocide of 8000 Muslims on European soil, the deaths of thousands of Afghani civilians, and the Palestinian and Iraqi casualties mentioned by Bin Laden, by contrast insignificant? Why do *Westerners* feel especially under siege, when so many Muslims have been dying?

I now return to the song, "I Reject," a laundry list that includes a number of issues that many western liberals and progressives might agree are worthy of rejection, such as the U.S. administration's "proof" of the existence of Iraqi weapons of mass destruction or the excessive pollution caused by gas-guzzling SUVs. An important example of the possibilities of such agreement between progressive secular forces and Muslims occurred during late 2002 and early 2003, when the Muslim Association of Britain served as one of the three organizers of London demonstrations against the impending invasion of Iraq, including one in February that was the largest ever mounted in the city (Modood 2005a: 204).

But although it is essential to acknowledge the possibility of such connections and cooperation, it is perhaps more critical, and more in keeping with Fun^Da^Mental's intentions, to recognize discomforting potential differences. For "I Reject" also manifests a profound skepticism toward the notion that modernity and the progress it heralds represent a straightforward destiny for everyone. It articulates opposition to the prevalent views that "freedom" to expose lots of skin represents the liberation of women, whereas Muslim women who make public displays of modesty and religious piety are behaving in a hostile manner.[16] It critiques the tolerance said to be an inherent value of liberalism, arguing instead that British liberalism is very *in*tolerant when it comes to Muslims, and reminding us that Muslimo- phobia is not the exclusive property of the far Right. It levels a criticism against secularism that demands that religious expression be limited to the private sphere. "I Reject" suggests that foreign policy "failings" (murder of civilians, pillaging, attacks on Islam) may be *inherent* to western liberalism, which regards its values as universal, not culturally specific, and which attempts to impose these so-called universal values on Muslims at home and abroad (Modood 2005a: 172).

Conclusion

I do not want to claim here that Fun^Da^Mental is in any way "representa- tive" or "typical" of Muslims in contemporary Britain. Nonetheless, they are of importance for a number of reasons. First, Fun^Da^Mental's music and views have a significant public presence, and therefore they are able to speak to audiences that include non-Muslims. (In fact, some have argued that Fun^Da^Mental's main audience is white Britons.) Moreover, because of the diverse backgrounds of the group, the variety of musical genres that they deploy, and the range of messages and concerns that they express, they offer a useful and more complex vision of Muslim identity in Britain today, one that is much more complex than the usual polarities of the assimilated and successful versus the ghettoized, inward-looking criminal and/or fundamentalist. Let me now try to sum up and tie together some of the dimensions of Fun^Da^Mental that I believe are worth underscoring.

First, Fun^Da^Mental raises issues that are not of exclusive concern to Muslims, although they very much speak from a Muslim orientation. They aim to educate by provocation, as well as to promote struggles linking Muslims to others, struggles over racial and class discrimination, against colonialism, and so on.

Second, the colonial past, rooted in histories of migration, is very impor- tant. Fun^Da^mental stresses the colonial experience in South Asia, but also links this history to similar ones, such as apartheid in South Africa and the enslavement of blacks in the Americas. Fun^Da^Mental thereby recalls and invokes shared, global colonial experiences of both oppression and struggles. Such traditions are not only potential points of linkage between nonwhite communities in Britain (particularly blacks and Asians), but they also very much inform understandings of the present, having to do with definitions of terrorism, the continued importance of western (especially U.S.) imperialism, and so on.

Third, and particularly in its more recent work, a critique of western liberalism and secularism is of great concern for Fun^Da^Mental, which attempts to expose liberal–secular hypocrisies and to highlight the intolerance of a supposedly tolerant Britain. By "foregrounding" Muslim beliefs and in advancing a defense of Muslim communities, in Britain and around the world, they challenge current resistance in Britain to public displays of piety and religiosity. In this they are in line with BrAsian critic Tariq Modood (2005a: 112), who asks: "Is the Enlightenment big enough to tolerate the existence of pre-Enlightenment religious enthusiasm, or can it only exist by suffocating all who fail to be overawed by its intellectual brilliance and vision of Man?"

Fourth, and despite the language of "rejection," Fun^Da^Mental is very much engaged with European culture, politics, and values. All the provocation and belligerence are cast in very British terms, in the idiom of punk. Aki Nawaz has also claimed the right to artistic freedom of expression, in defense of *All Is War*:

> We see people writing books about the global conflicts, we see films, documentaries, everybody's on about the issues so why can't I sing about them? . . . But people are saying to me, "Everybody else is allowed to say what they wish but Muslims are not allowed to say what they want because they face being arrested." . . . This is a democracy—is it such just for white folks, and fascism for everybody else? (Damien 2006)

Fifth, Fun^Da^Mental's Islamic orientations are wide ranging and global in scope. But if Fun^Da^Mental connects to a global *umma*, it is by no means an Orthodox one. In their early work, Fun^Da^Mental made reference to and sampled from the very heterodox tradition of the Nation of Islam (including Malcolm X and Louis Farakhan). In terms of its connection to Islamic trends of the subcontinent, it has recorded and performed with artists from the very popular, grassroots, and non-Orthodox *qawwali* Sufi tradition. For the song "Srebenica Massacre," Fun^Da^Mental uses the services of a female Bosnian Muslim who wears no headscarf. If Fun^Da^Mental's posture, in terms of lyrics and image, is very aggressive, if its members refuse to play the role of "moderate" Muslim, their relation to global Islamic trends is very open and heterogeneous.

In a time when Muslims in Britain, and particularly its youth, are being vilified and stereotyped, Fun^Da^Mental serves as an important correction to mainstream views. Militant yet inclusive and open, rejectionist yet deeply concerned with education and dialogue, Muslim and black and British/punk and global in their concern, they provide a very different, multiplexed, and more useful vision of what it might mean to be "Muslim" in today's Britain.

19

Maroc-Hop: Music and Youth Identities in the Netherlands

Miriam Gazzah

Dutch Moroccan hip-hop, or "Maroc-hop," was put on the musical map in the Netherlands in 2002 with the release of the hit record, *K*tmarokkanen (F*king Moroccans)* by the 25-year-old Dutch Moroccan rapper Raymzter. He wrote the song in reaction to a Dutch politician's remark that was accidentally picked up by a microphone and aired on national television in which he referred to Moroccan youths as "those f*king Moroccans." The enormous success of Raymzter's rap cleared the way for other rappers of Moroccan origin who have been active in the production of a growing hip-hop musical scene. In addition to hip-hop, a vibrant subculture has been constructed around Arab Moroccan popular folk music known as *Shaabi*, which includes dance events, websites, and magazines. Maroc-hop and Shaabi contribute in different ways to the construction of identity of Dutch Moroccan youths within the specific context of contemporary Dutch society. Although Shaabi music gets used as a way to reinforce elements of an ethnic past and celebrates a Moroccan identity, Maroc-hop is infused with an angst ridden edge and is becoming an important means for youths to voice their frustrations with Dutch society. Ever since 9/11, and even more so after the assassination of filmmaker Theo van Gogh in November 2004 by a Dutch Moroccan muslim radical, Dutch Moroccan youth have been in the political and media spotlights. This often negative attention for the Moroccan community has caused many Dutch people to associate Dutch Moroccan youth with crime, terrorism, and Islamic fundamentalism—an image that frustrates many Dutch Moroccans youths who feel stigmatized and have to defend themselves constantly.

Until recently, few scholars took an interest in studying the association between music and identity formation of ethnic minorities. During the 1970s and '80s, scholars tended to consider pop music as part of youth subcultures, of which the most famous example is Hall and Jefferson's *Resistance Through Rituals* (1976). The focus lay on how style and bricolage constituted forms of resistance to hegemonic society. As a result of the overconcentration on latent ideologies behind style and class differences, these studies mostly neglected the reasons why specific groups used certain kinds of style or music to express this resistance. The scholars working in this school of thought considered youth subcultures "magical solutions for class differences" (Brake 1980: 24). They focused on the "hidden meanings" behind certain symbols used by youth subcultures. For example, the so-called "punk rockers" in the United Kingdom in the 1970s, guided by the music of the Sex Pistols and Johnny Rotten, used to decorate themselves with utensils such as safety pins. This was explained as a hidden message of resistance against the hegemony of the British middle class. By adorning themselves with these "cheap" objects, the "punks" rebelled against the normative standard values of middle class, and symbolized and glorified the emptiness, hardness, and poverty of British lower class.

During the 1980s and '90s, scholars from different disciplinary vantage points, including anthropology, sociology, and economics, made new inroads into the study of pop music. Roughly speaking, two distinct approaches emerged: one that considered the role of the media and music industry as highly important in the study of pop music (Negus 1998, 1999; Thornton 1995), and another that took a more cultural approach. Those scholars who studied music from a cultural point of view often emphasized the connection between music and identity (Bennett 2000; Rose and Ross 1994; Stokes 1994). Within the context of immigration and multiculturalism, pop music has taken on other dimensions. The attention to immigrants and marginalized ethnic communities in the Netherlands and much of western Europe is often reduced to topics such as unemployment, religious fundamentalism, Islamism, and terrorism; topics having to do with the cultural influence of these groups have largely gone unnoticed.

This chapter, based on primary research, shows how second-generation Dutch Moroccan youths between 20 to 30 years of age use specific musical genres in distinctive social contexts to express identity. These young men and women listen to a wide variety of musical genres, two of which (Shaabi and hip-hop) hold a special position.

Dutch Moroccan Youth and Dutch Politics

Moroccan immigrants have been part of Dutch society for more than 30 years. Currently, in the Netherlands there are more than 329,000 people of Moroccan descent, of whom 161,000 are part of the second generation.[1] The Moroccan community is the third largest minority community after the Surinamese and the Turkish communities. The first Moroccans came to the Netherlands as "guest laborers" during the 1960s and '70s. As a consequense of a crisis in the Dutch labor market. Moroccan and Turkish guest workers were contracted do manual labor in Dutch factories and in other such sectors. These guest workers were supposed to stay in the Netherlands only temporarily. However, during the 1980s, it became clear that these workers would not return to their native countries, and most of them had their families join them in the Netherlands. As a result, many Dutch Moroccan youth were either born in the Netherlands or came to the Netherlands at a very young age. This is called the *second generation*. Most of the second-generation Dutch Moroccans have Dutch citizenship. The third generation of Dutch Moroccans is in the making, because many second-generation Dutch Moroccans are getting married (to other Moroccans) and starting their own families.

It is estimated that most people of Moroccan descent belong either to the Dutch middle or lower classes. Educational levels of Dutch Moroccans have improved during the past couple of years, in which Moroccan girls of the second generation increasingly attend and complete higher education.[2] Yet, in general, many Dutch Moroccans still find themselves in a social and economic marginal position. As a result of low or no education, and sometimes poors skills in the Dutch language, unemployment among Dutch Moroccan youth is quite high. In addition, poor housing circumstances and the lack of financial backup cause a large portion of the Dutch Moroccan community to be financially and sometimes socially isolated. In addition to this, Dutch Moroccans, and especially Dutch Moroccan young males, continue to be associated with unemployment and crime, and more recently with Islamic radicalism and terrorism.

A majority of the Moroccan guest workers arriving in the Netherlands during the 1960s and '70s originated from the Rif area in northern Morocco, and spoke a Berber language (Douwes et al. 2005: 29). It is roughly estimated that 60% to 80% of the Moroccans in the Netherlands trace their roots back to the mountainous Rif area (Benali and Obdeijn 2005: 211). The rest of them originate from various other regions in Morocco. This has produced a rather heterogeneous Dutch Moroccan population, which consists of Moroccan Berbers and non-Berbers, some speaking a Berber language and Moroccan Arabic (and Dutch), others speaking only a Berber language (and Dutch), and later generations only speaking Dutch.[3]

Concerning Dutch Moroccans' religiosity, the great majority of the Dutch Moroccan community presents themselves as Muslim. Of course, many differences in practicing Islam exist. The Dutch Moroccan community consists of many active practicing Muslims, but also of many "cultural" Muslims (i.e., people who call themselves Muslims, but do not actively practice Islam). In general, Phalet et al. (2004: 39) detected a trend of privatization of Islam among young Dutch Moroccans, meaning that although the participation in religious rituals and mosques is decreasing among second-generation Turks and Moroccans, their identification with Islam remains.

Regarding cultural traditions, Dutch Moroccans attribute great value to the preservation of what they perceive as Moroccan cultural traditions. This is reflected, for example, in the way they organize and celebrate weddings or religious holidays. The desire to conserve "Moroccan" traditions, which requires "Moroccan food, dress, music, and art," triggered the establishment of a Dutch Moroccan retail circuit in many Dutch cities. This circuit includes the foundation of many Dutch Moroccan shops and companies selling fruit, vegetables, and *halal*;[4] Moroccan art or hand crafts; Moroccan traditional dress and fashion; and Moroccan and Arab music shops.

Furthermore, the aspiration that exists among many Dutch Moroccans to celebrate family celebrations and especially weddings the "Moroccan way" set off the establishment of a commercial wedding circuit. This circuit includes shops selling or renting Moroccan wedding dresses and jewelry; shops selling Moroccan pastry and providing food catering, DJs, and music bands specialized in Moroccan music; and the surfacing of so-called *neggafas* or *ziyyanas* (i.e., personal makeup and dress assistants helping the bride) and wedding planners specialized in organizing Moroccan weddings (Essers and Benschop 2007). Moreover, several websites have recently appeared offering information on all kinds of issues relating to the organization of a Moroccan wedding in the Netherlands.

As a result of all kinds of socioeconomic and political circumstances, Dutch society has experienced a great deal of turmoil during the past decade. In particular, events such as 9/11, the murder of Dutch politician Pim Fortuyn in 2002, and that of film director Theo van Gogh in 2004 shook up the nation and instigated debates about the position of Islam and Muslims in the Netherlands. Moreover, within this debate the Dutch Moroccan community is frequently labeled as a problem group. Certainly, because van Gogh was murdered by a 26-year-old second-generation Dutch Moroccan born in Amsterdam, Dutch Moroccans have not been out of the public eye.

During the 1980s and '90s, Dutch Moroccans were predominantly stereotyped as youth delinquents, criminals, drug dealers, and those not willing to integrate into Dutch society and who were oppressive toward women. Dutch Moroccans were labeled an *ethnic minority*, and the most urgent question in political debates was how to "integrate" the newcomers into Dutch society. During the 1980s and '90s, integration was supposed to happen through foreigners learning the Dutch language, taking over Dutch norms and values, and becoming part of society through participation (i.e., work or education). Even now, the issue of integration is still a hot item in political discussions.

However, after 9/11 and especially since Theo van Gogh's murder, political debate does not revolve around integration alone, but focuses on the question of whether Islam and Islamic lifestyles are compatible with Dutch society. The fact that the muderer of van Gogh was a Dutch Moroccan, born and raised in the Netherlands, caused an increased fear of terrorism and Islamic radicalism among the Dutch Moroccan community. Since then, Dutch Moroccans are increasinlgy associated with Islamic fundamentalism, terrorism, and extremism. The Dutch Moroccan community has become "Islamized." Stefano Allievi (2006: 37) detected this trend of Islamizing immigrants in Europe during past years and explains how immigrants in public and political debates are categorized (e.g., as Muslims instead of Moroccans or Turks regardless of whether they are, in fact, practicing Muslims). A great deal of negative issues like terrorism, Islamic radicalism, oppression of women, dictatorial regimes, and so on are associated with this Muslim identity. Because identity is not only composed of self-definition, but also by how one is perceived by others, this process of labeling sometimes results in stereotyping and stigmatization; it has a great impact on the identity construction processes of Dutch Muslims and Dutch Moroccans in particular.

As a result of this Islamization, a sharp demarcation has emerged between Muslims and non-Muslims in the Netherlands, almost eliminating the option to be Muslim *and* Dutch. Religion has thus become the most important identity marker for people of foreign descent. Dutch Moroccans are no longer called *guest workers* or *ethnic minorities*, but are now either mainly distinguished by their religion or by their "otherness," referring to them as "Muslims" or *allochtonen* (the singular form is *allochtoon*).

It is important to note that Dutch Moroccans themselves also contributed to an identification based on religion. Although the first generation often did not emphasize their religious identity, second-generation Moroccans and Turks started to present themselves gradually more as Muslims, rather than as Turks or Moroccans. In fact, the rising visibility of Muslims in the Netherlands is the result of two trends taking place simultaneously. First, large parts of second-generation immigrants prioritize their Muslim identity over their cultural or ethnic background. Second, this inclination to be represented as Muslim is also triggered by government policies and public debates in media imposing a Muslim identity upon them.

Besides the term *Muslim*, the term *allochtoon* is often used by journalists, politicians, policy makers, and the general public in political debates on integration. The word *allochtoon* comes from the Greek root word *allochtonos*, which means "of foreign descent." The official definition of an *allochtoon*, according to the Dutch Central Bureau of Statistics, is someone who has at least one parent who is born abroad.[5] The word *allochtoon* has become the catchphrase for Dutch Moroccans and Dutch Turks, and is increasingly used as a synonym for the label *Muslim*. Usage of the term *allochtoon* is ambiguous, because the reference to "foreign descent" in many cases refers to people who are born and raised *in* the Netherlands. Furthermore, the use of the term as a synonym for *Muslim* is not accurate, because the term *allochtoon*, in principle, could refer to a wide variety of people with roots outside the Netherlands who are not necessarily Muslim. Nevertheless, the term *allochtoon* has become a very popular term in the public debate on integration, and has also acquired negative associations, connecting the term *allochtoon* to people who are not willing to integrate, who do not speak Dutch, and who are Muslim. Again, similar to the label *Moroccan*, the label *Muslim* itself also evokes negative connotations and is often used with a negative undertone. The objectification of Dutch Moroccans as *Muslims* and *allochtonen*, defining them consequently as non-Dutch, continues to highlight the distinction between Muslims and non-Muslims, and between Dutch Moroccans and the autochthonous Dutch.

The imposition of the labels *Muslim* and *allochtoon*, and the prominence of the Dutch Moroccan community in the public debate, could give the naive and indifferent Dutch citizen the impression that "it is all about those Moroccans." The highlighting of religious and ethnic differences created a hardened climate, which has become a hotbed for some factions in society to express freely racist and prejudiced opinions against Muslims, foreigners, Dutch Moroccans, or anybody who is different and perceived as a threat. In this situation, when boundaries between "us and them," on the face of it, seem to be ever more important, studying Dutch Moroccan youth and their musical activities and identities could provide interesting insights into their attitude toward Dutch society and their own position in it. To come to a better understanding of Dutch Moroccan youth, analyzing the social significance of two popular genres among Dutch Moroccan youth—Shaabi and Maroc-hop—is an excellent starting point.

Shaabi: A Return to the Mother Culture

The Arabic word *shaabi* literally means "of the people." *Shaabi* is also the term used for popular Moroccan folk music. Sung in either an Arabic Moroccan dialect or in Berber, and with North African rhythm patterns that allow people to show off their typical Moroccan dancing moves, Shaabi holds especial appeal to the Moroccan community. Within this musical category several subgenres exist, such as *Reggada* from the region of Oujda en Berkane in northeastern Morocco and *Rewaffa*, Berber music from the Rif region.

In the context of the Dutch Moroccan community, Shaabi originally dominated the private setting of family celebrations such as weddings. It has since spread to and gained a central place in the public parties for youth who identify with both the rhythm and lyrics. The traditional lyrics describe family celebrations such as weddings or the harvest. More recently the lyrics have shifted to themes around the experience of emigration and immigration. Many newer Shaabi songs that have proved popular outside Morocco are about separation and loss of a loved one, in many cases the loved one being an immigrant. The song "Bladi kif yansak al bal" (roughly translated: "My Country, How Could I Forget You?") by Yahia is about the difficulties of living far away from your native country and is dedicated to "all the [Moroccan] immigrants." The song glorifies all the beautiful cities and places of Morocco, and the singer remembers the weddings and pleasant times spent there with family and friends.

The continued and growing popularity of Shaabi music in the Netherlands can be attributed to many factors. To begin, the popularity of a musical genre is maintained through a complex interaction between supply and demand. Shaabi would not survive in the Netherlands if it did not have a growing audience and a set of mechanisms by way of markets and events to feed the demand. The presence of several Moroccan music shops in major Dutch cities, which predominantly sell Arabic and Moroccan music means that the product is locally available and publicly present. All four major Dutch cities (i.e., Amsterdam, Rotterdam, Utrecht, and The Hague) have at least one music shop specializing in Moroccan and Arab music. A good deal of this music is produced in Morocco and exported to Europe, yet there is also a growing market for Arabic music that is produced and distributed in Europe, especially in France and Belgium.

Dance events are also key to Shaabi's popularity among mainly second-generation Dutch Moroccans between the ages of 18 and 30 years. Organizers of these events attempt to create a Moroccan and Arab Islamic environment by providing, for example, Moroccan food and the famous mint tea, stands where people can sell Moroccan and Arab music, books on Islam, or jewelry. At most occasions there is no alcohol sold and people who are intoxicated are refused entrance. Dance parties, festivals, and concerts of famous Shaabi artists such as Najat Aatabou, Senhaji, or Daoudi commonly attract crowds of up to 3,000 people.

Different types of Shaabi events take place, among which are women-only parties, or *Hafla Annisa*. Mothers, friends, daughters, children, aunts, and nieces find in these women parties a space where they can enjoy themselves, dance, sing, and interact with other women without any kind of male interference. Although the main attraction of these gatherings is the performance of Shaabi music by both female and male musicians, the ingredients of these parties are somewhat different from the regular Shaabi events. For example, there might be a fashion show demonstrating the newest Moroccan fashion or a workshop on how to apply henna.[6]

Why does this music mobilize such large crowds of young people, sometimes up to 3,000 visitors? If you ask young Moroccans why they go to these parties or listen to Shaabi music, the answer often includes explanations such as,

"I feel Moroccan when I hear this music."

"It evokes a sense of solidarity with other listeners."

"It's a way for me to express my feelings."

"It makes me feel different from the Dutch. It distinguishes me from the rest."[7]

Thus, these events satisfy a desire to be in or return to Morocco, even though it is only for a short time. Shaabi parties, in other words, represent a celebration of Moroccan identity. The actual musical performance does not appear to be the central concern of the audience. The audience is usually more caught up in interacting with each other, and they often dance with their backs to the performers, seemingly not interested in what is happening on stage, but are more concerned with becoming absorbed in the atmosphere and losing oneself in the moment. The performance of the artist thereby becomes part of the background while the performance of the crowd moves to the foreground.

This losing oneself in the atmosphere of dancing enhances the feeling of solidarity. Shaabi musical events therefore enable youth to create a kind of coherent Dutch Moroccan community. The emphasis here is on *cohesive*, because outside the context of concerts and dance events, one can hardly speak of a unified and cohesive community. The Dutch Moroccan community is quite heterogeneous, with the majority representing Berbers from the

Rif, and the others a mix of mainly Arab-speaking peoples from different regions. Historically, the Berber-speaking population has had a strained relationship with the Arab population. When Dutch Moroccan youths come together in these musical contexts, internal differences seem to disappear temporarily.

Besides creating a community, music can also be used to create boundaries between groups of people. Implicit in the theory that music unites people and creates communities is the idea that it also *excludes* people. In this case, Shaabi concerts function as a tool to exclude any "Dutch" influences. Rarely can "native" or "white" Dutch be spotted at these dance events, which are one of the few meeting points within Dutch society where the vast majority of the visitors have a Moroccan background. The role of Shaabi within Moroccan youth culture in the Netherlands, then, is aimed at retrieving a Moroccan identity—that is, of expressing a "Moroccaness" and creating bonds of affiliation with other Dutch Moroccan youth. These events represent a space where young people who might otherwise be on the margins of the host society can freely be Moroccan, and can behave, dance, sing, and interact like "a Moroccan." In this way, Shaabi music also allows young people to incorporate elements of their parents' culture into their own youth cultures. Infused with nostalgia for Morocco, Shaabi plays a significant role in the assertion and preservation of a Moroccan identity among Moroccan Dutch youths, some of whom have never even been to Morocco. By means of music and events, these youths can express an identity that focuses more on being Moroccan in the Netherlands than on being Moroccan in Morocco. In addition, they can glorify part of the culture of their parents without actual interference from their parents, and thereby retain their autonomy and independence.

Shaabi clearly plays a significant role in the identity construction of Moroccan youths in the Netherlands and allows these youths to interact and connect with each other. When playing Shaabi music in the privacy of their home, they can relive the experience they had at a social event they visited in the past, reinforcing the solidarity expressed there. On a symbolic level, this music allows youths to integrate a part of their parent culture into their lives. At the same time, it serves as a direct, nonaggressive, and nonprovocative way to make a distinction between the Moroccan community and overall Dutch society. Many Dutch Moroccan youths perceive these dance events as social spaces created for Moroccans only, even though they are always public events and accessible to anyone. Still, these events and the subculture that has emerged around them, have the tendency to air a certain kind of exclusive Moroccan character. This subculture is, as it were, "something for Moroccan youths only."

Maroc-hop: Rap and Rage

Hip-hop music occupies another important arena of popular music for Dutch Moroccan youths. Hip-hop is an eclectic music known for its bricolage of sounds, beats, and text fragments. It originated in African American neighborhoods in New York when, in the 1970s, youths started the genre by rapping over drum-beats. Fans and historians often credit Kool Herc and Africa Bambaata as the orig-inal hip-hoppers (Rose 1994: 51). Hip-hop often incorporates fragments from other songs, films, television programs, commercials, and street sounds—a tech-nique referred to as *sampling* (Rose 1994: 2–3). Hip-hop can be divided into several subgenres, including the so-called *boast rap*, which thrives on materialism, and *message rap*. Boast rap deals with themes such as fast cars, money, women, and jewelry, thus conveying the message that getting or being rich is the ideal way of life. Message rap, on the other hand, is characterized by social engagement and social criticism. Minority groups worldwide have found in message rap a vehicle to articulate frustration about their oftentimes difficult positions in society.

Music critics and scholars agree that what attracts minority groups to hip-hop music is its expression of dissatisfaction and the way it allows a form of direct social engagement. This explanation alone does not tell us why certain minority groups are more prone to producing and utilizing hip-hop as a form of social engagement than others. In the Netherlands, second-generation Moroccans in particular create hip-hop; second-generation Turks, for example, are not as active in this milieu. In France, Maghrebi youth are also highly active in the hip-hop scene, whereas in the United Kingdom many young people with African or Caribbean roots are involved in hip-hop (Androutsopoulos and Scholz 2003; Heijmans and De Vries 1998; Mitchell 2001; Wermuth 2002). Equally interesting is the way that each of these groups interacts with and creates new forms of hip-hop in their own identity-specific way.

In the Netherlands, Dutch youths with strong identification to their Moroc-can roots have started a subgenre of hip-hop that I call *Maroc-hop*. Maroc-hop appropriates and adapts many elements from American hip-hop culture in specifically local ways. Even though Maroc-hop associates itself musically with the United States, it is a medium to reject and express disapproval of the poli-tics of the United States, especially the foreign policies of the Bush administra-tion. Musically speaking, Maroc-hop uses "ordinary" hip-hop beats, but frequently mixes them with Arab rhythms. In addition, Maroc-hop uses many Arabic melody fillers and sometimes samples of old classical Arab songs. On Raymzter's latest album, *Rayacties* (2005), several songs include samples of old Egyptian songs.

The emphasis on self-definition, whereby the artist chooses a stage name that defines his role and persona, is emblematic of global hip-hop. Stage names are a first step in self-definition and expression of an identity, a vitally important element in hip-hop culture. Tricia Rose (1994: 36) states that "hip-hop's prolific self-naming is a form of reinvention and self-definition. [DJs], rappers, graffiti artists . . . take on hip-hop names and identities that speak to their role, personal characteristics, expertise, or 'claim to fame.'" These nicknames serve as tools for marginalized youths who originate from lower class communities and have limited access to prestige and social status. These names enable hip-hoppers to obtain "street credibility" or "prestige from below" (Rose 1994: 36).

Rappers tend to choose names that relate to their coolness, power, street smarts, supreme qualities, or neighborhood. Naming and self-definition allow these artists to create links with American and global hip-hop cultures while also asserting their own local ethnic identity. Some rappers choose self-mocking names or names that implicitly comment on society. The best-known artist in this group is Ali Bouali who goes by the alias Ali B, which mocks the stereotypes of Moroccan youths as all criminals, as the Dutch press and media use first names and the first initial of family names to refer to criminal suspects to protect their privacy. Other rappers like Soesi-B and Yes-R deliberately use "Moroccan" names, thus opting for a direct alliance with their Moroccan background. Soesi-B refers to a region in southern Morocco, the Souss region, whereas Yes-R is a wordplay on his Arabic name Yasser.

Other rappers use familiar idioms from American popular culture. Three of the main Dutch Moroccan members of Den Haag Connections (DHC), an ethnically mixed rap group with Dutch and Dutch Moroccan members, go by the Latin names of Chilloh MC (Master of Ceremony), Rico, and Omar Montana. These names are inspired by the famous gangster movie *Scarface* (1983), which stars Al Pacino as Tony Montana. *Scarface* is the story of an illegal Cuban immigrant trying to live the American dream.[8] Montana works himself up from the streets to the leader of a criminal organization. It is a typical story of the underdog making it to the (illegal) top until the inevitable time of doom.

A large part of the Maroc-hop scene is an underground scene, meaning that most Maroc-hop rappers do not perform in actual venues; the scene is predominantly active on the Internet. Although the Internet itself is, of course, not an underground medium, to find the specific sites where one can find Maroc-hop music, one must be in the know of the names of the bands and the sites where they are active to find them. Knowledge of this underground circuit is therefore required. Most Maroc-hoppers are amateur musicians and rappers, and they use the Internet to distribute their own home-made productions, except those rappers who have been able to start a professional career and have record deals, such as Ali B, Yes-R, and Raymzter. The underground character of the Maroc-hop scene enables rappers to operate free from censorship, to a certain extent, and write and spit lyrics that are often on the edge of what is legally permissible. The repertoire of Maroc-hop consists of politically engaged themes often filled with youthful rebellion and voiced in very harsh and sometimes foul language.

Among the recurrent themes of Maroc-hop are racism, Dutch politics, the war in Iraq, 9/11, and the Israel–Palestine conflict, revealing a considerable political consciousness among hip-hoppers. Many rap bands have written songs about Bush and Sharon in especially angry terms. In the repertoire of underground bands whose music largely circulates on the Internet, such as *Nieuwe Allochtoonse Generatie* (New Foreign Generation) and DHC, several tracks blame Bush, Sharon, and the Jewish state for the misery of the Arab world. These songs reveal a strong identification with the Arab and Palestinian people, and with Muslims in general. Islam is passionately defended by rappers who lash out at everyone who "attacks" Islam in whatever form. Moreover, there are many songs dealing with local topics such as Dutch politicians Pim Fortuyn and Ayaan Hirsi Ali.[9] Both Fortuyn (murdered May 6, 2002, by an animal rights activist) and Hirsi Ali are known for their critical attitude toward Islam. Other rappers try to invalidate stereotypes about Moroccan youth, such as Ali B's song "Geweigerd.nl" ("Refused.nl"), which criticizes the policy of many Dutch discotheques to refuse entrance of groups of young Moroccans. Sometimes lyrics are more symbolic and metaphorical, such as Ali B's, *Leven van de straat* ("Life on the Streets"). Others have a more humorous way of addressing social issues, as illustrated in Samiro's rap "Couscous." This song hilariously tackles stereotypes harbored by both the Moroccan and Dutch communities of each other. In the following verse (which I translated from the original Dutch), Samiro sings in a broken Dutch accent, typical of a Moroccan migrant:

> He is fed up and only wants couscous
> No French fries with chicken and no applesauce either
>   [typical Dutch food]
> He is fed up and only wants to eat couscous
> They say: low fat, but that is just an excuse
> I do not like French fries or Brussels sprouts [typical
>   Dutch food]
> That is not good for me and I will never eat it again
> My friend invited me over for a fondue Bourguignon
> Afterwards I spent the night on the toilet
> Me, stomach-ache and nauseous, me shout: oh, no!
> I have to buy couscous, thank you very much, yes please[10]

A great deal of Maroc-hop's repertoire could thus be seen as a reaction to the exclusion of Moroccans in public debates about Islam, particularly since September 11, 2001. It represents an "artistic," if sometimes blunt, contribution to the public debates on integration and Muslim politics. Maroc-hop, however, does not limit itself to political topics. Many songs glorify sex, violence, crime, drugs, love, and women. Rather than present themselves primarily as Muslim or Moroccan, these rappers invoke identities based on local areas and boast and brag about their group of friends, their rap crew, and their rap qualities ("flow"). Members of this music culture, in other words, exhibit a strong identification with their Dutch context as well.

These songs contradict the assumption often voiced by Dutch media and politicians that Dutch Moroccan youth only identify with their Moroccan and Islamic background. As mentioned before, Dutch Moroccans are often labeled as *Muslims* or *allochtonen*, leaving little room for expression of other identities. This imposition of identity demonstrates how many Dutch people consider Dutch Moroccan youth to be Muslim and nothing else, as if these young people are only concerned with their Muslim or Moroccan backgrounds, which is often not the case. The term *allochtoon* and its association with people unwilling to integrate into Dutch society or attribute value to Dutch norms and values gives a negative spin to this. The themes of Maroc-hop resist this reduction of the Maroc-hoppers' identities to Moroccan or Muslim and indicate an annexation of a mix of global and local identities. Besides the lyrics, the names of rap bands such as DHC, referring to the band's Dutch hometown (The Hague), and Tuindorp Hustler Click, referring to the band's link to the Amsterdam district Tuindorp, are also signs of these multiple identifications and affiliations.

The roughness of Maroc-hop became nationally known when, in July 2004, Dutch police arrested the DHC rappers after the prime-time news program *NOVA* aired a report on the inflammatory lyrics of DHC's "Hirsi Ali Diss" rap, a song in which DHC allegedly threatened to kill the Somali born then parliamentarian.[11] DHC made the headlines. The "Hirsi Ali Diss" rap and many other songs expose a strong sympathy toward Muslims and Islam. In fact, all these songs originate from a feeling that Islam is "under attack" by people such as Ayaan Hirsi Ali, the late Pim Fortuyn, Ariel Sharon, and George Bush.

To answer the question why these rappers use such inflammatory lyrics, we should put these musical compositions in a wider perspective. Since September 11, 2001, the political debate on the position of Muslims in the Netherlands has taken a more hostile direction. In addition, the media hardly ever offer a platform to Dutch Muslims to contribute to this debate. As a result, the debate on

Islam and Muslims in the Netherlands takes place "over the heads of the Dutch Muslims," with limited input and involvement of the people in question. A great deal of Maroc-hop's repertoire could be seen as a reaction to this exclusion. The songs could be considered as contributions to this discussion of Moroccan youths who feel disenfranchised, to a large degree, by the Dutch. Their songs are their contribution to the national debate. The use of foul language is, on the one hand, an integral part of hip-hop culture and, on the other, an effective way of getting the attention of the media and a wider public.

Maroc-hoppers defend Islam wholeheartedly, although it remains to be seen to what extent they are practicing Muslims themselves. It is especially the political Islam that is defended in a national and international context. Regarding the rappers' own religiosity, their lyrics remain often vague. It seems that their identification with Islam is more political than cultural. The paradox that is created through rapping in one song about how they hate Pim Fortuyn because of his anti-Islamic attitude and in the next song about how they "crack a crib" or "smoke a joint" is not recognized by the Maroc-hoppers themselves. Maroc-hop's approach to Islam differs greatly from how other hip-hoppers incorporate Islam in their lyrics. In America, Islamic hip-hop is much more about experiences of being American and Muslim at the same time (Abdul Khabeer 2007), whereas Maroc-hop is a rebellious genre voicing rappers' frustrations about discrimination against Moroccans and Muslims, about Dutch policy regarding *allochtonen*, and about geopolitics in the Middle East.

Music of a Generation

"I think the next generations [of Moroccans in the Netherlands] will
keep listening to Moroccan music. But even if they don't, that is not so
bad. The point is that the next generation will listen to music
that fits their generation (Dutch Moroccan youth)."[12]

Shaabi and Maroc-hop permit young Moroccans in the Netherlands to express specific identities in local contexts. At Moroccan parties and family festivities, Shaabi music functions as a catalyst for the celebration of a very specific Moroccan identity. Central in these celebrations are feelings of nostalgia and pride in Morocco's cultural past and traditions. These social events are the appropriate and suitable places to enunciate loyalty to these cultural rituals and the identities connected to it. Although Shaabi music is directed more at the past (Morocco's cultural history), hip-hop music relates more to the present. Maroc-hop functions as a cultural reservoir from which young people can select their "favorite" identity. Moroccans are often stigmatized by the majority community as Muslims, thus denying other identities. Youths use hip-hop as a cultural repertoire from which they can express multiple identities, even when they may appear contradictory. Maroc-hop has attracted a growing audience because of its music and its ability to offer its listeners a collection of identities as a hip-hopper, a foreigner, a Muslim, a young Moroccan, or just a young person in the Netherlands. Maroc-hop can simultaneously support, strengthen, and deny all these identities, offering listeners the choice to select whichever identities suit the mood or the times. In its ability to adapt, respond, and innovate to the present, it is the music of the times, the music of a generation.

Acknowledgment

A shorter version of this article appeared under the same title in *ISIM Review* (2005 (16): 6–7).

20

Heavy Metal in the Middle East: New Urban Spaces in a Translocal Underground

Pierre Hecker

Heavy Metal and Muslim Youth

"The pull of Islam seems to be strong enough, even outside the Middle East, to preclude metal from getting a foothold among Moslem youth" (Weinstein 2000: 120). Or so assumed American sociologist Deena Weinstein in her book of almost 20 years ago, *Heavy Metal: A Cultural Sociology*, about the relation between Muslim youth and metal. Today, local metal scenes can be found throughout the Middle East, as in almost any other region of the world. Although still marginal in terms of numbers and public attention, the metal scene in the region, particularly in urban centers in Turkey, Lebanon, and Israel, has developed its own infrastructures consisting of bands, magazines, independent labels, distributors, festivals, and bars.

In all fairness to Weinstein, since the time of her research, enormous changes by way of technical and communication innovations have aided in the spread of heavy metal music and culture all over the globe. Nevertheless, it must be questioned why Islam in particular is supposed to serve as a force that somehow precludes youth from entering heavy metal. According to my research on heavy metal in the Middle East, it is not Islam or religion, but rather factors such as availability, economic capacity, and freedom of expression that influence the ways in which scene-specific cultures travel, and cultural codes are appropriated at the local level. Furthermore,

Weinstein (2000) ignored the fact that as far back as the mid 1960s, Turkey has had an indigenous rock tradition.

The emergence of local metal scenes in the Middle East has taken place within a wider context of globalization. Two aspects are central to the following investigation: the aspect of lifting out social relations from local contexts (Giddens 1990: 21),[1] and the aspect of making cultural resources globally available through the dissemination of modern media and communication systems (Hepp 2004). More specifically, the advent of the Internet and the evolution of technological means to convert sounds and images into digital data files that can be easily sent along a worldwide data highway significantly facilitated the global availability of cultural resources. New communication technologies further created the possibility to establish social relations beyond spatial or temporal boundaries. The communications revolution that gathered speed in the latter portion of the 20th century has far-reaching effects on the formation of knowledge in everyday life. Socialization can no longer be understood as something that happens primarily at the local or national level, for a considerable bulk of codes and meanings appropriated by the social subject are derived from sources that lay far beyond local reach.

In his recent work on media networks and globalization, *Netzwerke der Medien: Medienkulturen und Globalisierung*, Andreas Hepp (2004: 163) argues that locality, despite constant discussions on *disembeddedness, deterritorialization*, and *delocation*, remains a significant sphere in the study of globalization, because the social subject will always be physically embedded in a local context. Localities, then, do not dissolve, but provide a reference point for ongoing globalization processes. The global finds reflection in the local or, more precisely, the global availability of cultural resources is reflected in the form of locally appropriated cultural codes and meanings. Besides placing emphasis on the local embeddedness of globalization and the mutual impact between the global and the local, Hepp (2004: 143, 163) proposes a focus on aspects of *translocality*—that is, the increasing connectivity between different localities all over the world. In that sense, he comes close to Giddens (1990: 64), who defines globalization as "the intensification of worldwide social relations."

The appropriation of cultural codes and meanings is also a matter of constituting new social spaces and drawing boundaries in everyday life. The global "metal space," with boundaries that are made of distinct codes and meanings, is comprised of local scenes that constitute locally embedded, translocally connected social spaces. In other words, the codes that demarcate the metal space from its social surroundings consist of a specific set of symbols, sounds, and styles that include long hair, piercings, tattoos, black clothes, violently aggressive and distorted sounds, and symbols of human decay and evil. The codes and their meanings, however, are contextually dynamic and changeable.

This chapter, based on two case studies from Turkey, explores the impact of newly emerging metal spaces on already existing social spaces. It considers aspects of local embeddedness and of translocal connectivity, an investigation that illustrates how boundaries are negotiated in everyday life. The study is also a testament to the vitality of heavy metal in the context of the Muslim Middle East. The first case study focuses on the emergence of Turkey's very first rock bar; the second case sheds light on the connectivity among metalheads of different ethnic, religious, and national backgrounds.

From the Coffeehouse to the Rock Bar

The invasion of public space by young rockers and metalheads since the second half of the 1980s manifests in the form of rock bars, record labels, music shops, festivals, and groups of long-haired guys hanging around in the streets in certain parts of the city. This development, which signals the appropriation of new cultural concepts, does not come out of the blue. It is embedded in a wider transformation of public space in Turkish society that already began during the 19th century. The impact of this development is important to understand the presence of local metal spaces in Turkey today:

> I was still an easy-going adolescent with no other social outlet except third-class Hong Kong–made Karate films, when, one day, I heard about the existence of beer houses where girls and boys drank together. . . . When did these beer houses evolve into bars? I wasn't even aware . . . I had just heard rumors about a beer house under an Istanbul bridge which was playing music. . . . We were slaves to the music in a fantastic volatile world formed by alcohol. (Ofluoğlu 2005: 19)[2]

With an almost wistful longing, Şanver Ofluoğlu, who has been involved in quite a number of underground fanzines and radio shows during the past 15 to 20 years, portrays a nostalgic picture of the small and shabby place under the old Galata Bridge, which became known as Istanbul's very first rock bar, the *Kemancı Körpü Altı* (The Fiddler under the Bridge). The story of the Kemancı and how it evolved from an ordinary beer house to a rock bar represents a key narrative for the collective memory of Istanbul's local metal scene. The "golden times" of the old Kemancı are even remembered by those who never set foot in the place, either because they were too young or because they were not living in Istanbul at the time. One would be hard pressed to find an Istanbul metalhead who has never heard about the Kemancı (fig. 20.1).

The Kemancı's evolution into a rock bar is symptomatic for the changes in the concept of public space under the influence of European modernity. The European impact on the transformation of public space can be traced back to the era of *Tanzimat* reforms (1839–1876) and the incorporation of the Ottoman economy into the capitalist world market during the 19th century. The free trade agreements with Britain and France of 1838 mark the beginning of European economic penetration of the Ottoman Empire. British and French businessmen were granted an exemption from customs duties, bolstering foreign investment and imports throughout the second half of the 19th century (Raccagni 1980: 10; Zürcher 1993: 66). Along with the free trade agreements,

FIGURE 20.1. Wall painting at the Kemancı rock bar in Istanbul. (Pierre Hecker, 2005)

foreign investors also benefited from the capitulation treaties that had been signed between the Ottoman Empire and a number of western European states. The "capitulations" granted judicial immunity to foreign nationals, exempted them from the Ottoman tax system, and opened the internal market to foreign private investment. All this created a situation favorable to the emergence of a strong western European business community and the influx of previously unknown cultural concepts.

In terms of public space, modernization manifested in new forms of night-life and entertainment activities that became visible by the end of the 19th century. In the Ottoman capital of Istanbul, European–style coffeehouses, so-called *Kafe Şantan* (*Café Chantant*), cabarets, casinos, and beer gardens opened up. These places also introduced new forms of alcoholic beverages, such as cognac, liquor, whisky, champagne, and beer (Zat 2002: 139–148). This development, however, was mainly limited to the district of Pera (Beyoğlu). Here, on the northern shores of the Golden Horn, modernization efforts could be felt most. Not only was it home to numerous European businesses, embassies, and schools, but also to Istanbul's large Armenian and Greek Orthodox communities.[3] The latter maintained close ties to western Europe and were exempted from the Ottoman prohibition on alcohol, which applied to the Empire's Muslim citizens. The area alongside the main road *Cadde-i Kebir*, today's *Istiklal Caddesi*, saw the construction of modern European–style buildings that soon became home to Istanbul's middle and upper classes.

Up until that time, Istanbul's urban landscape in terms of public space and leisure activities was dominated by coffeehouses (*kahvehane*) and, to a lesser extent, wine houses (*meyhane*). Although today considered integral to Turkish tradition, the coffeehouse had once been an innovation that brought significant change to urban life. Coffee consumption in Anatolia dates back to the mid 16th century, with the first Istanbul coffeehouse opening in 1554 (Arendonk 1990: 451). Until then, leisure activities were largely confined to the private space; exceptions included the public bath and religious institutions such as mosques, churches, and Sufi orders. Nightlife was limited to taverns that were infamous for reckless alcohol consumption and gambling (Hattox 1985: 125). The coffeehouse soon attracted men from all levels of society who made it a common activity to go out, chat, and socialize within the new public atmosphere. The emergence of coffeehouses considerably changed men's social lives, everyday habits, and social relations. From early on, coffeehouses were also perceived as places of oppositional activity and immoral behavior, particularly for some clerics who considered coffee as a substance prohibited by Islamic law. This touch of subversiveness resulted in temporary bans and persecutions by the Ottoman authorities (Arendonk 1990: 451–452; Hattox 1985).

As a result of the Ottoman prohibition on alcohol, alcohol business lay completely in the hands of non-Muslims. Only non-Muslims were allowed to consume alcohol and to run a *meyhane*, the only place for alcohol consumption until the beginning of the *Tanzimat* era (Zat 2002: 13). The *meyhane*, which literally means "wine house," deduced from the Persian word for wine (*mey*), was a remnant from Byzantine times. In English literature it is often referred to as *tavern* (e.g., Hattox 1985). According to Vefa Zat's research, published in *Eski Istanbul Meyhaneleri* (*Early Istanbul Wine Houses*), taverns already existed under the sultanate of Mehmet II (1451–1481) and were only temporarily closed down under the reign of some of his successors (Zat 2002: 144, 190–191). Traditional Ottoman taverns were mainly small and shabby places. In addition to wine, they also served *rakı*, an anise-flavored alcoholic beverage similar to Greek *ouzo* or Arabic *araq*. With the beginning of the *Tanzimat* reforms, modern European–style drinking places gradually replaced the traditional *meyhane* (Zat 2002: 13).[4] This was also the time when the first beer houses (*birahane*) appeared on the scene.

Beer started to become popular during the second third of the 19th century. Istanbul's first beer houses (*birahane*) opened during the early 1840s with the beer still being imported from non-Ottoman Europe. This started to change when the first beer company, the Bomonti Beer Company, opened in the neighborhood of Feriköy in 1890. Founded by two brothers from Switzerland, Bomonti remained Istanbul's only brewery until 1909. That year, a second company, the Nektar Beer Company, opened in Büyükdere. In 1912, both companies amalgamated, forming the *Bomonti Nektar Şirketi* (Bomonti Nektar Corporation). Although beer did not become a product of mass consumption, Istanbul had several dozen beer houses and beer gardens by the end of the 19th century. The levels of beer production and consumption have been steadily rising in Turkey during the past century.

The Kemalist Revolution of the 1920s and '30s marks a new stage in the transformation of public space under the influence of European modernity. Far-reaching reforms that aimed at breaking with the Ottoman past by modernizing Turkish society from above also included the abolition of the prohibition on alcohol in 1926. Turkey's founding father, Mustafa Kemal, was a heavy drinker himself and died of liver cirrhosis in 1938. The new legal basis gave Muslims the right to produce, consume, and sell alcohol for the very first time. This had been an important step in gradually replacing Christian tavern and beer house keepers through Muslim ones. The transformation was accelerated by the fact that Istanbul's Christian communities had been continuously fading as a result of a number of pogroms and political crises throughout the 20th century.

With the beginning of the Kemalist era new public spaces such as theaters, opera houses, cinemas, restaurants, and pastry shops emerged as the favorite symbols of modern Turkey. As a result of the new modernist ideology gradually affecting people's minds and thinking, the traditional concepts of *meyhane*, *kahvehane*, and *birahane* started becoming contested. From an urban middle class perspective, the coffeehouse was increasingly linked to the lower, uneducated classes of society and therefore associated with attributes of traditionalism, provincialism, ignorance, and vulgarity (Kömeçoğlu 2004: 157–158). Particularly since the second half of the 1980s, Istanbul's old coffee and beer houses began being replaced by modern-type restaurants, bars, and cafés.

Istanbul's first rock bar, the Kemancı, can be seen as an indicator as well as an impulse for the transformation of public space in urban life. The 1990s saw modern, European–style bars, clubs, and cafés pop up all around Istanbul's modern city center, first and foremost in the districts of Taksim and Beyoğlu. In this area, modern bars and cafés have gradually been replacing the traditional coffeehouses and beer houses, which have almost vanished from that part of the city. Most of the new places deliberately adopted the label *bar* or *café* to separate themselves from the traditional, male-dominated *birahane* or *kahvehane*.[5] The intention of drawing this linguistic line is to separate clearly the modern urban space from the traditional urban space.

The new bars and cafés stand apart from their more traditional counterparts in how they dissolve the spatial line between the male and the female, for in them young men and women can meet, sit, and drink together in public. The traditional meaning of public space in Turkish society is based upon the moral principle of separating the masculine from the feminine. According to that, the public space of the coffeehouse as well as of the beer house is an exclusively male space; women are confined to the private. From that perspective, the opening of "beer houses where girls and boys drank together" (Ofluoğlu 2005: 19) must be seen as morally subversive.

Rockers Emerge under the Bridge

In the streets of Istanbul, young metalheads became visible for the first time in the mid 1980s. Their presence caused many controversies among the Turkish public. Because of their deviant appearance and behavior, they were mostly perceived as an epitome of moral subversiveness. Young men with long hair, weird beards, black clothes, and the habit of drinking lots of beer came as a challenge to traditional notions of morality. Countless media reports depicted metal as a threat to Turkey's national and religious identity. Although most of these reports, including accounts on Satanism, suicide pacts, and perverted sexual practices, were highly imaginative, metalheads were indeed violating particularly Islamic traditions. Having extramarital relationships, considering the drinking of alcohol as an integral part of their lifestyle, and deliberately seeking distance from religious practices in everyday life (e.g., daily prayers, attending religious ceremonies, wearing the headscarf, fasting during Ramadan, and so forth) are clear statements that Muslimness is not a relevant category for most of them. Turkish metalheads regard themselves mostly in a secular tradition that needs to be defended in the wake of Islamic revivalism. In that sense, global metal's antireligious and antitraditionalist attitudes fit well into Turkey's Kemalist worldview.

In the early days—in other words, during the 1980s and early '90s—young rockers and metalheads were nevertheless confronted with hostile, often violent reactions from the Turkish public. As a result of this situation, rock bars played an important role in defining their identities. The narrative of the Kemancı under the bridge is the story of how Istanbul's rockers and metalheads created a place of their own in the very heart of the city, a place where they felt free and safe from a hostile environment.

The old Galata Bridge, which spanned the Golden Horn since its inauguration in 1912 until its devastation in a fire in May 1992, connected the busy districts of Beyoğlu and Eminönü.[6] Its structure consisted of two separate levels, an upper floor carrying a wide road with tramway tracks in the middle and pedestrian sidewalks on each side, and a lower floor hosting a variety of small fish restaurants, coffeehouses, and beer houses. The area under the bridge was simultaneously famous and infamous, in particular for its evening and nighttime activities. The option of eating fresh fish from the Bosporus, playing backgammon or cards, and ending up drunk in one of the places selling cheap *rakı* and beer attracted many men from the surrounding quarters.

When the Kemancı opened under the old Galata Bridge in 1986, it would not have attracted "ordinary" citizens. Seyda Babaoğlu, a female metalhead who entered the Kemancı for the first time around 1990, describes the scene:

> There was no other rock bar then except the Kemancı, which was under the bridge. Actually, it was a small and totally run-down place, where you used to sit on barrels; and there were some kind of trays on them [instead of tables]. Everything constantly fell down; the guys fell into the sea because they were drunk and quarreling. . . .
> Concerning the stereo, there was only a very bad tape player with very bad loudspeakers. We used to listen to heavy metal there and all the

metalheads who listened to that music, this was only a handful of people, they all used to come to the old Kemancı under the bridge. . . . It had a super atmosphere, although it was totally run-down. It was a dive, but the atmosphere was super . . . . It was like a family.[7]

The Kemancı was run by two young men in their mid 20s who had bought the place by chance. Zeki Ateş and Ilyas Gürel were already regular guests of the beer houses under the bridge when they heard about one of them, the Yudum (Gulp), being for sale. The Yudum was one of the notorious localities where men frequented with the aim of finding cheap beer and getting drunk quickly. Although Ateş and Gürel wanted to start something different, they did not initially intend to open a rock bar when renaming Yudum to Kemancı. They opened a beer house that, under the influence of its customers, transformed into a bar. The Kemancı attracted a combination of local fishermen, artists, and intellectuals; some of the latter listening to rock and metal music. Its cosmopolitan atmosphere as well as its location within close proximity to Istanbul's modern city center was critical to the flourishing of rock and metal culture.

In retrospect, the area under the bridge makes an ideal location for a rock bar. Situated in the middle of the city's two most busy areas with thousands of people crossing it every day, a constant flow of customers was widely guaranteed. Sheltered under the old bridge and surrounded by the sea, the Kemancı lay at the center of public life, yet at the same time was hidden from curious eyes. One could easily sit down and have a beer without running the risk of being spotted by family members or feeling bothered by the open disapproval of passing pedestrians. During the daytime, a considerable percentage of the Kemancı's customers were (male and female) high school students heading from Beyoğlu, the location of some of the city's most prestigious high schools, to Eminönü, the city's main transportation center. Crossing the bridge on their way home to catch the bus, boat, dolmuş (minibus), or taxi, many students took the chance and stopped by the Kemancı for a beer.

The Kemancı's transformation started slowly with the rockers and metalheads bringing their own cassettes to the beer house. It was the first place in Turkey to play rock and heavy metal music publicly, an act that was seriously frowned upon by neighboring beer houses. Unlike the Kemancı, the other establishments under the bridge played Turkish popular music and its proprietors were not familiar with the intense sounds of heavy metal. Even more suspicious than the deviant music, was the deviant behavior of the Kemancı's clientele. The young rockers and metalheads, long-haired guys dressed in jeans and leather jackets shaking their heads to a violent noise of music, did not fit into any common category to which others could attach meaning. Moreover, the Kemancı, unlike other places in the area, provided a space where males and females were spotted sitting together, chatting, and drinking beer. With a combination of sound, style, and symbols, the young metalheads invaded the public, creating a new social space in the middle of Istanbul. The initially hostile reaction of local coffeehouse owners illustrates the audible and visible tangibility of space and boundaries. The tense situation, however, eased after a period of mutual acquaintance and noninterference.

An important impulse in the Kemancı's transformation process came from local metal bands. Thrash metal bands such as Pentagram and Kronik used to draw crowds of people to the Kemancı in aftershow parties. Özer Sarısakal from Kronik puts it the following way:

> After a concert at the [Harbiye] Open Air [Theater] the guys in the audience said, "We get out of here now, out of the concert and go to Kemancı." There was a place called Kemancı under the bridge; back then, there was a bridge. . . . It was nice there; a place that belonged to us. . . . After that, the Kemancı became very popular. We went there after the concert and it was pretty crowded. Later on, other places opened up. Then, the bridge burned down and they went to this area, to Taksim and to Beyoğlu. Here is Gitar and Caravan. A number of places opened up. They opened and closed, opened and closed.[8]

The Kemancı under the bridge represented a kind of safe haven for the metalheads who were exposed to considerable pressures and animosities in everyday life. With the Kemancı they had a public space of their own where they could meet, listen to music, and drink beer without being bothered from the outside. Until it opened in 1986, metalheads did not have a place to go and collectively share the music and its culture. As Zeki Ateş, the owner of the Kemancı, puts it: "People were in need of something like that. I mean these people were listening to music, but at home or at concerts. That time, there was no such place—a place where you could listen [to metal music]."[9]

The mere existence of the Kemancı strengthened the social cohesion of the metal scene and brought about a sense of community. When the old Galata Bridge burned down in 1992, the Kemancı relocated in Taksim on Sıraselviler Street at the northern end of Beyoğlu's main shopping road (*Istiklal Caddesi*). Emphasizing its link to the past, it officially adopted the name *Kemancı Köprü Altı* (Kemancı under the Bridge). Only a short time after relocating to Taksim, Zeki Ateş and Ilyas Gürel split their business. While Ilyas continued to operate the Kemancı Köprü Altı, a small, shabby, and smoky place, Zeki opened the new Kemancı, a bigger, three-story rock club in one of the neighboring buildings that provided different kinds of music and a concert stage on each floor. Because the new Kemancı directly opened as a rock club, it appropriated distinct codes from the very beginning. The hallway and staircase were completely covered with adaptations of the paintings of Swiss artist H. R. Giger, whose morbid images have been popular motifs in metal. Other paintings depict a barely dressed woman on a motorcycle or an adaptation of the Last Supper with Jesus and the disciples sitting a around table filled with a guitar and empty beer cans.

During the early years, the Kemancı had to cope with a notoriously negative public image. Rumors of drug abuse and prostitution gave it the stigma of being a den of immorality. Although this did not have much to do with reality, the bar became widely famous and infamous. According to Zeki Ateş, there had been almost constant trouble with the local authorities on issues of morality. Throughout the years, however, the authorities have fundamentally shifted their attitude towards the Kemancı. Local officials even started bringing international visitors to the place to show them Turkey's modern, European face. In that sense, the Kemancı turned from a morally unacceptable no-go area into an appreciated symbol of modern Turkey.

The Translocal Underground

Talking about translocal connectivity in terms of cultural globalization processes and its impact on already existing social spaces in the Middle Eastern cities may sound quite abstract, but it becomes tangible when contextualized at the local level. Before the advent of the Internet, the global metal scene had been relying on postal mail for sending and exchanging demo tapes, flyers, fanzines, or other information on local bands and scenes around the globe. Turkish metalheads started participating in that process during the early 1990s. Güray, publisher of several underground fanzines in Istanbul (e.g., *Yer Altı I Feel Like Nick Cave*) and one of the first to get intensively involved into the metal scene's worldwide tape-trading[10] network, describes his initial socialization with the global scene:

> Well, I think it was back in '91 or '92. There was *Laneth Magazine*,[11]
> you know, and I think I saw some demo reviews of Turkish bands. . . .
> I wrote them a letter, sent money, and got the demos. I received a
> couple of flyers of foreign bands, then, and I just wondered, if the . . .
> foreigners would write [back] as well. I just wondered, you know. I
> wondered about more underground acts. So, I just wrote my first
> letter . . . . I asked them for demos, prices, and [information], and

when I got some response I was shocked, because I didn't expect it!
You know, for the first time, I got in touch with foreign bands. And I
started to buy their demos; and later . . . you know when you got a
demo back 10 years ago, you received tons of flyers and lots of
addresses; and I started to write to everyone.[12]

Güray describes a common activity, at least, for those metalheads who had a
sufficient knowledge of English. Throughout the years, he established contacts
with metalheads around the world, getting access to musical and informational
material of bands that never made it to sign an official record deal. He
explains:

Well, first of all, it was good to have some stuff from really weird
places. You know in the beginning, you just know that there is metal
in Europe and America, but later I received flyers from Panama, from
South America, South Africa—Groinchurn,[13] I've been in touch with
them. And then, Japan, Indonesia, Malaysia, Russia. So, it was really
good. I just wanted to have at least one contact per country. So, I tried
to write to everyone, to Israel, South Africa, Brazil, Chile, Paraguay,
Argentina, everywhere.[14]

Within that context, he also tells about the initial contact with a then-
unknown Israeli metal band called Orphaned Land: "I think I got a flyer of their
demo. So, I wrote them and got their demo before they signed to Holy Records.
So, I only knew it by the underground way of flyer. And I was surprised when
they sent me a CD from Holy Records. It was strange."[15]

Orphaned Land, which had been an underground band until recently,
developed close ties to the Turkish scene and, despite widespread political
resentment in Turkish society toward Israel, they became one of the most
popular and respected bands among Turkish metalheads. Asked about the
band's relation toward Turkey, Orphaned Land's vocalist Kobi Farhi responded:
"We have many friends in Turkey. It is like our home . . . . We are bonded in love
with Turkey,"[16]—a love that the band expressed by playing cover versions of
Turkish music stars Ibrahim Tatlıses and Erkin Koray, and by printing T-shirts
depicting a patchwork of the band's logo and the Turkish national symbols: the
star and the crescent. In fact, Orphaned Land's general concept goes beyond
establishing social relations with fellow metalheads abroad. With their music
they propagate a reconciliation of the three monotheist religions. The band
released albums that were consequently appropriating symbols of all three religions. Later, Orphaned Land put emphasis on local embeddedness. Defining
their music as Oriental Doom Death or simply Middle Eastern Metal, they are

merging metal sounds with traditional tunes and instruments (e.g., *oud, saz, buzuki*). Actually, the music and concept of the band is appealing to metalheads throughout the Middle East.

When the band, in the aftermath of the second *Intifada*, initiated an online platform entitled *Protest the War*, fans from around the world left notes joining the protest. The following entries, among many others, were marked as coming from different Middle Eastern countries:[17]

> I know it is strange for an egyptian to write to u guys but i really like ur music and i really love u . . . this is the truth u may not believe me. . . . i hope u to write to me as a friend and the biggest fan of urs in the middle east . . . by the way there r many fans for u here in egypt (. . .) [sic] (Cairo, August 2002)

> Hey ORPHANED LAND im 13 male from lebanon i'm a big fan of u i don't care about the religions and about the atmosphere between lebanon and israel i wanted peace. [sic] (Beirut, June 2002)

> Hi there I am from syria, and I like O-L so much, and this band is loved in our country SYRIA, . . . I hate not jews or christians or any other religion, and we are all working together for peace. [sic] (Homs, November 2003)

> Hail my orphaned brothers i hope peace will spread among all of us and live in peace with our jews brothers, i would like to pay tribute to my orphaned brothers kobi and yossi wishing them all the best and progress. TAKE CARE MY ORPHANED BROTHERS. [sic] (Dubai, June 2002)

> Dear brothers kobi, yossi and all orphaned family . . . . I'm muslim, you know but i call you as friends . . . . It's not important to be a men from different language, RELIGION, RACE . . . for me . . . I LOVE U ORPHANED LAND, GOD SAVE YOU . . ." [sic] (Istanbul, April 2002)

Turkey plays a key role in the dialogue between Israeli and Arab metalheads. It is the only country of the region that, during the past couple of years, has been regularly organizing metal festivals in summer and has been easily accessible for metalheads from the Arab world as well as from Israel. Meeting on "neutral ground" with some Arab fans after a show at Istanbul's Rock the Nations Festival in 2004, Kobi Farhi (Orphaned Land) stated with enthusiasm:

> We are in contact with Arabic fans for years . . . and it was a fantastic
> sight to see people from Israel, Syria, Jordan, Lebanon, Saudi Arabia,
> Dubai, Turkey, Greece, and more singing together the lyrics of the
> same band together without any problem. . . . A lot of fans from
> those countries came to me after the show to say hello. I'm so happy
> about it.[18]

After talking to Orphaned Land at the festival, Rawad Abdel Massih from the
Syrian–Lebanese band The Hourglass gave a statement that is quite similar to
that of Kobi Farhi:

> I met them here. I can tell you so honestly, I'm not faking anything,
> these guys, they are the nicest band I met over here. Really, these
> guys are so nice! . . . In music there is no politics! . . . We are not
> Bush or anyone else. I don't fucking care . . . my problem is music,
> and as I wrote a song about Palestine, I can write a song about the
> Holocaust. . . . I don't believe in nationalism at all. I believe in
> universality, in globalization. I believe in the unity of human beings,
> not Arabic nationalism or so.[19]

All these words of warmth and friendship exchanged between people who are
supposed to hate each other as a result of a long history of political and religious
conflict in the region illustrate a new dimension of social relations within the realms
of global metal. In that sense, the lines separating different religious, national, and
ethnic spaces from each other are being transgressed and contested.

Conclusion

The purpose of this chapter was to prove that metal is a global culture. Its dissemination does not follow any essentialist categorization along religious, ethnic, or
nationalist lines. Global metal appeals to the young in a Muslim context in the
same way that it appeals to the young in any other religious or national context.
Talking about global metal also means that young metalheads establish social relations across religious, ethnic, and national divides, fostering the emergence of
transnational communities. I do not claim that global metal is free of political controversies, but it provides a separate space for common identification and mutual
understanding. The example of early tape-trading networks also gives insight into
the translocal connectivity among metalheads; it proves that cultural globalization
is not solely bound to the realm of economic interests represented by the cultural
industry. There is a world beyond MTV and the multinational record companies.

As already stated at the beginning of this chapter, the global availability of cultural resources provides new identity options at a local level. The emergence of local metal scenes in the Middle East is an example of how the younger generation opts for identities that formerly lay beyond the local reach. The global gets tangible in the form of new urban spaces formed by rock bars, music shops, festivals, and, above all, young metalheads who are negotiating their identities in everyday life. The history of Istanbul's first rock bar gives testimony to how the appropriation of cultural resources brings about change to the traditional concept of public space in Turkish society. The Kemancı's transition from a formerly stigmatized, shunned place to a symbol of modern Turkey indicates a shift of meaning with regard to public space. From that perspective, we witness the transgression and shift of formerly relevant moral boundaries, particularly in terms of gender relations. This brings me to the final point of this chapter: Metal provides the young with a means for individual emancipation from traditional lines. This includes seeking distance from religious conservatism and traditional concepts of morality. Muslimness is not a relevant category in their everyday lives.

21

Music VCDs and the New Generation: Negotiating Youth, Femininity, and Islam in Indonesia

Suzanne Naafs

Young Women and Popular Culture

Traveling by bus from central Padang in West Sumatra to Andalas University on the outskirts of the city is hardly a relaxing journey. One is surrounded by bright colors, loud noises, chatting students, and, most of all, a screen showing music videos on video compact disk (VCD), with the sound system full blast. During the first six weeks of my stay in Padang, this was a rather overwhelming experience. Later I found that this screening of music videos in public buses was reserved to those buses to Andalas filled with high school and university students. Commuting to the university turned out to be an excellent introduction to the VCDs I was going to research. So what were we looking at and why were these music videos shown in these particular buses?

This chapter deals with the images of young female artists prevalent in music VCDs of national and regional music genres in Indonesia and what they reflect about youth lifestyles, desires, and generational shifts. Just like many of their peers in other parts of the world, young middle class Indonesians connect with fashion, music, and entertainment to create subcultures and achieve a sense of self. In particular, an analysis of VCDs can tell us about realities of being young, female, and Muslim in Indonesian society today. The music videos of these young female artists reflect a variety of cross-cultural influences that are imported, adapted, recreated, and blended.

These influences do not always correspond with prevailing norms about proper behavior and clothing styles for young Muslim women in Indonesia. It is often through style of dress and the body that they set themselves aside from the adult world and may challenge "dominant forms of moral regulation and sexual containment" (Giroux 1998: 28–29). VCDs, therefore, provide insights regarding how the politics of the body and sexuality are gendered, changing, and contested in contemporary Indonesia. Among the questions posed are: which lifestyles for young women do the clips in music VCDs refer? How are these images, drawing on both westernized and local influences, adapted to a Muslim society? How are the contradictory images in these VCDs interpreted by both youth and adults?

The introduction of VCDs in the mid 1990s quickly added a new dimension to popular culture in Indonesia and many other Southeast Asian countries.[1] The music VCD, a disc that combines audio and visual capabilities, is closely tied to two other phenomena found in this part of the world: the region's pirating industry and the popularity of *karaoke*.[2] Most VCDs in Indonesia are pirated, which means not only that they are made without the consent of the artist or its producer, but that their distribution and market are not regulated. Almost all music VCDs are produced as *karaoke* videos in which the lyrics of the song are printed on the screen for sing-along *karaoke* style.[3]

New technologies such as VCD, the Internet, and mobile phones form a means for young Indonesians to express their desire for modernity (Barendregt and Van Zanten 2002: 91). For youth who have access to these new kinds of media, these technologies provide new opportunities to connect themselves to a wider world in ways that their parents often do not understand. VCDs do not carry an entirely positive connotation. Since their appearance, Indonesian authorities have battled against the circulation of pornographic films and images that often circulate via pirated VCDs.[4]

Despite attempts at censorship and regulation, VCDs have rapidly become part of the daily lives of people from many different backgrounds. In the city of Padang on the island of Sumatra, VCDs had pervaded many parts of public space. Padang is a moderate-size provincial city with a population of about 800,000 people and is the capital of West Sumatra, the homeland of the Muslim Minangkabau people. The city has its own harbor and airport, a large cement factory, as well as several universities, shopping malls, cinemas, and a museum of Minangkabau culture. In Padang, VCDs are sold at the market, in cassette stores, and shopping malls; rented through video rentals; and played in *karaoke* clubs, public buses, and at home. Consumers of VCDs from a stall at the central market ranged from *becak* drivers (bike cab drivers) to bank personnel. Although some mall stores and VCD stalls (fig. 21.1) at the market specifically target

FIGURE 21.1. VCD stand in Jakarta. (Asef Bayat, 2008)

students and teenagers, others appealed to a much broader market with their selection of western pop and rock, *pop Indonesia, pop Minang* (Minangkabau pop music produced in West Sumatra), and *dangdut* (Indonesia's most popular music genre), as well as VCDs with cartoons and nature documentaries, which cater to the taste of families with young children.

The three music genres highlighted are *pop Indonesia, dangdut*, and *pop Minang*, the more popular music genres in Padang, in addition to western pop and rock. Clips in these VCDs are often directly aimed at teenagers and young adults; the artists portrayed promote not only their music, but a lifestyle as well (Andsager 2006). Even though the appropriation of trends and influences from abroad is nothing new in Indonesian pop music,[5] these VCDs are breaking new ground by combining images of global youth culture in a distinctive Indonesian context, thus adding a visual dimension to the music that previously was not there.

This research is based on fieldwork conducted in 2003. It includes 35 in-depth interviews with middle class teenagers, students, and adults, most of whom had a higher education, and interviews and ethnographic observations among VCD sellers and consumers at the market, cassette, and mall stores. I went to *karaoke* clubs and video rentals, and regularly rode in city buses that almost continuously screened music VCDs. Whenever possible, I tried to watch

VCDs with people in their homes, but because many people did not own their own VCD player, I was not able to talk about the content of music VCDs directly with them as often as I had wanted. I worked around this by asking VCD vendors at the central market in Padang (*Pasar Raya*) to put on VCDs of female artists so that I could ask customers their views about the images of young women in the clips.

Media, Gender, and the State: A Changing Terrain

Images of young women in popular media are not created in a vacuum, but are closely linked to broader developments in the national arena, such as political and economic change, the reduction of censorship by the government, the introduction of new technologies, the current Islamic revival, and the often contradictory gender ideologies that confront young women.

During the 32 years of president Suharto's authoritarian New Order regime (1966–1998), media in Indonesia were regulated from Jakarta through a body of state censorship laws. During the post-Suharto era, the strict regulation of the media has been largely abandoned, as a result of the removal of a number of restrictive censorship and licensing laws (Hill and Sen 2005: 6). The diminishing of centralized rule from Jakarta combined with the emergence of new technologies such as the Internet and VCDs in the 1990s, have provided openings for many ethnic groups to express their identities, as long as they do not strive for independence from Indonesia. In West Sumatra, this has led to discussions about what it means to "be Minang" and what Minangkabau culture should look like. For instance, discussions have focused on drug use, pornography, crime, and the question of whether Islamic law should be installed in West Sumatra. Apart from these discussions, Minangkabau identity is increasingly expressed through popular culture, including specific Minangkabau websites and Minangkabau pop music (*pop Minang*). This locally produced pop music has become a booming industry and is distributed to Minangkabau living in West Sumatra as well as those living in other parts of the world (Barendregt 2002: 416; Suryadi 2003: 63).

The increased freedom of expression during the post-Suharto period creates new opportunities and tensions in the realm of gender representations. Suharto's New Order held up a gender ideology in which women were taught to support their husbands, raise children, and safeguard society.[6] Popular women's magazines of this period that targeted a middle and upper class public offered Indonesian women a range of lifestyle possibilities, such as "the happy consumer housewife, the devoted follower of Islam, the successful career woman, the model citizen of the nation-state and the alluring sex symbol" (Brenner 1999: 17). These lifestyle choices were not just considered a personal matter, but a public one as well. Discussions in the media about what it means to be a young, modern Indonesian woman often reflect anxieties about the future of society (Allen 2007: 101; Warburton 2007) as the attitudes and behavior of (young) women are considered to be symptomatic of "the moral climate of the nation" (Brenner 1999: 32).

Although these images remain during the post-Suharto period, alternative representations have emerged. Indonesian women in their teens and (late) 20s are presented with a range of conflicting images of femininity. Popular teen magazines[7] and films offer increasingly less dependent female role models for teenage girls, by showing young women who have boyfriends and who have more autonomy in decision making. Apart from the earlier mentioned ideal of becoming a good wife and mother, with connotations of chastity and submissiveness, films and magazines feature the popular image of girl power, projecting an image of independent and sexually liberated young women (Sastramidjaja 2001). In literature there is the recent trend of *sastra wangi* literature (fragrant literature) in which young female authors write about the sexual emancipation of women (Garcia 2004). At the same time there is a growing Muslim youth culture, which combines global trends in popular culture with Islamic faith. Ranging from music sung by Islamic boy bands (Barendregt 2006), to *halal* makeup and Muslim girl magazines, this hybrid youth culture offers images of young women who veil and adhere to their religion, but also engage in flirting and having fun (Nilan 2006: 94–104).

Changing Youth Lifestyles and Islam

The array of lifestyle choices in the media reflects changes in youth lifestyles and morality. During the past 15 years, as young men and women spent longer amounts of time on education and training, the period between puberty and marriage has been prolonged in many (urban) parts of Indonesia. Dating and having a boy- or girlfriend have become more common, but this puts many young men and women at odds with the widespread notion that sexuality should be limited to marriage. Smith-Hefner (2005) has illustrated how young educated women in the city of Yogyakarta on Java see themselves confronted with contesting views about "western-type" and "Islamic-type" sexuality. On the one hand, "modern social change offers young women new opportunities and an important degree of autonomy, while at the same time they are expected to control themselves, limit their desires and remain chaste" (Smith-Hefner

2005: 453–454). In Padang, where the majority of inhabitants is Muslim, this normative view of "Islamic-type" sexuality prevails. This does not necessarily mean that young people in Padang never date or refrain from sex before marriage. However, their ability to adopt freely from global youth culture, which emphasizes "the body of the young person as a kind of marketable sexual commodity"(Giroux 2000, quoted in Nilan 2006: 93), is contained in a context where too much sexual content is perceived as a break with local values.

Moreover, the setting of Padang also creates its own opportunities and limitations. Padang is a city that most inhabitants imagined to be more "modern" than other parts of West Sumatra, but less "advanced" (*maju*) than metropolitan cities such as Jakarta. Padang's middle and upper class citizens had access to electricity and communication technologies such as the Internet and VCDs that had not yet arrived in parts of the countryside, which had remained "old fashioned" and "backward." At the same time, they romanticized the countryside as a place where a strong sense of community still prevailed, whereas Minangkabau in Padang had become too individualistic. They warned against the rampant individualism and hedonism in Jakarta, something from which they felt Minang culture should be protected. Given this context, young women in Padang cannot freely imitate the wide range of images available in music VCDs, but they do selectively choose some aspects of popular youth culture to incorporate in their own lives.

Angels and Femmes Fatales: Images of Female Artists in Music VCDs

The clips under discussion belong to several music genres, but can be roughly divided into two main categories: that of national pop music and that of regional pop music, in this case pop music produced in West Sumatra, *pop Minang*. The two most well-known genres that appeal to a nationwide audience in Indonesia are *pop Indonesia* and *dangdut*.

Pop Indonesia refers to Indonesian pop music that is (strongly) influenced by Anglo-American pop music and global trends in current rock and pop music. *Pop Indonesia*, which features male and female bands and singers, is sung in the Indonesian language and is produced in Indonesia. The music is primarily meant for the national market, even though many *pop Indonesia* artists dream to "go international" (Wallach 2002: 16–17).

Agnes Monica, a 17-year-old soap opera actress, was gaining fame as a *pop Indonesia* singer in 2003.[8] Musically, her style resembles that of young western female artists such as Christina Aguilera and Britney Spears. She is especially popular with teenagers and students, although opinions about her differ. Most of the songs on the album deal with themes such as falling in love, having a boyfriend, or suffering from a broken heart. Recurrent themes in these clips are urban backdrops,[9] trendy haircuts, stylish teenagers, cell phones, fast cars, attractive people drinking cocktails in a bar and enjoying themselves, and boys and girls walking hand in hand.

Agnes Monica herself has adopted various styles of dress. Overall, her image appeals to a cosmopolitan, self-reliant, and hip lifestyle in the big city. On the cover photo of her album, both her hair and clothes seem to be styled in a punk and urban street style. But, she can also adapt a more hip-hop style when she wears, for example, purple hair extensions and is dressed in cargo pants and a short tank top that reveals part of her belly. This effect is enhanced by the male dancers surrounding her, who resemble rappers. In fact, her chameleonlike ability to change her image is one of the qualities that appeals to many fans. Dewi, 22, a female student and a genuine fan of Agnes Monica commented:

> Agnes Monica is only 17, but she's already rich. Despite her young
> age, she knows how to perform. She is a presenter, acts in a soap on
> TV and in several commercials. She is not afraid to choose her own
> style and she is a trendsetter with her hairstyle. I like to read about
> her profile in magazines. She is already well known in Indonesia and
> wants to go international.

But when I asked Dewi if she would wear clothes in the trendy style of Agnes Monica in Padang, she had reservations: "Agnes Monica is from Jakarta, where there is more freedom compared to Padang. I don't expect her clothing style to become a trend here. People would find it strange and I wouldn't dare to go out dressed like that. I usually wear jeans, T-shirts, and sneakers."

Iwan (18, male student) says of the clip in which Agnes Monica dances together with a few male dancers: "A girl on a stage surrounded by only men is *jelek*." When asked to clarify this term, he explained that a *wanita jelek* is a girl or woman whose clothes are too vulgar and clash with local culture, who exploits her body, smokes, and/or uses drugs. Nineteen-year-old Budi was more moderate in his comments, saying that Agnes Monica is of Chinese descent and that he therefore could not tell for sure what a proper clothing style for her would look like.

Budi and Iwan's remarks imply that notions about what is considered inappropriate for girls in Padang might be considered normal for other parts of Indonesia—for instance, in Indonesia's capital (Jakarta), in other social settings (show business), for people of another religion (non-Muslims), or for people from other ethnic groups (girls and women of western or Chinese descent). Although teenage girls and young women such as Agnes Monica are often portrayed in media wearing sexy outfits, in everyday life Muslim fashion is becoming popular (Champagne 2004). The more popular everyday dress code for many female teenagers and students in Padang consists of tight jeans and T-shirts with a headscarf (*jilbab*). Variations on this style occur as well, ranging from not wearing a *jilbab* at all (like Dewi), to more covered forms of Islamic dress. This might explain Dewi's reluctance to wear clothes in the style of her idol, because she is part of a Muslim society that teaches young women to keep certain parts of their body covered (their *aurat*) and that monitors the interactions between unrelated boys and girls, because premarital sex is taboo (Smith-Hefner 2005: 442). An open display of her body and sexuality would defy local norms. Moreover, in some ways, Agnes Monica's independence and rebelliousness, more commonly associated with masculine youth cultures, do not match with prevailing notions of femininity, which emphasize qualities like caregiving and modesty (Kearney 1998: 149). Yet female students such as Dewi liked her music and were attracted by her independent and trendy image, rather than her sexy appearance. The fact that this type of imagery appeals to young women such as Dewi could be a sign of changing lifestyles and aspirations, because most Minangkabau parents would not raise their daughters to be independent at such a young age. Male students did not object to Agnes Monica's music, but rather to her performing while surrounded by men only. At the same time, one wonders if some of the young men watch her as a kind of sexual fantasy in a society where they are supposed to be modest and where sex before marriage is taboo.

One of the most popular music genres in Indonesia, *dangdut*—an energetic mix of Indonesian, western, and Arab sounds—attracts large audiences of both youth and adults in villages and cities throughout the country. In addition to nationally well-known *dangdut* artists such as Rhoma Irama[10] and Anisa Bahar, many regions in Indonesia have their own *dangdut* groups who sing in their local language, such as Javanese, *bahasa Medan*, or *bahasa Minang*. *Dangdut* has become a regular item in the selection of VCDs displayed at market stalls in Padang.

Dangdut's most celebrated and notorious female artist is Inul Daratista. Her dancing style, characterized by dynamic and sensual movements of her hips (referred to by the Indonesians as *ngebor*, meaning "drilling"), stirred a national controversy when she rose to fame in 2003 at age 24. Since then, conservative Muslim authorities have condemned Inul's shows as being pornographic and banned her from performing in several cities. Her erotic dancing has been cited as one of the reasons for a much-contested antipornography bill that captured the national debate in 2005–2006 (Allen 2007: 103) and was passed as a law in 2008. At the same time, feminists, human right activists, and intellectuals have defended Inul's right to artistic freedom (Suryakusuma 2003). Despite this controversy, *dangdut* in all its varieties continues to be widely popular.

Inul's videos are characterized by bright colors and rich stage decor, as exemplified in her VCD *Karaoke Goyang Inul*. Inul's band consists of male musicians who play at the side of the stage. She often records her music in front of a studio audience, which includes women wearing the *jilbab* (head-scarf) in the front rows of the studio audience. Perhaps they are strategically placed there to suggest that Inul's live performances are not that controversial as some might think and that it is all right for people to watch her shows.[11] Yet Inul never interacts with the audience in front of her, but directly addresses the viewers of her VCD through the lyrics of her songs. In the first song on one VCD she asks them not to become upset by her sexy dancing style: "*Para penonton . . . Bapak-bapak, Ibu-ibu, semuanya. Jangan heran kalau Inul sedang goyang. Rada panas, agak seksi. Ma'afkanlah*" ("Viewers, ladies and gentlemen, all of you. Do not be surprised when I am swinging my hips. Rather hot, quite sexy. My apologies.").

The clothes of female *dangdut* artists not only differ greatly from everyday dress, but also from the styles of pop and rock stars on MTV (Wallach 2002: 297). Inul is always wearing tight tops and trousers that are decorated with fringes on her waist, rear, and upper legs, that twirl when she shakes her hips. Inul's dancing, more so than her singing, forms the attraction of her perfor-mances. Each time Inul shakes her hips, the camera zooms into this part of her body. This is probably the reason why this VCD is considered inappropriate for young viewers.

Many people I interviewed about this VCD had strong ideas about Inul and her performances. Ricky, a 27-year-old man who worked for a nongovernmen-tal organization in Padang, was one of the few people I met who readily admit-ted to being a huge fan of Inul:

> Inul is entertainment. Her voice . . . the way she dances . . . I think
> she is really talented. Even my mother, who is a strict Muslim, says,
> "It is a gift when someone can dance like that." I have been a fan
> from the start. It is boring to watch so many people imitate her style,
> because she is the original.

However, most people were less positive about Inul. Ibu Siti, 56, female and owner an aerobic center, comments:

I like Inul's voice, but not her dancing. I think sex is too dominantly part of her performances. Because of their background in Islam and *adat* (local custom), most Minang would disapprove of Inul's performances. I think that many people with a low level in education, such as *becak* drivers, would like Inul's style, but that higher educated people with strong faith don't like her.

Achmad, 22, an economics student, was very strict in his remarks about Inul: "It is wrong for someone to desire Inul, but it is OK for someone to think of her music and style of dancing as art. But for Muslims, Inul is not art."

Although some watch Inul merely as entertainment, others are offended by her erotic dancing or find the music tacky and lower class. However, the many claims from people who said to disapprove of the erotic dancing of female *dangdut* artists did not always precisely reflect reality. Elements of *dangdut*-style dancing were occasionally incorporated in the aerobic classes in which I participated.[12] The number of disapproving comments about Inul or *dangdut* in general forms a striking contrast to the many *dangdut* shows on national television or the presence of local *dangdut* imitators in Padang.

A third form of locally produced pop music is *pop Minang*, "a cover term for various popular music genres from the West Sumatran region that utilize songs, melodies and tunings from a huge reservoir of older genres" (Barendregt 2002: 415). *Pop Minang* encompasses everything from more or less traditional songs to trendy Minangkabau–style dance music. Because of this variety, an analysis of some of the subgenres in *pop Minang* reveals much about generational shifts as youth and adults select and respond to different aspects of lifestyles portrayed in this music.

Pop Minang is sung in the Minangkabau language and functions as a means for expressing and discussing notions of Minang culture (Barendregt 2002). Because of the phenomenon of *merantau* (going abroad) and the large numbers of Minang migrants who live outside West Sumatra, many *pop Minang* songs cover themes such as longing for home (Barendregt 2002: 430), love, hope, and unfulfilled expectations. Visually the "sound of longing for home" is evoked through images of well-known places in West Sumatra. An example of this kind of *pop Minang* featuring a female artist, is a VCD called *Saluang Talempong Minang, Volume 3*. This *Misramolai* series is produced and recorded by a local record company named Minang Record.

The clips in this VCD show a young woman (the female singer) filmed in various locations in West Sumatra, ranging from lake Maninjau to *Istana Pagaruyung*, a replica of the palace of a former Minangkabau king. The girl in the video appears calm and reserved, either sitting or slowly walking while performing the song. Her dress as well as those of her female background dancers is neat and covered, but not necessarily traditional. A typical outfit the singer would be wearing is a red shawl with golden embroidery, a little makeup, and a golden hair ribbon. The tempo of the music and the dancing is relatively slow, with a lot of repetition. Keyboard and the *saluang*, a bamboo flute that is often used in Minangkabau music, are the main instruments in this VCD.

This VCD is an example of a semitraditional genre of *pop Minang* music in which more classical songs are mixed with modern influences, such as keyboard, and contemporary clothes and choreography. This type of *pop Minang* VCD seems to be aimed at an audience of mostly adult or elderly Minangkabau. Most teenagers and students I interviewed did not like this type of *pop Minang* and told me they found it boring, old fashioned, or *kampungan* (backward, something for the lower classes). For that reason this type of music was never played in the public buses en route to Andalas University.

In general, many young people thought this type of Minang clip was outdated compared with the clips in national pop music. A female VCD seller at the market remarked: "Maybe the people here are less modern. In Jakarta there is money to make modern clips by using computer effects. That takes a lot of financial investment. Here in West Sumatra there is less money available for such things." Agus (19, male student) told me: "The *pop Minang* music that is released on VCD is already more modern than it used to be. VCDs are more modern than cassette tapes. The songs sound less monotone because other 'colors' (*warna*) such as keyboard are added to traditional instruments such as the flute." But still, the text, lyrics, and the images in this type of VCD were too old-fashioned for him: "Minang culture is a habit and habits are hard to change."

With regard to the images of women in this VCD, most people I interviewed (youth as well as adults) agreed that the woman in the clip looked pretty ordinary and not too sexy. They noticed that the director of the clips had used a mix of traditional and contemporary elements to accompany the music. Because the music contains a mix of both traditional and contemporary music styles and instruments (for instance a more upbeat tempo compared with traditional Minangkabau music), most people thought the appearance of the female singer did fit the music. They recognized her clothes as a variation on traditional Minangkabau dress and felt that although the clip was not "real" (*asli*) enough to feel completely authentic, it was accurate enough to evoke a feeling of "Minangness."

Record companies in West Sumatra also release VCDs with other subgenres of *pop Minang*. Next to following trends in national pop music, producers of *pop Minang* also incorporate international elements in the music to create a more trendy sound. Although VCDs such as the *Misramolai* series make use of clear symbols of Minang identity (for instance, specific instruments such as the *saluang* [bamboo flute], traditional or semitraditional dress and dancing styles, tourist locations in West Sumatra, lyrics in the Minang language),[13] the other end of the spectrum of *pop Minang* music contains subgenres like Minang *house* or *triping* music, in which these markers are less clearly pronounced. The musical style of these genres might best be described as house music, but the lyrics are sung in the Minangkabau language. This type of music is sometimes played in the small taxi buses (*angkot*) that ride in Padang and occasionally in the Andalas buses, but sometimes also at weddings and parties in West Sumatra.

An example of Minang *triping* music is the VCD *Triping Dangdut*. What is striking about this VCD is an odd contradiction in the layout of the cover. The front side of the cover shows a picture of the four female artists that perform on this VCD. Combined with the bright colors of the layout, it almost seems one is looking at the cover of a VCD with children's pop music. However, the back side shows the silhouette of what appears to be a naked woman wearing stiletto heels. Clearly, this sends a whole different message than the innocent images depicted on the front side of the cover.

The clips in this VCD are recorded in a disco, a cave, and in the open air. Overall, the images evoke an atmosphere of nightlife, partying, and *triping*.[14] In all clips there are two young men and two girls dancing. The girls wear tight jeans and short tops or skirts and dresses with high-laced boots underneath. Their hair is loose and they wear bright-red lipstick. The men are dressed in jeans or trousers with a short blouse or T-shirt. One of them is wearing a T-shirt printed with the whiskey brand Jack Daniels. This stands out, because the vast majority of the people in Padang is Muslim and not allowed to drink alcohol. He has loosely put a pair of black sunglasses in his hair, adding to his nonchalant appearance. The clothes of the girls also differ from the type of dress people wear in everyday life. Although tight jeans are normal dress for teenagers and students, it is regarded inappropriate for women to show their bare shoulders. The ultrashort skirts in the clip, but also the way these girls dance, is controversial for Indonesian standards. They move their hips, twist their bodies, and look sensuously into the camera. The camera is often filming their bodies in close-up.

Pak Nurdin, a male resident of Padang and owner of a foundation that produces local documentaries, has a clear opinion about this type of Minang VCD: "This VCD is only meant to sell erotic images, the lyrics of the songs are not much. The technical quality of the VCD is very good. This producer might be the best in Padang." After having watched the first clip, Pak Nurdin continues:

This VCD is not at all relevant for Minang culture, but the paradox is that this type of VCD sells a lot, also outside West Sumatra. The producer of this VCD knows the market well. *Triping* music is controversial, but there are also a lot of people who like it. *Triping* music is also increasingly used as live music, for instance at weddings. The clothes of the girls in the videos look just like in Jakarta. I do not consider this Minang and I do not like it.

Triping videos like these mostly seem to be intended for youth who like to party. According to Pak Nurdin, this type of clip underlines the difference between two cultures: that of the older generation and that of cosmopolitan youth. However, this is not to suggest that all youth would like this type of clip. Two high school girls whom I interviewed during a bus ride to Andalas while a *triping* video was playing said they were annoyed by the pornographic images of the sexy girls in the *triping* and disco clips. They would rather just listen to a cassette instead of having to watch these clips. Personally they preferred VCDs with Indian music that showed women in pretty clothes or the VCD of the popular teen movie *Ada Apa Dengan Cinta? (What's up with Love?)*.

Negotiating Being Young, Female, and Muslim

Music VCDs in Indonesia are not just part of a thriving commercial industry, they have a cultural impact as well. Drawing on a wide variety of westernized and local images, the videos in these VCDs portray different youth lifestyles, at times defying local norms about proper behavior for young Muslim women. Presented with images of female artists that range from modest and innocent to very erotic ones, young women in Padang choose selectively what they can and cannot incorporate into their own lives, while in the process negotiating what it means to be young, female, and Muslim in contemporary Indonesia. These young women maneuver between images of female artists who openly show off their body and sexuality, and Minangkabau values that prescribe Minang girls and women to dress neat and behave politely. Some of the more erotic images of female artists in the VCDs under discussion were a source of anxiety to youth and adults who perceive these videos as being "not authentic" and portraying the "wrong" kind of youth culture, breaking with local cultural and religious values. Although sexy images are an important part of music VCDs, because they help establish an artist's image and advance the sales of her music (Andsager 2006: 31), this was not necessarily the aspect young people picked up from these videos. Notions of self-reliance and financial independence, the cosmopolitan and flashy lifestyles portrayed, or the modern computer effects used in these clips were sometimes more interesting to them, because these aspects could be incorporated in their own lives.

Even though young people choose selectively what they can and cannot copy from these videos, lifestyle choices for young women (not men!) continue to be discussed in highly moral and political terms, reflecting anxieties about the future of the nation. Debates in the national arena, such as the debate about the controversial antipornography bill (Allen 2007) in 2005–2008 and the upheaval about the introduction of *Playboy* magazine in 2006 indicate that the politics of the body and sexuality are gendered and contested in Indonesia. Critics who blame these sexy images on the West seem to forget that "nearly all traditional dances in Indonesia feature sensual movements, bare shoulders and tight-fitting costumes, and many traditional visual art works allude to fertility and physical beauty" (Allen 2007: 107–108). Meanwhile, in an attempt to counter a range of social ills including "immoral behavior," the mayor in Padang has issued legislation that prescribes Islamic dress for men and women (2004) and compulsory Islamic education for children and youth (2007), which is "designed to equip them for life with the values of Islam" (Hooker and Huda 2007). These developments suggest that the last word has not been said about youth lifestyles, proper behavior for women, Minangkabau identity, and the future of West Sumatra. Further research into this dynamic area could enhance our understanding of the complex ways in which the global, the national, and the local are linked when it comes to the construction of youth lifestyles, morality, and generational change in Indonesia.

Acknowledgment

Research was conducted in 2003 in Padang, West Sumatra, for my MA thesis in cultural anthropology at Leiden University, The Netherlands (2005). Andalas University in Padang provided support during fieldwork.

I am grateful to Bart Barendregt, Annelies Moors, Linda Herrera, and Asef Bayat for commenting on earlier versions of this chapter. The thesis on which this chapter is based has benefited from the encouragement and helpful suggestions of Patricia Spyer.

22

Conclusion:
Knowing Muslim Youth

Linda Herrera and Asef Bayat

In recent years there has been a proliferation of interest in youth issues in general and Muslim youth in particular. A plethora of publications from academia, nongovernmental and governmental organizations, international institutions, and development organizations examine youth conditions, youth behaviors, and their roles as conduits of development and change. Shifting paradigms since the end of the Cold War about human rights and global citizenship within a prevailing neoliberal global order have informed much of the policy, academic, and political interest in youth. The "question of youth" often gets articulated as a paradox, as a problem and an opportunity. The problem relates to security, anxiety over the youth bulge (sometimes called *population bomb*), unemployment, inequality, civil and regional conflicts, HIV and AIDS, drug use, extremism, and gang violence. These conditions, which exist widely, take on a unique urgency in the global South, where the nation-state is arguably undergoing a crisis of authority and legitimacy. Governments often cannot adequately support, regulate, influence, or incorporate the young into their institutions, nor convince them of their ideologies. Writing with reference to the African continent, Jean and John Comoroff persuasively argue, "one of the hallmarks of the present moment, of the age of globalization and postcoloniality, has been a diminishing of the capacity of governments —if not the market forces they foster—to control adolescent bodies, energies, or intentions. . . . [T]he nation-state plays host to forces that it can no longer ade-quately rein in" (Comaroff and Comaroff 2005: 22).

A good deal of youth-related policy and research coming out of establish-ment institutions—such as United Nations agencies, the World Bank, the U.S. State Department, European Union, and U.S. think tanks—that work closely with nation-states place a strong emphasis on the economy (i.e., trade) and security within a discourse of democracy and human rights. In much of this framework, youth are treated as a group that needs to be understood and trained for purposes of political containment, ideological monitoring, and economic reform. Massive projects of social engineering, from global educa-tional reforms and related human capital planning, are imaged by their architects as the way to move human societies on paths of poverty alleviation, international security, and economic and political liberalization (Herrera 2008).

The Millennium Development Goals' (MDGs), for instance, derived from the Millennium Declaration adopted by 189 nations in 2000, are part of a United Nations–led global process of poverty eradication and sustainable development in which children and youth in the global South are at the core. The eight goals, which are supposed to be achieved by 2015, are: to eradicate extreme poverty and hunger; achieve universal primary education; promote gender equality and empower women; reduce child mortality; improve maternal health; combat HIV/AIDS, malaria, and other diseases; ensure envi-ronmental sustainability; and develop a global partnership for development (see the United Nations Web site at http://www.un.org/millenniumgoals/global. shtml). Whereas MDG projects and policies make an effort to involve youth as advocates, the young are allowed little to no scope to question, reject, or offer alternative visions, demands, and arrangements for sociopolitical, cultural, and economic development.

A similar prescriptive approach to youth and development can be found in the highly influential *World Development Report 2007: Development and the Next Generation* (World Bank 2007). Despite the report's abundant reference to youth agency and participation, youth more often than not are treated as objects rather than as agents of development. As a critic of the report sums, this approach "does a disservice to the authentic concerns of young people who seek a better world—the report offers no hope in this direction and instead positions young people as a valuable resource that nations can leverage to build competitiveness in the global economy" (Kamat 2007: 1216). In the above grand development narratives, the young are supposed to join, not question, a consolidated global framework for economic and political development.

In the post–September 11, 2001, period, security issues joined poverty eradication as the global development concern. Muslim youth, especially

Muslim males, were thrust onto the international stage. As raised in the introduction, much of the mainstream policy analysis and research on security has focused on Islamic extremism and terrorism. Terrorism is often understood as a pathology of the individual, of a culture (Muslim or Arab for instance), of a demographic situation (i.e., the youth bulge), or a condition of poverty. The subsequent field of terrorism studies, which has proliferated since 9/11, in many respects parallels the 1960s sociological work on youth deviance and delinquency, the difference being that it is not concerned with urban crime in the West, but with international security in an interconnected global order. Alternative approaches to security studies are emerging, as evidenced by the incipient field of Critical Studies on Terrorism (Jackson et al. 2009), with a new journal by the same name (est. 2009). This critical approach of inquiry is primed to take up the issue of youth with a lens to deconstructing the discourse of security and to investigate the "youth threat" in a context of power, inequality, and geopolitics in a global order, and hopefully with deeper understanding of youth lives, conditions, and trajectories.

Much of the grand planning and development narratives about youth are informed ideologically by the normative economic and political liberalization frameworks noted above, and methodologically by statistical analysis, economic models, and quantitative methods. To be sure, quantitative data such as sociological surveys can be extremely useful in providing a more comprehensive idea about the identity features (e.g., gender, class, ethnicity, location) in relation to employment, housing, leisure time, political participation, crime, attitudes, media use patterns, and many other important domains of youth life. Yet youth can also be objectified and treated as passive objects of policy objectives, exhortation, or guidance; they can get stripped of having an authentic voice of their own, and denied the right of setting the terms of the discussion about their current lives and future aspirations.

Young and Muslim

In this volume we embarked on exploring the cultural politics of Muslim youth by trying to understand how the young maneuver and negotiate the terms between being young and Muslim—how they do so within the political and economic settings that offer both opportunities as well as serious challenges to their livelihoods, expressions of their identities, lifestyles, and life projections. The category of "Muslim youth" has been used in an inclusive way insofar as it comprises secular Muslims, hybrid Muslims, non-Muslim minorities in Muslim majority societies, and religious Muslims who take part in Muslim youth cultural politics. Methodologically, we have attempted to balance between providing detailed understanding at the micro sites in which youth live their everyday existence, while theorizing about how their choices, movements, interactions, activities, and attitudes often make up an arena of contestation for power. Using biographical interviews, oral histories, participant observation, and critical ethnography have allowed us to get directly acquainted with the lives, lifestyles, attitudes, aspirations, and habitus of youth themselves. The chapters take us to the public spaces of youth sociability; a Dunkin' Donuts in Brooklyn, an Egyptian restaurant in Bangkok, a mosque in The Gambia, a public bus in Indonesia—each micro location tells something about how youth are navigating their lives, identities, and choices in light of global processes.

We have discussed the ways in which Muslim youth assert their youthfulness within the constraints posed by authoritarian states and by the moral and political authorities in the global South. We have also dealt with the ways youth attempt to realize their Muslimness in western political–cultural environments where they are oftentimes considered a security threat in addition to cultural and economic liabilities. Whether in the global North or South, young Muslims are deeply engaged in struggles for citizenship in a localized and broader global sense. Thus, the chapters deal with two general populations of youth: those in the "global North" and those in the "global South." Although these two populations share many common points of identification and collectively take part in multiple aspects of belonging to a global generation, their actual physical location in different parts of the world holds great significance, especially when it comes to issues involving citizenship, livelihoods, and lifestyles.

Muslim youth in Europe and North America are forming identities in at least partial response to belonging to a minority group in the context of public debates and policies about security, integration, multiculturalism, and citizenship. Despite sometimes empirical evidence to the contrary, minority Muslim youth are being positioned by the dominant society as a troublesome population. The perceived problem is not that there are too many young people, as is the case in countries of the South with a youth bulge; indeed, many countries in Europe suffer from a demographic deficit and encourage higher birth rates and youth immigration to supplement the labor force. The problem, rather, is that Muslim youth are viewed as disruptive and even dangerous elements about whom something should be done. The nature of the presumed problem differs according to gender. Young Muslim men are under especial scrutiny as security threats and economic liabilities, whereas Muslim women, especially those who don headscarves and opt for pious "youthhoods," are seen more as posing threats to the cultural traditions and integrity of European societies.

Young Muslim men, including converts to Islam, have to deal with omnipresent stereotypes and images of them as dangerous and prone to extremism, and of being unproductive members of society. In the United Kingdom, for instance, Muslim men in the 16- to 24-year-old age group reported an unemployment rate three times higher than the national average—and Muslim women twice the national average—even though they participate in postcompulsory education at higher than average rates (Hussain and Choudhury 2007: 6; Modood 2004). On the point of extremism, there is no denying that Muslim men were perpetrators of the 9/11 terrorists attacks in the United States; the March 11, 2004, Madrid train attacks; the July 21, 2005, London subway bombings; and the 2004 murder of Theo van Gogh, all of which were not only devastating on national levels, but spectacular global media sensations. But it needs to be better acknowledged that these events, while they clearly point to serious problems in certain circles, should not be understood as embodying the culture of the Muslim minorities who make up large and heterogeneous populations. For the most part, Muslim youth exert their energies in pursuit of education, jobs, stability, justice, family, fame, and fortune—the stuff of ordinary youth in most parts of the world.

Are moral panics by the dominant society and power holders about Muslim youth justified? When confronted with a population that is perceived to be trouble, we must always ask: trouble for whom? Who is defining the problem? What political, economic, cultural, or moral order is this group perceived to be disturbing? A "problem" cannot be investigated solely by dissecting the presumed objects of the problem—namely, the youth themselves. More critical research where Muslims are a minority is needed on the majority societies to investigate how discourses about and representations of Islam and youth get formed, whose interests they serve, and their historical basis (see Mazawi, this volume).

Whether in New York, London, or Berlin young Muslims are responding to and asserting roles in the whirlwind of events and politicized gaze on their lives. The research in this volume demonstrates that young Muslims are acting on their worlds in meaningful ways, but their lives, especially when they do not fit into dominant representations about Islam, identity, and development, often get overlooked. Some fuse a politics of piety and group solidarity with a "version of Islam that is consistent with their multicultural and globalized vision of the faith" (Bayoumi, this volume). Others assert themselves in the minefield of identity politics. They take ownership of how they are represented through means of creative expression, whether in the realms of fashion, literature, film, comedy, or music. As we have seen in the case of music, rappers from London to The Hague repackage Muslim stereotypes with acerbic wit and irony. The *"Jihad* Rap" of Fun^Da^Mental serves as one of the many avenues through which counternarratives are spreading about not only what it is like to be young and Muslim in the UK, but of the underlying inequities of the dominant society from a minority vantage point. Musical groups often use their public platform as a pedagogical space to "provide a very different, multiplexed, and more useful vision of what it might mean to be 'Muslim' in today's Britain" (Swedenburg). The popular arts, grassroots movements, Arab and Muslim student associations (figure 22.1), and cyber communities represent some of the avenues where youth are taking a more proactive stance and setting the terms of debates, thereby bringing about an alternative consciousness and action about issues of citizenship, justice, and multiculturalism.

In Muslim majority countries of the global South, whether in West Africa, Asia, or the Middle East and North Africa, youth are shaping identities, forming communities, and taking action more around issues of employment, political and economic marginalization, and intergenerational conflict with the older generation, all while struggling to assert their youthfulness. Ben Soares' observation in this volume about youth in Mali as often being "marginalized in relation to an older generation in the interconnected realms of politics, economics, and religion" rings true for youth throughout the postcolonial states.

FIGURE 22.1. Students at San Francisco State University dancing the Dabke during Arab Culture Week. (Shiva, 2008)

The chapters in this volume testify that youth coming of age in the post-colonial global South, in already difficult circumstances brought about by poverty, fragile economies, conflict, authoritarian and corrupt governments, globalism, and intergenerational strife, are highly critical, frustrated, and sometimes overwhelmed by powerlessness. They speak of the ubiquity of political corruption and cronyism, economic exclusion, moral discipline and suppression of lifestyle, and the gross injustices and aggressions associated with free market economics. The conditions of contemporary life can lead youth to display extremist, inflexible, and conservative tendencies when compared with their parents' generation. In the West African country of The Gambia, for instance, traditional generational relations are being inverted as the youthful male members of the Tabligh Jama'at challenge the authority of their elders. In their pursuit of power, opportunities, and religious authority, the young shun local practices in favor of more rigid interpretations of religion and social practice.

Similarly, as Hasan argues in his portrait of male youth who took part in the Lakshar Jihad in Indonesia, some educated youth try to confront conditions of contemporary life by challenging the power and authority of the older generation. The Salafi movements, with their transnational reach, attract youth and offer them, if not hope, a sense of pride in belonging to an Islamic brotherhood. Some youths, by joining these groups, may satisfy an immediate need to "establish identify and claim dignity," and thereby feel relevant and powerful, but in the longer term these movements do not transform structural forces or bring about the conditions that will lead to livelihoods, economic opportunities, and secure futures. Such movements in actuality are not an alternative to a socioeconomic and political order, but a reaction to it. At a point in their lives, these young men in The Gambia and Indonesia considered that the only way to access opportunities was to establish an alternative cultural and political order, even if that meant supporting a project that was repressive, exclusionary, or politically regressive.

But many other young male youths, such as the "Rasta Sufis" in Mali and the globalized Muslims in Niger, are experiencing new avenues of cultural expression, openness, and awareness as their economic opportunities and chances at securing a future are constricting. Male youth in Niger embrace and experiment with "anti-Islamic" cultural products and lifestyles by listening to hip-hop music and dressing in ghetto fashion, as they simultaneously identity with the "global *umma*." But while they experiment with and assert multiple identities, they face barriers of being unable to earn a living. Like scores of youth in similar situations, they live the impossibility of being "connected to the world, yet excluded from it" (Masquelier).

At the same time, masses of other young people experience a kind of over-mobility in search of livelihoods, or as political and environmental refugees escaping conflict and persecution, or environmental degradation. They move to and between cities, nations, and regions, below and above the radar, in the pursuit of survival and some future stability. But with the many barriers they encounter, they are no longer seeking a path to adulthood in the traditional sense of attaining future stability and a decent standard of living. They are, rather, struggling for "a means of envisioning a future that enables youth to become something other than youth, but without relying upon the customary means for resolving this transformation—particularly as the transformation into adulthood is something increasingly problematic" (Simone).

In both the global North and South, Muslim youth navigate between assert-ing their youthfulness and oftentimes their Muslimness. But this maneuvering is mediated by a host of social, economic, and political settings within which these youths operate. The expression of identities and realization of youthful dreams are affected and profoundly complicated by a plethora of global, national, and local processes that render the reality of Muslim youth much more complex than is often portrayed. However, this complex identity forma-tion is by no means peculiar to Muslims, nor is Muslim youth an exceptional entity. We have argued against essentializing Muslim youth, as treating them as a unique group that might somehow be trapped in a maze of a supposedly stagnant culture and religion while the rest of the world changes. As the chap-ters in this volume unequivocally demonstrate, Muslim youth, located in pro-cesses of globalization in this period of late neoliberalism, share many significant points of convergence with their global generational counterparts, especially when it comes to concerns about livelihood, struggle for political in-clusion, intergenerational conflicts, coming of age in an era of global discourses about human rights, and rapidly changing new media and communications technologies. But it cannot be denied that certain structural factors and condi-tions of the contemporary period have brought Muslim youth into the interna-tional spotlight, thereby making this group important actors and a category of inquiry in its own right.

Future Directions

Even though this volume covers diverse critical themes pertinent to contempo-rary Muslim youth, we do not claim that it is exhaustive. The field is in its for-mative phase and many issues still need rigorous scholarly attention. We have already emphasized the importance of transcending an exceptionalist approach to the study of Muslim youth, while at the same time understanding the features that might differentiate this population from others at this historic global moment. Much of the current research stems from a problem-centered approach (culture, social, security, health, economic, or demographic). It is, however, important also to look at the young on their own terms, as a particular social group that is increasingly becoming the "new proletariat" of our times. It may appear that youth are merely reacting to difficult situations of poverty, unemployment, political exclusion, corruption, and Islamophobia, but this is not the whole story. They are also shaping the terms of debate on issues and structures that affect their lives, and they are creating and disseminating messages and images to define themselves on a public stage. Finally, the new information and communication technologies, especially "mobile communication," is transforming our working life and life-worlds (Castells et al., 2007), and youth are the most avid recipients, producers, and innovators of such technologies.

Tackling these themes requires innovative methodologies and comparative, interdisciplinary, and intergenerational collaborations. There is a real need for anthropologists, sociologists, political economists, social historians, scholars of cultural studies, development studies, media studies, and law to undertake research around common pertinent questions. Qualitative research should provide an understanding of the everyday practices, negotiations, and decisions at the micro level, while remaining attuned to the larger tensions associated with neoliberal development and the paradoxes of globalization. Our approach in this volume has been largely under the rubric of cultural politics. However, it is important to delve into and complement such studies with a political economy approach. Other macro analyses that look at large processes defined as globalization, development, and modernization are important, provided they are grounded in a micro understanding of everyday lives and realities of young people. There is also a need for more cross-generational research to be able to better understand if, for instance, attitudes about religion, politics, and society are a product of a particular time or life stage, or if these are more an outcome of educational background and environment. Finally, research in the area of youth necessitates not only research *about* the young, but collaborations and initiatives *with* the young.

These studies have affirmed that young people are highly discerning about issues of justice and equity and that they agree on the need for change. But awareness of an issue is not enough to stimulate change. As Bennani-Chraïbi argues in her survey of Moroccan youth, "action comes about as the result of a particular type of socialization, involvement in networks, and experience in micro events that allow ideas to translate into actions." Today's young people, the most numerous, educated, and globally connected generation in history, are simultaneously objects, victims, and agents of change. How deeply youth cultural political activities can transform the social order toward social justice, equity, livelihoods, and other opportunities is yet to be seen. Muslim youth are struggling to exert their youthfulness in the present, charting out courses for a future, and acting on their world in ways that demand awareness and attention. As a new generational consciousness is in the making, understanding and engaging youth will inevitably continue as a vital arena for research and action.

Notes

CHAPTER 1

1. One of the authors explored issues of youth politics from an intergenerational perspective in relation to Africa in some depth while supervising the Masters of Arts thesis of Eyob Balcha at the International Institute of Social Studies on youth and politics in Ethiopia. See (Balcha 2009).

2. For a video explaining the introduction of Google Knol in Arabic, see www.youtube.com/watch?v=dDXmcMj8KQY.

CHAPTER 2

1. For Mao Tse-tung, *youth movement* meant the political participation of students in the anticolonial (Japan) struggle (Mao 1969: 241–249). For a listing of such youth organizations and movements, see www.youthmovements.org/guide/globalguide.htm.

2. See Ashraf and Banuazizi (1985). Out of a sample of 646 people killed in Tehran in the street clashes during the revolution (from August 23, 1977, to February 19, 1978), the largest group after artisans and shopkeepers (n = 189) were students (n = 149) (Bayat 1997: 39).

3. See Rahnavard in daily *Bahar*, June 18, 2000: 2). A one-day symposium was organized to discuss why the youth showed such a disinterest in religious lessons.

4. See http://dailynews.yahoo.com, July 25, 2000.

5. According to a July 2000 report authored by Muhammad Ali Zam, the director of cultural and artistic affairs for Tehran; see daily Bahar, July 5, 2000. This became a highly controversial survey, because the conservatives disputed its authenticity and negative impact on their image.

6. Reported by the Sina News Agency (2004a).

7. Conducted by psychologist Dawood Jeshan on 120 runaway girls in Tehran, reported by the Sina News Agency cited in Iran Emrooz website on June 17, 2004.

8. Interview with an anonymous medial anthropologist working on the subject (Spring 2001).

9. Ibid.

10. A contribution of Muhammad Hadi Taskhiri, of the Organization of Islamic Culture and Communication in the Second International Seminar on Hijab, Novemebr 19, 1997, reported in *Zanan*, no. 26, September/October (Meh/Aban) 1997, pp. 8–9.

11. A survey of the Supreme Council of Youth reported in the 2nd International seminar on hijab cited in Zanan, no. 26, September/Otober (Mehr/Aban) 1997.

12. This finding was reported by the National Radio and TV, Organization of Islamic Propaganda, and the Organization of the Friday Prayers (*Setad-e Namaz*); cited by Emad Eddin Baaqui in *Payam-e Emrooz*, no. 39, April/May (Ordibehesht) 2000, p. 14.

13. As reported by the head of Tehran's cultural and artistic affairs (July 5, 2000, www.nandotimes.com).

14. Survey conducted by the National Organization of Youth, reported in *Aftab*, April 28, 2001.

15. Interview with Azam, an anonymous participant, June 2002.

16. See the article in the *Christian Science Monitor* (December 5, 1997 by Scott Peterson, "Ecstasy in Iran, Agony for Its Clerics.")

17. This is well illustrated in an editorial of a reformist daily. See "The Mystery of Firecrackers," *Aftab* March 15, 2001, p. 2.

18. See "Leisure Time and Amusement," *Aftab-e Yazd*, April 3, 2001, p. 9; "Shad Zistan-e Zanan," *Dowran-e Emrooz*, February 9, 2000, p. 2.

19. Report on seminar on the 'Approaches to the Concept of Living,' cited in *Aftab-e Yazd*, 9 January 2001, p. 7; and 11 January 2001, p. 7.

20. See Jean-Michel Cadiot, August 20, 2001, IranMania.com.

21. This seemed to be confirmed by a large-scale survey (Kian-Thiebaut 2002).

22. Interviews with youth conducted by Rime Naguib, American University in Cairo (AUC) sociology student (Spring 2002).

23. The ages of Egypt's political leaders by their birth date: President Mubarak, born in 1928; Dia Eddin Dawoud (Naser Party), 1926; Khalid Mohyeddin (leader of Tajammo' Party), 1922; Mustafa Mashur (leader of Muslim Brothers), 1921; Ibrahim Shukri (leader of Labor Party), 1916. Noman Gom'a, the youngest opposition leader of the Wafd Party was born in 1934.

24. In a survey, only 16% of Cairo University students expressed interest in party politics. In addition, some 87% of elders did not trust the youth to do politics (Abdel-Hay 2002: 117–118).

25. Drawn on the conclusion of a debate in Majlis el-Shura, reported in *Al-Ahram*, July 14, 2000, p. 7.

26. This information is based on my interview with the Minister of Youth and Sports, Dr. Ali Eddin Hilal, November 3, 2001, Cairo.

27. The Ministry of Social Affairs reported to have extended some EL30 million between 1997 and 2000. See *Al-Ahram*, July 14, 2000.

28. The Ministry of Local Development was to extend some of these loans. See ibid.

29. I have especially relied on Muhammad Shalabi's, "Egypt's Youth Centers: Between Ideals and Reality," unpublished, AUC, Spring 2003.

30. They often represented prestaged shows where the young attendees were carefully picked, questions rehearsed, and the oratory and flattery by which students addressed the president left little genuine interaction.

31. Hoda's statement in response to my question: What is it like to be young in today's Egyptian society? (Spring 2003, Cairo, Egypt).

32. The ticket costs ranges from LE75 to 150, with alcohol drinks for LE20 and water, LE10.

33. The figure for the country was 22% (based on a survey of 14,656 male high school students in 1990 [Soueif et al. 1990: 71–72]).

34. Reportedly, the quantity seized by the police jumped from 2,276 hits in 2000 to 7,008 hits in 2001; see *Cairo Times*, March 14–20, 2002, p. 16.

35. Active sexuality of youth is also confirmed by al-Dabbaqh (1996).

36. Interviews with youngsters by Rime Naguib, sociology student, AUC (Spring 2002).

37. Ironically, the partially segregated trains made the traditional young women more mobile. Parents would not mind if their daughters took trains because segregated trains were thought to protect their daughters from male harassment. See Seif Nasrawi, "An Ethnography of Cairo's Metro," unpublished, Fall 2002, AUC.

38. See Rime Naguib, "Egyptian Youth: A Tentative Study," unpublished, Spring 2002.

39. Rime Naghib, interview with youth, Spring 2002, AUC.

40. CAPMAS reported more than 5 million bachelor boys and 3.4 million girls caused uproar in the media about the moral consequences of the state of these unmarried adults. Indeed, the age of marriage reached 30 to 40 years for men and 20 to 30 years for women. See *Al-Wafd*, January 1, 2002, p. 3.

41. For an analysis of the Amr Khaled "phenomenon," see Bayat (2007b: 151–155).

CHAPTER 3

1. For a further account on the conflict, see, for example, International Crisis Group (2000), Trijono (2001), and van Klinken (2001).

2. DDII is a *da'wa* organization established in 1967 by former leaders of Masyumi, Indonesia's first and largest banned Islamic party, as a strategy to deal with various political impasses that had blocked their ambition to reenter the political arena of Indonesia during the early years of Suharto's administration (see Husin 1988).

3. Ikhwan al-Muslimin (The Muslim Brotherhood) is a multinational Sunni Islamist movement and the world's largest, most influential political Islamist group.

Founded by the Sufi schoolteacher Hassan al-Banna in Egypt in 1928, the movement claims that it seeks to instill the Quran and Sunnah as the sole reference point for ordering the life of the Muslim family, individual, community, and state, and ultimately to reestablish a Caliphate or unified Muslim state (see Mitchell 1993: 260–261). Another influential political Islamist group, the Hizb al-Tahrir was established by Taqiy al-Din al-Nabhani in Palestine in 1953 and actively espoused the creation of the *khilafa islamiyya* (Taji-Farouki 1996). Unlike the two movements, the Tablighi Jama'at is originally a nonpolitical Indian Islamic movement that was established by Maulana Muhammad Ilyas al-Kandahlawi in the 1930s and actively encouraged members to conduct *khuruj*, traveling around to advocate *da'wa* causes (Masud 2000).

4. The term *Salafi* generally refers to the reform movement in Egypt introduced by Jamal al-Din al-Afghani (1839–1897), Muhammad 'Abduh (1849–1905), and Muhammad Rashid Rida (1865–1935). Yet, unlike any reformist, modernist Muslim organizations that emerged across the Muslim world, the Salafi *da'wa* campaign is squarely within the puritanical classic Salafi–Wahhabi tradition, marked by its concern with matters of creed and morality, such as strict monotheism, divine attributes, purifying Islam from accretions, and anti-Sufism, and developing the moral integrity of the individual. To a large extent, it can be conceptualized as a form of reconstituted Wahhabism, the official religion of Saudi Arabia. In fact, its proliferation has directly been sponsored by this kingdom. The term *Salafi* has been used as the banner of the movement because of the pejorative connotation of the term *Wahhabi* among many Muslims in the world, thus crucial for political convenience (see Hasan 2007).

5. The Salafi doctrine has one primary concern: to urge a return to the Quran and the Sunna in accordance with the understanding and example set by the *Salafi al-Salih* (pious ancestors) to steer Muslims away from various forms of polytheism (*shirk*), reprehensible innovation (*bid'a*), and superstition (*khurafa*).

6. Despite the fact that the rebellion had targeted the Saudi royal family for its corruption, it reflected a more general backlash against the effects of the oil boom during the 1970s on Saudi society. As a result of the boom, westerners had poured into the Saudi kingdom, threatening the conservative Wahhabi way of life (see Gold 2003: 108).

7. Interview with Abu Nida, Yogyakarta, December 2002.

8. Concerning the al-Haramayn Foundation and the Jam'iyyat Ihya' al-Turath al-Islami, see Benthall and Bellion-Jourdan (2003: 36, 73).

9. The passing of this bill reinforced the existence of the Islamic courts within the Indonesian legal system. Previously, it ranked the second-class court after the public, military, and administrative courts.

10. On the concept of risk society, see Beck (1992).

11. Interviews with Abdul Fatah and Mohammad Sodik, members of the Laskar Jihad from nonuniversity backgrounds, December 2002.

12. See the *Jakarta Post* article (November 7, 2006 by Max Ridwan Sijabat, "Youth Unemployment to Get Worse over Next Decade").

13. For a detailed discussion of this term, see Cook (2001).

14. There is abundant literature on social movement explaining the dynamic of contention (see, for instance, Tarrow [1998]).

CHAPTER 4

1. Pascal Ménoret (2007) used the expression "dangerous classes of globalization."

2. These attacks occurred simultaneously in several places in Casablanca (e.g., restaurant, hotel). They were attributed to kamikazes, belonging to the Salafiyaa Jihadiyya, close to the Qaeda. There were 45 deaths (33 civilians and 12 kamikazes).

3. *Morock* refers to a Franco Moroccan film, produced by Laïla Marrakchi and debuted in 2005, filmed after the attacks of May 16, 2003, in Casablanca. It represents a wealthy youth who attends the French Lycée in Casablanca and transgresses religious prohibitions. On one hand, it recounts a love story between a Muslim young girl and a Jewish adolescent. On the other hand, it suggests the "return of religion" for the heroine's brother, which is a worry for her. This cinematic event provoked an extremely stormy public debate.

4. This is a counterelite that intervenes in the political field by making an ideological reference to Islam.

5. After consultations that began during the early 1990s, the members of the al-Islam wa at-Tawhid (Reform and Uniqueness) movement were integrated by Dr. Khatib, a close associate of the palace, into the Popular Constitutional and Democratic Movement, an empty shell he had been leading since 1967. Following the general elections of 1997, the party was renamed the Justice and Development Party in 1998.

6. The Justice and Development Party won 42 seats in Parliament. Nevertheless, in a spirit of self-limitation, it only presented candidates in some constituencies. In 2007, it became the second force in Parliament.

7. The most important points were raising the age of marriage from 16 to 18 for both men and women, abolition of matrimonial guardianship over a woman and her duty of obedience to her spouse, the possibility of making marriage contracts, the establishment of joint responsibility for the family, a limitation on repudiation and polygamy, the possibility for a woman to ask for a divorce, the care for children being made a prerogative of both parents, and protection for children born out of wedlock (see *Le Matin du Sahara:* 11 October 2003).

8. The National Plan of Action for the Integration of Women into Development, initiated by the feminist movement, was proposed by the Secretary of State for Social Welfare, the Family and the Child of the government under the left-wing leader Abderrahmane Youssoufi.

9. Malika Zeghal recalls that Mohammed V left the domain of education in the hands of both the "modernists" and the *'ulamâ* (Zeghal 2003: 9), but it seems that religious education was totally entrusted to *'ulamâ*. This situation is currently changing. Following the example of the Charfi reform in Tunisia, a reform of the educational system occurred in Morocco in 2000.

10. According to Dale Eickelman and James Piscatori (1996), it is not necessary to have Islamic references, nor even to be a Muslim to be in "Muslim politics."

11. It should be remembered that, according to the analysis of schoolbooks carried out by El Ayadi (2000), the *shari'a* contains, in its essence, the principles of democracy, human rights, and social justice.

12. Al-Qardâoui is a famous Egyptian *'âlim* and former advocate of the Muslim Brothers who has excellent relationships with the monarchies of the Gulf states.

13. The root of the word is *khubz* (bread) means opportunism moved by the quest for bread.

14. Jump (*hregu*) refers to crossing illegal frontiers, in particular using small boats.

CHAPTER 5

1. Previous Grand Mufti of the kingdom and a highly popular figure, he died in 1999.

2. According to a poll published by the website www.camrynet.com and quoted by *Al-Sharq al-Awsat* (December 13, 2003) *"tafhit*, a mortal hobby in Saudi Arabia."

3. The colloquial bedouin verbs *fahhata, hajja,* and *tafasha* denote flight or running. A *mufahhat* is literally a fugitive; *tafhīt* also means the shrilling of skidding tires, as well as the shouting of young children. *Hajwala* is still used as a synonym of confusion, anarchy. A *muhajwil* is a tramp. Young people reverted the term; a *muhajwil* is a tough guy, a street hero.

4. See, for example, "4 Youngsters Burnt Alive after a *Mufahhat*'s Car Collides with Another Car," (*Al-Watan*, March 16, 2006).

5. "The Leaders of the *Tafhit* Dissent Arrested in Riyadh," (*Al-Jazira* April 11, 2006).

6. Tawfîq al-Zâydî, *Al-Jarīma al-murakkaba* (The Composite Crime), documentary movie, al-Ikhbariyya national news TV channel, December 2006.

7. Personnal observation during a conference on *tafhīt*, Riyadh, April 2007.

8. See www.alamal.med.sa/.

9. Anonymous, "Akhīran, al-kitācb al-mamnū': Al-hajwala fī 'ilm al-'arbaja" [At Last, the Forbidden Book: "The *tafhīt* in the Science of Hooliganism], http://maqhaa. com/forums/showthread.php?t=1561.

10. See "A Leader of the *mufahhatīn* Calls His Followers to Avoid Certain Places in All the Kingdom's Provinces," (*Al-Sharq al-Awsat*, November 27, 2005).

11. Rakan, "Al-'arbaja, nash'atuhā wa namūhā" [Hooliganism, Its Genesis and Evolution], January 8, 2004, www.alqasir.net.

12. See "Nahwi tatwīr nizām naql 'amm āmin wa fa"āl fī madīnat al-Riyād" [Toward the Development of a Secure and Fast Public Transportation System in Riyadh], High Comity to the Development of Riyadh, 2000, p. 3.

13. Rakan.

14. The *kasrāt* are songs young people write and sing during their reunions. They probably get this name (derived from the verb *kassara,* to break) because the young people who write them break down the traditional versification. Another explanation is that *kasrāt* singers perform vocal competitions in which they are supposed to retort to one another with wit and eloquence to tear their challenger into pieces.

15. See www.t2bk.com/vb/showthread.php?t=272.

16. The Committee of Defence of the Legitimate Rights is a political association created in Riyadh in 1993 by Islamic intellectuals and activists who demanded political, juridical, and economic reforms in Saudi Arabia. The Committee, closed down by the authorities, was recreated in 1994 by its exiled spokesman, Muhammad al-Mas'ari, in London.

17. Abu Zegem, "Min qiṣaṣ at-tā'ibīn Abū ziqim wa Abū ḥasan" [Stories of the Repented *Mufahhatin* Abu Zegem and Abu/Hasan]. Video bought on a sidewalk of Tâ'if on December 28, 2005.

18. Rakan.

19. Compare with Faris bin Hizam, "Qissat ta'sīs al-Qā'ida fī-1 -Su'ūdiyya" [The Story of the Creation of al-Qaeda in Saudi Arabia], (*Al-Riyadh*, September 27, 2005).

20. See note 17.

21. Pre-Islamic Bedouin warrior and poet, he wrote one of the *mu'allaqât* (6th century AD). His hostility to the sedentary Banu Tamim tribe, which is nowadays one of the pillars of the Saudi modern state, is not the least reason for his popularity among young Bedouins.

22. See www.t2bk.com/vb/showthread.php?t=272.

CHAPTER 6

1. To guarantee my informants' privacy, most of the names used in this article are pseudonyms. Names of prominent religious leaders, however, have not been changed because they are public figures.

2. Worldwide, *Mashalas* are known as *Tablighis*, adherents of the reformist Islamic movement Tabligh Jama'at. Because *Mashala* has a negative connotation and because my informants called themselves *Tablighis*, the latter term will be used in this chapter.

3. A well-known *hadith* (account of what the Prophet Muhammad said or did) reports that the Prophet was displeased with men wearing long garments (Sahih Bukhari, vol. 4, book 56, no. 692, www.usc.edu/dept/MSA/reference/searchhadith.html).

4. Although many of the "traditionalist" Muslims whom I interviewed did not formally affiliate themselves with any Sufi brotherhood, I take them to be part of a Sufi tradition, because they involve themselves in mystical practices and use special litanies of prayer and techniques of invoking God's names as ways of approaching God (see Soares 2005: 37). Most of them have been trained in traditional Quranic schools in which the emphasis is on the recitation of Quranic verses by heart. Knowledge is structured in this system in a hierarchical way, and its dissemination is restricted to a few specialists. The reformist tradition, represented by my interpreter's cousin, calls much of the Sufi tradition into question and seeks to change the way Islam is practised locally. In the reformist tradition, knowledge is theoretically available to everyone, and the individual's intellectual development is no longer associated with divine intervention (Brenner 2000: 7–8; Soares 2005: 9–10).

5. Meeting in Brikama, April 24, 2005.

6. The Gambia has a long-standing history of Islam, which may be explained by its geographical location. The River Gambia is one of Africa's most navigable waterways, and has always provided traders easy access to the country's interior. Trade has been extremely important in introducing Islam and attracting people to it. Propelled by the proliferation of *jihad* during the 19th century, Islamic beliefs spread rapidly in The Gambia. British colonialist policy further enhanced its spread and consolidation. Nowadays, more than 90% of the Gambian population is Muslim.

7. In this chapter I focus on young men using religion to free themselves from the hegemony of the Muslim elders. This does not mean, however, that Islam does not play a role for women, who become part of the Tabligh Jama'at through marriage with a male Tablighi. Earlier it was stated that Ilyas, the founder of the Tabligh Jama'at, encouraged Islamic missionary work also among women. For more information on gender dynamics within the movement, see Janson (2005; 2008; forthcoming).

8. Although the Tabligh Jama'at advocates an apolitical stance for its adherents (Sikand 2003), my field research showed that the religious behavior of Tablighi youth represents a new arena of contestation for power in The Gambia.

9. The Serahuli were propagators of Islam, spreading the religion during their trade missions in West Africa.

10. This designation refers to the adherents of the Saudi reformist movement of Mohammad Ibn 'Abd al-Wahhab, who developed a doctrine that emphasized the oneness of God and condemned all popular forms of piety. *Wahhabiyya* emerged as an identifiable group in West Africa during the 1940s and early '50s within the network of both students and merchants who had contacts with the Middle East (Amselle 1985; Kaba 1974).

11. Al-Falah is a Muslim cultural and religious association that was founded by Al Haji Mahmoud Ba in Dakar in 1956. Despite the weight of French colonial surveillance, Ba managed to establish educational institutes in Senegal, where reformist ideas were taught, modeling them after the schools he himself attended in Saudi Arabia (Brenner 2000: 72–73, 91; Gomez-Perez 1998: 143–144).

12. Unlike the Kuwaiti office of the Revival of Islamic Heritage Society, the offices of this Kuwait–based nongovernmental organization in Pakistan and Afghanistan are officially designated as terrorist organizations (http://wid.ap.org/documents/detainees /fenaitelaldaihani.pdf).

13. Young women are denied access to *Markaz*. They have their own meeting place in a compound close to the mosque, where they gather every Sunday to get instruction in the Islamic principles (Janson 2008: 20–27).

14. This Sufi order was established in Fez, Morocco, during the last decade of the 18th century. It was founded by the Algerian Ahmad al-Tijani. During the mid 19th century, Al Haji Umar Tal disseminated its doctrine in Senegal, where it spread to other West African countries.

15. Nevertheless, Reetz (2006) demonstrates that their ideologies are quite incomparable. Although *Wahhabiyya* is marked by an outspoken anti-Sufi

orientation, the Tabligh Jama'at borrowed from Sufi practices such as *dhikr*, the remembrance of God.

16. This difference in perception between Tablighis and Wahhabis leads to different *da'wa* (call to Islam) methods, see note 32.

17. I did not ask Dukureh's followers how old they were because elderly people normally do not know their exact age. Birth certificates did not exist when they were born, but I took them to be in their late 60s.

18. Although the Tablighis lay claim to the *marabouts'* power, I do not think they want to lay claim to their resources. I heard several stories of *marabouts* who were rewarded with cars and even compounds by their customers. However, wealth is not something the Tablighis aim for. Their lifestyle is characterized by simplicity and austerity, because in their opinion only poverty and hardship can bring them closer to God.

19. Interview in Siffoe, April 20, 2005.

20. A survey conducted in South Africa indicates that middle-age persons are the age group to whom the Jama'at holds the most appeal (Moosa 2000: 212).

21. Interview in Sukuta, March 26, 2006.

22. Interview in Brikama, April 1, 2006.

23. For women's participation in missionary tours, see Janson (2008, forthcoming). For more information on the Tablighi activities in which Gambian youth are involved, see Janson (2005; 2009).

24. Interview in Gunjur, April 12, 2006.

25. Interview in Serrekunda, May 7, 2006.

26. During my field research I came across a great number of ghettos with sometimes very creative (English) names, indicating the activities they are engaged in and the ways the members see themselves. To name just a few: *L. A. Ghetto, Outlaw Ghetto, One Love Ghetto, Arsenal Ghetto, Rasta Crew Ghetto,* and *Ganja Ghetto (ganja* is the local term for marijuana).

27. Interview in Brikama, May 9, 2006.

28. The demonstrations went ahead despite a refusal by the authorities to grant the Gambian Students Union a permit, and became violent when the security forces used excessive force to break it up. At least 14 youth were killed (Amnesty International 2001).

29. The desire of leaving the country for Europe or the United States is so strong among numerous youth that there is a special word for it in Gambian slang: "having nerves." Out of frustration with visa rejections, some start to drink or, more often, use drugs, and I have seen quite a number of youth contending with serious psychological problems because of this. When my research assistant consulted a doctor because of a stomachache, the first thing she asked him was whether he "had nerves."

30. Interview in Gunjur, April 16, 2005.

31. Interview in Banjul, March 29, 2006. For Ahmed's full conversion story, see Janson (2009).

32. According to my informants, Wahhabis use a more direct *da'wa* method, which explains why they are less successful in "converting" youth to their ideology.

A Tablighi student expressed it as follows: "Unlike Wahhabis, Tablighis don't condemn or attack people. One may compare the difference in their ways of doing *da'wa* with doctors' different ways of approaching a patient. A doctor shouldn't tell his patient plainly: 'You are ill and going to die.' Instead, he must say: 'Take your medicine and you will recover.' *Tabligh* is like that; the softer the approach, the better the results. Tablighi preachers don't tell the youth bluntly to stop smoking *ganja* (marijuana). Instead, they try to be role models in the hope that the youth realize that smoking is not good and get out of their bad habits. *Tabligh* is our medicine; it's the only thing that can cure."

33. Interview in Siffoe, April 20, 2005.

34. Interview in Brikama, May 20, 2005.

CHAPTER 7

1. The population of the 1967 occupied Palestinian territories reached 3,761,646 inhabitants divided into two major areas: the West Bank with 2,345,107 and the Gaza Strip with 1,416,539. A total of 48.8% of the population is younger than 15 years of age. The percentage of persons 10 years and older who use the Internet is 49.5%.

2. In July 2006, BZU ranked "third . . . among all universities" (http://www.birzeit.edu/news/16627/news) in the Arab countries according to a webo-metric ranking, and ranked 1,781 among the top 5,000 universities in the world (www.webometrics.info/top3000.asp-offset=1750.htm and http://www.birzeit.edu/news/16627/news). BZU is the first Arab university and the "third university among universities in the Arab world" (http://www.birzeit.edu/news/16627/news./http www webometrics info top3000 asp offset 1750 htm) in the realm of "web publications and in its commitment to open access to knowledge. The American University in Beirut (AUB) came first with the rank of 1325 followed by the American university in Cairo (AUC) with the rank of 1518." (http://www.birzeit.edu/news/16627/news)

3. See articles by BZU's first webmaster Nigel Parry at www.birzeit.edu/web also.

4. The Cisco Networking Academy Program is a partnership between Cisco Systems and education, business, government, and community organizations around the world. The Networking Academy curriculum centers on teaching students to design, build, and maintain computer networks.

5. www.birzeit.edu/news/news-d?news_id=5328.

6. First launched in February 1999, by students in partnership with BZU's computer center.

7. This includes the Dheisha refugee camp in the West Bank and the Khan Yunis camp in the Gaza Strip (www.palestinian-rights.org/projects/media.html).

8. See www.mohe.gov.ps/Factsfgrs.html.

9. Data taken from an internal memo circulated by Maan Bseiso of PalNet CHECKCommunications Ltd., via Palestinaian Information Technology Association (PITA), on September 16, 2002.

10. See www.pcbs.gov.ps/DesktopDefault.aspx?tabID=3951&;lang=en.

11. For a 2003 report on Israeli high technology and investment, see www.ishitech.co.il/0403ar5.htm and www.export.gov.il/Eng.

12. These figures are from the most recent household survey on ICT, which was released in August 2006 (www.pcbs.gov.ps/Portals/_pcbs/PressRelease/CommTeco6e.pdf).

13. See, for example, the initiative for Palestinian youth managed by UNICEF (www.unicef.org/voy/discussions/member.php?u=4730).

14. See www.infoyouth.org and www.pngo.net.

15. See www.palestinian-rights.org/projects/media.html.

16. See www.it4youth.org and www.nextbillion.net/archive/activitycapsule/2583.

17. Seewww.enlighten-palestine.org/pdf/information_pack.pdf.

18. See www.pyalara.org.

19. Contributors include Glenn Kalnasy, Cord Aid, TAMKEEN, the Canadian Representatives Office, Brains Unlimited, UNICEF, the European Commission, Ragdoll Ltd., Dalhousie University, P.G. MEYER VIOL, Willy Brant Center, Save the Children-UK, the Heinrich Böll Foundation, and others. To support and perhaps influence the way in which the Palestinian ICT sector and policy are evolving, numerous international donors, NGOs, and governments have been cooperating with the various sectors pertinent to ICT among Palestinians.

20. See Ministry of Youth, www.wafa.ps.

21. See www.pyalara.org.

22. See www.shabab.ps.

CHAPTER 8

1. According to Assaad and Barsoum (2007), from the British mandate period to the present, unemployment has been "primarily a problem of educated youth." But the problem has become more pronounced during the past decade. They note: "Youth with a secondary education or above made up 95 percent of youth unemployment in 2006, up from 87 percent in 1998. . . . In fact, university graduates are the only educational group whose unemployment rates increased since 1998" (Assaad and Barsoum 2007: 19).

2. I first came across the phrase *a transition to nowhere* by International Institute of Social Studies (ISS) PhD student Rekopantswe Mate in her research design paper (2009).

3. For accounts of the everyday practices in Egyptian schools and ethnographic descriptions of some of the abuses and struggles that take place in classrooms, see Herrera and Torres (2006).

4. A nationwide survey of 6,006 households in Egypt found that children in 64% of urban households and 54% of rural homes attending both public and private schools take private lessons (Egypt Human Development Report 2005: 55–56). Egyptians spend the equivalent of 1.6% of the gross domestic product (LE4.81 million) on private tutoring at the preuniversity level (World Bank 2002: 26). See Mark Bray (2009) for a comprehensive analysis of the effects of private tutoring on education systems worldwide.

5. In his work on middle class Indian men, Nisbett (2007) calls this phenomenon of the ways young men use escapist means to pass their time as "timepass."

6. Adel Iman is a celebrated Egyptian comedian who starred in the enormously popular comedy *Terrorism and Kebab*, directed by Sherif Arafa in 1993. The film is a hilarious satire of the frustrations of an everyday Egyptian man who takes the *Mugama*, the symbol of state bureaucracy, hostage, only to demand kebab for everyone.

7. By *generational location* I refer to Karl Mannheim's seminal essay on generations. He writes: "Individuals who belong to the same generation, who share the same year of birth, are endowed, to that extent, with a common location in the historical dimension of the social process" (Mannheim 1952: 105).

8. For detailed country-specific and regionwide statistics on Internet users worldwide, see Internet World Stats at www.internetworldstats.com/stats5.htm 2009)

9. Some youth use their newly acquired consciousness and daring that the Internet seems to have provided to get involved in organized movements for democratic and economic reform. The Egyptian Movement for Change, more popularly referred to as *Kifaya* (Enough), formed in 2004 with a prodemocracy, antiregime platform. It carried out rare and daring anti-Mubarak demonstrations during which slogans such as "No to extension [of Mubarak's presidency]; No to hereditary succession" were chanted (see http://weekly.ahram.org.eg/2005/759/eg8.htm). *Kifaya* attempted to build a national opposition coalition based on a platform of action for mass civil disobedience. Although it has lost momentum since 2007 for a number of reasons, not the least being a state crackdown on it, *Kifaya* provided an important example that confronting the regime head-on is possible.

10. At the time these interviews were conduced in 2006, there were some high-profile cases of Egyptian bloggers who suffered arrest and persecution for publicizing unsavory opinions about the government and Islam (Sandals 2008). Since then, Internet users have increased by the millions, and the social networking website Facebook was used for an act of mass civil disobedience in support of the April 6, 2008, strike of textile workers in Mahala al-Kubra (Benin and el-Hamalawy 2007). The two 20-something masterminds of this action—Israa Abel-Fattah (dubbed the president of the "Facebook Republic") and Ahmed Maher—were both arrested and jailed. Israa's Facebook activism abruptly came to an end after being released from an ordeal of 18 days in jail. Ahmed, who has by now had a few encounters with state security, including hours of vicious beating by the police until he disclosed his Facebook password, remains committed to continuing a Facebook-facilitated political movement (El-Sayed 2008).

CHAPTER 10

1. I have changed the names of some people who are in my book to protect their privacy.

2. Also, see the population demographic pamphlet titled *New York* by the Arab American Institute (2003), which estimates a population of 405,000 Arab Americans

in New York with 29%, or 117,450 people, living in Brooklyn. www.aaiusa.org/page/file/6a268f88611a0ed6f2_yzemvy7hy.pdf/NYdemographics.pdf.

3. Also see de la Cruz and Brittingham (2005: 19). The median age of 30.8 is derived by factoring in Arab Americans with mixed ancestries with Arab Americans generally. Arab Americans alone, according to the 2000 Census, have a median age of 33.1 years.

4. See CBS News/Associated Press. (June 18, 2003, "Bush Orders Racial Profiling Ban, Critics Worry Loopholes Will Still Allow Profiling of Some Groups").

5. See USA Today article (August 10, 2006 by Marilyn Elias, "USA's Muslims under a Cloud.").

6. I have encountered this repeatedly in my study. See also Muslims Weekly (2004).

7. This usually requires a command of English and Arabic, with an ability to narrate stories with an intellectual and emotional content, and with some sense of humor. In certain ways, the style suggests to me a preaching format reminiscent of the Egyptian lay preacher Amr Khaled and American evangelical Christians.

8. See www.almaghrib.org/aboutus.php#Page_1.

9. See www.almaghrib.org/curriculum.php.

CHAPTER II

1. About 10 million Muslims live in western Europe, half of them in France, with the majority of North African origin.

2. The term laïc (from which laïcité is derived) originates from the Greek word, laikos, which means, according to the Petit Larousse (2003: 581), "which belongs to the people" and "which does not belong to the clergy." In the field of schooling, laïcité refers to a mode of organization that aims to administer schools in a "neutral" and "nonpartisan" way with regard to denominational or communitarian affiliations, avoiding reference to any judgments in relation to faith-based knowledge claims.

3. The secular humanist traditions associated with laïcité were also revoked during the Vichy government during the interlude of the occupation, and religious instruction in public schools was reinstituted (Wykes 1967: 224).

4. These are the lois Marie (1951), Barangé (1951), Debré (1959), and Guermeur (1977) (see Poucet 2001).

5. The reference here is to the loi Debré (loi no. 59-1557 from December 31, 1959). Two major types of "contracts" are defined under this law (and its subsequent amendments introduced since the early 1970s): "simple" (for elementary schools) or "by association," mainly for postelementary schools. The law establishes "reciprocal" principles that regulate the relations between private schools and the state (see Poucet 2001).

6. About 17% of the French school population studies in private educational institutions, a total of more than two million students enrolled in about 10,000 private educational institutions (Catholic schools are the majority), 26,000 in Jewish schools,

2,500 in Protestant schools, and 1,000 in Muslim schools (www.education.gouv.fr/systeme_educatif/enseignement_prive.htm).

7. The *Commission de réflexion sur l'application du principe de laïcité dans la République* was appointed in July 2003 and submitted its recommendations regarding the principles underpinning the application of *laïcité* in December. Its recommendations led to the enactment of law 2004–228 of March 15, 2004, which regulates the display of religious symbols in public schools (www.senat.fr/dossierleg/pj103–209.html).

8. The Académie de Bordeaux covers the region of Aquitaine (southwest France), with a total population of about three million inhabitants. Its jurisdiction extends over the *départements* (districts) of Dordogne, Gironde, Landes, Lot-et-Garonne, and Pyrénées-Atlantiques.

9. See the article in *Le Monde* by Sylvie Chayette (December 18, 2006, "A l'attaque de la carte scolaire!").

10. See the article in *Le Monde* (September 17, 2006 by Nicola Sarkozy, "La carte scolaire est devenue l'instrument de la ségrégation sociale").

11. See the article in *Le Monde* (September 6, 2006 by Martine and Catherine Rollot, "Haro sur la 'carte scolaire,' mais sans alternative").

12. Cited in Fadéla Amara's article, "La carte scolaire, une hypocrisie" in *Libération* (Septermber 7, 2006 http://www.liberation.fr/tribune/010159616-la-carte-scolaire-une-hypocrisie) The French text reads: "*une libéralisation sauvage du système, avec pour conséquence un enseignement à deux vitesses.*" Following the 2007 presidential elections, Amara, a self-identifying leftist activist, joined Sarkozy's government, headed by François Fillon, as Secretary of State in Charge of Urban Policies.

13. This school signed a "contract" with the state in 2008, thus becoming a state-"assisted" private Muslim school.

14. Created in 1981, ZEPs refer to socioeconomically disadvantaged areas in which schools are provided with additional resources. In 2003, one fifth of all school students in France studied in educational institutions located within ZEP areas (www.association-ozp.net/article.php3?id_article=2672).

15. Reportedly, two additional Muslim schools are under consideration at Vitry-sur-Seine and Marseille.

16. Founded in 1983, the UOIF is depicted by some media outlets as a "radical" Islamist platform that seeks to act as a dominant voice on the *Conseil français du culte musulman*. The latter was created in 2003, among others following the involvement of Nicolas Sarkozy, then Minister of the Interior, "to give the French state a Muslim counterpart for practical discussions of policy" (Bowen 2007b: 48).

17. The original French text reads: "*former des cadres de référence musulmane, avec une triple culture: française, arabe et musulmane.*" See the article in *Le Figaro* (August 29, 2006 by Cécila Gabizon, "Incertitudes sur l'ouverture du collège-lycée al-Kindi.")

18. *Le Collectif des Jeunes Musulmans de France*, initially founded in 1992, took its current name as *Le Collectif des Musulmans de France* (CMF) in 2002. The CMF charter states that the Collectif "attempts to struggle against all extremisms, and to bring

together Muslim citizens and public authorities and society in general" (see Charte du CMF, www.lecmf.fr).

CHAPTER 12

1. I rely, here, mostly on the work of Saba Mahmood (2005), who has theorized on the emerging forms of piety within female mosque movements in Egypt. Her approach is particularly challenging because she critically engages with (liberal) feminist thought, and more generally with some of the founding principles of political modernity, especially individual autonomy. Mahmood's notion of piety as observed in the mosque movement in Egypt most notably contains the self-willed obedience to certain religious conventions anchored in a constant cultivation of virtues and practices.

2. I conducted my fieldwork between 2000 and 2001 and in autumn/spring 2006/2007 with women who were part of a Muslim organization either as "simple" members and users or who held leading positions as teachers or as representatives of the administrative body within female sections of the organization. The examples provided for Germany are taken from the *Islamische Gemeinschaft Milli Görüs*, the *Verein der Islamischen Kulturzentren*, and *Anstalt für Religion e.V./Diyanet Isleri Türk Islam Birligi*. The young women in France were predominantly part of the *Institut Musulman Français*, a center for Islamic instructions, located in Marseille and/or engaged in the *Jeunes Musulmans de France*.

3. I use the concept of the secular here not primarily in terms of a separation between political and religious spheres but rather as conceptualized by Talal Asad (2003) as a practice that regulates religious sensibilities in public realm.

4. In France a law prohibiting "ostentatious" religious symbols in sate schools was adopted in 2004 after a long process of public discussions and knowledge gathering in the so-called *Commission Stasi* (2003). In Germany, several federal departments gradually adopted laws legitimizing the ban of covered teachers from state schools after the decision of the Constitutional Court in 2003, which, although relying on the principle of religious freedom, opened the path for distinctive laws by the federal departments.

5. It goes without saying that this kind of discourse reproduces an inherent contradiction. Although articulating the attempt to overcome the dichotomy between body and mind by hiding the female body and thereby getting closer to the mind, which is implicitly associated with the other sex, the women, in fact, reinforce these boundaries by following dress codes that are exclusively attributed to the feminine sphere: The headscarf incorporates the taboo of displaying femininity, whereas it is itself a strong expression of femininity. On the other hand, the attempt to "return" to the noblest dimension of the person, the mind, by hiding markers of one's sexuality, presupposes the existence of a certain essence "responsible for the reproduction and naturalisation of the category of sex itself" (Butler 1990: 20).

6. In 2005, a local court in Hamburg, for example, rejected the demand by a nine-year-old schoolgirl to abstain from swimming lessons (http://fhh.hamburg.de/stadt/Aktuell/justiz/gerichte/oberverwaltungsgericht/aktuelles/presseerklaerungen/pressearchiv-2005/pressemeldung-2005–06–16-ovg-01.html).

CHAPTER 13

1. According to Year Census Book (*Salnameh Amari*), Markaz Amar Iran.*1375/1996 A*. 552,000 students graduated from high schools in 1996 (including those who got diplomas or preuniversity certificates) whereas admission to BA and college-level programs at all higher education centers was limited to 170,000, regardless of their age.

2. See interviews with Moghadam (2006) and Pour Mohamadi(2007) for the different approaches to mandatory veiling.

3. There were also other important efforts to indoctrinate the ethical Islamic vision, including the education system, state-owned radio and television, and war-related cinema known as "Holy Defense Cinema."

4. According to *Etelaat newspaper (Bahman, 11 1360/February 1 1981)*, in 800 cases followed by the *Mobarezeh ba Monkarat* court in January 1981, 629 person were released, 24 were prisoned, 390 were lashed and some were sent to work in special workshops for criminals.

5. For this interview see (*Keyhan* 1360, 12 Azar /1981, December 12: 4. "Goft-e-go ba reeis-e dadgah Mokerat" [Interview with the supreme judge of Mokarat court])

6. As cited in *Etelaat* 1358,15 Farvardin/ 1979, April 4, Khomeini, Roohollah, Farman-e tashkil-e daereh mobarezeh ba monkerat [Order to form mobarezeh in mokerat court]).

7. See *Etelaat* 1358, Ordibehesht 3/1979, April 23, Qotbzadeh, Sadegh. Mosahebeh ba Qotbzadeh [Interview with Qotbzadeh]).

CHAPTER 14

1. The great majority of Dogondoutchi residents are Mawri, a local subgroup of the larger Hausa ethnolinguistic entity.

2. The official name of the reformist Muslim association is the *Jama'atu Izalat al-Bid'a wa Iqamat al-Sunna*.

3. Aside from encouraging personal mystical experiences, Sufis approve the use of amulets and the performance of certain rituals (such as the celebration of the Prophet's birthday), and promote, along with the veneration of saintly figures, the redistributive ethos around which much of everyday life is ordered in Nigérien communities. Izala followers reject these practices as innovations (*bidea*) that have no place in Islam.

4. By focusing on Izala as a counterdiscourse to mainstream Sufism, I do not mean to say that these are the only two alternatives for Nigériens in search of a Muslim identity. Nor do I imply that there is a clear opposition between *'yan* Izala and

so-called *'yan darika*. In Dogondoutchi specifically, a novel form of Sufism has emerged, running officially counter to both Izala reformism and the orientation of those Muslims who oppose Izala. Because it borrows both from conventional Sufi performances of piety and Izala's concern with frugality and asceticism, the newly founded Awaliyya acts as a destabilizing category, undermining the distinctiveness of other Muslim orientations (Masquelier 2009b). In Niger (and Nigeria), the emergence of divergent Muslim perspectives has resulted in the proliferation of Islamic organizations (see Charlick 2004; Glew 1996; Laitin 1982; Umar 2001).

5. The two major Sufi orders in Niger are the Tijaniyya and the Qadiriyya. Although the Tijaniyya counts more members than the Qadiriyya, many of the wealthiest merchants in Niger belong to the Qadiriyya.

6. In addition to Muslim reformists and those Muslims who oppose Izala, Meunier (1998) presents a third category, the "rationalists," composed of mainly French-educated Muslims who consider Islam a personal religion and insist that religion should remain separate from politics. In documenting the diversity of religious orientations among Muslims in Niger, we must avoid privileging formalist definitions of religious engagement, but instead attend to the diverse, sometimes informal, and often contradictory ways in which Nigériens define their Muslim identities.

7. Marriage marks the transition to adulthood. Only married men and women can be truly considered adults.

8. The role of media in the dissemination of models of religious reform and counterreform, and in the contestation of religious authority has been amply documented elsewhere (see Eickelman and Anderson 1999; Hirschkind 2006; Meyer and Moors 2006).

9. Not all parents show leniency to their children when it comes to the performance of religious duties, however. Members of Izala are anxious to foster a strong sense of piety among their progeny. They insist that their children engage in regular acts of worship.

10. In my experience, Muslims frequently move in and out of formal, as well as informal, religious groups. They may well shift alliances because of the popularity of a preacher or a life crisis that forces them to reconsider the form that religious participation should take (Masquelier 2009b).

11. During the early 1990s, where one should pray was a burning issue, forcefully demonstrated in 1992 when a violent dispute erupted between Izala members and their Muslim opponents over the ownership of Dogondoutchi's *grande mosquée*, the site of Friday prayers (Masquelier 1999). Because the mosque is the most visible symbol of a Muslim community, its control has important implications for the formation of the religious landscape and the fashioning of religious identities.

12. Note that it is often difficult to identify clearly the factors that promote political participation, especially among youths. During the 2004 campaign, candidates, hoping to gain votes, courted youth with gifts of tea, sugar, and radio cassette players. Young men told me that they voted for a particular candidate because,

thanks to the gift of a boom box or cash for a thatched shelter, they thought this individual was particularly sensitive to their predicament.

CHAPTER 15

1. There is an expanding body of literature on youth in contemporary Africa relevant to this discussion (see, for example, Abbink 2005; Argenti 2002; Diouf 2003; Hansen 2008; Weiss 2005). On the current neoliberal era in Africa, see Ferguson (2006), Otayek and Soares (2007), and LeBlanc and Soares (2008).

2. On Mali's student movement in the early to mid 1990s, see Smith (1997).

3. See the statistics from UNICEF (www.unicef.org/infobycountry/ mali_statistics.html#46).

4. Although such popular culture in Mali has not received much scholarly attention, see the Malian youth magazine *Grin-Grin*. See also the appeal of rap music and culture in neighboring Senegal (Niang 2006) and Niger (Masquelier 2007).

5. On Chérif Haïdara, his career, and organization Ançar Dine, see Soares (2004, 2005, 2006), on which this section draws (cf. Schulz 2006).

6. On similar modernist Islamic organizations in Côte d'Ivoire, see LeBlanc (2006).

7. However, after September 11, 2001, there have been attempts to identify presumed Islamists and radicals in Mali, as elsewhere (Soares 2006).

8. On these "traditional" and modern forms of Islamic education in Mali, see Brenner (2000).

9. Such elements of style may have also come from the presence of small numbers of the Muslim Baye Fall, a subgroup of the Mourides, a Senegalese Sufi order. On the Baye Fall, see Roberts and Roberts (2003) and Pezeril (2008). On the Mourides, see Diouf (2000; cf. Soares 2007a).

10. I have analyzed some of these pamphlets elsewhere (Soares 2007b).

11. The Web site was defunct for several years, but it has been recently revived and is much more sophisticated. See http://soufibilal.org.

12. This is reminiscent of Ibrahim Niasse and his method of *tarbiyya* (spiritual training) in the Tijaniyya (Seesemann and Soares 2009; Seesemann 2010).

CHAPTER 16

1. According to the 2000 census data, out of a total population of 67,803,927, the median age in Turkish society is 24.83 years. That is, half the population is younger and half the population is older than this age (see *Turkey's Statistical Year Book 2004*, p. 37, www.die.gov.tr/yillik/03-Nü;fus.pdf).

2. The ways in which a group of the young intellectuals who became known as *Muslim intellectuals* during the 1980s and particularly during the first half of the 1990s, how they set the stage both for fellow intellectuals and Muslim youth in Turkey, and the characteristics of their works, as well as their socioeconomic and cultural backgrounds, were discussed extensively by Michael Meeker (1991, 1994). Meeker

focuses only on male Muslim intellectuals and hence omits the importance of their female counterparts. For a different account, see Ayşe Saktanber (2002b: 261–262).

3. This survey was conducted in 11 provinces of the country in 1998. Its sample size was set at 2,200 and was distributed among selected provinces according to population size. These provinces were also clustered on the basis of a series of economic, social, and cultural variables. Consequently, in addition to the three largest metropolitan areas—Istanbul, Ankara, and Izmir—two provinces were selected from each of four clusters. These were Denizli and Trabzon, Sivas and Diyarbakır, Antalya and Edirne, and Gaziantep and Tokat. Among these 2,200 respondents, 48.9% were female, 51.1 male, 75% single, 20.2% married, and 4.5% engaged. About 51.3% of all the respondents were in the age group of 15 to 20, and 48.7% of them were between the ages of 21 to 27. The survey used face-to-face interviews of respondents in their home environments, in addition to some focus group discussions conducted in Istanbul. For further information about how this survey was carried out and, in particular, the details on the basis of which economic, social, and cultural variables the clusters were selected, see Konrad Adanauer Foundation (1999: 2–4).

4. Regarding Karl Mannheim's arguments on the role of traumatic events in creating generational consciousness, June Edmunds and Bryan S. Turner (2005) argue that political generations identify themselves in terms of historical and cultural traumas, which are created and recreated through a variety of social processes by members of national, social, or global groups (see also Mannheim 1997).

5. Turkish novelist Elif Safak is a graduate of METU, where she received her PhD in political science. She signs her name as Shafak in this novel, which was originally written in English and published in the United States. This novel is published in Turkish under the name of *Araf* (Safak 2004).

6. For more on Islamist fashion shows, see Yael Navaro-Yashin (2002). For more on newly emerging restaurants, coffee houses, tea gardens, and summer resorts that basically cater to religious people, particularly in Istanbul, see Christopher Houston (2002), Alev Çınar (2005), and Mücahit Bilici (2000).

7. For example, Nilüfer Göle is one of those who evaluates this novel as an autobiographical account. Göle also sees this novel as an indication of the prevalence of multiple modernities through which changing Muslim subjectivities are usually evaluated as an outcome of a mutually productive relationship between Islam and modernity, placing the following question into the core of her arguments: How do Muslims situate themselves vis-à-vis modernity? However, here, as a subtext, she also assumes that, in epistemological terms, Muslims actually experience an entirely different life-world than westernized secular people. Nevertheless, within the framework of this specific novel, Göle traces such a relation of compatibility between Islam and modernity within the resistant attitude of young Islamists towards the deindividualizing effects of Islamist political ideology when they come to terms with love and intimacy, with which the I agree (Göle 2000: 103–108).

8. Izniki's ancient book of manners was anonymously called the "book of manners with a lance" among the people of Anatolia, for it is believed that there was a

figure of a lance on the cover of the original book. For a contemporary Turkish version of this book, see Kara (1989).

9. *Conversations Across the Bosphorus,* is a film by Jeanne C. Finley, in collaboration with Mine V. Ternar, Gökcen Hava Art, and Pelin Esmer (1995).

10. See, for example, a highly sensible discussion about how Muslim students have navigated their own and others' sense of them at a college campus in northern California, dealing with being seen as potential threat and with negative stereotypes about Islam, such as "Muslim terrorist" or "oppressed woman" (Nasır and Al-Amin 2006).

CHAPTER 17

1. The generation gap includes items such as youth self-identification, lifestyle, life expectancy, different visions toward history, collective action, familial relationships, politics, religion, and many others (Ministry of Islamic Guidance 2001, 2003).

2. Information obtained in interviews with Iranian women by author in 2005 through 2006; all translations are by author. See also Miriam Cooke (2001: xi).

3. In June 2007, the Ministry of Internal Affairs of Mahmoud Ahmadinejad's government declared that this kind of marriage must be strongly encouraged

4. However, it is very surprising that despite the huge advertising of Fatima, none of the religious interviewees in my research mentioned Fatima as their role model.

5. Camron Michael Amin (2002) similarly argues that Reza Shah's unveiling was an attempt to remove the supervision of women from the men in their family and to transfer that supervision to the men of the state.

CHAPTER 18

1. See *The Sun* article (June 29, 2006) by Grant Rollings, "The Jihad Rap."

2. The term *BrAsian* "refuses the easy decomposition of the British and Asian dyad into its western and nonwestern constituents. BrAsian is not merely a conflation of the British and the Asian, it is not a fusion but is a confusion of the possibility of both terms" (Sayyid 2005: 7).

3. The clear reference here is to the traditional U.S. folk song, "She'll Be Coming 'Round the Mountain." Interestingly, some claim that the "she" in question is Mother Jones, coming around the mountain to organize the miners.

4. African-American slang for "authentic" blacks.

5. The (standard) account of this phenomenon, exemplary for an analysis that is as attentive to the political as it is to the cultural dimensions, is *DisOrienting Rhythms* (Sharma et al. 1996).

6. See the *New York Times* article (October 22, 2006 by Alan Cowell, "For Multiculturalist Britain, Uncomfortable New Clothes").

7. It should be noted that Aki has made it clear in interviews that he doesn't support any kind of terrorism, including state terrorism (Damien 2006).

8. The interview, conducted by Taysir Alluni, was broadcast on January 31, 2002. It can be found online at archives.cnn.com/2002/WORLD/asiapcf/south/02/05/binladen.transcript/ and in Lawrence (2005: 117–118).

9. Mohamed M. Ali et al. (2003), in *Population Studies,* estimated that between 400,000 and 500,000 Iraqi children younger than the age of five years died from 1991 to 1998, during the United Nations (UN) sanctions regime. A UNICEF survey, issued in August 1999, estimated half a million deaths of children younger than five during the same period (UNICEF 1999). The U.S. Ambassador to the UN, Madeleine Albright's response when asked about the UNICEF figures by Leslie Stahl, responded, "We think the price is worth it."

10. I quote the translation of bin Laden's words as provided on Fun^Da^Mental's website (www.fun-da-mental.co.uk/), which are substantially the same as those on cnn.com (see note 7). The translation in Lawrence (2005: 117–118) reads as follows: "Who said that our children and civilians are not innocents, and that the shedding of their blood is permissible? Whenever we kill their civilians, the whole world yells at us from east to west, and America starts putting pressure on its allies and puppets. Who said that our blood isn't blood and that their blood is blood? More than 1,000,000 children died in Iraq, and they are still dying. . . . How is it that these people are moved when civilians die in America, and not when we are being killed every day? Every day in Palestine, children are killed. . . . We kill the kings of disbelief and the kings of the Crusaders and the civilian among the disbelievers, in response to the amount of our sons they kill: this is correct in both religion and logic."

11. See *The Times* (London) article (August 4, 2006), by Stephen Dalton, "Angry in the UK."

12. Bruce Lawrence (2005: xxiii), in his introduction to *Messages to the World,* also compares bin Laden to Che. "If captured alive he will doubtless be killed on the spot, as Che Guevara was forty years ago. . . . His posthumous legend will live, like that of Guevara, to inspire other such knights, until such time as different, more humane heroes can attract the idealism of Muslim youth."

13. Mental's website does not provide translations of the two songs from *All Is War* that are sung in Zulu.

14. According to a study by University of New Hampshire Professor Marc Herold, 3,800 Afghan civilian died between October 7 and December 7, 2001, during the course of the U.S.-led occupation (BBC News 2002).

15. Not only did the U.S. and western European powers stand by as these massacres were taking place, but it now appears that the United States, the UN, and NATO may have been complicit in permitting Serb forces to occupy Srebrenica (as well as Gorazde and Zepa), and hence complicit in the massacres, and that ever since they have been covering up their complicity (Perlman 2008).

16. See Joan Scott's (2007) very important discussion of these issues in the French context, in her *The Politics of the Veil,* especially chapter 5.

CHAPTER 19

1. Centraal Bureau voor de Statistiek (Dutch Central Bureau for Statistics), Voorburg/Heerlen, (www.cbs.nl).

2. Integration Map 2005 (www.cbs.nl, pdf).

3. It is estimated that 40% to 50% of the Dutch Moroccan community speak a Berber language (Chafik 2004: 129).

4. *Halal* and *haram* are Arab Islamic terms referring to things that are permissible (*halal*) and forbidden (*haram*). *Halal* often refers to meat coming from animals slaughtered according to Islamic regulations.

5. www.cbs.nl.

6. Henna is a coloring product used in northern Africa but also in African and Indian cultures to adorn the body, usually the hands and feet.

7. The author translated the interview fragments from Dutch to English, summer 2004.

8. The movie *Scarface*, directed by Brian de Palma and written by Oliver Stone (1983), has inspired more rappers. The song "Kogel vangen voor je mattie" ("Catching a Bullet for Your Homie") by the Tuindorp Hustler Click (Tuindorp is a district in northern Amsterdam) includes several samples of scenes from the movie *Scarface*. Other maroc-hop songs and rap songs from other genres feature references to this movie as well.

9. Dutch Somali politician Ayaan Hirsi Ali used to be a left-wing politican, but in 2002 she made a controversial shift to right-wing party VVD. Together with Fortuyn, she dominated much of the political debate on Islam in the Netherlands from 2002 to 2006. Her views on Islam, and especially Dutch Muslims, were highly critical. Although she claimed that her political aim was to emancipate Muslim women in the Netherlands, she was not liked by Dutch Muslims, who, most of the time, disapproved of the way in which she wanted to "help" Muslim women. Dutch Muslims were suspicious of her ever since it became clear that Hirsi Ali had forsworn her religion (i.e., Islam). She was thus not a Muslim herself anymore. After she had insinuated in an interview with the Dutch newspaper *Trouw* that the Prophet Muhammad was a pedophile, describing him as "a pervert" in January 2003 (Douwes et al. 2005: 150), she lost all her credibility among Dutch Muslims. Her cooperation with Theo van Gogh in 2004 resulted in the production of a controversial film about abuse of Muslim women called *Submission,* which only added to her bad reputation among Dutch Muslims (Moors 2005: 8–9). This controversial film showed naked women dressed in see-through *burqas* with Quranic writings on their bodies. It was meant to make public how women in Islamic communities are oppressed and abused, linking Islam and Muslim men with aggressive and inhumane behavior.

10. The song "Couscous" was released in 2003.

11. Dutch news program *NOVA* aired reports on the "Hirsi Ali Diss" on June 29, 2004, and July 5, 2004.

12. Interview fragment from Dutch to English translated by the author in July 2004.

CHAPTER 20

1. Anthony Giddens (1990: 21) subsumes this process under the term *disembedding,* which he defines as "the 'lifting out' of social relations from local contexts and their restructuring across indefinite spans of time–space."

2. This paragraph was originally published in Turkish (English translation: Pierre Hecker).

3. To the present day, Beyoğlu houses the British, Swedish, French, German, and Russian consulates as well as Istanbul's French and German high schools (*Galatasaray Lisesi, Özel Alman Lisesi*).

4. Today's meaning of *meyhane* can hardly be compared with the meaning of *meyhane* in Ottoman times. In present-day Turkey, *meyhane* has a wider meaning in the sense of restaurant or bar serving all kinds of alcoholic beverages and food. The traditional *meyhane* generally did not serve food.

5. Uğur Kömeçoğlu (2004: 158), in a recent study on Islamic cafés in Istanbul, also pointed toward the phenomenon of adopting the term *café* rather than *kahvehave* in order give the place a modern touch.

6. The bridge connected the Karaköy Square in the north with the Ragıp Gümüşpala Caddesi in the south (a main road surrounded by the Egyptian Bazaar, the Mısır Çarşı, and the New Mosque, the Yeni Cami). The old bridge was replaced by a new one in 1994; its remains were moved upstream and relocated to an area between the districts of Balat and Hasköy. Even though the bridge is inoperative still, it, meanwhile, hosts the annual Istanbul Design Week, which offers an international platform for all sorts of artistic design (fashion, architectural, graphic, and so forth).

7. The interview with Seyda Babaoğlu was held in Istanbul November 28, 2003. Originally conducted in German, I later translated it into English.

8. The interview with Özer Sarısakal was originally conducted in Turkish in Istanbul on June 14, 2004 (English translation by the author).

9. Personal interview with Zeki Ateş conducted in Istanbul on December 12, 2003 (translated by me from Turkish to English).

10. The term *tape trading* stands for the nonmonetary exchange of demo tapes among bands, independent labels, and distributors. Turkish record labels specializing in metal music, such as Istanbul's *Hammer Müzik,* still apply this strategy to distribute their recordings and get (cheap) access to the outputs of foreign labels. This, however, happens on a small scale.

11. *Laneth* was one of Turkey's first metal fanzines sold in a number of local shops around Turkey. It started as a do-it-yourself project that required only a small budget.

12. Personal interview conducted in Istanbul in August 2004.

13. *Groinchurn* was a South African grind core band from Johannesburg formed during the early 1990s and later signed by the German independent label Morbid Records.

14. Personal interview conducted in Istanbul in August 2004.

15. Ibid.

16. Taken from a personal interview with Kobi Farhi conducted via e-mail in July 2004.

17. All entries from Orphaned Land's Web site (www.orphaned-land.co.il).

18. Personal interview with Kobi Farhi conducted via e-mail in July 2004.

19. The interview with Rawad Abdel Massih was conducted in Istanbul on July 4, 2004.

CHAPTER 21

1. VCDs are widely available in most Southeast Asian countries except for Japan. They are also popular among Chinese communities living in Australia, Canada, the United States, and other western countries. In addition to these countries, India and Pakistan increasingly appreciate VCDs as well (Hu 2004: 206).

2. *Karaoke* means "empty orchestra" and is nowadays most commonly known as "commercially produced and marketed equipment, with a microphone mixer, that provides prompt selection of prerecorded instrumental accompaniment," but can also refer to the act of "singing to recorded music for entertainment" (Mitsui, 2001: 31–33).

3. In addition to VCDs, music videos are also broadcasted on MTV Indonesia and other television channels. It is only in music videos on VCD that the lyrics of the song are printed on screen, implying that these VCDs are specifically intended for *karaoke* use.

4. Reports about police actions against the sale of adult magazines and pirated porn VCDs and DVDs in markets in Jakarta and elsewhere regularly appear in local and national newspapers. See, for instance, (*The Jakarta Post,* April 13, 2006, http://www.thejakartapost.com/news/2006/04/13/protesters-attack-039playboy039-editorial-office.html. and November 19, 2005, http://www.thejakartapost.com/news/2005/11/19/police-raid-centers-pirated-vcds.html.).

5. This point may be exemplified by looking at the careers of two of Indonesia's most well-known male performers, *dangdut* singer Rhoma Irama, and singer–songwriter Iwan Fals, who both have used influences from outside the country to produce their music styles. During the 1970s, Rhoma Irama created his style by mixing "Middle Eastern and Indian musical elements . . . with [w]estern rock, modern electric instruments and stage effects, Islamic morality, and an exoticized Arabic style of dress." A decade later Iwan Fals "drew upon [w]estern folk and country music along with the ethos of the Indonesian *ngamen* (itinerant street singer) tradition" in his songs that criticized social injustices (Bodden 2005: 15).

6. See the *International Herald Tribune* article, (May 14, 2003 by Julia L. Suryakusuma, "A Singer's Gyrating Rattles Indonesia.").

7. For a discussion on the types of images of women in teen magazines, see Perempuan (2004); and Swastika (2004).

8. Agnes Monica's second album *Whaddup A?!*, released in 2005, was an even bigger hit than her debut and won her several awards in 2006. After gaining popularity in southeast Asia, she now wants to go international (see *The Jakarta Post* of January 24, 2008, http://www.thejakartapost.com/news/2005/11/19/police-raid-centers-pirated-vcds.html).

9. This resembles a preliminary analysis of the relation between image, text, and sound in *pop Indonesia* VCDs (Barendregt and Van Zanten 2002: 91).

10. See Frederick (1982) for a detailed account of the rise of Rhoma Irama and the history of *dangdut* in Indonesia.

11. Especially, pirated VCDs with registrations of her live performances added to Inul's fame and notoriety. However, the VCD described here is an officially produced VCD aimed at a national audience, showing a registration of a studio performance.

12. Inul used to work as an aerobic teacher herself.

13. See Barendregt (2002) for a discussion of the expression of Minangkabau identity through popular music.

14. The term *triping* carries connotations of drug use (mostly Ecstacy) in nightlife and at parties (Sastramidjaja 2000: ix).

References

Abaza, Mona. (2001) "Perception of Urfi Marriage in the Egyptian Press." *ISIM Newsletter* 7: 20–21.

Abaza, Mona. (2002) *Debates on Islam and Knowledge in Malaysia and Egypt: Shifting Worlds.* New York: Routledge.

Abbas, Tahir. (2005) "British South Asian Muslims: Before and After September 11." In Tahir Abbas, ed., *Muslim Britain: Communities under Pressure,* 3–17. London: Zed Books.

Abbink, Jon. (2005) "Being Young in Africa: The Politics of Despair and Renewal." In Jon Abbink and Ineke van Kessel, eds., *Vanguard or Vandals: Youth, Politics and Conflict in Africa,* 1–34. Leiden: Brill.

Abdel-Hay, Ahmed Tahami. (2002) "Al-Tawajjohat al-Siyasiyya Lil-Ajyal al-Jadida," *Al-Demokratiya* 6.

Abdul Khabeer, Suad. (2007) "Rep That Islam: The Rhyme and Reason of American Islamic Hip Hop." *The Muslim World* 97(1): 125–141.

Abdullah, Zaky. (2004) "Indonesia, Leading the Way in Tackling the Youth Employment Challenge." Presented at JILPT International Labour Information Project Liaison Meeting, Tokyo, Japan, September 27–28.

Abdul-Rahman, Mustafa. (2001) "Sex, Urfi Marriage a Survival Strategy in Dahab." The American University in Cairo, unpublished Sociology term paper, Fall.

Abu-Lughod, Lila. (1989) "Zones of Theory in the Anthropology of the Arab World." *Annual Review of Anthropology* 18: 276–306.

Adam, André. (1962) *Une Enquête auprès de la jeunesse Musulmane au Maroc.* Aix-en-Provence: Annales de la Faculté des lettres.

Agier, Michel. (1999) *L'invention de la ville: Banlieues, townships, invasions et favelas.* Paris: Éditions des Archives Contemporaires.

Ahmad, Mumtaz. (1995) "Tablīghī Jamā'at," in John L. Esposito, ed., *The Oxford Encyclopedia of the Modern Islamic World*, Vol. 4, 165–169. New York: Oxford University Press.

Al-Dabbaqh, Mona (1996) "Addiction among Egyptian Upper Class." MA thesis, American University in Cairo.

Alexander, Claire E. (2000) *The Asian Gang: Ethnicity, Identity, Masculinity.* Oxford: Berg.

Alexander, Claire E. (2005) "Imagining the Politics of BrAsian Youth." In Nasreen Ali, Virinder S. Kalra, and Salman Sayyid, eds., *A Postcolonial People: South Asians in Britain*, 258–271. London: Hurst.

Al-Ghazzami, Abdallah. (2004) *ḥikāyat al-ḥadātha fī-1 -mamlaka al-'arabiyya al-su'ūdiyya [The Story of Modernity in Saudi Arabia].* Beirut: Al-Markaz al-Thaqafi al-'Arabi.

Ali, Mohamed M., John Blacker, and Gareth Jones. (2003) "Annual Mortality Rates and Excess Deaths of Children under Five in Iraq, 1991–98." *Population Studies* 7(2): 217–226.

Allen, Christopher. (2003) *Fair Justice: The Bradford Disturbances, the Sentencing, and the Impact.* London: Forum.

Allen, Pam. (2007) "Challenging Diversity?: Indonesia's Anti-Pornography Bill." *Asian Studies Review* 31: 101–115.

Allievi, Stefano (2006) "How and Why 'Immigrants' became 'Muslims.'" *ISIM Review* 18: 37.

Al-Rumayh, Sâli/h. (2006) "Al-'awāmil al-mu'aththira fī irtifā' ẓāhirat al-tafḥīṭ bayna al-shabāb al-Su'ūdī wa ṭuruq al-wiqāya minhā. Dirāsat muqārina li-wāqi' al-ẓāhira fī kul mīn al-Riyāḍ, Jidda wa al-Dammām" [The Factors Leading to an Increase of *Tafḥīṭ* among Saudi Youth and the Means to Prevent it: Comparative Study in Riyadh, Jeddah, and Dammam]. Riyadh: Majallat al-buḥuth al-amniyya(15) 34: 171–229.

AlSayyad, Nezar and Manuel Castells, eds. (2002) *Muslim Europe or Euro-Islam: Politics, Culture, and Citizenship in the Age of Globalization.* Lanham, Md.: Lexington Books.

Amin, Camron Michael. (2002) *The Making of the Modern Iranian Woman: Gender, State Policy, and Popular Culture, 1865–1946.* Gainesville: University Press of Florida.

Amir-Moazami, Schirin. (2005) "Muslim Challenges to the Secular Consensus: A German Case Study," *Journal of Contemporary European Studies* 13(3): 267–286.

Amir-Moazami, Schirin. and Armando. Salvatore. (2003) "Gender, Generation, and the Reform of Tradition: From Muslim Majority Societies to Western Europe," in Joergen Nielsen and Stefano Allievi, eds., *Muslim Networks, Transnational Communities in and Across Europe*, 32–77. Leiden, Brill.

Amnesty International (2001) Amnesty International Report 2001: Annual Report Summaries 2001. (http://www.amnesty.org/en/library/info/ POL10/006/2001/en)

Amselle, Jean-Loup. (1985) "Le Wahabisme à Bamako (1945–1985)." *Canadian Journal of African Studies* 19(2): 345–357.

Anderson, Jon W. (2003) "New Media, New Publics: Reconfiguring the Public Sphere of Islam," *Social Research* 70(3): 887–905.

Androutsopoulos, Jannis and Arno Scholz. (2003) "Spaghetti Funk: Appropriations of Hip-Hop Culture and Rap Music in Europe." *Popular Music and Society* 26(4): 463–479.

Andsager, Julie. (2006) "Seduction, Shock, and Sales: Research and Functions of Sex in Music Video." In Tom Reichert and Jacqueline Lambiase, eds., *Sex in Consumer Culture: The Erotic Content of Media and Marketing*. Mahwah, N.J.: Lawrence Erlbaum Associates.

Anonymous. (1998) "Rap interview." *British Muslims Monthly Survey* 4: 3 (artsweb. bham.ac.uk/bmms/1998/03March98.html#Rap%20interview).

Appadurai, Arjun. (1996) *Modernity at Large: Cultural Dimensions of Globalization*. Minneapolis.: University of Minnesota Press.

Arendonk, C. van. (1990) "Kahwa." In E. van Donzel et al., eds., *The Encyclopaedia of Islam*, 449–453. Leiden: Brill.

Argenti, Nick. (2002) "Youth in Africa: A Major Resource for Change." In Alex de Waal and Nick Argenti, eds., *Realizing the Rights of Children and Youth*, 123–154. Trenton, N.J.: Africa World Press.

Asad, Talal. (2005) Reflections on *Laïcité* and the Public Sphere." *Social Sciences Research Council, Items and Issues* (5/3): 1–11.

Ashraf, Ahmad and Ali Banuazizi (1985) "The State, Classes, and Modes of Mobilization in the Iranian Revolution." *State, Culture and Society* 1(3): 3–30.

Assaad, Ragui and Farzaneh Roudi-Fahimi. (2007) *Youth in the Middle East and North Africa: Demographic Opportunity of Challenge?* Washington, DC: Population Reference Bureau.

Assaad, Raguie and Ghada Barsoum. (2007) "Youth Exclusion in Egypt: In Search of 'Second Chances.'" Middle East Youth Initiative Working Paper. Wolfensohn Center for Development and Dubai School of Government.

Associated Press. (2006) "Le recteur de Lyon s'oppose à l'ouverture d'un établissement scolaire musulman dans le Rhône." Lyon, August 30. (http://web.ifrance. com/actu/france/25878)

Ayubi, Nazih. (1991) *Political Islam: Religion and Politics in the Arab World*. London: Routledge.

Aziz, Abdul, Imam Tholkhah, and S. Soetarman, eds. (1989) *Gerakan Islam Kontemporer di Indonesia*. Jakarta: Pustaka Firdaus.

Balasescu, Alexandru. (2004) "Fashioning Subjects, Unveiling Modernity." PhD diss., University of California at Irvine.

Balcha, Eyob. (2009) "Youth and Politics in Post 1974 Ethiopia: Intergenerational Analysis." Masters of Arts Thesis in Development Studies. International Institute of Social Studies of the Erasmus University Rotterdam.

Bamberg, Michael. (2004) "Positioning with Davie Hogan: Stories, Tellings and Identities." In Collette Daiute and Cynthia Lightfoot, eds., *Narrative Analysis: Studying the Development of Individuals in Society*, 135–158. Thousand Oaks: Sage.

Barendregt, Bart. (2002) "The Sound of 'Longing Home': Redefining a Sense of Community through Minang Popular Musics." *Bijdragen Koninklijk Instituut Taal Land en Volkenkunde* 158(3): 411–451.

Barendregt, Bart. (2006) "The Art of No-Seduction: Muslim Boy-Band Music in Southeast Asia and the Fear of the Female Voice," *IIAS Newsletter* 40: 10. www.iias.nl/nl/40/IIAS_NL40_10.pdf.

Barendregt, Bart and Wim van Zanten. (2002) "Popular Music in Indonesia since 1998: In Particular Fusion, Indie and Islamic Music on Video Compact Discs and the Internet." *Yearbook for Traditional Music* 34: 67–110.

Baubérot, Jean (2000): *Histoire de la laïcité française*. Paris: Presses Universitaires de France.

Bayat, Asef. (1997) *Street Politics: Poor People's Movements in Iran*. New York: Colombia University Press.

Bayat, Asef. (2005) "What Is Post-Islamism?" *ISIM Review* 16: 5.

Bayat, Asef. (2007a) "Islamism and the Politics of Fun," *Public Culture* 19(3): 433–459.

Bayat, Asef. (2007b) *Making Islam Democratic: Social Movements and the Post-Islamist Turn*. Stanford: Stanford University Press.

Bayoumi, Moustafa. (2006a) "A Light in Brooklyn." *The Nation*, September 25, 23.

Bayoumi, Moustafa. (2006b) "Racing Religion." *New Centennial Review* 6(2): 267–293.

Bayoumi, Moustafa. (2008) *How Does It Feel To Be a Problem?: Being Young and Arab in America*. New York: The Penguin Press.

Beck, Ulrich. (1992) *Risk Society: Towards a New Modernity*, trans. Mark Ritter. London: Sage.

Beehner, Lionel. (2007) "The Effects of 'Youth Bulge on Civil Conflicts.'" The Council on Foreign Relations. April 27, 2007. www.cfr.org/publication/13093/.

Benali, Abdelkader and Herman Obdeijn. (2005) *Marokko door Nederlandse Ogen. 1605–2005, Verslag van een Reis door de Tijd*. Amsterdam: Arbeiderspers.

Benin, Joel and Hossam el-Hamalawy. (2007) "Egyptian Textile Workers Confront the New Economic Order." *Middle East Report Online*. March 25. www.merip.org/mero/mero032507.html.

Bennani-Chraibi, Mounia. (1994) *Soumis et rebelles, les jeunes au Maroc*. Paris: CNRS éditions.

Bennani-Chraibi, Mounia, and Iman Farag, eds. (2007) *Jeunesses des sociétés Musulmanes: Par-delà les menaces et les promesses*. Paris: Aux lieux d'être/CEDEJ.

Bennett, Andy. (2000) *Popular Music and Youth Culture: Music, Identity and Place*. London: MacMillan Press.

Benthall, Jonathan and Jerome Bellion-Jourdan. (2003) *The Charitable Crescent: Politics of Aid in the Muslim World*. London: I. B. Tauris.

Beriss, David. (1996) "Scarves, Schools and Segregation: The *Foulard* Affair." In Anne Corbett and Bob Moon, eds. *Education in France: Continuity and Change in the Mitterrand Years, 1981–1995*, 377–387. London: Routledge.

Berque, Jacques. (1982) *Ulémas, fondateurs, insurgés du Maghreb, XVII e Siècle*. Paris: Sindbad.

Beshkin, Abigail. (2001) "SIPA Conference Discusses New York City's Growing
    Muslim Population." *Columbia News.* May 3. http://www.columbia.edu/cu/
    news/01/05/muslim.html

Bhattacharyya, Anindya. (2006) "Aki Nawaz from Fun-Da-Mental Talks about
    Imperialism and His Album *All Is War.*" *Socialist Worker,* August 5. www.
    socialistworker.co.uk/article.php?article_id=9369.

Biaya, Tshikala K. (2005) "Youth & Street Culture in Urban Africa: Addis Ababa, Dakar
    & Kinshasa." In Alcinda Honwana and Filip De Boeck, eds., *Makers & Breakers:
    Children & Youth in Postcolonial Africa,* 215–228. Oxford: James Currey.

Bilal, Cheick Soufi, n.d.a *La Qadria.* Np.

Bilal, Cheick Soufi. n.d.b *La célébration du Maouloud.* Np.

Bilici, Mücahit. (2000) "Islam in Bronzlaşan Yüzü: Caprice Hotel Örnek Olayı"
    ["Tanning Face of Islam: The Case of the Caprice Hotel"]. In Nilüfer Göle, ed.,
    Islam'ın Yeni Kamusal Yüzleri [New Public Faces of Islam]. Istanbul: Metis.

Blackman, Shane. (2005) "Youth Subcultural Theory: A Critical Engagement with
    Concept, Its Origins and Politics, from the Chicago School to Postmodernism."
    Journal of Youth Studies 3(1): 1–20.

Bodden, Michael. (2005) "Rap in Indonesian Youth Music of the 1990s: 'Globaliza-
    tion,' 'Outlaw Genres,' and Social Protest." *Asian Music,* Summer/Fall: 14.

Bonnenfant, Paul. (1982) "La capitale saoudienne: Riyad." In Paul Bonnenfant, ed.,
    La Péninsule Arabique D'aujourd'hui, Vol. 2, 655–705. Paris: CNRS editions.

Boontharm, Davisi. (2005) *Bangkok: Formes du Commerce et Evolution Urbaine.* Paris:
    Editions Recherches.

Borradori, Giovanna. (2003): *Philosophy in a Time of Terror: Dialogues with Jürgen
    Habermas and Jaques Derrida.* Chicago, Ill.: The University of Chicago Press.

Boudarbat Brahim and Aziz Ajbilou. (2007) Youth Exclusion in Morocco: Context,
    Consequences, and Policies. Middle East Youth Initiative Working Paper.
    Wolfensohn Center for Development, Dubai School of Government.

Bourdieu, Pierre. (1971) "Genèse et structure du champ religieux." *Revue Française de
    Sociologie* XII(3): 295–334.

Bourdieu, Pierre. (1977) *Outline of a Theory of Practice.* Cambridge: Cambridge
    University Press.

Bourdieu, Pierre. (1980) "Le capital social: Notes provisoires." *Actes De La Recherche
    En Sciences Sociales* 31: 2–3.

Bourdieu, Pierre. (1984) "La Jeunesse n'est qu'un Mot." In *Questions de Sociologie,*
    143–154. Paris: Les éditions de Minuit.

Bourdieu, Pierre. (1992) *The Logic of Practice.* Stanford: Stanford University Press.

Bourdieu, Pierre. (1993) *Sociology in Question.* London: Sage.

Bourdieu, Pierre. (1994) *Distinction.* London: Routledge and Kegan Paul.

Bourdieu, Pierre. (1997) *Méditations pascaliennes.* Paris: Seuil.

Bourqia, Rahma, Mohamed El-Ayadi, Mokhtar El Harras, and Hassan Rachik. (2000)
    Les Jeunes et les valeurs religieuses. Casablanca: EDDIF.

Bowen, John R. (2002). "Islam in/of France: Dilemmas of Translocality." Presented at
    the 13th International Conference of Europeanists. Chicago, Ill.: March 14–16.

Bowen, John R. (2007a) "A View from France on the Internal Complexity of National Models." *Journal of Ethnic and Migration Studies* 33(6): 1003–1016.

Bowen, John R. (2007b) *Why the French Don't Like Headscarves: Islam, the State, and Public State.* Princeton, N.J.: Princeton University Press.

Brah, Avtar. (2005) "The 'Asian' in Britain." In Nasreen Ali, Virinder S. Kalra, and Salman Sayyid, eds. 35–61. London: Hurst.

Brake, Mike. (1980) *The Sociology of Youth Culture and Youth Subcultures: Sex, Drugs and Rock 'n' Roll?* London: Routledge and Kegan Paul.

Bray, Mark. (2009) *Confronting the Shadow Education System: What Governments Policies for What Private Tutoring?* Paris: United Nations Educational, Scientific, and Cultural Organization (UNESCO), International Institution for Educational Planning (IIEP).

Brenner, Louis. (2000) *Controlling Knowledge: Religion, Power and Schooling in a West African Muslim Society.* London: Hurst.

Brenner, Suzanne. (1999) "On the Public Intimacy of the New Order: Images of Women in the Popular Indonesian Print Media." *Indonesia* 67: 13–37.

Brinton, Crain. (1965) *The Anatomy of Revolution.* New York: Random House.

Broder, Henryk M. (2007) "The Voice of a Silent Majority. Muslim Bloggers and Journalists Speak Out." *Spiegel Online International,* 4 November. http://www. spiegel.de/international/world/0,1518,476644,00.html

Brown, Wendy. (2006) *Regulation Aversion: Tolerance in the Age of Identity and Empire.* Princeton: Princeton University Press.

Brubaker, Rogers. (1992) *Citizenship and Nationhood in France and Germany,* 9–42. Brunswick: Transaction Publishers.

Bundy, Colin. (1987) "Street Sociology and Pavement Politics: Aspects of Youth and Students Resistance in Cape Town, 1985." *Journal of Southern African Studies* 13(3): 303–330.

Bunt, Gary R. (2003) *Islam in the Digital Age: E-Jihad, Online Fatwas and Cyber Islamic Environments* (Critical Studies on Islam). London: Pluto Press.

Burke, Edmund III. (1972) "The Moroccan Ulema, 1860–1912." In Nikkie Keddie, ed. *Scholars, Saints and Sufis,* 93–126. Berkeley: University of California Press.

Cable News Network. (2007) "Poll: For Christians' Identity: It's Faith First, U.S., Second." August 23. www.cnn.com/2007/US/08/22/gw.poll/.

Caeiro, Alexandre. (2005) "An Imam in France: Tareq Oubrou." *ISIM Newsletter* 15 (Spring):48–49.

Cainkar, Louise. (2004) "Islamic Revival among Second-Generation Arab American Muslims: The American Experience and Globalization Intersect." *Bulletin of the Royal Institute for Inter-faith Studies* 6(2): 99–120.

Calhoun, Craig. (1995) *Critical Social Theory.* Oxford: Blackwell.

Campion, Chris. (2006) "Fun-Da-Mental, All Is War." *The Observer.* July 16. observer. guardian.co.uk/omm/10bestcds/story/0,1818107,00.html.

CAPMAS. (1999) *The Statistical Year Book, 1992–1998.* Cairo: Central Agency for Public Mobilization And Statistics.

Castells, Manuel. (1999) *The Information Age: Economy, Society, and Culture, Vol. II: The Power of Identity.* Oxford: Blackwell.

Castells, Manuel. (2002) *The Internet Galaxy: Reflections on the Internet, Business and Society*. Oxford: Oxford University Press.

Castells, Manuel, Mireia Fernandez-Ardevol, Jack Linchuan Qiu, and Araba Sey, eds. (2007) *Mobile Communication and Society: A Global Perspective*. Cambridge, Mass: MIT Press.

Chaaban, Jad. (2008) "The Costs of Youth Exclusion in the Middle East," Wolfensohn Center for Development, working paper no. 7, Washington, D.C. www.shababinclusion.org/content/document/detail/983/.

Chaambi, Adbedlaziz. (2007) "Interview d'un militant: Abdelaziz Chaambi." *Le Collectif Musulman de France*, January 2007. www.lecmf.fr.

Chafik, Mohammed. (2004) *Imazighen: De Berbers en hun geschiedenis*. Amsterdam: Bulaaq.

Champagne, Jessica. (2004) "Jilbab Gaul." *Latitudes* 46: 14–23.

Chandler, Neil. (2006) "Rap of Hate: Maniac's Rant over Bombers Is Banned." *Sunday Star* August 20, 8.

Chaney, David. (1996) *Lifestyles*. London: Routledge.

Charlick, R. B. (2004) Niger. *African Studies Review* 47(2): 97–108.

Chérifi, Hanifa. (2005) "*Islam et intégration à l'école*," *Revue européenne des migrations internationales* 17(2). http://remi.revues.org/document1974.html.

Chu, Jeff. (2001) "We Don't Want to Convert You." *Time* (Europe edition), December 24. http://www.time.com/time/world/article/0,8599,188722,00.html

Çınar, Alev. (2005) *Modernity, Islam and Secularism in Turkey: Bodies, Places, and Time*. Minneapolis: University of Minnesota Press.

Cincotta, Richard P., Robert Engelman, and Danielle Anastasion. (2003) *The Security Demographic: Population and Civil Conflict after the Cold War*. Washington D.C.: Population Action International.

Çizmeci, Şule. (2005) "Kahve Bahane" ["Coffee is the Excuse"]. *Radikal Cumartesi Eki* [*Radical Saturday Supplement*] January 19.

Coburn, Jo. (2006) "Straw Gets the Debate He Wanted." BBC News, October 6. http://news.bbc.co.uk/go/pr/fr/-/2/hi/uk_news/politics/5413012.stm

Cockburn, Alexander and Robin Blackburn, eds. (1969) *Student Power: Problem, Diagnosis, Action*. London: Penguin Books.

Cohen, Stanley. (2002) [1972]. *Folk Devils and Moral Panics*. 3rd ed. London: Routledge.

Cole Ardra L. and J. Gary Knowles, eds. (2001) *Lives in Context: The Art of Life History Research*. Walnut Creek, Calif.: Altamira Press.

Cole, Jennifer and Deborah Durham (2007) *Generations and Globalization: Youth, Age, and Family in the New World Economy*. Bloomington and Indianapolis: Indiana University Press.

Comaroff, Jean, and John Comaroff. (1999) "Occult Economies and the Violence of Abstraction: Notes from the South African Postcolony," *American Ethnologist* 26(2): 279–303.

Comaroff, Jean and John Comaroff (2005) "Reflections on Youth: From the Past to the Postcolony in Africa." In Alcinda Honwana and Filip De Boeck, eds., *Makers & Breakers: Children & Youth in Postcolonial Africa*, 19–30. Trenton, NJ & Asmara, Eritrea: Africa World Press.

Cook, Michael. (2001) *Commanding Right and Forbidding Wrong in Islamic Thought.* Cambridge: Cambridge University Press.

Cooke, Miriam. (2001) *Women Claim Islam: Creating Islamic Feminism through Literature.* New York: Routledge.

Cooper, Barbara M. (2003) "Anatomy of a Riot: The Social Imaginary, Single Women, and Religious Violence in Niger." *Canadian Journal of African Studies* 37(2–3): 467–512.

Cruise O'Brien, Donal. 1996. "A Lost Generation? Youth Identity and State Decay in West Africa," in R. Werbner, ed., *Postcolonial Identities in Africa,* 55–74. London: Zed Books.

Daftere Motale'ate Farhangi [Cultural Studies Bureau]. (1385/2007) "A View on Budget Bill: Situation of Youth National Organization; Women and Family." Tehran: Markaze Pajooheshshaye Majlese Shoraye Eslami [Iranian Parliament Research Center].

Dağı, İhsan D. (2004) "Rethinking Human Rights, Democracy, and the West: Post-Islamist Intellectuals in Turkey." *Critique: Critical Middle Eastern Studies* 2(2): 136–139.

Damien, Steffan. (2006) "'Benefits of G-Had': Muslim Rapper's Album Raises Eyebrows in Britain." *AFP-English* July 21. http://www.amren.com/mtnews/ archives/2006/07/benefits_of_gha.php

Darboe, Momodou. (2004) "ASR Focus: Islamism in West Africa—Gambia." *African Studies Review* 47(2): 73–82.

Davis, Mike. (1992) *City of Quartz: Excavating the Future in Los Angeles.* London: Vintage Books.

De Boeck, Filip. (2005) "The Divine Seed: Children, Gift & Witchcraft in the Democratic Republic of Congo." In Alcinda Honwana and Filip De Boeck, eds., *Makers & Breakers. Children & Youth in Postcolonial Africa,* 188–214. Oxford: James Currey.

De Certeau, Michel. (1984) *The Practice of Everyday Life.* Berkeley: University of California Press.

De Galembert, Claire and Nikola Tietze. (2002) "Institutionalisierung des Islam in Deutschland: Pluralisierung der Weltanschauungen." *Mittelweg* 36(11/1): 43–62.

de la Cruz, Patricia and Angela Brittingham. (2003) "The Arab Population." Census 2000 Brief. U.S. Census Bureau, December: 7.

de la Cruz, Patricia and Angela Brittingham. (2005) "We the People of Arab Ancestry Arab Population." Census 2000 special reports, U.S. Census Bureau.

de Noray, Marie-Laure and Oumar Maïga. (2002) *Bamako, génération vingt ans: Panorama et témoignages de la jeunesse bamakoise des années 2000.* Bamako: Éditions Donniya.

De Waal, Alex, ed. (2004) *Islamism and Its Enemies in the Horn of Africa.* Bloomington: Indiana University Press.

Deeb, Lara. (2006) *An Enchanted Modern: Gender and Public Piety in Shi'i Lebanon.* Princeton: Princeton University Press.

Dekmejian, R. Hrair. (1995) *Islam in Revolution.* Syracuse: Syracuse University Press.

Deltombe, Thomas. (2005) *L'islam imaginaire: La construction médiatique de l'islamophobie en France, 1975–2005*. Paris: La Découverte.

Denis, Eric and Asef Bayat. (2001) "Egypt: Twenty Years of Urban Transformation, 1980–2000," International Institute of Development and Urbanization, London, unpublished.

Devisch, René. (1995) "Frenzy, Violence, and Ethical Renewal in Kinshasa." *Public Culture* 7: 593–629.

Diarra, B. S. (2002) "Aïd al-Fitr à Magnambougou: Le jihad." *Aurore* December 9, 2.

Dicko, Abdrahamane. (2005) "Solidarité islamique: L'AMJM offre plus de 300 poches de sang au CNTS," *Les Echos*, June 27, www.afribone.com/article.php3?id_article=1112.

Dicko, G. A. (2004) "Soufisme: Bamako: le nouveau départ." *L'Essor* December 22,.

Diouf, Mamadou. (1996) "Urban Youth and Senegalese Politics: Dakar 1988–1994." *Public Culture* 8: 225–249.

Diouf, Mamadou. (2000) "The Senegalese Murid Trade Diaspora and the Making of a Vernacular Cosmopolitanism." *Public Culture* 12(3): 679–702.

Diouf, Mamadou. (2003) "Engaging Postcolonial Cultures: African Youth and Public Space." *African Studies Review* 46(1): 1–12.

Douwes, Dick, Martijn De Koning, and Welmoet Boender, eds. (2005) *Nederlandse Moslims: Van Migrant tot Burger*. Amsterdam: AUP/Salomé.

Douzinas, Costas. (2007) *Human Rights and Empire: The Political Philosophy of Cosmopolitanism*. New York: Routledge-Cavendish.

Durham, Deborah. (2000) "Youth and the Social Imagination in Africa: Introduction to Parts 1 and 2." *Anthropological Quarterly* 73(3): 113–120.

Durham, Deborah. (2004) "Disappearing Youth: Youth as a Social Shifter in Botswana." *American Ethnologist* 31(4): 589–605.

Duru-Bellat, Marie and Annick Kieffer. (2000) "Inequalities in Educational Opportunities in France: Educational Expansion, Democratization or Shifting Barriers?," *Journal of Education Policy* 15(3): 333–352.

Edmunds, June and Bryan Turner. (2002) *Generations, Culture and Society*. Buckingham: Open University Press.

Edmunds, June and Bryan S. Turner. (2005) "Global Generations: Social Change in the Twentieth Century." *The British Journal of Sociology* 56: 559–577.

Efe, Mehmet. (1993) *Mızraksız Ilmihal [Book of Manners without a Lance]*. Istanbul: Yerli Yayınları.

Egypt Human Development Report. (2005) *Choosing our Future: Towards a New Social Contract*. Cairo: UNDP and The Institute of National Planning.

Eickelman, Dale F. (1989) "National Identity and Religious Discourse in Contemporary Oman." *International Journal of Islamic and Arabic Studies* 6(1): 1–20.

Eickelman, Dale F. and Jon W. Anderson, eds. (1999) *New Media in the Muslim World: The Emerging Public Sphere*. Bloomington: Indiana University Press.

Eickelman, Dale F. and James Piscatori. (1996) *Muslim Politics*. Princeton: Princeton University Press.

Eisenstadt, Shmuel N. (2003) *From Generation to Generation*, 3rd ed. New Brunswick: Transaction Publishers.

El Ayadi, Mohamed. (2000) "La jeunesse et l'Islam: Tentative d'Analyse d'un Habitus Religieux Cultivé." In Rahma Bourquia, et al., eds., *Les Jeunes et les Valeurs Religieuses*, 87–165. Casablanca: EDDIF.

El Ayadi, Mohamed. (2007) "Les jeunes et la Religion." In Mohamed El Ayadi, Hassan Rachik, and Mohamed Tozy, eds. *L'Islam au Quotidien: Enquête sur les Valeurs et les Pratiques Religieuses au Maroc*, 99–175. Casablanca: Editions Prologues.

Eliasoph, Nina. (1998) *Avoiding Politics. How Americans Produce Apathy in Everyday Life*. Cambridge: Cambridge University Press.

El-Sayed, Mohamed. (2008) "Virtual Politics." *Al-Ahram Weekly Online*. August 7–13. http://weekly.ahram.org.eg/2008/909/fe1.htm.

Esposito, John L. (1983) *Voices of Resurgent Islam*. New York: Oxford University Press.

Esposito, John and Dalia Mogahed. (2007) *Who Speaks for Islam? What a Billion Muslims Really Think*. New York: Gallup Press.

Essers, Caroline and Yvonne Benschop. (2007) "Enterprising Identities: Female Entrepreneurs of Moroccan and Turkish Origin in the Netherlands." *Organization Studies* 28: 49–70.

Etchegoin, Marie-France and Claude Askolovitch. (2008) "Une nouvelle alliance du trône et de l'autel: Le croisé de l'Elysée," *Le Nouvel Observateur*. http://hebdo. nouvelobs.com/hebdo/parution/p2258/articles/a366441.html.

Etling, Bruce, John Kelly, Rob Faris, and John Palfrey. (2009) Mapping the Arabic Blogosphere: Politics, Culture, and Dissent. Berkman Center Research Publication No. 2009–06. The Berkman Center for Internet & Society at Harvard University. http://cyber.law.harvard.edu/publications/2009/Mapping_the_Arabic_Blogosphere

Farahi, Mozhgan. (1382/2003) "You Cannot Resolve Sexual Misconduct by Exhortation." *Gozaresh* 148, Tir.

Felouzis, Georges, Françoise Liot, and Joëlle Perroton. (2003) "La Ségrégation ethnique au Collège." *Ville-École-Intégration Enjeux* 135: 123–135.

Felouzis, Georges. (2003) "La ségrégation ethnique au collège et ses consequences." *Revue Française de Sociologie* 44: 413–447.

Ferguson, James. (1999) *Expectations of Modernity: Myths and Meanings of Urban Life on the Zambian Copperbelt*. Berkeley: University of California Press.

Ferguson, James. (2006) *Global Shadows: Africa in the Neoliberal World Order*. Durham: Duke University Press.

Ferrándiz, Francisco. (2004) "The Body as Wound: Possession, *Malandros* and Everyday Violence in Venezuela." *Critique of Anthropology* 24: 107–133.

Fillieule, Olivier. (2006) "Requiem pour un Concept: Vie Et Mort De La Notion de 'Structure Des Opportunités Politiques.'" In Gilles Dorronsoro, ed., *La Turquie Conteste*. Paris: CNRS Éditions.

Finkielkraut, Alain. (2003) "M. Alain Finkielkraut, philosophe." In "Assemblée nationale, Mission d'information sur la question des signes religieux à l'école,

Commission des Affaires culturelles, familiales et sociales, Compte rendu no. 41bis, Jeudi 22 mai." Paris: Assemblée nationale.

Forst, Rainer. (2002) "A tolerant Republic?" In Jan-Werner Müller, ed., *German Ideologies since 1945: Studies in the Political Thought and Culture of the Bonn Republic*. 209–220. New York: Palgrave.

Foucault, Michel. (1976) *The History of Sexuality, Vol. 1: The Will to Knowledge*. London: Penguin.

Foucault, Michel. (1979) *Discipline and Punish*. New York: Vintage Books.

Frederick, William H. (1982) "Rhoma Irama and the Dangdut Style: Aspects of Contemporary Indonesian Popular Culture." *Indonesia* 34: 102–130.

Friedman, Jonathon (1994) "Introduction," in Jonathan Friedman, ed., *Consumption and Identity*. 1–22. London: Harwood Publishers.

Fuad, Midhat. (2001) "Youth Centers without Youths." *Sawt ul-Azhar* September 14.

Gaborieau, Marc. (2000) "The Transformation of Tablīghī Jamā'at into a Transnational Movement." In Muhammad Khalid Masud, ed., *Travellers in Faith: Studies of the Tablīghī Jamā'at as a Transnational Islamic Movement for Faith Renewal*, 121–138. Leiden: Brill.

Gamson, William. (1992) *Talking Politics*. Cambridge: Cambridge University Press.

Garcia, Michael Nieto. (2004) "More Than Just Sex: Three Women Take the Indonesian Literary World by Storm." *Inside Indonesia* 80: 26–27. http://insideindonesia.org/content/view/217/29/.

Garratt, Daren. (2004) "Youth Cultures and Sub-cultures." In Jeremy Roche, Stanley Tucker, and RachelThomson, eds. *Youth in Society: Contemporary Theory, Policy and Practice*, 145–152. London: Sage Publications.

Gerhardt, Marcus. (2004) "Varzesh va Jaameh Madani dar Iran" ["Sport and Civil Society in Iran"]. *Goftogu* 42: 45–55.

Giblin, Béatrice. (2006) "Ghettos américains, banlieues françaises," *Hérodote* 122: 1–14.

Giddens, Anthony. (1990) *The Consequences of Modernity*. Cambridge: Polity Press.

Giddens, Anthony. (1991) *Modernity and Self-Reflexivity: Self and Society in the Late Modern Age*. Stanford: Stanford University Press.

Giroux, Henry A. (1998) "Teenage Sexuality, Body Politics, and the Pedagogy of Display." In Jonathan S. Epstein, ed., *Youth Culture: Identity in a Postmodern World*, 24–55. Oxford: Blackwell.

Glew, Robert S. (1996) "Islamic Associations in Niger." *Islam et sociétés au sud du Sahara* 10: 187–204.

Goffman, Erving. (1956) *The Presentation of the Self in Everyday Life*. New York: Doubleday.

Goffman, Erving. (1967) *Stigma*. Frankfurt/Main: Suhrkamp.

Gold, Dore. (2003) *Hatred's Kingdom: How Saudi Arabia Supports the New Global Terrorism*. Washington, D.C.: Regnery Publishing.

Göle, Nilüfer. (1997) *The Forbidden Modern: Civilization and Veiling (Critical Perspectives on Women and Gender)*. Ann Arbor: University of Michigan Press.

Göle, Nilüfer. (2000) "Snapshots of Islamic Modernities." *Deadalus* 129(1): 91–117.

Göle, Nilüfer. (2002) "Islam in Public: New Visibilities and New Imaginaries." *Public Culture* 14(1): 173–190.

Göle, Nilüfer (2003) "The Voluntary Adoption of Islamic Stigma Symbols." *Social Research* 70(3): 803–828.

Gomez-Perez, Muriel. (1998) "Associations islamiques à Dakar." In Ousmane Kane and Jean-Louis Triaud, eds., *Islam et islamisme au sud du Sahara*, 137–153. Aix-en-Provence: Iremam.

Gorton Ash, Timothy. (2005) "Soldiers of Hidden Imam." *New York Review of Books* 52(17).

Grégoire, Emmanuel. (1993) "Islam and the Identity of Merchants in Maradi (Niger)." In Louis Brenner, ed., *Muslim Identity and Social Change in Sub-Saharan Africa*, 106–115. Bloomington: Indiana University Press.

Gresh, Alain and Michel Tubiana. (2005) "Vivre ensemble." In *1905–2005: Les enjeux de la laïcité*, 7. Paris: L'Harmattan.

Guénif-Souilamas, Nacira and Eric Macé. (2004) *Les féministes et le garçon arabe*. Paris: Éditions de l'Aube.

Guevara, Che. (1998) *Guerilla Warfare*. Lincoln: University of Nebraska Press.

Gunn, T. Jeremy. (2004) "Religious Freedom and *Laïcité*: A Comparison of the United States and France." *Brigham Young University Law Review* Summer: 419–506.

Gunn, T. Jeremy. (2005) "French Secularism as Utopia and Myth." *Houston Law Review* 42(1): 81–102.

Haenni, Patrick. (2005) *L'autre Revolution Conservatrice*. Paris: Éditions du Seuil et La République des Idées.

Haeri, Shahla. (1993) *Law of Desire: Temporary Marriage in Shi'i Iran*. London: I. B. Tauris.

Haïdara, Alou B. (2007) "L'ancien président de la République sur la voie du soufisme: Moussa Traoré invité d'honneur de Cheick Soufi Bilal pour le Maouloud 2007" *Bamako-Hebdo*, 14 April 2007.

Haïdara, Alou Badra. (2008) "Opération Maouloud de la Fondation pour l'Enfance: Des vivres d'une valeur de 11 millions FCFA distribués aux associations musulmanes et aux mosquées de Bamako." *L'Indépendant* March 21. www.maliweb.net/category.php?NID=28707&;intr=

Hall, Stuart and Tony Jefferson, eds. (1976) *Resistance Through Rituals: Youth Subcultures in Post-War Britain*. London: Hutchinson.

Hamdani, Hassan. (2007) "Maroc contre Marock: La liberté des uns offense les autres." *Tel quel* 278: 42–48.

Hammond, Andrew. (1998) "Campuses Stay Clear of Politics." *Cairo Times* October: 15–28.

Hammoudi, Abdellah. (2007) *Master and Disciple. The Cultural Foundations of Moroccan Authoritarianism*. Chicago: University of Chicago Press.

Hanieh, Adam. (1999) "The WWW in Palestine: An Informational and Organising Tool." *Middle East Report* Winter: 41–44.

Hansen, Karen Tranberg. (2008) *Youth and the City in the Global South*. Bloomington: Indiana University Press.

Hasan, Noorhaidi. (2006) *Laskar Jihad: Islam, Militancy, and the Quest for Identity in Post-New Order Indonesia*. Cornell, N.Y.: SEAP Cornell University.

Hasan, Noorhaidi. (2007) "The Salafi Movement in Indonesia: Transnational Dynamics and Local Development." *Comparative Studies of South Asia, Africa and the Middle East* 27(1): 83–94.

Hassan, Riaz. (2002) *Faithlines: Muslim Concepts of Islam and Society.* Oxford: Oxford University.

Hattox, Ralph S. (1985) *Coffee and Coffeehouses: The Origin of a Social Beverage in the Medieval Near East.* Seattle: University of Washington Press.

Hebdige, Dick. (1981) *Subcultures: The Meaning of Style.* London: Routledge.

Heijmans, Toine and Fred De Vries. (1998) *Respect! Rappen in fort Europa.* Amsterdam: De Balie and De Volkskrant.

Hendri, Havy. (2008) "Pemuda dan 'Pro-Youth' Pembangunan." *Media Indonesia* January 12.

Hepp, Andreas. (2004) *Netzwerke der Medien: Medienkulturen und Globalisierung.* Wiesbaden: VS Verlag für Sozialwissenschaften.

Hermann, Rainer. (2003) "Political Islam in Turkish Society." *Islam and Christian Muslim Relations* 14(3): 265–276.

Herrera, Linda. (1992) "Scenes of Schooling: Inside a Girls' School in Cairo." *Cairo Papers in Social Science* 15(1): 1–89.

Herrera, Linda. (2006a) "What's New about Youth?" *Development and Change* 37(6): 1425–1434.

Herrera, Linda (2006b) "When Does Life Begin? Youth Perspectives from Egypt." In *DevIssues.* 8 (2/December): 7–9.

Herrera, Linda. (2008) "Education and Empire: Democratic Reform in the Arab World?" *International Journal of Educational Reform* 17(4): 355–374.

Herrera, Linda. (2009) "Youth and Generational Renewal in the Middle East." *International Journal of Middle East Studies* 41(3): 368–371.

Herrera, Linda and Carlos Alberto Torres, eds. (2006) *Cultures of Arab Schooling: Critical Ethnographies from Egypt.* New York: State University of New York Press.

Hesmondhalgh, David. (2005) "Subcultures, Scenes or Tribes? None of the Above." *Journal of Youth Studies* 8(1): 21–40.

Hesse, Barnor and S. Sayyid. (2005) In Nasreen Ali, Virinder S. Kalra, and Salman Sayyid, eds., *A Postcolonial People: South Asians in Britain,* 13–31. London: Hurst.

Hill, David and Krishna Sen. (2005) *The Internet in Indonesia's New Democracy.* London: Routledge.

Hirschkind, Charles. (2006) *The Ethical Soundscape: Cassette Sermons and Islamic Counterpublics.* New York: Columbia University Press.

Ho, Enseng. (2004) "Empire from Diasporic Eyes: A View from the Other Boat." *Comparative Studies in Society and History"* 46(22): 210–246.

Holland, Janet, Caroline Ramazanoglu, Sue Sharpe, and Rachel Thomson. (1994) "Power and Desire: The Embodiment of Female Sexuality." *Feminist Review* 46: 21–38.

Honwana, Alcinda and Filip De Boeck, eds. (2004) *Makers and Breakers, Made and Broken: Children and Youngsters as Emerging Categories in Postcolonial Africa.* London: James Currey.

Honwana, Alcinda and Filip De Boeck, eds. (2005) *Makers and Breakers: Children and Youth in Postcolonial Africa*. Trenton: Africa World Press.

Hoodfar, Homa. (2000) "Iranian Women at the Intersection of Citizenship and the Family Code: The Perils of Islamic Criteria." In Suad Joseph, ed., *Gender and Citizenship in the Middle East*, 287–313. Syracuse, N.Y.: Syracuse University Press:

Hooker, Virginia and Huda Yasrul. (2007) "Starting Early." *Inside Indonesia* 90. http://insideindonesia.org/content/view/605/47/.

Houston, Christopher. (2002) "The Brewing of Islamist Modernity: Tea Gardens and Public Space in Istanbul." *Theory, Culture and Society* 18(6): 77–97.

Hu, Kelly. (2004) "Chinese Re-makings of Pirated VCDs of Japanese TV Dramas." In Koichi Iwabuchi, ed., *Feeling Asian Modernities: Transnational Consumption of Japanese TV Dramas*, 205–226. Hong Kong: Hong Kong University Press.

Hudson, Rex A. (1999) "The Sociology and Psychology of Terrorism: Who Becomes a Terrorist and Why?" A report prepared under an Interagency Agreement by the Federal Research Division. Washington D.C.: Library of Congress, September.

Human Rights Watch. (2002) *We Are Not the Enemy: Hate Crimes Against Arabs, Muslims, and Those Perceived to be Arab or Muslim after September 11*. New York: Human Rights Watch.

Hunwick, John O. (2003) *Arabic Literature of Africa, Vol. IV: The Writings of Western Sudanic Africa*. Leiden: Brill.

Huq, Maimuna. (1999) "From Piety to Romance: Islam-Oriented Texts in Bangladesh." In Dale F. Eickelman and Jon W. Anderson, eds., *New Media in the Muslim World: The Emerging Public Sphere*, 133–161. Bloomington: Indiana University Press.

Husin, Asna. (1988) "Philosophical and Sociological Aspects of Da'wah: A Study of Dewan Dakwah Islamiyah Indonesia." PhD diss., Columbia University.

Hussain, Serena and Tufyal Choudhury. (2007) *Muslims in the EU: Cities Report, United Kingdom*. Open Society Institute, EU Monitoring and Advocacy Program.

Hutnyk, John. (2005) "The Dialectic of 'Here and There': Anthropology 'At Home.'" In Nasreen Ali, Virinder S. Kalra, and Salman Sayyid, eds., *A Postcolonial People: South Asians in Britain*, 74–90. London: Hurst.

Hyder, Rehan. (2004) *Brimful of Asia: Negotiating Ethnicity on the UK Music Scene*. Aldershot: Ashgate.

Ibn Ekhvah. (1367/1988) *Aaein Shahrdare dar Gharn-e Haftom* [*Ruling the City in Thirteenth Century*]. Tehran: Entesharat-e Elmi-farhangi.

Ibrahim, Barbara and Hind Wassef. (2000) "Caught between Two Worlds: Youth in the Egyptian Hinterland." In Roel Meijer, ed., *Alienation or Integration of Arab Youth*, 161–185. London: Curzon Press.

International Crisis Group. (2000) "Indonesia: Overcoming Murder and Chaos in Maluku." *Asia Report*. Jakarta/Brussels: International Crisis Group.

Ismail, Salwa (2008) "Muslim Public Self-Presentation: Interrogating the Liberal Public Sphere." *Political Sciences and Politics* 41: 25–29.

Jackson, Richard, Marie Breen Smyth, and Jeroen Gunning, eds. (2009) *Critical Terrorism Studies: A New Research Agenda*. Abingdan: Routledge.

Jahad Daneshgahi Daneshgah Tehran. (1378/1999) *Baresi Zamineh-haye Ehyaa*
Farhange Amre be M'aroof va Nahi az Mokar [*A Study on the Conditions of*
Revitalization of the Tradition of 'Commanding the Just and Prohibiting the
Forbidden']. Tehran: Jahade Daneshgahi Tehran University.

Janson, Marloes. (2005) "Roaming about for God's Sake: The Upsurge of the *Tablīgh*
Jamā'at in The Gambia." *Journal of Religion in Africa* 35(4): 450–481.

Janson, Marloes. (2006) "'We Are All the Same, Because We Are All Worshipping God':
The Controversial Case of a Female Saint in The Gambia." *Africa* 76(4): 502–525.

Janson, Marloes. (2008) "Renegotiating Gender: Changing Moral Practice in the
Tablīghī Jamā'at in The Gambia." *Journal for Islamic Studies* 28: 9–36.

Janson, Marloes. (2009) "Searching for God: Young Gambians' Conversion to the
Tabligh Jama'at." In Mamadou Diouf and Mara Leichtman, eds., *New Perspectives*
on Islam in Senegal: Conversion, Migration, Wealth, Power, and Femininity, 139–168.
New York: Palgrave Macmillan.

Janson, Marloes. (Forthcoming) "Guidelines on Becoming a Perfect Woman: The
Interplay between Gender Ideology and Praxis in the *Tablīgh Jamā'at* in The
Gambia." In Margot Badran, ed., *Gender and Islam in Africa* (provisional title).
Leiden: Brill.

Jenkins, Richard. (1994) "Rethinking Ethnicity: Identity, Categorization and Power."
Ethnic and Racial Studies 17(2): 197–223.

Jennings, Jeremy. (2000) "Citizenship, Republicanism and Multiculturalism in
Contemporary France." *British Journal of Political Science* 30: 575–598.

Jessen, Frank and Ulrich von Wilamowitz-Moellendorff. (2006) *Entschleierung eines*
Symbols? Konrad-Adenauer-Stiftung.

Johnston, Michael. (2005) *Syndromes of Corruption, Wealth, Power, and Democracy.*
Cambridge: Cambridge University Press.

Jones, Gavin W. and Chris Manning. (1992) "Labour Force and Employment during
the 1980s," in Anne Booth, ed., *The Oil Boom and After: Indonesian Economic*
Policy and Performance in the Soeharto Era, 363–407. Kuala Kumpur: Oxford
University Press.

Jouili, Jeanette S. (2007) "Being a Pious French Muslim Woman." *ISIM Review* 19:
32–33.

Jouili, Jeanette and Schirin Amir-Moazami. (2006) "Knowledge, Empowerment and
Religious Authority among Pious Muslim Women in France and Germany." *The*
Muslim World 97(4): 615–640.

Jugé, Tony S. and Michael P. Perez. (2006) "The Modern Colonial Politics of
Citizenship and Whiteness in France." *Social Identities* 12: 187–212.

Kaba, Lansiné. (1974) *The Wahhabiyya: Islamic Reform and Politics in French West*
Africa. Evanston, Ill.: Northwestern University Press.

Kahen, Mojgan. (1997) *Barrasiye tatbighiye masa'le jensi beyne Iraniha va Beljikiha* [*A*
Comparative Study on Sexual Behaviors between Iranians and Belgians]. www.
iranianuk.com/article.php?id=15256.

Kalra, Virinder S. (2000) "Vilayeti Rhythms: Beyond Bhangra's Emblematic Status to a
Translation of Lyrical Texts." *Theory, Culture & Society* 17(3): 80–102.

Kalra, Virinder S. (2005) "Policing Diversity: Racialisation and the Criminal Justice System." In Nasreen Ali, Virinder S. Kalra, and Salman Sayyid, eds., *A Postcolonial People: South Asians in Britain*, 234–243. London: Hurst.

Kalra, Virinder, and S. Sayyid, eds. (2005) *A Postcolonial People: South Asians in Britain*, 1–10. London: Hurst.

Kamat, Sangeeta. (2007) "Populism Repackaged: The Word Bank's Perspective on Equity and Youth." *Development and Change* 38(6): 1209–1218.

Kara, İsmail. (1989) *Mızrakh İlmihal* [Book of Manners with a Lance]. Istanbul: Dergah Yayınları.

Karpin, Michael and Ina Friedman. (1988) *Murder in the Name of God: The Plot to Kill Yitzhak Rabin*. New York: Metropolitan Books.

Kastoryano, Riva. (2003) "Der Islam auf der Suche nach 'seinem Platz' in Frankreich und Deutschland." In Michael Minkenberg and Ulrich Willems, eds., *Politik und Religion. Politische Vierteljahresschrift, Sonderheft*, 184–206. Wiesbaden: Westdeutscher Verlag.

Kazemipour, Abdolsamd. (2003) *Baava-rha va Raftar-haye Mazhabi dar Iran 1353–1379* [*The Religious Believes and Practices in Iran 1974–2000*]. Tehran: Vezaarate farhang va Ershaad eslami.

Kearney, Mary C. (1998) "'Don't Need You': Rethinking Identity Politics and Separatism from a Grrrl Perspective." In Jonathan S. Epstein, ed., *Youth Culture: Identity in a Postmodern World*, 148–188. Oxford: Blackwell.

Keaton, Trica Danielle. (2006) *Muslim Girls and the Other France: Race, Identity Politics, and Social Exclusion*. Bloomington: Indiana University Press.

Kepel, Gilles. (2002) *Jihad: The Trail of Political Islam*. London: I. B. Tauris.

Kepel, Gilles. (2003) *Muslim Extremism in Egypt: The Prophet and Pharaoh*, 2nd ed. Berkeley: University of California Press.

Khalifa, Ayman (1995) "The Withering Youth of Egypt." *Roya* 7: 6–10.

Khatam, Azam. (1384/2005) "Fazaa-haye Omomi va Ghalaroo Hamegani" ["Public Sphere and Public Spaces"]. *Iranshahr* 3: 3.

Khatam, Azam. (1385/2006) "Eslaah Talabi va farhang Omomi" ("Reformism and Popular Culture"). *Goftogu* 47: 99.

Khedimellah, Moussa. (2002) "Aesthetics and Poetics of Apostolic Islam in France." *ISIM Newsletter* 11: 20–21.

Khomeini, Ayatollah. (1370/1991) *Sahifeye Nour* [*The Book of Light*]. Tehran: Ministry of Islamic Guidance, AH, 134.

Khosrokhavar, Farhad. (2002) "Postrevolutionary Iran and the New Social Movements." In Eric J. Hooglund, ed., *Twenty Years of Islamic Revolution*, 3–18. Syracuse: Syracuse University Press.

Khoury-Machool, Makram. (1987) "Makram Zeh Lo Mered, Zo Milhama." *Ha'ir* December 18: 1.

Khoury-Machool, Makram. (1988) "This Is Not a Revolt—This Is a War." *Journal of Palestinian Studies* 17(3): 91–99.

Khoury-Machool, Makram. (2002) "The Globalisation of Media: The First Cyberwar in the Middle East." *The Middle East in London, Stacy International:* 70–83.

Kian-Thiebaut, Azadeh. (2002) "Political Impacts of Iranian Youth's Individuation: How Family Matters." Presented at MESA, Washington D.C., November 24 [unpublished].

Kilani, Monther. (2002) "Équivoques de la religion et politiques de la laïcité en Europe." *Archives des Sciences Sociales des Religions* 121: 69–86.

Kilani, Monther. (2005) "Il faut déconfessionnaliser la laïcité: Le religieux imprègne encore les imaginaires." *Journal des Anthropologues* 100–101: 37–48.

Klinken, Gerry van. (2001) "The Maluku Wars: Bringing Society Back." *Indonesia* 71: 1–26.

Klinkhammer, Gritt. (2000) *Moderne Formen islamischer Lebensführung: Eine qualitativ empirische Untersuchung zur Religiosität sunnitisch geprägter Türkinnen in Deuschland*. Marburg: Diagonal Verlag.

Knight, Michael Muhammad. (2007) *The Five Percenters: Islam, Hip-hop and the Gods of New York*. Oxford: Oneworld Publications.

Kömeçoğlu, Uğur. (2004) "Neue Formen der Geselligkeit: Islamische Cafés in Istanbul." Nilüfer Göle and Ludwig Ammann, ed., *Islam in Sicht: der Auftritt von Muslimen im öffentlichen Raum*, 147–177. Bielefeld: Transcript-Verlag.

Konrad Adanauer Foundation. (1999) *Turkish Youth 98: The Silent Majority Highlighted*. Ankara: Ofset Fotomat.

Krastev, Ivan and Alan L. McPherson. (2007) *The Anti-American Century*. Budapest: Central European University Press.

Kundnani, Arun. (2001) "From Oldham to Bradford: The Violence of the Violated." *Race & Class* 43(2): 105–131.

Kurzman, Charles. (2005) "A Feminist Generation in Iran?" Working paper. University of North Carolina at Chapel Hill.

Laïcité et République, Commission présidée par Bernard Stasi. (December 11, 2003) Paris, La Documentation française. http://lesrapports.ladocumentationfrancaise. fr/BRP/034000725/0000.pdf

Laitin, David P. (1982) "The Shari'ah Debate and the Origins of Nigeria's Second Republic." *Journal of Modern African Studies* 20: 411–430.

Laroui, Abdellah. (1977) *Les Origines Sociales et Culturelles du Nationalisme Marocain, (1830–1912)*. Paris: François Maspero.

Last, Murray. (1992) "The Power of Youth, Youth of Power: Notes on the Religions of the Young in Northern Nigeria." In Hélène d'Almeida-Topor, ed., *Les jeunes en Afrique: La politique et la ville*, Vol. 2, 375–399. Paris: L'Harmattan.

Launay, Robert. (1992) *Beyond the Stream: Islam and Society in a West African Town*. Berkeley: University of California Press.

Launay, Robert and Benjamin F. Soares. (1999) "The Formation of an 'Islamic Sphere' in French Colonial West Africa." *Economy and Society* 28(4): 497–519.

Lawrence, Bruce, ed. (2005) *Messages to the World: The Statements of Osama Bin Laden*. London: Verso.

LeBlanc, Marie-Nathalie. (2000) "From *Sya* to Islam: Social Change and Identity among Muslim Youth in Bouaké, Côte d'Ivoire." *Paideuma* 46: 85–109.

LeBlanc, Marie Nathalie. (2006) "De la tradition à l'Islam: L'orthodoxie à l'encontre des rites culturels." *Cahiers d'Etudes Africaines* 182(2): 417–436.

LeBlanc, Marie Nathalie and Benjamin F. Soares, eds. (2008) "Muslim West Africa in the Age of Neoliberalism." *Africa Today* 54: 3.

Leccardi, Carmen and Elisabetta Ruspini, eds. (2006) *A New Youth? Young People, Generations and Family Life*. Hampshire: Ashgate.

Leigh, B. (1999) "Learning and Knowing boundaries: Schooling in New Order Indonesia." *Sojourn* 14: 1.

Leruth, Michael F. (1998) "The Neorepublican Discourse on French National Identity." *French Politics and Society* 16(4): 46–61.

Levtzion, Nehemia. (1987) "Rural and Urban Islam in West Africa: An Introductory Essay." In Nehemia Levtzion and Humphrey J. Fisher, eds., *Rural & Urban Islam in West Africa*, 1–20. Boulder, Colo.: Lynne Rienner Publishers.

Lewis, Philip. (1994) *Islamic Britain: Religion, Politics and Identity among British Muslims—Bradford in the 1990s*. London: I. B. Tauris.

Liddle, R. William. (1996) "The Islamic Turn in Indonesia: A Political Explanation." *Journal of Asian Studies* 55: 3.

Liederman, Lina Molokotos. (2000) "Pluralism in Education: The Display of Islamic Affiliation in French and British Schools." *Islam and Christian-Muslim Relations* 11(1): 105–117.

Limage, Leslie. (2000) "Education and Muslim Identity: The Case of France." *Comparative Education* 36(1): 73–94.

Liqueur, Walter. ([1962] 1984) *Young Germany: A History of the German Youth Movement*. New York: Transaction Publishers.

Loimeier, R. (1997) "Islamic Reform and Political Change: The Example of Abubakar Gumi and the 'Yan Izala Movement in Northern Nigeria." In David Westerlund and Eva E. Rosander, eds., *African Islam and Islam in Africa: Encounters between Sufis and Islamists*, 286–307. Athens: Ohio University Press.

Lynch, Mark. (2006) *Voices of the New Arab Public: Iraq, al-Jazeera, and Middle East Politics Today*. New York: Columbia University Press.

Mahmood, Saba. (2005) *Politics of Piety: The Islamic Revival and the Feminist Subject*. Princeton: Princeton University Press.

Mahmoud, Golzari. (2004) Paper Presented at the workshop, "Young Girls and the Challenges of Life," May 2004, cited in ISNA News agency, 22 Urdibahasht 1383, womeniniran.com.

Maira, Sunaina and Elisabeth Soep. (2004) *Youthscapes: The Popular, the National, the Global*. Philadelphia: University of Pennsylvania Press.

Mannheim, Karl. (1952) "The Problem of Generations." In Paul Kecskemeti, ed. *Essays on the Sociology of Knowledge*, 276–322. New York: Oxford University Press.

Mannheim, Karl. (1997) *Collected Works of Mannheim*. London: Routledge.

Mansell, Robin and Uta When, eds. (1998) *Knowledge Societies: Information Technology for Sustainable Development*. Oxford: Oxford University Press.

Marcuse, Herbert. (1969) "On Revolution." In Alexander Cockburn and Robin Blackburn, eds., *Student Power: Problems, Diagnoses, Action*, 367–372. London: Penguin Books.

Marshall-Fratani, Ruth. (2006) "The War of 'Who Is Who': Autochthony, Nationalism, and Citizenship in the Ivoirian Crisis." *African Studies Review* 49(2): 9–43.

Masquelier, Adeline. (1996) "Identity, alterity, and ambiguity in a Nigerién community: Competing definitions of true Islam." In Richard Werbner, *Postcolonial identities in Africa*, 222–244. London: Zed Press.

Masquelier, Adeline. (1999) "Debating Muslims, Disputed Practices: Struggles for the Realization of an Alternative Moral Order in Niger." In John L. Comaroff and Jean Comaroff, eds., *Civil Society and the Political Imagination in Africa: Critical Perspectives*, 219–250. Chicago: University of Chicago Press.

Masquelier, Adeline. (2001) *Prayer Has Spoiled Everything: Possession, Power and Identity in an Islamic Town in Niger*. Durham, N.C.: Duke University Press.

Masquelier, Adeline. (2005) "The Scorpion's Sting: Youth, Marriage, and the Struggle for Social Maturity in Niger." *Journal of the Royal Anthropological Institute* 11: 59–83.

Masquelier, Adeline. (2007) "Islam, Youth, and the State in Niger." In Benjamin F. Soares and René Otayek, eds., *Islam and Muslim Politics in Africa*. New York: Palgrave.

Masquelier, Adeline. (2009a) "Lessons from *Rubì*: Love, Poverty, and the Educational Value of Televised Dramas in Niger." In Jennifer Cole and Lynn Thomas, eds., *Love in Africa* 204–228. Chicago: University of Chicago Press.

Masquelier, Adeline. (2009b) *Women and Islamic Revival in a West African Town*. Bloomington: Indiana University Press.

Massey, Doreen. (1998) "The Spatial Construction of Youth Cultures." In Tracey Skelton and Gill Valentine, eds., *Cool Places: Geographies of Youth Cultures*, 121–129. London: Routledge.

Massignon, Bérengère. (2000) "Laïcité et gestion de la diversité religieuse à l'école publique en France." *Social Compass* 47(3): 353–366.

Masud, Muhammad Khalid. (2000a) "The Growth and Development of the Tablīghī Jamā'at in India." In Muhammad Khalid Masud, ed., *Travelers in Faith: Studies of the Tablīghī Jamā'at as a Transnational Islamic Movement for Faith Renewal*, 3–43. Leiden: Brill.

Masud, M. Khalid, ed. (2000b) *Travelers in Faith: Studies of the Tablighi Jama'at as a Transnational Islamic Movement for Faith Renewal*. Leiden: Brill.

Matar, Nadia. (1997) "Glows Ticks and Grooves." *Cairo Times* March 14–20.

Mate, Rekopantswe (2009). "Discourses of Youth Sexuality in the Context of HIV and AIDS in Beitbridge in Zimbabwe" (Unpublished paper) The Hague: International Institute of Social Studies of Erasmus University Rotterdam (ISS).

Meeker, Michael. (1991) "The New Muslim Intellectuals in the Republic of Turkey." In Richard L. Tapper, ed., *Islam in Modern Turkey*. London: I. B. Tauris.

Meeker, Michael. (1994) "Muslim Individual and His Audience: A New Configuration of Writer and Reader among Believers in the Republic of Turkey." In Serif Mardin ed., *Cultural Transitions in the Middle East*, 153–188. Leiden: Brill.

Meer, Nasar. (2006) "'Get Off Your Knees': Print Media, Public Intellectuals and Muslims in Britain." *Journalism Studies* 7(1): 35–59.

Metiner, Mehmet. (2004) *Yemyeşil Şeriat Bembeyaz Demokrasi* [*All Green Shari'a, All White Democracy*]. Istanbul: Dogan Kitap.

Mehran, Golnar. (1991) "The Creation of the New Muslim Woman: Female Education in the Islamic Republic of Iran." *Convergence* 23(4): 42–52.

Melucci, Alberto. (1989) *Nomads of the Present: Social Movements and Individual Needs in Contemporary Society*. London: Hutchinson.

Ménoret, Pascal. (2007) "La Constitution Imaginaire de La Jeunesse Saoudienne: Islam et Révolte en Arabie Saoudite." In Mounia Bennani-Chraibi and Iman Farag, eds., *Jeunesses des sociétés Musulmanes: Par-delà les menaces et les promesses*, 195–221. Paris: Aux lieux d'être.

Ménoret, Pascal. (2008) "Thugs and Zealots: The Politicization of Saudi Youth, 1965–2007." PhD diss., Paris-1 University.

Metcalf, Barbara D. (2002) *'Traditionalist' Islamic Activism: Deoband, Tablighis, and Talibs*. ISIM papers. Leiden: ISIM.

Meunier, Olivier. (1998) "Marabouts et courants religieux en pays Hawsa." *Canadian Journal of African Studies* 32(3): 521–557.

Meyer, Birgit and Annelies Moors. (2006) *Religion, Media, and the Public Sphere*. Bloomington: Indiana University Press.

Miller, D. (1994) "Style and Ontology." In Jonathan Friedman, ed., *Consumption and Identity*, 71–96. Chur, Switzerland: Harwood Academic Publishers.

Ministry of Culture and Islamic Guidance. (1994) *An Introduction to Behaviorology of the Youth*. Tehran: Ministry of Culture and Islamic Guidance.

Ministry of Islamic Guidance. (2001) *Results of Survey in Twenty-Eight Centers of Iranian Provinces: Iranians' Values and Attitudes* Tehran: Ministry of Islamic Guidance.

Ministry of Islamic Guidance. (1382/2003) *Data Analysis of Iranians' Values and Attitudes: Generation Gap and Continuity*. Tehran: Tarh-haye Melli [National Plans], AH.

Mintz, John and Douglas Farah. (2002) "Small Scams Probed for Terror Ties: Muslim, Arab Stores Monitored as Part of Post-Sept. 11 Inquiry." *The Washington Post* April 12.

Mitchell, Richard P. (1969) *The Society of the Muslim Brothers*. Oxford: Oxford University Press.

Mitchell, Tony, ed. (2001) *Global Noise: Rap and Hip-hop outside the USA*. Middletown: Wesleyan University Press.

Mitsui, Toru. (2001) "The Genesis of Karaoke: How the Combination of Technology and Music Evolved." In Toru Mitsui and Shuhei Hosokawa, eds., *Karaoke Around the World: Global Technology, Local Singing*, 29–42. London: Routledge.

Modood, Tariq. (2004) "Capital's Ethnic Identity and Educational Qualifications." *Cultural Trends* 13(2): 87–105.

Modood, Tariq. (2005a) *Multicultural Politics: Racism, Ethnicity and Muslims in Britain*. Minnesota: University of Minnesota Press.

Modood, Tariq. (2005b) "Politics of Blackness and Asian Identity." In Nasreen Ali, Virinder S. Kalra, and Salman Sayyid, eds., *A Postcolonial People: South Asians in Britain*, 64–71. London: Hurst.

Mohsen-Finan, Khadija. (2002) "Promoting a Faith-Based Citizenship: The Case of Tariq Ramadan." In Rémy Leveau, Khadija Mohsen-Finan, and Catherine Wihtol de Wenden, eds., *New European Identity and Citizenship*, 133–141. Aldershot: Ashgate.

Moors, Annelies. (2005) "Submission." *ISIM Review* 15: 8–9.

Moosa, Ebrahim. (2000) "Worlds 'Apart'" Tablīghī Jamā'at in South Africa under Apartheid, 1963–1993." In Muhammad Khalid Masud, ed., *Travelers in Faith: Studies of the Tablīghī Jamā'at as a Transnational Islamic Movement for Faith Renewal*, 206–221. Leiden: Brill.

Moruzzi, Norma Claire. (2006) "Trying to Look Different: *Hejab* as the Self-Presentation of Social Distinctions." Presented at the Iranian Studies Conference, London, August 2–7.

Moruzzi, Norma Claire and Fatemeh Sadeghi. (2006) "Out of the Frying Pan, into the Fire: Young Iranian Women Today." *Middle East Report* 241: 22–28.

Morvan, Alain. (2008) *L'Honneur et les honneurs: Souvenirs d'un recteur "kärcherisé."* Paris: Grasset.

Muslims Weekly. (2004) "Columbia Presents First Study on Muslim Political, Social, Religious Identity." Jamaica, Queens, NY: Muslims Weekly. October 8. www.indypressny.org/nycma/voices/139/briefs/briefs_4/.

Müstecaplıoğlu, Barış. (2005) *Şakird [Disciple]*. Istanbul: Metis.

Naafs, Suzanne. (2005) "Beelden van Vrouwen in VCD's: Een Onderzoek naar Ideeën over 'Minang zijn.' Traditie en het Moderne." MA thesis, Leiden University.

Naguib, Kamal. (2008) *Thaqafat al-Shabab al-Misri: Al-ihbatat wa 'l-tattalu'at wa-ab'ad al-muqawama. [The Children Have Grown Up: The Disappointments, Ambitions, and Scope of the Resistance in Egyptian Youth Culture]*. Cairo: Mahrousa Press.

Nasır, Na'ila Suad and Jasiyah Al-Amin. (2006) "Creating Identity-Safe Spaces on College Campus for Muslim Students." *Change* (March/April): 23–27.

Nasr, Seyyed Vali Reza. (2001) *Islamic Leviathan: Islam and the Making of State Power*. Oxford: Oxford University Press.

Navaro-Yashin, Yael. (2002) "Market for Identities: Secularism, Islamism, Commodities." In Deniz Kandiyoti and Ayse Saktanber, eds., *Fragments of Culture: The Everyday of Modern Turkey*. New York: I. B. Tauris.

Negus, Keith. (1998) "Cultural Production and the Corporation: Musical Genres and the Strategic Management of Creativity in the US Recording Industry." *Music, Culture and Society* 20(3): 359–379.

Negus, Keith. (1999) *Music Genres and Corporate Cultures*. London: Routledge.

Neyzi, Leyla. (2001) "Object or Subject? The Paradox of the 'Youth' in Turkey." *International Journal of Middle East Studies* 33(3): 411–432.

Niandou-Souley, Abdoulaye. and Gado Alzouma. (1996) Islamic Renewal in Niger: From Monolith to Plurality. *Social Compass* 43(2): 240–265.

Niang, Abdoulaye. (2006) "Bboys: Hip-Hop Culture in Dakar, Sénégal." In Pam Nilan and Charles Feixa, eds., *Global Youth: Hybrid Identities, Plural Worlds*, 167–185. London: Routledge.

Nilan, Pam. (2006) "The Reflexive Youth Culture of Devout Muslim Youth in Indonesia." In Pam Nilan and Charles Feixa, eds., *Global Youth: Hybrid Identities, Plural Worlds*, 91–110. London: Routledge.

Nilan, Pam and Charles Feixa. (2006) *Global Youth: Hybrid Identities, Plural Worlds*. London: Routledge.

Nisbet, Erik C. and James S. Shanahan. (2004) "Restrictions on Civil Liberties: Views of Islam & Muslim Americans." Media and Society Research Study Group, Cornell University.

Nisbett, Nicholas. (2007) "Friendship, Consumption, Morality: Practicing Identity, Negotiating Hierarchy in Middle-Class Bangalore." *Journal of the Royal Anthropological Institute* 13: 935–950.

Nóvoa, António. (2002) "Ways of Thinking about Education in Europe." In António Nóvoa and Martin Lawn, eds., *Fabricating Europe: The Formation of an Educational Space*, 131–155. Dordrecht: Kluwer Academic Publishers.

Oberti, Marco. (2007) *L'école dans la ville: Ségrégation, mixité, carte scolaire*. Paris: Sciences Po.

Ofluoğlu, Şanver. (2005) "*Kemancı* Gülleri." *Kuzey Ormanı* 1: 19.

Orhan, Pamuk. (2000) *Kar* [Snow]. İstanbul: İletişim Yayınları.

Osella, Filippo and Caroline Osella. (2008) "Introduction: Islamic Reformism in South Asia." *Modern Asian Studies* 42: 317–346.

Otayek, René and Benjamin F. Soares. (2007) "Introduction: Islam and Muslim Politics in Africa." In Benjamin F. Soares and René Otayek, eds., *Islam and Muslim Politics in Africa*. New York: Palgrave.

Palestinian Central Bureau of Statistics. (2005) *Women and Men in Palestine*. Ramallah: he Palestinian Central Bureau of Statistics.

Palestinian Central Bureau of Statistics. (2006) *Palestine in Figures 2005*. Ramallah: he Palestinian Central Bureau of Statistics.

Pamuk, Orhan. (2000) *Kar* (Snow), İstanbul: İletişim Yayınları.

Panahi, Mohamad Hossein. (1375/1996) "Nezame Farhangh, karkard-ha va Degarghoni-ha" ["Cultural System: Functions and Changes"]. *Tahajome Farhangi, Nameh Pajopesh* 2&3.

Pascon, Paul, and Mekki Bentaher. (1969) "Ce que Disent 296 Jeunes Ruraux" *BESM* January–June: 112–113.

Peach, Ceri. (2005) "Britain's Muslim Population: An Overview." In Tahir Abbas, ed., *Muslim Britain: Communities under Pressure*, 18–30. London: Zed Books.

Penamas. (1995) *Jurnal Penelitian Agama dan Masyarakat*, 20, 7. Jakarta: Board of Research and Development of the Department of Religious Affairs.

Perempuan, Maria Rosari Dwi. (2004) "Kami Ingin Jadi Diri Sendiri." *Jurnal Perempuan* 37: 7–16.

Perlman, Marc. (2008) "Western Promises." *The Nation* January 7. http://www.thenation.com/doc/20080107/perelman.

Petit Larouse. (2003) Grand Format. Paris: Larousse.

Pew Research Center. (2007) *Muslim Americans: Middle Class and Mostly Mainstream*. Washington, D.C.: Pew Research Center.

Pezeril, Charlotte. (2008) Islam, mysticisme et marginalité: Les Baay Faal du Sénégal. Paris: L'Harmattan.

Phalet, Karin, Jessika Ter Wal, and Carlo S. Van Praag, eds. (2004) *Moslim in Nederland: Een Onderzoek naar de Religieuze Betrokkenheid van Turken en Marokkanen.* Den Haag: Sociaal en Cultureel Planbureau.

Piven, Frances Fox and Richard A. Cloward. (1979) *Poor People's Movements: Why They Succeed, How They Fail.* New York: Vintage Books.

Pizzorno, Alessandro. (1986) "Some Other Kind of Otherness: A Critique of Rational Choice Theories" In Alejandro Foxley, ed., *Development, Democracy and the Art of Trespassing*, 355–373. Notre Dame: University of Notre Dame Press.

Population Council. (1999) *Transitions to Adulthood: A National Survey of Egyptian Adolescents*, Cairo,: The Population Council.

Poucet, Bruno, ed. (2001) *La loi Debré: Paradoxe de l'état éducateur?* Amiens, Champagne-Ardennes: Centre régional de documentation pédagogique (CRDP) de l'Académie d'Amiens.

Qotbi, Mansour. (1379/2000) "Causeless Rebellion in the Land of Iran." *Iran Javan* 166, Mehr.

Qvortrup, Jen, Marjatta Bardy, Giovanni Sgritta, and Helmut Wintersberger, eds. (1994) *Childhood Matters: Social Theory, Practice and Politics.* Wien: Avebury.

Raccagni, Michelle. (1980) "The French Economic Interests in the Ottoman Empire." *International Journal of Middle East Studies* 11(3): 339–376.

Ralph, Michael. (2008) "Killing Time." *Social Text* 26(4): 1–29.

Recknaged, Charles and Azam Gorgin. (2000) "Iran: New Morality Police." *Radio Free Europe*, July 26. http://www.rferl.org

Reetz, Dietrich. (2006) "Sûfî Spirituality Fires Reformist Zeal: The Tablîghî Jamâ'at in Today's India and Pakistan." *Archives de sciences sociales des religions* 135: 33–51.

Reuter, Astrid. (2007) "Säkularität und Religionsfreiheit: Ein doppeltes Dilemma." *Leviathan.* 2(35): 178–192.

Reynolds, Pamela. (1995) "Youth and the Politics of Culture in South Africa." In Sharon Stephens, ed., *Children and the Politics of Culture*, 218–240. Princeton: Princeton University Press.

Rheingold, Howard. (1994) *The Virtual Community: Surfing the Internet.* London: Minerva.

Roberts, Allen F. and Mary Nooter Roberts. (2003) *A Saint in the City: Sufi Arts of Urban Senegal.* Los Angeles: UCLA Fowler Museum of Cultural History.

Robinson, Kathryn. (2000) "Indonesian Women: From *Orde Baru* to *Reformasi*." In Louise Edwards and Mina Roces, eds., *Women in Asia: Tradition, Modernity and Globalisation*, 139–169. Ann Arbor: University of Michigan Press.

Robison, Richard and Vedi R. Hadiz. (2004) *Reorganising Power in Indonesia: The Politics of Oligarchy in an Age of Markets.* London: Routledge.

Roitman, Janet. (2005) *Fiscal Disobedience.* Princeton, N.J.: Princeton University Press.

Roland, Mark. (1998) "Erotic Terrorism." *Melody Maker* March 28, 46.

Roman-Amat, Béatrice. (2007) "La réussite exemplaire d'Aubervilliers." August 5. www.histoiresdememoire.org.

Rose, Tricia. (1994) *Black Noise: Rap Music and Black Culture in Contemporary America.* Middletown: Wesleyan University Press.

Rose, Tricia and Andrew Ross, eds. (1994) *Microphone Fiends: Youth Music and Youth Culture.* New York: Routledge.

Roy, Olivier. (2004) *Globalized Islam: The Search for a New Ummah.* New York: Columbia University Press.

Sadria, Mojtaba. (1384/2005) "Jonbesh-haye Ejtemaei Farhangi va tahavolat Farhangi" ("Sociocultural Movements and Cultural Transformation"). *Iranshahr* 3: 11.

Safabakhsh, Mohsen. (1382/2003) *Nataiej-e Nazar Sanji dar bareh Khoshoonat dar Football (Result of Poll Report on Violence in Football).* Tehran: Sazeman-e Tarbiat Badani Keshvar.

Safak, Elif. (2004) *Araf,* trans. Aslı Bilici. Istanbul: Metis.

Safak, Elif. (2004) *The Saint of Incipient Insanities.* New York: Farrar, Straus and Giroux.

Saint-Blancat, Catherine. (2002) "Islam in Diaspora: Between Reterritorialization and Extraterritoriality. *International Journal of Urban and Regional Research* 26: 138–151.

Saint Sauveur, Charles de. (2007) "Les familles de plus en plus." *Le Parisien* March 5.

Saktanber, Ayşe. (1997) "Formation of a Middle Class Ethos and Its Quotidian: Revitalizing Islam in Urban Turkey." In Ayşe Öncü and Petra Weyland, eds., *Space, Culture and Power: New Identities in Globalizing Cities,* 140–156. London: Zed Books.

Saktanber, Ayşe. (2002a) *Living Islam: Women, Religion and the Politicization of Culture in Turkey.* New York: I. B. Tauris.

Saktanber, Ayşe. (2002b) "'We Pray Like You Have Fun': New Islamic Youth between Popular Culture and Intellectualism in Turkey." In Deniz Kandiyoti and Ayse Saktanber, eds., *Fragments of Culture: The Everyday of Modern Turkey.* pp. 294–307. New York: I. B. Tauris.

Saktanber, Ayşe. (2006) "Women and the Iconography of Fear: Islamization in Post-Islamist Turkey." *Signs: Journal of Women in Culture and Society* 32(1): 21–31.

Salehi-Isfahani, Djavad and Navtej Dhillon. (2008) "Stalled Youth Transitions in the Middle East: A Framework For Policy Reform." Middle East Youth Initiative Working Paper. Wolfensohn Center for Development Dubai School of Government.

Salih, Ruba. (2004) "The Backward and the New: National, Transnational, and Post-National Islam in Europe." *Journal of Ethnic and Migration Studies* 30(5): 995–1011.

Salvatore, Armando. (2004) "Making Public Space: Opportunities and Limits of Collective Action among Muslims in Europe." *Journal of Ethnic and Migration Studies* 30(4): 1013–1031.

Samhan, Helen. (2003) "By the Numbers." *Arab American Business* October: 27–35.

Sami, Bill. (2005) "Iran Youth Movement Has Untapped Potential." Radio Free Europe. April 13. www.rferl.org/features/features_Article. aspx?m=04&;y=2005&id=3D5DCD40–3EBC-4343-A1C9–5BF29FFE7BB.

Sandals, Alexandra. (2008) "Arab Bloggers Defy Arrest." *Aljazeera.net*. March 11. http://english.aljazeera.net/NR/exeres/6CAD7AE3–608B-455A-AC08–90B4CB0AEF4A.htm.

Sastramidjaja, Yatun L. M. (2000) *Dromenjagers in Bandung: Twintigers in het moderne Indonesië*. Amsterdam: Het Spinhuis.

Sastramidjaja, Yatun L. M. (2001) "Sex in the City: Between Girl Power and the Mother Image: Young Urban Women Struggle for Identity." *Inside Indonesia*: 64.

Savishinsky, Neil J. (1994) "Rastafari in the Promised Land: The Spread of a Jamaican Socioreligious Movement among the Youth of West Africa." *African Studies Review* 37(3): 19–50.

Sayyid, Salman. (2005) "Introduction: BrAsians: Postcolonial People, Ironic Citizens." In Nasreen Ali, Virinder S. Kalra, and Salman Sayyid, eds., *A Postcolonial People: South Asians in Britain*, pp. 1–10. London: Hurst & Company.

Schler, Lyn. (2003) "Ambiguous Spaces: The Struggle over African Identities and Urban Communities in Colonial Douala, 1914–45." *Journal of African History* 44: 51–72.

Schulz, Dorothea. (2006) "Morality, Community, Publicness: Shifting Terms of Public Debate in Mali." In Birgit Meyer and Annelies Moors, eds., *Religion, Media, and the Public Sphere*, 132–151. Bloomington: Indiana University Press.

Scott, Jean Wallach. (2005) "Symptomatic Politics: The Banning of Islamic Headscarves in French Public Schools." *French Politics, Culture and Society* 23(3): 106–127.

Scott, Joan Wallach. (2007) *The Politics of the Veil*. Princeton: Princeton University Press.

Seale, Bobby. (1970) *Seize the Time: The Story of the Black Panther Party and Huey P. Newton*. Random House.

Seesemann, Rüdiger. (2010) *The Divine Flood: Ibrahim Niasse and the Roots of a Twentieth-Century Sufi Revival*. New York: Oxford University Press.

Seesemann, Rüdiger and Benjamin F. Soares. (2009) "'Being as Good Muslims as Frenchmen': On Islam and Colonial Modernity in West Africa." *Journal of Religion in Africa* 39(1): 91–120.

Sennet, Richard. (1992) *The Fall of Public Man*, New York: W. W. Norton.

Serajzadeh, Seyed Hossein. (1999) "Non-attending Believers: Religiosity of Iranian Youth and Its Implications for Secularization Theory." Presented at the World Congress of Sociology, Montreal.

Shadid, W. and P. S. van Koningsveld. (2005) "Muslim Dress in Europe: Debates on the Headscarf." *Journal of Islamic Studies* 16(1): 35–61.

Shari'ati, Ali. (1983) "Zan" ["Woman"]. In *Mamjoo'e asar, Collected Works*, 2nd ed. Tehran: Sabz.

Shari'ati, Ali. (2004) *Results of Survey in Twenty-Eight Centers of Iranian Provinces: Iranians' Values and Attitudes*. Tehran: Ministry of Islamic Guidance.

Sharma, Sanjay, John Hutnyk, and Ashwani Sharma, eds. (1996) *DisOrienting Rhythms: The Politics of the New Asian Dance Music*. London: Zed Books.

Shirky, Clay. (2008) *Here Comes Everybody: How change Happens when People Come Together*. New York: Penguin.

Sikand, Yoginder. (2002) *The Origins and Development of the Tablighi-Jama'at (1920–2000): A Cross-Country Comparative Study.* New Delhi: Orient Longman.

Sikand, Yoginder. (2003) "The Tablighi Jama'at and Politics." *ISIM Newsletter* 13: 42–43.

Silver, Hillary. (2007) "Social Exclusion: Comparative Analysis of Europe and Middle East Youth." Middle East Youth Initiative Working Paper. Wolfensohn Center for Development and Dubai School of Government.

Silverman, Max. (2007) "The French Republic Unveiled." *Ethnic and Racial Studies* 30(4): 628–642.

Silverstein, Paul A. 2004. Algeria in France: Transpolitics, Race, and Nation. Bloomington: Indiana University Press.

Singerman, Diane. (1995) *Avenues of Participation: Family, Politics, and Networks in Urban Quarters of Cairo.* Princeton, New Jersey: Princeton University Press.

Singh, Amar. (2006) "Muslim Rapper Defends His Suicide Bomber Lyrics." *The Evening Standard* June 28, 9.

Sivanandan, A. (2006) "Race, Terror and Civil Society." *Race and Class* 47(3): 1–8.

Smith, Susan. (2007) AlMaghrib Institute: Motivating People to Learn More about Islam." *Arab News* April 10, http://arabnews.com/?page=5&section=0&article= 94818&d=10&m=4&y=2007.

Smith, Zeric Kay. (1997) "'From Demons to Democrats': Mali's Student Movement 1991–1996." *Review of African Political Economy* 72: 249–263.

Smith-Hefner, Nancy J. (2005) "The New Muslim Romance: Changing Patterns of Courtship and Marriage among Educated Javanese Youth." *Journal of Southeast Asian Studies* 36(3): 441–459.

Soares, Benjamin F. (2004) "Islam and Public Piety in Mali." In Armando Salvatore and Dale F. Eickelman (eds.), *Public Islam and the Common Good,* 205–226. Brill, Leiden.

Soares, Benjamin F. (2005) *Islam and the Prayer Economy: History and Authority in a Malian Town.* Edinburgh: Edinburgh University Press for the International African Institute.

Soares, Benjamin F. (2006) "Islam in Mali in the Neoliberal Era." *African Affairs* 104: 77–95.

Soares, Benjamin F. (2007a) "Rethinking Islam and Muslim Societies in Africa." *African Affairs* 106: 319–326.

Soares, Benjamin F. (2007b) "Saint and Sufi in Neoliberal Mali." In Martin van Bruinessen and Julia Howell, eds., *Sufism and the 'Modern' in Islam,* 76–91. London: I. B. Tauris.

Soares, Benjamin F. and Filippo Osella. (2009) "Islam, Politics, Anthropology." *Journal of the Royal Anthropological Institute* (N.S.) 15(S1): 1–23.

Soueif, M. I., et al. (1990) "Use of Psychoactive Substances among Male Secondary School Pupils in Egypt: A Study of a Nationwide Representative Sample." *Drug and Alcohol Dependence* 26: 63–79.

Soysal, Yasemin Nuboğlu. (2000) "Citizenship and Identity: Living in Diasporas in Post-war Europe?" *Ethnic and Racial Studies* 23(1): 1–15.

Soysal, Yasemin. (2002) "Locating European Identity in education." In António Nóvoa and Martin Lawn, eds. *Fabricating Europe: The Formation of an Educational Space*, 55–66. Dordrecht: Kluwer Academic Publishers.

Stokes, Martin, ed. (1994) *Ethnicity, Ideuntity and Music: The Musical Construction of Place*. Oxford: Berg Publishers.

Stratham, Paul and Ruud Koopmans. (2004) "Resilient or Adaptable Islam? Migrants' Claims Making for Group Specific Demands in Britain, France, Germany and the Netherlands," Presented at the Conference of Europeanists: Europe and the World: Integration, Interdependence, Exceptionalism? Chicago, Ill., March 11–13.

Suryadi. (2003) "Minangkabau Commercial Cassettes and the Cultural Impact of the Recording Industry in West Sumatra." *Asian Music* XXXIV(2): 50–89.

Suryakusuma, Julia L. (1996) "The State and Sexuality in New Order Indonesia." In Laurie J. Sears, ed., *Fantasizing the Feminine in Indonesia*, 93–119. Durham: Duke University Press.

Swastika, Alia. (2004) "Apakah Saya Feminis? Mengaja *Girl Power* Dalam Majalah Gadis." *Jurnal Perempuan* 37: 65–76.

Sweetman, Paul. (2003) "Twenty-First Century Dis-Ease? Habitual Reflexive of the Reflexive Habitus." *The Sociological Review* 51: 4.

Taji-Farouki, S. (1996) *A Fundamental Quest: Hizb al-Tahrir and the Search for the Islamic Caliphate*. London: Grey Seal.

Tarrow, Sidney. (1994) *Power in Movement: Social Movements, Collective Action and Politics*. New York: Cambridge University Press.

Tarrow, Sidney. (1998) *Power in Movement: Social Movements and Contentious Politics*, 2nd ed. Cambridge: Cambridge University Press.

Teczan, Levent. (2003) "Das Islamische in den Studien zu Muslimen in Deutschland." *Zeitschrift für Soziologie* 32(3): 237–261.

The Iranian Presidency and the Management and Planning Organization. (2004) *Quarter Century Report of the Islamic Republic Performance (1977–2001)*. Tehran: Sazmane Modiriat va Barname Rizi.

Thompson, E. P. (1963) *The Making of the English Working Class*. London: Victor Gollancz.

Thornton, Sarah. (1995) *Club Cultures: Music, Media and Subcultural Capital*. Cambridge: Blackwell.

Tincq, Henri. (2008) "Sarkozy et Dieu." *Le Monde* February 15.

Tozy, Mohamed. (1999) *Monarchie et Islam politique au Maroc*. Paris: Presses de Sciences Po.

Trijono, Lambang. (2001) *Keluar dari Kemelut Maluku: Refleksi Pengalaman Praktis Bekerja Untuk Perdamaian Maluku*. Yogyakarta: Pustaka Pelajar.

Tse-tung, Mao. (1967) "The Orientation of the Youth Movement." In Mao Tse-tung, *Selected Works of Mao Tse-tung*, Vol. 2, 241–249. Peking: Foreign Languages Press.

Ulrich, Brian. (2009) "Historicizing Arab Blogs: Reflections on the Transmission of Ideas and Information in Middle Eastern History." *Arab Media and Society* www.arabmediasociety.com/?article=711.

Umar, Muhammad S. (1993) Changing Islamic Identity in Nigeria from the 1960s to the 1980s: From Sufism to Anti-Sufism. In Louis Brenner, ed., *Muslim Identity and Social Change in Sub-Saharan Africa*, 154–178. Bloomington: Indiana University Press.

Umar, Muhammad S. 2001. Education and Islamic Trends in Northern Nigeria: 1970–1990s. *Africa Today* 48(2): 128–50.

UNICEF. (1999) "Iraq Surveys Show 'Humanitarian Emergency.'" www.unicef.org/newsline/99pr29.htm.

United Nations Department of Economic and Social Affairs (UNDESA). (2005) *World Youth Report 2005: Young People Today, and in 2015.* New York: UNDESA.

United Nations Department of Economic and Social Affairs (UNDESA). (2007) *World Youth Report 2007: Young People's Transition to Adulthood: Progress and Challenges.* New York: United Nations Press Release.

United Nations Development Programme. (2002) *Arab Human Development Report 2002: Creating Opportunities for Future Generations.* New York: United Nations Publications.

United Nations Development Programme. (2003) *Arab Human Development Report 2003: Building a Knowledge Society.* New York: United Nations Publications.

United Nations Office for West Africa (UNOWA). (2005) *Youth Unemployment and Regional Insecurity in West Africa.* Dakar, Senegal: UNOWA.

Vahdat, Farzin. (2005) "Religious Modernity in Iran: Dilemmas of Islamic Democracy in the Discourse of Mohammad Khatami." *Comparative Studies of South Asia, Africa and the Middle East* 25: 650–664.

Van Bruinessen, Martin. (1996) "Islamic State or State Islam? Fifty Years of State-Islam Relations in Indonesia." In Ingrid Wessel, ed., *Indonesien Am Ende Des 20. Jahrhunderts*, 19–34. Hamburg: Abera.

Van Klinken, Gerry. (2001) "The Maluku Wars: Bringing Society Back In, "*Indonesia* 71 (April): 1–26.

van Zanten, Agnes. (1997) "Schooling Immigrants in France in the 1990s: Success or Failure of the Republican Model of Integration?" *Anthropology & Education Quarterly* 28(3): 351–374.

Varzi, Roxanne. (2000) *Warring Souls, Youth, Media, and Martyrdom in Post-Revolution Iran.* Durham, N.C.: Duke University Press.

Vasconcellos, Maria Drosilla. (2003) "Asociologia da educação na França: Um percurso produtivo." *Educação & Sociedade* 24(83): 553–573. www.cedes.unicamp.br [Currently published online as *Jornal de Educação*].

Vatikiotis, Michael R. J. (1998) *Indonesian Politics under Suharto: The Rise and Fall of the New Order.* London: Routledge.

Venel, Nancy. (1999) *Musulmanes Française: Des pratiquantes voilées à l'université.* Paris: L'Harmattan.

Veyne, Paul. (1982) *Les Grecs ont-ils Cru à Leurs Mythes? Essai sur l'Imagination Constituante.* Paris: Seuil.

Vezaarat-e Farhang va Ershad-e Eslami. (1371/1992) *Osoule Syasate FarhangiJomhuri-ye Islami-ye Iran.* [*The Charter of Cultural Policy in Islamic Republic of Iran*]. Tehran: Ministry of Guidance, Supreme Council of Cultural Revolution.

Vezaarat-e Farhang va Ershad Eslami. (1380/2001) *Arzesha va Negaresh-haye Iranian* [*Iranian Values and Norms*].Tehran: Ministry of Guidance, Bureu of National Projects.

Victims of Crime. (2003) "Hate and Bias Crimes Report, U.S. Department of Justice." Office for Victims of Crime. www.ojp.usdoj.gov/ovc/ncvrw/2003/pg5j.html.

Wallach, Jeremy. (2002) "Modern Noise and Ethnic Accents: Indonesian Popular Music in the Era of Reformasi." PhD diss., University of Pennsylvania.

Walzer, Michael. (1997) *On Toleration*. New Haven: Yale University Press.

Warburton, Eve. (2007) "No Longer a Choice: Veiling Has Become a Highly Politicised Practice in Indonesia." *Inside Indonesia* 89. http://insideindonesia.org/content/view/16/29

Weinstein, Deena. (2000 [1991]) *Heavy Metal: The Music and Its Culture*. Revised edition. New York: Da Capo Press.

Weiss, Brad. (2002) "Thug Realism: Inhabiting Fantasy in Urban Tanzania." *Cultural Anthropology* 17(1): 93–124.

Weiss, Brad. (2005) "The Barber in Pain: Consciousness, Affliction and Alterity in Urban East Africa." In Alcinda Honwana and Filip De Boeck, eds., *Makers & Breakers: Children & Youth in Postcolonial Africa*, 102–120. Oxford: James Currey.

Wermuth, Mir. (2002) *No Sell Out: De Popularisering van een Subcultuur*. Amsterdam: Aksant.

Willaime, Jean-Paul. (2000) "L'enseignement religieux à l'école publique dans l'est de la France: Une tradition entre déliquescence et recomposition." *Social Compass* 47(3): 383–395.

Windle, Joel. (2004) "Schooling, Symbolism and Social Power: The Hijab in Republican France." *The Australian Educational Researcher* 31(1): 95–112.

Wohl, Robert. (1979) *The Generation of 1914*. Cambridge, Massachusetts: Harvard University Press.

Wolfsensohn Center, The Brookings Institution. (2008) "From Oil Boom to Youth Boon: Tapping the Middle East Demographic Gift." Washington, D.C., January 7, 2008.

World Bank. (2002) *Arab Republic of Egypt Educational Sector Review: Progress and Priorities for the Future*, Vol. I. http://eric.ed.gov:80/ERICWebPortal/custom/portlets/recordDetails/detailmini.jsp?_nfpb=true&_&ERICExtSearch_SearchValue_0=ED474423&ERICExtSearch_SearchType_0=no&accno=ED474423.

World Bank. (2004) *Unlocking the Employment Potential in the Middle East and North Africa Toward a New Social Contract*. Washington D.C.: World Bank Publication.

World Bank. (2007) *World Development Report 2007: Development and the Next Generation*. Washington D.C.: World Bank Publications.

World Bank (2008) *The Road Not traveled: Education Reform in the Middle East and North Africa*. Washington D.C.: World Bank Publications.

Wulff, Helena. (1995) "Introducing Youth Culture in Its Own Right: The State of the Art and New Possibilities." In Vered Amit-Talai and Helena Wulff, eds., *Youth Cultures: A Cross-Cultural Perspective*, 1–18. London: Routledge.

Wykes, Olive. (1967) "The Decline of Secularism in France." *Journal of Religious History* 4(3): 218–232.

Yaghmaian, Behzad. (2002) *Social Change in Iran: An Eyewitness Account of Dissent, Defiance, and New Movements for Rights*. Albany, N.Y.: State University of New York Press.

Yellow Peril. (1995) "Fun-Da-Mental: A Revolution of the Consciousness." *3D World*. www.cia.com.au/peril/texts/features/Fundamental.htm.

Zat, Vefa. (2002) *Eski Istanbul Meyhaneleri*. Istanbul: Iletişim Yayınları.

Zeghal, Malika. (2005) *Les Islamistes Marocains*. Paris: La Découverte.

Zubaida, Sami. (2003) "Islam in Europe." *Critical Quarterly* 45(1–2): 88–98.

Zürcher, Erik J. (1993) *Turkey: A Modern History*. London: I. B. Tauris.

NEWSPAPERS CITED

Al-Ahram Weekly
Al-Hayat
Al-Jazira
Al-Riyadh
Al-Sharq al-Awsat
Al-Wafd
Al-Watan
Aftab
Aftab-e Yazd
Bahar
Dowran-e Emrooz
Etelaat
Foroyaa
International Herald Tribune
Iran
Iran-e Emrooz
Keyhan
Le Figaro
Le Matin du Sahara
Le Monde
Libération
Nowrooz
Payam-e Emrooz
Resalat
Salam
Spiegel International
The Christian Science Monitor
The Independent (The Gambia)
The Jakarta Post
The New York Times
The Sun
The Times
USA Today

Index

Abdelaziz, king, 86
Abu Zegem, 88–89
Activism, 7, 86–88, 221, 247–8
  Communist youth, 28
  German Youth Movement, 29
  Internet, 16, 116
  Ba'ath Party, Iraqi, 29
  in Mali, 247–8
  Radicalism, 7, 107
  Social Movement Theory, 7
  among Students, 8, 108
al-Adal wal-Ehsan, 5
Adulthood, 28, 30, 208, 362
Afghanistan, 90
Ahmadinejad, Mahmoud, 218–20, 278, 283
AIDS (or HIV), 7, 229, 355–6
Ali B (Dutch Moroccan hip-hopper), 22, 319–20
Allochtoon, 313–4, 321–2
American Muslims, 163
  Identity, 166, 169
  Islamic education, 169. *See also* education

Leadership, 167, 170
Practicing Islam, 170–1
as Youth, 168
Ashura, 34, 286
Asian Cool, 296–8
Asian Economic Crisis, 49
al-Azhar, 19

Ba'ath Party, Iraqi, 29
Ba'athism, 29
Basiji, 37, 211–2, 215–6, 219–21
Baz, Shaykh Abd al-'Aziz bin, 77
Bin Laden, Osama, 20, 73, 234–8, 292, 302, 304
Bir Zeit University (BZU), 114–16
Bourdieu, Pierre, 6, 14, 30, 57, 65, 106, 194. *See also* habitus
BrAsian Muslims, 292–9. *See also* United Kingdom
British National Party (BNP), 294–5, 298

Cameroon, 148
  Education, 149
  Unemployment, 149

Castells, Manuel,
    and mobile communication, 363
Chador (Iranian women veil), 273–7,
    283–5
Childhood, 28, 30
Citizenship, 179, 198–9, 201–4, 246
    Political participation, 179
    in European Union, 185–6
    in Mali, 246
    and Religion, 203
Comaroff Jean, 227, 356
Comaroff John, 227, 356
Communautarisme, 177
Communist youth, 28
Corruption, 57, 82, 86, 134–5, 137–8,
    142, 236, 363

Daratista, Inul, 348–50
Da'wa, 51–54, 58–59, 248
    and Internet, 172–3
    in USA, 170–1
Development, 60, 62, 357, 355, 359
    Agricultural, 56
    Human, 6
    Impact on youth, 56
    Neoliberal, 363
Diab, Amr, 46
Diallo, Bilal, 249, 251–7
    in Media, 253–4
Diversity,
    Education, 182
    Sociocultural, 180, 182
Dogondoutchi, 226, 228, 230–1, 234–7
Drugs (ecstasy, cannabis), 37, 43–44,
    131, 134, 142
al-Durra, Muhammad, 117, 118
Dutch Moroccans, 309–23
    Cultural traditions, 312
    Education, 311
    Immigration, 315
    Integration, 313
    Moroccan identity, 316–7
    Music, 315

Muslim identity, 313–4, 321
Racism, 320
Radicalism, 311, 313
Religiosity, 312
Second generation, 311
Unemployment, 311

Economy and youth, 227–8, 235–6, 243,
    328–9
Education, 67, 117, 104, 132–3, 138, 149,
    169, 208–9, 244, 278, 311.
    See also Higher Education
    among American Muslims, 169
    Bir Zeit University (BZU), 114–6
    Catholic schools vs. Muslim schools,
        178–9, 183
    collèges ghetto, 182
    Dutch Moroccans, 311
    E-learning, 115
    in Iran, 208–9, 278
    madrasa, 55, 249, 255
    Muslim schools 177.
        See also France
    Muslim Student Association [MSA],
        167, 169, 171–2
    Palestine Education Initiative, 116
    Pesantren, 55
    Schoolbooks, 67
    Secular Islam, 184
    in Turkey, 259
Egypt, 9, 127–43
    al-Azhar, 19
    Corruption, 134–5, 137–8, 142
    Drugs (ecstasy, cannabis), 37, 43–4,
        131, 134, 142
    Education, 132, 133, 138
    Gender, 30, 38, 41, 133
    Hizb al-Tahrir, 52
    Internet, 134, 140, 142
    Mubarak regime, 130, 134, 139
    Muslim Brotherhood (Ikhwan
        al-Muslimin), 52, 135–6
    Patriarch, 132, 133

Human Rights, 136–142
Unemployment, 128
and USA, 134, 139
Empire, 63
Erdoğan, Tayyib, 260
Ethnography, 358
Europeanness, 185
Europe, 185–6
    Arabic music, 315
    Radical religion, 27–8
    Youth activism, 7

Fahd, King, 77
Fascism, 29
Feminism, 191–4, 198, 345–6,
    348–51
Finkielkraut, Alain, 180–1
France, 177–88, 189–205
    Catholic schools, 178–9
    Citizenship, 179, 198, 201–4
    Communautarisme, 177
    Frenchness, 179, 183
    Muslim schools, 177–9, 182–4
    "Other," the, 179, 181
    Secularism, 178
Fun^Da^Mental, 22, 291–307, 360
Fundamentalism, 36–37, 39, 294, 296

al-Gama'a al-Islamiya, 5
Gambia, The, 95–112
    Drugs, 108–9
    Dukureh, Karammoko, 99–103
    Education, 104
    Markaz, 105–6
    Poverty, 107
    Tabligh Jama'at, 96–111, 361
    Unemployment, 108
Generation, 8, 165, 169, 189, 263, 275,
    285, 311
    9/11, 20
    Boom, 84, 208
    Consciousness, 8, 227
    in Egypt, 9

e-generation, 10
Gap, 273–5, 285
Global, 8
"i"-generation,
    as Intergenerational Struggle, 193,
        195
    in Iran, 275, 285
    and Mannheim, Karl, 8, 263, 275
    Muslim immigrants, 165, 169, 189,
        192
    Muslim women, 192
    Religiosity, 163–4
    Vanguard, 168
Gender relations, 30, 38, 41, 133, 265,
    268–9, 276, 278, 280–2, 284–5,
    344–5
    Education, 181
    Equality, 195–6
    in Indonesia, 344–5
    Social division, 172, 181
German Youth Movement, 29
Germany, 29, 189–206
    Ausländer, 199
    Citizenship, 198–9
    German Youth Movement, 29
    Muslim immigrants, 199. *See also*
        generation
    Tolerance, 200. *See also* tolerance
Globalization, 63, 69, 298, 326, 335, 355,
    363
    "Cheap," 17
    and Networks, 326
    and Neoliberalism, 3, 362
Gogh, Theo van, 309, 312–3, 359
Gortz, Andre, 29
Guevara, Che, 301–2

Habitus, 6, 57, 106–7, 139, 216
Hadith, 105–6, 212
Haïdara, Chérif Ousmane Madani, 247,
    249, 251, 257
Hamas, 122
Hassan II, King, 66, 73

Higher Education, 128
  and Injustice, 138
  in Iran, 209–210
  and Youth Unemployment, 64, 128
Hip-hop, 228–9, 232, 296, 309–10, 318–23, 361
HIV (or HIV/AIDS), 7, 229, 355–6
Hizb al-Tahrir, 52
Homosexuality, 80, 87, 91
  in Iran, 279
  and Secular Islam, 169
Hussein, Imam, 18

Ijtihâd, 66, 68
Ilyas, Mawlana, 96, 98
Immigration,
  among Dutch Moroccans, 315
  in Iran, 209
  in Mali, 246
  in Netherlands, the, 311, 313, 315
  Second generation, 189. *See also* generation
  Social exclusion, 180. *See also* integration
Indonesia, 49–62, 343–6, 348–51. *See also* Suharto
  Corruption, 57
  Dangdut, 343, 346, 348–50
  Dress culture, 347–52
  Feminism, 345–6
  Gender relations, 344–5
  Identity crisis, 58
  New Order regime, 55, 344–5
  Pelita, 55
  Pirated music, 342
  Pop, 343, 346
  Pop Minang, 343–4, 346, 350–2
  Sexuality, 345–6, 348–51
  Unemployment, 58
  VCD, 341–54
Information and communication technology (ICT), 7, 9, 10, 16, 139–140, 362, 363

in Egypt, 140–142
in Middle East and Africa, 139
in Palestine, 114–123
Rural youth, 7
in Turkey, 264
Integration, 10, 13, 22, 181, 313, 314, 321
  in France, 181
Internet. *See* Information and communication technology
Intifada, 113–121
Iran, Islamic Republic of, 32, 52, 207–21, 274–83, 285
  Ashura, 34, 286
  Cultural invasion, 215–6, 218
  Cultural Revolution, 32
  Demography, 208
  Dress culture, 274, 282–4
  Education, 208–9, 278
  Feminine identity, 275–7
  Gender relations, 276, 278, 280, 284–5
  Human rights, 221
  Immigration, 209
  Moral society, 210–4, 219–11
  Nongovernmental organizations (NGOs), 38, 40, 42
  Pahlavi regime, 276
  Post-Islamism, 32, 38, 207, 221. *See also* Islamism
  Poverty, 208
  Prostitution, 212–3, 218, 277
  Reform, 217–8
  Sexual desire, 274–7, 280–3, 285. *See also* sexuality
  Sexuality, 212–3, 279, 283, 285
  Teenage runaways, 34
  Temporary marriage, 35, 277, 281, 285
  Unemployment, 209–10
  Young generation, 275, 285. *See also* generation
  Youth crisis, 210
  Youth identity, 280

Islamic Revolution, Iran, 32, 52, 207–21, 274, 276, 278

Islamism (or political Islam, or radical Islam, or Islamic Movements), 27, 32, 38, 64, 207, 221, 312

Fanaticism, 64, 297

and Political participation, 41

Post-Infitah, 41

Post-Islamism, 207, 221

Radicalism, 7, 27–8, 107, 129, 141–2, 311, 313

and schoolbooks, 67

Islamophobia, 16, 20, 164, 295, 299, 305, 363

Issoufou, 235–6

Jahiliyya, 59–60

Jammeh, Yahya, 100

Jihad, 50–51, 61, 73–74, 90, 249, 292, 302–3

Jihad Rap, 292, 360

Justice and Development Party (JDP), 67–72

Karbaschi, Gholam Hussein, 34

Khalid, Amr, 46

Khamenehei, Ayatollah Ali, 211

Khomeini, Ayatollah, 211, 213–4, 276, 286, 294

Khatami, Mohammad, 38–9, 217–8

al-Khattab, 'Umar, 77, 86

Laïcité, 178–180, 201–3

Locality, 326

Laskar Jihad, 15, 50–51, 56, 61, 361

Laskar Mujahidin, Indonesia, 49

Laskar Pembela Islam, 49

Literacy,
in Iran, 208

madrasa, 55, 249, 255

Mali,
Citizenship, 246

Consumerism, 244–5

Coup d'état, 243

Dress culture, 242

Economy, 243

Education, 244

Immigration, 246

Laïc, 241

Media, 243

Rasta Sufi, 242–3, 361

Religiosity, 247–8

Youth activism, 247–8. *See also* Activism

Unemployment, 245

Mannheim, Karl. *See* generation

Marabouts, 97, 99–103, 110

Marcuse, Herbert, 29

Maroc-hop, 309, 314, 318–23

Mashala, 95, 108

Mawdudi, Mawlana, 67

Metal (music), 23, 326, 331, 333–5

Internet, 335

Metalheads, 332–4, 336–8

in Israel, 336–8

Methodology, 357

Militant Islamist groups. *See also* al-Qaeda, 5, 15, 49, 50–51, 96, 98, 101, 103, 105, 361

al-Adal wal-Ehsan, 5

al-Gama'a al-Islamiya, 5

Laskar Jihad, 15, 50–51, 61, 361

Laskar Mujahidin, Indonesia, 49

Laskar Pembela Islam, 49

Tabligh Jama'at, 96, 98, 101, 103, 105, 361

Millennium Development Goals (MDGs), 356

Monica, Agnes, 346–8

Morocco, 63–76

Al-'Adl wa Al-Ihsân, 68–71

Ali B (Dutch Moroccan hip-hopper), 22, 319–20

Drugs (cannabis), 69

Education, 67

Morocco (*continued*)
  Hip-hop, 22, 309–10, 318–23
  Justice and Development Party (JDP),
    68–72
  Maroc-hop, 22, 309, 314, 318–23
  Monarchy, 65–68, 73
  and Palestine, 72, 74, 76
  Radical Islam, 27
  Shaabi, 309–10, 314–7
  'Ulamâ, 65–68
Muhammad, Prophet, 18, 52, 60, 95, 251
Muharram, 19
  Hussein parties, 19, 286
Multiculturalism, 10, 13,177, 180, 299,
    310
Music,
  Arabic, 315
  Dangdut, 343, 346, 348–50
  Feminism, 346–7
  Fun^Da^Mental, 22, 291–307
  Hip-hop, 103, 157, 228–9, 232, 296,
    309–10, 318–23, 361
  Identity, 310
  Jihad Rap, 292, 360
  Maroc-hop, 22, 309, 314, 318–23
  Metal, 23, 326, 331, 333–5
  Pop Indonesia, 343, 346
  Pop Minang, 343–4, 346, 350–2
  Rap, 228–30, 232
  Shaabi, 22, 309–10, 314–7
  VCD, 341–54
Muslim Brotherhood (*Ikhwan al-
  Muslimin*), 52, 135–6
Muslim schools,
  in France, 177–9, 182–4
Muslim Student Association [MSA], 167,
    169, 171–2

Nakba, 113
Nawaz, Aki (Aki Nawaz Qureishi), 293–8,
    302–3
Neoliberalism, 17, 23, 127, 130, 149, 232,
    246,257, 277

Netherlands, the,
  Arabic music, 315
  Dutch Moroccans, 309, 311
  Immigration, 311, 313
  Islam, 312
  Maroc-hop, 309, 314, 318–23
  Racism, 320
New Media. *See* Information and
    communication technology
Niger, 225–40
  AIDS, 229
  Corruption, 236
  Economy, 227–8, 235–6
  Hip-hop, 228–9, 232
  Izala, 227–8, 230–1, 234–6, 238
  Media, 232–3
  Muslim identity, 226–7, 230–2,
    234, 238
  Rap, 228–30, 232
  Religiosity, 226–7, 233, 238
  STD, 229. *See also* sexuality
  Tolerance, 231
  And USA, 234–6
Nowrooz, 37

Palestine, 113–125, 295, 302
  Bir Zeit University (BZU).
    See Education
  Cyber resistance, 113, 118–123
  al-Durra, Muhammad, 117, 118
  Education, 117
  ICT. *See* Information and
    communication technology
  Intifada, 113–121
  Media, 118, 122
  Nakba, 113
  NGOs, 114, 120
  Palestine Education Initiative, 116
  Palestine Liberation Organization,
    113
Palestine Education Initiative, 116
Palestine Liberation Organization, 113
Pesantren, 55

Polygamy, 63
Pornography, 44–45, 141
Post-Islamism, 32, 38, 207, 221.
    See Islamism
Poverty, 107, 208, 356–7, 363

Qadiriyya, 249, 251, 254
al-Qaeda, 90, 136, 234
al-Qardâoui, Youssef, 71
Qutb, Sayyid, 52, 59–60, 67

Rabin, Yitzhak, 114
Racism, 293–5, 298, 320
Radicalism, 7, 27–28, 107, 129,
    141–2, 311, 313
    and Youth activism, 7
Rafsanjani, Ali Akbar Hashemi, 35, 216,
    219, 277
Rap, 228–30, 232
Rastafarian, 250
Rasta Sufi, 242–3, 361
Raves, 43
Rock Against Racism, 293
Rural youth, 7

Sahwa, 16, 82–88
Salaf al-Salih, 50, 52–53, 60–61
Sarkozy, Nicolas, 179, 182
Satanism, 43, 45
Saudi Arabia, 77–94
    Bedouin, 80, 82, 90–1
    al-Haramayn, 54
    Drugs, 80–81, 83, 87
    Political activism, 86–88
    Radical Islam, 27
    Sahwa, 16, 82–88
    Tahfit, 16–17, 77–94
    Wahhabism, 52–3
Scarface, 319
Secularism, 169, 178, 184, 260–1
Ségou, 249–52
Sexuality, 191, 193–4, 197
    and Gender relations, 280–2

Homosexuality, 80, 87, 91, 279.
    See also homosexuality
    in Indonesia, 345–6, 348–51
    in Iran, 212–3, 274–7, 279–83, 285
    Sexual liberation, 193–4
    STD, 229
Shaabi, 22, 309–10, 314–7
al-Sharari, Mish'al, 77–78, 85, 89
Shari'a, 50, 53–54, 68–71, 279
Shirazi, Ayatollah Ha'eri, 35
Shi'ite, 52
Shirky, Clay, 10
Shûra, 69
Social Movement Theory, 7
Sufi, 95, 97, 101–2, 105, 227–8, 242,
    247–9, 252–6
Suharto, 49, 51, 54–55, 57, 344–5
Sunni (or Sunna), 52, 60, 96–97, 100,
    102, 110
Symmetrical Participation, 10

Tabligh Jama'at, 96–111, 361
Tuftn (or musuhhuum), 16–17,
    77–94
Tawhid, 148
Temporary marriage, 35, 277, 281, 285
Terrorism, 5, 129, 135, 142, 357. See also
    USA
Thalib, Ja'far Umar, 50
Thanawiyya Amma, 138
Tijaniyya, 249, 254
Touré, Amadou Toumani, 243
Translocality, 326, 335–6
Traoré, Moussa, 243–4, 246, 256
Ṭufush, 16, 81–93
Turkey,
    and Alcohol, 329–30
    Economy, 328–9
    Education, 259
    Feminism, 267
    Gender, 265, 268–9
    ICT, 264–5
    and Israel, 336–8

Turkey (*continued*)
  Masculine vs. Feminine, 331
  Media, 264
  Metal, 326, 331, 333–5
  Metalheads, 332–4, 336–8
  Muslim identity, 260–2, 264–5, 267–9
  Public spaces, 329–31
  Religiosity, 261–2, 264, 268–9
  Rock bar, 327, 331, 333–5
  Secularism, 260–1
  Youth identity, 263, 267

Umma, 153, 169, 171, 186, 225, 235, 361
Unemployment, 3–5, 12, 23, 64, 148, 238,
    243, 361
  in Cameroon, 149
  among British Asian Men in UK, 292
  among Dutch Moroccans, 311
  in Egypt, 128
  in Gambia, The, 108
  in Indonesia, 49, 58
  in Iran, 209–10
  in Mali, 245
  and rap, 229
United Kingdom (or Britain), 294–8
  BrAsian Muslims, 292–9
  British National Party (BNP), 294–5,
    298

Immigrants, 22
  Muslim identity, 296, 299
Urf, 210–11, 279
Urfi marriage, 19
USA134, 139, 170–1, 234–6
  Generation, 8
  Immigrant generation, 165, 169.
    See also generation
  Islam Awareness Week, 171–2
  Muslim Student Association [MSA],
    167, 169, 171–2. *See also*
    education
  and Niger, 234–6
  Post-9/11, 21
  Racism, 165
  Terrorism, 161
  Youth activism, 7

Video Compact Disk (VCD), 341–54

Wahhabi, 52–53, 99–102, 252, 255
Wasta (connections), 138
World Bank, 127, 128, 139, 356

Youth activism, 7
Youth Bulge, 4, 23, 127–8, 208, 355, 358
Youthfulness, 7, 190–8, 226, 360, 362,
    364